Gender in the Workplace

Gender in the Workplace

CLAIR BROWN *and* JOSEPH A. PECHMAN
Editors

THE BROOKINGS INSTITUTION
Washington, D.C.

Library of Congress Cataloging-in-Publication data
Gender in the workplace.
  Includes index.
  1. Sex discrimination in employment—United States.
2. Sex role in the work environment—United States.
3. Sex discrimination in employment.   4. Sex role
in the work environment.   I. Brown, Clair, 1946–
II. Pechman, Joseph A., 1918–   .   III. Brookings
Institution.
HD6060.5.U5G46   1987   331.13'3   87-668
ISBN 0-8157-1170-0
ISBN 0-8157-1169-7 (pbk.)

9 8 7 6 5 4 3 2 1

THE BROOKINGS INSTITUTION is an independent organization devoted to nonpartisan research, education, and publication in economics, government, foreign policy, and the social sciences generally. Its principal purposes are to aid in the development of sound public policies and to promote public understanding of issues of national importance.

The Institution was founded on December 8, 1927, to merge the activities of the Institute for Government Research, founded in 1916, the Institute of Economics, founded in 1922, and the Robert Brookings Graduate School of Economics and Government, founded in 1924.

The Board of Trustees is responsible for the general administration of the Institution, while the immediate direction of the policies, program, and staff is vested in the President, assisted by an advisory committee of the officers and staff. The by-laws of the Institution state: "It is the function of the Trustees to make possible the conduct of scientific research, and publication, under the most favorable conditions, and to safeguard the independence of the research staff in the pursuit of their studies and in the publication of the results of such studies. It is not a part of their function to determine, control, or influence the conduct of particular investigations or the conclusions reached."

The President bears final responsibility for the decision to publish a manuscript as a Brookings book. In reaching his judgment on the competence, accuracy, and objectivity of each study, the President is advised by the director of the appropriate research program and weighs the views of a panel of expert outside readers who report to him in confidence on the quality of the work. Publication of a work signifies that it is deemed a competent treatment worthy of public consideration but does not imply endorsement of conclusions or recommendations.

The Institution maintains its position of neutrality on issues of public policy in order to safeguard the intellectual freedom of the staff. Hence interpretations or conclusions in Brookings publications should be understood to be solely those of the authors and should not be attributed to the Institution, to its trustees, officers, or other staff members, or to the organizations that support its research.

Foreword

THE number of women in the paid labor force increased dramatically between 1920 and 1980, reaching almost 60 percent of all women aged 25–64 by 1980. But women still face obstacles to equality in the workplace: their wages remain at approximately 60 percent of men's wages, and they are predominantly in lower-paying jobs with fewer opportunities for promotion.

The economic and social forces that propelled women into the work force and those that have determined their treatment on the job are the focus of the papers in this volume, which grew out of a conference in November 1984 sponsored by the Brookings Institution and the Committee on the Status of Women in the Economics Profession. The volume contains an introduction by editors Clair Brown and Joseph A. Pechman, followed by eight papers analyzing specific gender issues. The papers examine changing consumption patterns of families as more women entered the labor force; segregation by sex in a large firm and a service occupation; subcontracting as a method of reducing women's wages; the effect of unionization on the male-female wage gap; occupational segregation among part-time workers; enforcement of child support awards to improve the economic condition of single mothers; and the use of subsidies to encourage firms to meet sex-based employment quotas.

Clair Brown is associate professor of economics and associate director of the Institute of Industrial Relations at the University of California at Berkeley. Joseph A. Pechman, director of the Economic Studies program at Brookings from 1962 to 1983, is a senior fellow at Brookings. They wish to thank the Committee on the Status of Women in the Economics Profession for its cooperation in organizing this project. They are also grateful to Nancy Davidson for editing the manuscript; Victor M. Alfaro, Kathleen M. Bucholz, and Carolyn A. Rutsch for verifying its factual content; Diana Regenthal for preparing the index; and Dawn R. Emery and Susan L. Woollen for secretarial and administrative assistance. The Rockefeller Foundation provided funding for the project.

The views expressed in this book are those of the authors and the conference participants and should not be ascribed to the Rockefeller Foundation or the trustees, officers, or other staff members of the Brookings Institution.

BRUCE K. MACLAURY
President

February 1987
Washington, D.C.

Contents

Tables

Figures

Gender in the Workplace

CLAIR BROWN *and* JOSEPH A. PECHMAN

Introduction

SOCIAL SCIENTISTS generally agree that one of this century's most important developments in the U.S. labor market has been the dramatic shift in women's work roles, from primarily unpaid work at home to a combination of paid market work and traditional unpaid work. In 1920 fewer than 20 percent of prime-aged women (25–64 years) engaged in any paid labor; by 1980 almost 60 percent did. Even with the dramatic increase in female participation, women's wages have remained at about 60 percent of men's wages. This major transformation in female work roles raises important questions. How has it affected family life and the standard of living? How have women fared in the labor market? Why are they predominantly in lower-paid, less desirable jobs? How have unions affected female jobs? What are the prospects for future occupational mobility and earnings growth for women workers?

This volume, which grew out of a conference sponsored by the Brookings Institution and the Committee on the Status of Women in the Economics Profession, brings together economists with a broad range of viewpoints to discuss the economic impact of women's changing work roles. The papers, using a variety of tools, provide an array of approaches to studying gender issues. However, they fall into two basic categories. The first four papers explicitly analyze the structural foundations of the economy by studying various aspects of the social structure in which the economy is embedded. The use of this type of institutional economic analysis to study women's work roles is still in its infancy. Changing sex roles offer an unusual opportunity to study the social structure within which the economy functions. The last four papers empirically analyze the recent outcomes of specific labor market activities in order to identify and measure the important factors involved. This approach is useful in prescribing or evaluating labor market policies, while the first one is useful for understanding and influencing long-run structural shifts.

1

Consumption, Work, and Growth

In the first paper, Clair Brown examines the changes in consumption patterns over the past sixty-five years to assess the impact of increasing incomes on the well-being of America's families. She uses an institutional analysis to study the relationships between consumption norms, work roles of men and women, and economic growth. The basic data for the analysis come from the consumer expenditure surveys taken in 1918–19, 1934–35, 1950, 1960–61, 1972–73, and 1980–81.

There have been major shifts in the occupational distribution of workers in the U.S. economy as real incomes have risen, albeit sporadically, since the end of World War I. The number of farmers has declined sharply, while the number of adult male workers in relatively high-paying white-collar occupations has increased. There has also been a large rise in the number of workers per family, reflecting the increase in the labor force participation rate of women.

Consumption norms changed dramatically during this period, largely as a result of a drop in the relative importance of food and a rise in the importance of transportation expenditures in the family budget. Between 1918 and 1973 food expenditures declined from 40 percent of the average budget to 19 percent, while transportation-related expenditures rose from a little more than 2 percent to almost 19 percent. Thus economic growth in the United States has produced a more mobile and socially active population.

Brown finds that, over the decades studied, changes in consumption norms had a substantial effect on women's work roles. She argues that economic growth pulled women into the paid labor force after the basic family needs in food, transportation, and housing were filled. Nutritional standards were basically met by 1950, sound housing with full plumbing facilities became almost universal by 1960, and almost all families owned at least one car by 1960. Thereafter, eating out became more popular, more comfortable housing was sought through such amenities as air conditioning and home appliances, and more convenient transportation was obtained by the purchase of second cars. Greater emphasis was placed throughout the post–World War II period on economic security through increased savings and membership in public and private retirement systems.

A major element in U.S. economic development has been the rise in women's labor force participation, which has improved the position of women in society while allowing families to buy more amenities. Although economic growth has brought women into the labor force, growth alone cannot bring about equality between working men and women as long as growth cannot equalize work roles at home. Since income is regarded as the main determinant of well-being and status, there is no economic motivation for decreasing the standard work week and allowing both husbands and wives to spend time maintaining families. Brown concludes that the equalization of work roles at home and in the marketplace will require a lengthy process to change government policies, employer practices, and the norms governing behavior within the family.

The Roles of Gender in an Internal Labor Market

Heidi I. Hartmann explores the role of gender in the institutional theories of internal labor markets and labor market segmentation. Most of the work on these theories has focused on men. The application to women is not straightforward since the division of labor by sex divides segments of the labor market, including internal labor markets in the primary sector. Greater emphasis on the social phenomena of class struggle and the labor process at the workplace has deepened the analysis of labor market operations, but even this more holistic approach has usually not incorporated gender. The processes of de-skilling jobs and assigning jobs are interrelated, and differential use of male and female workers is an integral part of these processes. Men and women struggle over who will get which jobs, while management and workers struggle over the design of the job structure and working conditions as well as the assignment of workers to jobs. More recent research has shown how the internal labor market structures differ for women from the structures originally described for men. The outward symbol of these different structures by gender is the high degree of sex segregation within firms by title. Men and women have profoundly different labor market experiences within the same firm although firms treat workers in the same job category equally.

Hartmann empirically analyzed the operation of gender in the internal labor market of a large insurance company. She found sex segregation by occupation and by pay grade, so that sex segregation by grade existed even within occupational groups. Overall, the lower-paid occupations are disproportionately female, and the better-paid occupations are disproportionately male. Furthermore, women are paid better than men in the "women's" occupations and less than men in the "men's" occupations, even though women have more company experience than men in both cases. Few women are promoted past grade level 16 (out of 28 grades).

In her regression analysis of promotion prospects, Hartmann found that promotion was *negatively* related both to having an outstanding or good performance rating and to the female percentage in the occupation/ grade. In addition, Hartmann found that salary growth was *positively* related to performance evaluation and to the female percentage. Overall, women workers were disadvantaged relative to men with respect to promotion, but appeared to be somewhat compensated with salary increases. However, salary growth does not compensate for lack of promotion, especially since men start at the the middle of the job structure and move to the top while women start at the bottom and move to the middle. Hartmann found racial discrimination to be even more pervasive than sex discrimination, since race was negative in explaining promotion *and* salary growth. The rules of "equal" treatment in specific jobs within the internal labor market seem to apply to women but not to minorities.

Occupational Segregation among Bank Tellers

Myra H. Strober and Carolyn L. Arnold analyze the creation and perpetuation of occupational segregation with their case study of bank tellers, an occupation that has changed from male to female. They use an institutional theory of occupational segregation, which assumes that (1) social rules and customs as well as profit maximizing govern employers' personnel decisions; (2) male workers as a group decide, within race and class constraints, which jobs will be theirs; and (3) male workers maximize their economic gain in making this decision. The feminization of bank telling was consistent with these assumptions.

Women were hired as tellers during World War II to fill the positions of men who left for military service. But the banks did not make permanent job commitments to these women until it became clear after the war that enough men did not want these jobs as other occupations became more attractive to them. Strober and Arnold argue that although telling was probably not de-skilled, the job was "declassed" as banking services became increasingly used by the masses as well as the elite.

As telling became more female intensive, it also was being performed by younger workers, especially among male employees. Around one-fourth of the male tellers were less than 25 years old in 1950, compared with over one-half in 1980. Apparently men came to use telling jobs as a step to other occupations. In contrast, one-third of the female tellers were less than 25 years old in 1950, compared with two-fifths in 1980. Women over 35 were another one-third of the female tellers in 1980, compared with only one-fifth of the male tellers.

The female-male earnings ratio remained remarkably stable, however, at about 75 percent from 1950 to 1980. Changes in the relative work experience of men and women and in the gender distribution of teller assignments probably contributed to an increase in the female-male earnings ratio, while stability in the relative education levels and the ratio of alternative opportunities for women and men probably contributed to keeping the earnings ratio constant. Strober and Arnold conclude that although blatant wage discrimination declined as it became illegal, wage norms incorporating subtle discrimination seemed to have worsened.

Tellers' earnings declined over this period relative to those of other occupations. Strober and Arnold explain this as a result of the decline in the relative education of male tellers, the decline in educational requirements for tellers, the feminization of telling per se, and the decline between 1970 and 1980 in the proportion of women workers in other female-intensive occupations.

Overall, Strober and Arnold show that price variables alone explain very little of the changes observed for bank tellers. However, these changes are understandable in the context of their broader institutional theory of occupational segregation.

Gender, Skill, and the Dynamics of Women's Employment

Lourdes Benería examines how homework and subcontracting affect the female labor market and gender differentiation in the labor market in Mexico City. Her study covers 1981–82, a transition period from economic growth to economic crisis.

Benería analyzes subcontracting as a process of decentralization of production to reduce labor costs by shifting production to labor market segments that are part of the secondary and informal markets. This shift facilitates the access to an increasingly more flexible labor supply without rigid contract restrictions. Gender plays an important role in this sector; in her sample, the proportion of employees who are female has been increasing.

Benería shows how the feminization of certain jobs can be linked to both technical and social skills related to gender. Employers prefer women workers not only because their wages are lower but also because the employers believe that gender characteristics affect women's work performance. These gender characteristics translate into social skills that are used to assign men and women workers to the hierarchy of positions.

Benería uses the labor process approach, which assumes that the capitalist organization of production and its corresponding division of labor is hierarchical in order to facilitate management control and to lower wages through skill differentiation and de-skilling. The use of a subcontracting chain allows this process to be finely developed since the typical chain has four levels: the large multinational, which subcontracts the majority of its production to firms funded by domestic capital, which then subcontract a minority of their production to illegal sweatshops, which then provide homework to a fluctuating number of women. The ratio of average monthly wages (not including fringe benefits) for unskilled workers between the multinational and homework levels was around 7:1 in a chain producing electric coils.

Benería sees the increase in female employment in Mexico City and the feminization of certain types of jobs as the result of lower women's wages (which in turn partially reflect the artificiality of skill definition) and the assumed characteristics of women workers, which include less militancy and more reliability, manual dexterity, and discipline than men.

Her analysis implies that a flattening of the labor hierarchy both among and within firms would increase gender equality since women are concentrated in the bottom jobs in both cases. For example, legalization of underground operations would help reduce the differences between the lower levels and the upper levels of the subcontracting process.

Unions and the Female Work Force

Richard B. Freeman and Jonathan S. Leonard analyze how women workers have fared in unions in recent years. Their main conclusion is that women have fared differently in unions in the public sector and those in the private sector.

Between 1973 and 1984, the percentage of women who were union members in the public sector almost doubled. This is the one sector in which unions have recently succeeded in organizing. The overall gap in unionization between men and women results largely from differences in the occupations and industries where men and women work, rather than from any innate differences in propensity to unionize.

Freeman and Leonard show that the widely held view that unions raise the wages of women by about as much as they raise the wages of men is true for the private sector and for blue-collar workers. However, in the public sector and among white-collar workers unionization raises women's wages *more* then men's wages. Even so, unionization does not reduce the male-female pay gap in the economy as a whole. The concentration of male unionists in the blue-collar sector, which has the greatest union premium, offsets the higher wage premium unions win for women in the public sector. Overall, they find that unionism has an insubstantial effect on the male-female pay gap.

Freeman and Leonard also compared termination, promotion, and employment growth of women workers in union and nonunion plants in the private sector, and they found no noticeable differences in the treatment of women. Unions also appear to have had no impact on affirmative action programs.

Seeing comparable worth as potentially the most important development affecting women workers in American history, Freeman and Leonard discuss how comparable worth presents a policy that can help unions organize, especially in the public sector where comparable worth is being effectively incorporated in the collective bargaining process.

Part-Time Work and Occupational Segregation

Occupational segregation of men and women declined somewhat during the 1970s, largely as a result of the entry of more women into the so-called male occupations (for example, managerial and professional jobs). Nevertheless, the traditionally male occupations remain bastions of male employment and the degree of occupational segregation is still very high.

Relatively more women work part time than men, but little is known about the influence of part-time work on occupational segregation. Karen C. Holden and W. Lee Hansen examine census employment data for 1971, 1976, and 1981 to see whether changes in segregation in part-time jobs have contributed to recent changes in segregation for the work force as a whole. An occupation is identified as male or female when the percentage of all workers in that occupation who are male and female exceeds the average percentages for those in regular full-time work by more than 10 percentage points. All other occupations are regarded as integrated.

Holden and Hansen find that there is a higher degree of occupational segregation among part-time job holders than among full-time job holders, but segregation declined more in the 1970s for the part-time work force. According to their figures, this decline was the result partly of a decline in segregation of some part-time jobs and partly of the growth of occupations in which part-time work had a favorable sex mix in 1971.

However, the decline in occupational segregation for the labor force as a whole was the result largely of a decline in the segregation of occupations of full-time job holders who were younger than 50 years old in 1971. Females more than doubled their share of full-time jobs (though from a small base of only 5 percent) in those occupations that were predominantly male. The experience of part-time job holders was mixed. Occupational segregation actually increased for part-time workers who were 25–29 years old in 1971 and declined for those who were 30 years or older in that year. Holden and Hansen speculate that employers of part-time workers seem to be more willing to move women into male-dominated occupations as their child care and other family responsibilities diminish.

Despite the improvement in the 1970s, occupational segregation is still a major problem. Women continue to find it extremely difficult to break into male-dominated occupations, and this is true of women who work part time as well as those who work full time. Holden and Hansen conclude that there is a need to expand employment opportunities for women in part-time as well as full-time work. Institutional arrangements such as flextime, job sharing, and affirmative action might help if they were focused on those occupations in which male part-time workers seem to have a comparative advantage. But most of these arrangements are being developed in the female occupations, so, unless there is a change, these efforts will do little to ease the problem of occupational segregation.

Child Support and Welfare

About one-fifth of all children are living with only one parent (most of them with their mothers), and the number has been growing rapidly. Half of the families headed by single mothers were on welfare at some time in 1978. One reason there is so much poverty in this group is that many fathers are not contributing to the support of their children. About half of these single mothers had no child support payments from the absent fathers. For those who received awards, the average award was slightly less than $2,000 for the entire year, of which an average of only 70 percent was actually collected by the mothers.

Barbara R. Bergmann and Mark D. Roberts attempt to estimate, through a series of simulations, how increases in the number, level, and enforcement of child support awards might improve the economic condition of single-mother families. Their estimates are based on the 1978 experience of over 1,260 single mothers surveyed by the Census Bureau in early 1979.

According to the first of the simulations, if all child support currently owed by absent fathers were actually collected, child support payments would rise by over 22 percent and welfare costs would decline by about 10 percent. However, there would be very little change in the number of independent mothers and the number of families in poverty. The discrepancy between the increase in child support payments and the drop in welfare costs occurs because some of the child support payments would go to mothers not on welfare.

A second simulation provides an estimate of the effect of giving child support payments to all mothers who did not receive them, on the assumption that the new awards are equal to the average of existing awards. Such an effort would almost double the amount of child support, cut welfare costs in half, and reduce the number of welfare families by about two-thirds. However, the number of families in poverty would decline by only about 18 percent, because most of the child support payments would simply substitute for welfare payments.

If the child support awards were increased to $1,800 per child per year (more than 50 percent higher than the average currently awarded), welfare costs would be cut by two-thirds and the number of poverty families would fall by over two-fifths. Part of the reduction in poverty would be the result of a 20 percent increase in the number of independent mothers. Finally, doubling the awards to $3,600 per child would reduce welfare costs by seven-eighths and reduce the poverty rate by roughly the same proportion, but it would not increase the number of independent mothers.

Bergmann and Roberts conclude that merely improving the enforcement of currently existing child support awards would not have a large effect on welfare expenditures or on the proportion of single mothers in poverty. To eliminate poverty among single mothers by child support payments alone would require payments that probably exceed absent fathers' ability to pay. Thus other programs, including training, job creation, and affirmative action, are needed as a supplement to child support to lift single mothers out of poverty.

Sex-Based Employment Quotas

The Swedish regional development program provides capital and other subsidies to firms that reserve for each sex at least 40 percent of the additional jobs created with this aid. The program, which began in 1974, applied to 358 firms in 1983–84, with planned increases in employment of 2,095 persons. Firms are expected to consult with local market boards and employment offices to meet these quotas. Charles Brown and Shirley J. Wilcher examine the experience with this program to see whether sex-based employment programs can help to reduce or eliminate sex discrimination in the workplace.

The available statistics suggest that, although a significant number of firms were legally exempt from the quota (for example, because they planned increases of three or fewer workers), employment of women increased appreciably at establishments receiving regional assistance. In the early years of the program, the planned increase in female employment by both exempt and nonexempt projects was 36 percent of the total planned increase in employment. In more recent years, the planned employment increase of women averaged 44 percent. In firms subject to the quota, women were estimated to account for 45 percent of new employment.

Brown and Wilcher believe, on the basis of three pieces of evidence, that the quota requirement has had an effect on hiring practices. First, they visited a number of firms that reported that the quota had made a difference. Second, a small number of firms are sanctioned each year for failing to meet the quota, and they uniformly respond by satisfying the enforcement authorities. Third, they find that half of the seventy-eight projects approved in 1976 just met the required level of female employment, which suggests that the quota requirement did have an effect on hiring practices.

Brown and Wilcher develop a model to estimate the effect of the quota on the employment practices of the firms approved for regional aid. Their best estimate is that about half of the firms increased their hiring of women to meet the quota. The implied increase in female employment for the firms directly affected amounted to 3 or 4 percent. While this seems to be a small change, Brown and Wilcher point out that it is larger than most studies find for the U.S. firms subject to the regulations of the Office of Federal Contract Compliance Programs.

Brown and Wilcher believe that a number of lessons can be drawn by the United States from the Swedish experience with sex quotas. First, affirmative action officials should encourage firms with federal contracts to employ workers who have completed federally financed employment and training programs. Second, affirmative action will not be successful unless adequate and effective resources are provided for the enforcement of regulations governing the hiring of women. Third, affirmative action will work only if there is a visible commitment by the government to equality between men and women in the labor market.

Conclusion

As a group, these papers shed new light on how gender functions in the economy. Specifically, they increase understanding of the evolution of institutions that both accompanied and forced the shift in women's work roles. They also show how labor market segmentation by gender functions, especially through occupational segregation. They analyze how the specific institutions of trade unions and the time structure of work affect women workers, as well as how certain government policies, such as collection of child support or an attempt to reserve more jobs for women, affect women's economic outcomes. Overall, they point the direction that future research should take as well as pose the questions that still need to be addressed.

CLAIR BROWN

Consumption Norms, Work Roles, and Economic Growth, 1918–80

THE standard of living in the United States improved dramatically between 1918 and 1980 as a rural agricultural economy was transformed to an urban industrial one with a gradually more professionalized work force. These changes in the economy affected women's and men's work roles and the distribution of the growing output. In addition, economic growth and the shift in work roles wrought changes in consumption norms. This essay uses an institutional analysis to study the relationships between consumption norms, work roles, and economic growth and to assess the impact of economic growth on well-being across classes.

Well-being, comfort, and status together compose the standard of living. Well-being is judged in practical terms by social norms, rather than assumed to be maximized individually through idiosyncratic preferences.[1] Consumption for well-being includes expenditures that ensure health, reproduction, and social integration sufficient to allow adults to engage regularly in work, family, and community life. Income level cannot be used to measure well-being because income is also spent to provide class-defined standards for comfort and status. However, given the existence of social norms that define basic health and welfare needs, the differences in well-being across classes can be measured and used to evaluate policies for redistributing income.

I would like to thank David Matza, Kathy Mooney, and Tibor Scitovsky for comments on an earlier version. David Brauer provided excellent research assistance. Both research support and staff support were provided by the Brookings Institution and the Institute of Industrial Relations, University of California, Berkeley.

1. This line of reasoning is compatible with Alfred Marshall, *Principles of Economics: An Introductory Volume,* 8th ed. (London: Macmillan, 1930); and A. C. Pigou, *The Economics of Welfare,* 4th ed. (London: Macmillan, 1932). These were termed the "material welfare school" by Robert Cooter and Peter Rappoport, "Were the Ordinalists Wrong About Welfare Economics?" *Journal of Economic Literature,* vol. 22 (June 1984), pp. 507–30.

An Institutional Framework

An institutional approach, defining institutions as the social rules and customs that provide the framework by which people order their everyday lives and resolve conflicts, assumes that a family's activities are primarily determined by the societal norms that govern its class. Maintaining class position, which includes maintaining relative income position, is the family's primary goal; improving class position is seldom a realistic goal.

This study focuses on white families in three classes, defined by the husband's occupation and by family income, and black families in one class, defined by family income.[2] For whites, the three occupational groups, which are distinguished by type of payment of earnings, are: (1) salaried managers and professionals (termed "salaried"), who are paid by the year rather than by the hour and suffer little job insecurity; (2) skilled and semiskilled workers (termed "wage earners"), also known as craft and operative workers, who are paid hourly wages and suffer cyclical unemployment; and (3) unskilled workers, laborers, and service workers (termed "laborers"), who are paid by the hour and have insecure jobs.

For each occupation, the median urban family income group is used to define the class. The median urban family income is also used to define the black class, but no occupation description is included since blacks generally are confined to the lowest occupational groups.[3]

In this model, economic growth is distributed through the differential access families have to paid work; this market access determines the class and income level of families. Expenditures are set by the consumption norms for an income class. Periods of rapid economic growth ease the rationing of access to paid work and allow the lower classes to improve their relative income, while periods of low economic growth do the opposite.

2. Throughout this paper, the term *white classes* is used to mean white families in the income-occupation groups outlined here. Likewise, *black class* refers to black families in the designated income group.

3. Although the black families studied are representative of black families over time, they include mostly husband-wife families. They are not representative of the growing group of black female-headed families, who are in the poorest class. The bottom 20 percent and the top 10 percent of the income distribution are excluded from this study; no data were compiled for them before 1950.

Since the productive and reproductive modes of a society are inter-related and interact dynamically over time, the work roles for women must be studied by looking at how their position in the market economy and the household has evolved over time.[4] Economic growth and the transformation of consumption norms directly affect women's work roles.[5] Since a family's housework time and money needs are determined primarily by social norms, and possibilities of substitution between time and money in maintaining the family's prescribed standard of living are limited, a wife's work decisions are not based on efficiency principles. Rather, such decisions are governed by social norms within a historical process. Specifically, in the period studied here, as the main components of the family's budget shifted away from food, clothing, and housing toward transportation, recreation, and personal insurance, the focus of women's work roles shifted from housework to a combination of housework and paid work. These shifts reflected the decline in family size as well as the impact of economic growth.

The Data

Expenditure data given here are from the consumer expenditure surveys conducted by the Bureau of Labor Statistics in 1918–19, 1934–35, 1950, 1960–61, 1972–73, and 1980–81. The data were revised to be compatible over the years surveyed. Although the population surveyed specifically ignored certain groups (such as recent immigrants and slum dwellers in 1918 and relief families in 1935), the selection does

4. Jane Humphries and Jill Rubery, "The Reconstitution of the Supply Side of the Labour Market: The Relative Autonomy of Social Reproduction," *Cambridge Journal of Economics*, vol. 8 (December 1984), pp. 331–46, discusses various approaches to studying the relationship between the productive and reproductive spheres. The impact of industrialization on the demand for women as workers and as childbearers and child rearers is examined in Louise A. Tilly and Joan W. Scott, *Women, Work, and Family* (Holt, Rinehart and Winston, 1978).

5. Claudia Goldin, "The Changing Economic Role of Women: A Quantitative Approach," *Journal of Interdisciplinary History*, vol. 13 (Spring 1983), pp. 707–33, also sees the process of economic development as the major factor in increasing female participation rates. However, many of the changes described here as institutional she sees as economic. Earlier, Clarence D. Long, *The Labor Force under Changing Income and Employment* (Princeton University Press, 1958), argued that the female labor force had grown primarily as a result of the release of females from housework and childbearing, the increase in female longevity and in the relative education of women, and the reduction in the normal workweek.

Table 1. *Occupational Status and Family Income, 1918–80*[a]

Current dollars unless otherwise indicated

	1918		1935		1950		1960		1973		1980	
Occupation of family head[b]	Median family income	Percent of white total	Median family income	Percent of white total	Median family income	Percent of white total	Median family income	Percent of white total	Median family income	Percent of white total	Median family income	Percent of white total
Salaried	1,770	12	2,280	9	4,930	12	8,720	19	17,900	25	32,920	29
Self-employed	1,830	10	1,650	11	4,380	10	6,910	10	15,230	5	27,530	4
Clerical and sales	1,160	10	1,710	15	3,950	12	6,590	14	12,780	14	23,690	15
Craft and operative workers	1,290	30	1,330	29	3,800	41	6,250	38	12,170	39	23,190	35
Laborers and service workers	990	18	1,070	10	2,730	13	4,700	12	9,150	13	17,520	13
Farmers and farm managers	910	18	970	26	2,000	10	2,970	7	8,960	3	13,730	2
Farm laborers and foremen	660	12			1,580	2	2,530	2	5,650	1	12,240	1
Black urban families[c]	n.a.	7	680	8	2,270	10	3,840	9	7,610	11	13,970	12
Addenda												
Total median income	1,140[d]	...	1,160	...	3,320	...	5,680	...	11,580	...	21,705	...
Total median income (1972–73 dollars)	3,270	...	3,650	...	5,950	...	8,270	...	11,580	...	10,800	...

Sources: For 1918, author's calculations based on Simon Kuznets, *National Income and Its Composition, 1919–1938* (New York: National Bureau of Economic Research, 1941); for 1935, data from National Resource Committee, *Consumer Incomes in the United States: Their Distribution in 1935–36* (Government Printing Office, 1938); for years since 1935, U.S. Bureau of the Census, *Current Population Reports*, series P-60, various issues.

n.a. Not available.

a. Income is annual median family income in current dollars, estimated from distributions and rounded to the nearest $10. Data for 1918 is not comparable to that for other years because income is average earnings (including all workers) and occupational distribution is for all males aged 10 and over from the 1920 census and only selected occupations are used.

b. Occupational groups include all families.

c. Population percentages represent urban population that was black in 1918, 1935, and 1950, and urban families that were black in 1960, 1973, and 1980.

d. For all personal incomes (excluding soldiers, sailors, and marines); estimated from Wesley C. Mitchell and others, *Income in the United States: Its Amount and Distribution 1909–1919* (Harcourt, Brace, 1921–22), table 26.

not pose a problem for this study, which, like the original surveys, focuses on urban families with an employed head. Temporary unemployment is included since an unemployment spell results in a lowering of the median income of the occupation. However, because relief families are excluded, the widespread chronic unemployment of the Depression era is not reflected in the 1934–35 median income by occupation. The impact of the Depression on the unemployment of various classes is noted, but the 1935 data are not strictly comparable to that of other years, when chronic unemployment was a much less serious problem.

Other data problems, such as the family types interviewed and the difference between the income group used and the actual income of the class, are specifically recognized and adjusted whenever possible. Overall, the adjusted data appear to provide a useful measure of expenditures for the four classes being studied.

The years being studied are representative of important points in America's economic history:

—the end of World War I in Europe and the beginning of massive industrialization with assembly line production in the United States (1918);

—the beginning of the recovery from the depths of the Depression and the end of the period without national social security programs in effect (1935);

—the beginning of the rebuilding of Europe after World War II and of U.S. supremacy in the world economy (1950);

—the beginning of active government fiscal policy using Keynesian theory and of government commitment to decrease poverty (1960);

—the beginning of major structural shifts, both domestically and internationally, as the result of large increases in energy prices and the restructuring of the international financial system (1973);

—the beginning of deregulation, lower taxes, and cutbacks in government income support programs (1980).

Income Distribution, Work Roles, and Budgets

From 1918 to 1980, the median real income of families increased more than threefold (see table 1). The occupational distribution of family heads changed dramatically. In 1918, 30 percent of employed family heads worked on farms, while 12 percent were professionals and managers. By 1980, only 3 percent of employed heads worked on farms, while 33 percent were professionals and managers. Over the same period, the percentage of employed family heads who were craft workers, operatives, laborers, or service workers remained fairly constant at about 50 percent.

These occupational shifts reflect economic growth; adult male workers went into relatively high-paying, white-collar occupations, while relatively low-paying farm work almost disappeared. But economic growth, interacting with social norms, also changed other work roles. Families without employed heads were approximately one-fifth of the families during the Depression and after World War II, but almost one-third of the families during the 1970s. Increasingly, these families had low incomes because they were headed by single women; in 1973, 36 percent of the families with incomes under $5,000 were female-headed.[6] Fewer families were low income owing to retirement, because social security and private pensions prevented a substantial decline in retirees' standard of living. Meanwhile, the number of workers per white family grew—from 1.2 in 1918 to 1.6 in 1980 for laborers, from 1.2 to 1.7 for craft and operative wage earners, and from 1.6 to 2.0 for salaried workers (see table 2). These changes reflect the continued rise in the participation rate of adult women and of teenaged girls after 1940.

Relative incomes shifted somewhat during the Depression, as the earnings of salaried professionals and managers continued to rise while the earnings of production workers in manufacturing and services fell.[7] Since World War II the earnings distribution across occupations has remained fairly stable. Black families and retired people, however, made substantial gains during the 1960s as a result of government income support programs.

Between the Depression and the mid-1970s, the proportion of family income from earnings did not rise, although the number of paid family workers did. In 1973 the proportion of income from earnings fell as a result of the rise in income support payments, especially social security benefits, during the 1960s (see table 3). Since 1935, personal earnings and government support programs have accounted for 94 to 98 percent of income for the three white classes, but the proportion of each of the

6. U.S. Bureau of the Census, *Current Population Reports,* series P-60, no. 97, "Consumer Income" (Government Printing Office, 1975).

7. See Simon Kuznets, *National Income and Its Composition, 1919–1938,* 2 vols. (New York: National Bureau of Economic Research, 1941).

Table 2. *Average Number and Distribution of Earners per Family, by Class of Workers, 1918–80*

Class	1918	1935ᵃ	1950	1960	1973	1980
	Average number per family					
Black	n.a.	n.a.	n.a.	n.a.	1.66	1.46
White laborer	1.20	1.00	1.31	1.44	1.51	1.56
White wage earner	1.21	1.17	1.39	1.54	1.76	1.73
White salaried	1.57	1.31	1.40	1.79	2.06	1.97
	Percentage distribution of earners per family					
White laborer						
0	n.a.	n.a.	3	2	6	9
1	n.a.	n.a.	67	58	46	37
2	n.a.	n.a.	26	34	40	47
3 or more	n.a.	n.a.	5	6	8	8
White wage earner						
0	n.a.	n.a.	1	0	2	5
1	n.a.	n.a.	64	52	35	32
2	n.a.	n.a.	30	39	51	52
3 or more	n.a.	n.a.	5	8	12	11
White salaried						
0	n.a.	n.a.	1	0	1	3
1	n.a.	n.a.	51	35	24	22
2	n.a.	n.a.	40	49	51	56
3 or more	n.a.	n.a.	8	15	24	19

Sources: For 1918 and 1935, U.S. Department of Labor, Bureau of Labor Statistics, Consumer Expenditure Surveys; for subsequent years, Bureau of the Census, *Current Population Reports*.

n.a. Not available.

a. Adjusted to include urban relief families. Unadjusted CES data, which included only nonrelief families, were: black, 1.37; laborer, 1.23; wage earner, 1.29; and salaried, 1.35. The estimates were made using the average income for the relief population (Works Progress Administration, *Source of Income of Former Urban Relief Cases*, Research Bulletin series I, no. 22, [WPA, 1936]), and the relief population by occupation.

two sources has varied. The higher the class, the greater the percentage of income from earnings and the less from government benefits. Generally, the average age of the family head was the same for the three classes, but the number of children under eighteen increased with class, as did the number of earners per family.[8]

The higher-class families were able to improve their relative income position because of their greater access to paid work and because of the husbands' higher earnings. Although laborer families averaged only 66

8. In 1972–73 the laborer group averaged 1 child; 22 percent received social security or railroad retirement payments and 88 percent received wage income. The salaried group averaged 1.4 children; 10 percent received social security or railroad retirement payments and 97 percent received wage income. Fourteen percent of both classes received some self-employment income. Calculated from Bureau of Labor Statistics, *Consumer Expenditure Survey Series: Interview Survey, 1972–73* (GPO, 1978), table 1.

Table 3. *Sources of Income, by Class of Workers, 1918–80*
Percent of total income

Class and income source	1918	1935ᵃ	1950	1960	1973	1980
Earningsᵇ						
Black	n.a.	n.a.	n.a.	n.a.	79	n.a.
White laborer	97	82	85	86	77	84
White wage earner	96	91	91	89	88	91
White salaried	95	96	91	93	90	92
Transfer paymentsᶜ						
Black	n.a.	n.a.	n.a.	n.a.	20	n.a.
White laborer	n.a.	15	9	8	17	13
White wage earner	n.a.	5	5	6	9	7
White salaried	n.a.	1	4	3	7	5

Source: Bureau of Labor Statistics, Consumer Expenditure Surveys, various years.
n.a. Not available.
a. See note a, table 2. Unadjusted CES earnings data were: black, 98; white laborer, 96; white wage earner, 96; white salaried, 96.
b. Excludes self-employed income.
c. Includes social security, railroad and government retirement, private pensions, veterans' payments, unemployment compensation, welfare and public assistance, and other stipends. Child support, alimony, and disability included after 1973. Food stamps and workers' compensation included in 1960 and 1980.

to 72 percent of the total earnings of wage-earner families, laborer families' earnings per worker averaged 73 to 79 percent of those for wage-earner families. Government support payments can be viewed as partially making up for the lack of access to market work and for the lower wages paid to laborer families.

The importance of access to market work for the determination of family income is evident in the comparison of the number of earners per family shown in table 2. The proportion of salaried families with only one worker fell by more than one-half between 1950 and 1980, while the proportion with more than two workers tripled between 1950 and 1973 and then declined somewhat between 1973 and 1980. Changes for the other classes are in the same direction but not as sharp.

These figures mask differences by class in family composition as well as differences in family members' work roles. For example, in 1973, 84 percent of laborer families included married couples with 47 percent of the wives in the labor force; 94 percent of salaried families included married couples with 63 percent of wives in the labor force. Additionally, 36 percent of salaried families included an earner other than the husband or wife.[9]

9. Calculated from U.S. Bureau of the Census, *Current Population Reports*, series P-60, no. 97, "Consumer Income" (GPO, 1975), tables 32, 37–39.

Consumption norms changed dramatically as real incomes grew, as can be seen in the changing family budgets. The most remarkable changes in the daily structure of economic life occurred with the shift in the relative importance of food and transportation: the share spent on food declined and transportation-related expenditures rose. After car ownership became almost universal, ownership of a second car became important. Less dramatic but still fundamental changes occurred in the relative positions of clothing, recreation, and personal insurance in the family budget. These trends are discussed in detail in the following section.

The Dynamics of Economic Growth, Work Roles, and Consumption Norms

Economic growth is distributed as income through the assignment of work roles, which include the occupation of the family head, the access of other family members to paid work, and the unpaid work that goes on in the home. The amount of the wife's unpaid work time is primarily reflected in the size of the family, which varies by class. A family's money income, which is primarily from earnings, determines its expenditures and savings. I assume here that in the absence of technological change expenditures are made according to traditional consumption norms. As income rises and expenditures increase, each class imitates the consumption norms of a higher class. This process is not socially disruptive: the pattern of consumption is new to those just adopting it, but it is socially acceptable and familiar, having been practiced previously by a higher class.[10]

However, economic growth usually occurs through technological change, which alters the market goods and services available. Departures from the traditional ways of consuming occur, which can be socially disruptive. Instead of merely emulating the consumption patterns of higher classes, families may spend more (or less) for a given category

10. This approach draws upon Veblen's pecuniary emulation, Duesenberry's relative income approach, and Kuznets's work on growth and structure of consumption. See Thorstein Veblen, *The Theory of the Leisure Class* (Houghton Mifflin, 1973); James S. Duesenberry, *Income, Saving, and the Theory of Consumer Behavior* (Harvard University Press, 1949); and Simon Kuznets, "Quantitative Aspects of the Economic Growth of Nations: The Share and Structure of Consumption," *Economic Development and Cultural Change*, vol. 10 (January 1962, pt. 2).

than would be predicted by traditional norms. When real expenditure growth is rapid, families are able to imitate the consumption norms of higher classes in categories that did not change, as well as spend more than expected in categories where there were innovations as a result of technological change. When real expenditure growth is slow or negative, families may want to keep apace with market innovations, so they may have to spend less in some categories in order to spend more in others.

The dynamics of economic growth, work roles, and consumption produced major changes over each of the subperiods between 1918 and 1980. These changes are revealed by the data shown in tables 4–8.

1918 to 1935

The most salient characteristic of the period between 1918 and 1935 is, of course, the economic havoc wrought by the Depression. The differences in income between classes widened during this period, primarily as a result of differential unemployment. The wages of laborers and semiskilled and skilled workers fell relative to those of salaried workers. For nonrelief families, the average number of earners became more equal across class. If unemployed families are included, the average number of workers per family declined between 1918 and 1935.[11]

Children, rather than wives, were likely to be an important source of secondary income for families in both 1918 and 1935, and their earnings increased the income divergence between classes.[12] In 1918 laborers' wives had a participation rate of 11.3 percent, but annual average earnings of only $101. Wives of wage earners or salaried workers had a partic-

11. In 1935 the relief rate was 40 percent for laborers, 25 percent for craft and semiskilled workers, 5 percent for salaried workers, and 60 percent for urban black families. Overall, 16.5 percent of urban families were on relief in 1935. Calculated from occupational distribution of 1935 relief cases (F.L. Carmichael and Stanley L. Payne, *The 1935 Relief Population in 13 Cities: A Cross Section*, Works Progress Administration Research Bulletin, series 1, no. 23 [WPA, 1936], table 7), employed head distribution in table 1, and black relief distribution in National Resources Planning Board, *Family Expenditures in the United States—Statistical Tables and Appendixes* (GPO, 1941), tables 55, 360.

12. Earnings of male subsidiary earners were much higher than female subsidiary earnings. Males averaged $888 in laborer families and $1,164 in wage-earner families, while females averaged $140 and $136 respectively. The males earned 91 percent (laborers) to 96 percent (wage earners) of their fathers' earnings. For blacks, males averaged $678 and females $64, with male subsidiary earners making 98 percent of their fathers' earnings. Calculated from BLS, *Cost of Living in the United States, 1917–19,* Bulletin 357 (GPO, 1924), table 1, p. 4.

ipation rate of 9 percent, with respective earnings of $160 and $304. Children contributed far more: 8.5 percent of laborers' families reported children's earnings that averaged $140, 12.3 percent of wage earner families reported $215, and 46 percent of salaried families reported $739.

In 1935 subsidiary earners—again more likely to be children—earned an average of $229 for one-fifth of laborer families and $331 for one-fourth of wage-earner families. Salaried families averaged only slightly more gainful workers per family than wage-earner families, but their subsidiary earnings were 2.4 times greater. One-third of black families had a subsidiary earner, but their earnings averaged only $152, so that black additional workers contributed less than one-half as much to family income as did those in wage-earner families.

Real disposable per capita personal income was only 2 percent lower in 1935 than in 1918,[13] but real expenditures were about 20 percent higher for white nonrelief urban families and 8 percent higher for black nonrelief urban families. All classes experienced a decline in family size, so that although the percentage of their budgets spent on food, housing, and transportation declined, the per capita amount generally increased.[14] Per capita expenditures on clothing declined for laborer and wage-earner families and increased for salaried and black families. Black families' clothing expenditures had been far below those required by social norms; the substantial increase in their expenditures was a prerequisite to greater social integration.

1935 to 1950

World War II brought economic recovery and a restructuring of labor market institutions. Real per capita GNP was 76 percent higher in 1950 than in 1935, and real disposable personal income was 59 percent higher. This period witnessed the largest increase in wives' labor market participation of the subperiods studied, as women were called upon to replace men who were serving in the military. The increase was greatest among women aged 45–64; there was only a slight increase among those aged 25–44 and a decline among those aged 20–24.[15] The number of

13. These and all following output (or national income) figures are calculated from the national income and product accounts.

14. These comparisons are made only for families with a husband, wife, and at least one child since this was the group surveyed in 1918. The family size effect for blacks is exaggerated because it compares families with children in 1918 to all families in 1935.

15. The comparison given here is from the 1940 and 1950 censuses.

Table 4. *Distribution of Family Budget Expenditures, by Class of Workers, 1918–80*

Percent

Class and expenditure	1918	1935	1950	1960	1973	1980
Black						
Food[a]	47.5	35.5	34.1	26.1	23.9	22.1
Clothing	13.2	9.3	12.0	11.1	11.2	6.3
Shelter	22.3	31.1	22.1	23.1	39.4	28.1
Housing	12.7[b]	18.1	10.2	14.1	30.0	16.4
Fuel and light	6.0	9.6	5.0	4.1	5.3	8.2
Furnishings	3.6	3.4	7.0	5.0	4.1	3.5
Miscellaneous	17.0	24.1	31.8	39.7	47.0	43.5
Transportation	n.a.	4.5	7.6	8.7	19.8	19.6
Recreation and education[c]	n.a.	5.0	6.8	8.3	6.5	6.2
Household operation	n.a.	2.4	3.6	5.5	4.2	2.6[d]
Medical care	n.a.	3.8	3.5	4.8	4.3	3.6
Personal care	n.a.	2.2	3.0	3.8	1.3	1.1
Gifts and contributions	n.a.	2.5	2.2	3.1	3.3	1.7
Personal insurance[e]	n.a.	3.3[f]	3.8	4.6	6.8	7.6
Other	n.a.	0.4	1.2	0.9	0.8	1.2
White laborer						
Food[a]	43.0	34.4	31.7	24.1	20.0	20.8
Clothing	14.6	8.8	9.2	8.6	6.4	5.2
Shelter	24.3	30.5	22.2	21.4	24.2	26.1
Housing	13.9[b]	18.6	12.0	12.6	15.7	15.5
Fuel and light	6.0	8.5	4.4	4.3	4.6	6.8
Furnishings	4.5	3.3	5.8	4.4	3.9	3.9
Miscellaneous	18.0	26.4	36.8	45.9	49.4	47.9
Transportation	2.0	5.8	10.1	13.6	18.1	21.5
Recreation and education[c]	3.1	5.2	7.2	8.3	8.9	6.8
Household operation	2.4	2.8	3.9	5.2	3.2	1.9[d]
Medical care	4.3	3.6	5.2	6.0	6.1	4.4
Personal care	1.0	1.9	2.1	2.6	1.0	0.9
Gifts and contributions	1.9	2.4	3.3	4.2	4.2	3.0
Personal insurance[e]	2.8	4.3[f]	3.7	4.8	6.8	7.8
Other	0.6	0.3	1.4	1.3	0.9	1.6
White wage earner						
Food[a]	40.1	32.8	30.0	23.6	19.4	19.9
Clothing	15.8	9.5	9.7	8.5	6.5	5.2
Shelter	24.6	28.6	20.4	21.4	22.5	25.8
Housing	14.6[b]	17.0	10.3	12.3	13.7	15.4
Fuel and light	5.3	7.7	4.0	4.4	4.5	6.3
Furnishings	4.6	3.8	6.1	4.7	4.3	4.1

Table 4 *(continued)*

Class and expenditure	1918	1935	1950	1960	1973	1980
White wage earner						
Miscellaneous	19.5	29.2	39.8	46.6	51.6	49.1
Transportation	2.3	7.3	12.3	13.7	18.6	21.7
Recreation and education[c]	3.8	5.6	8.0	8.1	9.7	7.2
Household operation	2.7	3.1	3.7	5.0	3.1	2.0[d]
Medical care	4.4	3.7	5.2	6.0	5.2	3.9
Personal care	1.0	1.9	2.1	2.7	1.0	0.9
Gifts and contributions	1.7	2.6	3.1	4.8	4.0	2.5
Personal insurance[e]	2.8	4.7[f]	4.3	5.2	9.1	9.5
Other	0.6	0.3	1.0	1.1	0.9	1.4
White salaried						
Food[a]	35.1	26.4	28.3	22.5	19.0	18.6
Clothing	18.7	10.1	10.4	9.9	7.0	5.7
Shelter	22.3	24.1	20.2	18.9	21.6	25.5
Housing	12.1[b]	14.9	9.8	10.4	12.9	15.6
Fuel and light	4.5	6.0	3.6	3.8	4.2	5.5
Furnishings	5.7	3.2	6.8	4.7	4.5	4.5
Miscellaneous	23.8	39.4	41.0	48.7	52.4	50.2
Transportation	4.5	10.6	13.1	14.0	18.0	20.5
Recreation and education[c]	4.5	8.1	8.6	9.5	10.5	7.7
Household operation	3.2	4.7	3.8	4.9	2.9	2.4[d]
Medical care	4.3	4.5	4.8	5.7	4.9	3.7
Personal care	0.9	2.1	2.0	2.5	1.1	0.9
Gifts and contributions	2.9	3.4	3.4	4.8	4.2	3.4
Personal insurance[e]	2.8	5.5[f]	4.3	6.0	9.9	10.2
Other	0.8	0.4	1.1	1.2	0.8	1.5

Sources: For 1918 (blacks), *Monthly Labor Review*, vol. 9 (August 1919), p. 119; for 1918 (whites), Bureau of Labor Statistics, *Cost of Living in the United States, 1917–19*, Bulletin 357 (GPO, 1924). For 1935, all classes except salaried, Faith M. Williams and Alice C. Hanson, *Money Disbursements of Wage Earners and Clerical Workers, 1934–36: Summary Volume*, Bureau of Labor Statistics Bulletin 638 (GPO, 1941); for salaried families, Bureau of Labor Statistics, Bulletins 643–49. For 1950, *Study of Consumer Expenditures, Incomes and Savings, Statistical Tables: Urban U.S.—1950*, Bureau of Labor Statistics and Wharton School of Finance and Commerce (University of Pennsylvania, 1956). For 1960, BLS, *Survey of Consumer Expenditures, 1960–61*, Report 237–38 (GPO, 1964). For 1973, BLS, *Consumer Expenditure Survey Series: Interview Survey, 1972–73*, Bulletin 1985 (GPO, 1978). For 1980, "Consumer Expenditure Survey: Results from the 1980–81 Interview," *BLS News*, December 19, 1984, and BLS, *Consumer Expenditure Survey: Diary Survey, 1980–81*, Bulletin 2173 (GPO, 1983).

n.a. Not available.

a. Includes liquor.

b. Excludes homeowners.

c. Includes tobacco.

d. Telephone, estimated from the National Income and Product Accounts, was shifted from fuel and light to household operation.

e. Personal insurance includes employee withholding for social security (OASDI). The contribution rate (with maximum taxable earnings) was 1 percent ($3,000) in 1937, 1.5 percent ($3,000) in 1950, 3 percent ($4,800) in 1960, 5.85 percent ($10,800) in 1973, and 6.127 percent ($25,900) in 1980. The percent of workers covered increased from 55 percent in 1940 to 85 percent in 1980.

f. Personal insurance was estimated from 1935 NRC data; it was added to expenditures and subtracted from assets.

workers per family increased for all classes and also became more equal across classes.

The gap in income between classes narrowed sharply as a result of greatly reduced unemployment rates for heads of lower-class families, a growth in subsidiary earners in lower-class families, and greater equalization of earnings across nonfarm occupations. In 1950 the typical black urban family with an employed worker had 83 percent of the income of a white laborer family, but the black family had more members and more earners than the white family.[16] Wage-earner families received 78 percent of the income of salaried families in 1950, compared with 57 percent in 1935. After 1950 the income differential between wage-earner and salaried families widened, while the differential between laborers and wage earners remained fairly constant at about 75 percent.

The family size of laborers and wage earners decreased, but the size of black and salaried workers' families remained the same or increased very little.[17] Reported expenditures for housing declined among all classes, but this reflected to a large degree the gains in ownership, which caused housing expenditures to be recorded as investments. Meanwhile, expenditures for furnishings increased substantially. Black families made substantial gains in their standard of living; better nutrition, clothing, and transportation aided their continuing social integration. White families made major improvements in food, transportation, clothing, home ownership, and medical care. By 1950 families with employed heads were living on a high plane by historical standards; this era of personal material improvements continued for another decade.

1950 to 1960

The period from 1950 to 1960 witnessed the largest increase in real expenditures of the subperiods studied. Expenditures grew almost 43 percent for salaried families, 20 to 25 percent for wage-earner and laborer families, and 17 percent for black families, even though real disposable per capita income was only 15 percent higher at the end of the decade.[18]

16. Calculated from consumer expenditure surveys, comparing black and white families with incomes of $2,000–$3,000.

17. The survey population was families (two or more people) for 1935 and households (including single individuals) for 1950. The implicit *family* size for 1950 is 3.6 for blacks, 2.9 for laborers, 3.3 for wage earners, and unchanged for salaried workers.

18. Calculated from U.S. Bureau of the Census, *Historical Statistics of the United States, Colonial Times to 1970*, pt. 1 (GPO, 1975), pp. 320–27.

The number of earners per family continued to grow, and at a faster rate as one went up the class ladder. One-half of wage-earner families and two-thirds of salaried families had two or more paid workers in 1960, while three-fifths of laborer families had only one paid worker. Overall, the income differences among the four classes grew slightly, as blacks fell slightly relative to laborers and salaried workers moved ahead relative to wage earners.[19] However, the divergence in incomes across class was smaller in this period than it was in 1918–35. Although the 1935–50 and 1950–60 subperiods had the largest growth in the number of workers per family, the growth in the former period acted to narrow the income gap between classes and in the latter it acted to widen the gap.

As in the previous decade, the female participation rate rose 12 percent, with the largest growth for women aged 45–64. In addition, the participation rate of mothers, even those with children under 6, began to rise. Wives were now more important than children as earners.[20] At the same time that the female participation rate was increasing, family size was also increasing for all classes. Work roles and consumption norms were coming into conflict.

One result was that market goods and services most closely related to housework became less important in the families' budgets. Average expenditures for food, clothing, and household operations shrank from 43 percent of each of the white classes' family budgets in 1950 to 37 percent in 1960. For blacks, the decline was from 50 to 43 percent. Salaried families did spend more on food on a per capita basis, but the other three classes spent less. Housing was the area where expenditures increased from 1950 on for all classes; and home ownership rates increased dramatically except for blacks, probably because of residential segregation and discrimination in credit allocation. As in the previous

19. As Joseph Pechman has pointed out, income inequality for the entire population showed a slight decline between 1950 and 1960. However, this reflects the improvement for the lowest fifth and the worsening for the highest fifth of the families, which are largely excluded from the occupational classes used here. See Bureau of the Census, *Current Population Reports,* series P-60, no. 142, "Consumer Income" (GPO, 1984), table 17. Jeffrey G. Williamson and Peter H. Lindert, *American Inequality: A Macroeconomic History* (Academic Press, 1980), found inequality changed very little between 1950 and 1972. However, they also found that between 1950 and 1960 the variance in the log of male incomes increased. Between 1950 and 1960 and between 1960 and 1972, the earnings of public school teachers and physicians rose relative to nonfarm unskilled laborers. Both of these findings are consistent with my income measures.

20. Tilly and Scott, *Women, Work, and Family,* also noted this switch in work roles between mother and children in England and France after World War II.

Table 5. Selected Characteristics of Families, by Class of Workers, 1918–80

Class and year[a]	Income range (current dollars)[b]	Average expenditures[c]		Ratio of expenditures to net income[d]	Ratio of taxes to gross income	Average family size (persons)[e]
		Current dollars	1972–73 dollars			
Black						
1918	Less than 900	791	2,268	99	n.a.	4.2
1935	600–900	785	2,468	104	0.1	3.4
1950	2,000–3,000	2,756	4,939	110	3.3	3.4
1960	3,000–4,000	3,949	5,754	113	3.6	3.5
1973	7,000–8,000	6,665	6,665	98	9.3	3.7
1980	f	12,440	6,189	87	n.a.	2.9
White laborer						
1918	900–1,200	1,075	3,080	100	0.1	4.5
1935	900–1,200	1,165	3,663	109	0.1	3.4
1950	2,000–3,000	2,947	5,821	116	5.0	2.6
1960	4,000–5,000	4,954	7,218	110	9.3	2.9
1973	8,000–10,000	7,772	7,772	98	11.8	2.7
1980	15,000–20,000	16,065	7,993	93	n.a.	2.7

White wage earner

Year	Income range					
1918	1,200–1,500	1,298	3,723	97	0.1	4.7
1935	1,200–1,500	1,439	4,524	106	0.1	3.5
1950	3,000–4,000	3,874	6,942	111	5.9	3.2
1960	5,000–6,000	5,827	8,490	106	9.8	3.4
1973	12,000–15,000	10,193	10,193	89	14.4	3.3
1980	20,000–30,000	20,330	10,114	83	n.a.	3.1

White salaried

Year	Income range					
1918	2,100–2,500	2,053	5,796	90	0.2	5.7
1935	2,250–2,500	2,285	7,184	103	0.3	3.3
1950	4,000–5,000	4,835	8,664	108	7.1	3.4
1960	7,500–10,000	8,476	12,350	99	12.4	3.8
1973	15,000–20,000	12,393	12,393	85	15.7	3.6
1980	g	25,334	12,604	74	n.a.	3.3

Sources: BLS, Consumer Expenditure Surveys, various years.

a. Class is defined by occupation and empirically measured by income of median group in each occupation.

b. After taxes in 1950 and 1960.

c. Expenditure patterns for 1980 reflect a small number of black households in data for whites because data were not analyzed separately by race and income.

d. Taxes have not been published for 1980 CES, so ratio given represents expenditures to *total* (pre-tax) income.

e. 1918 includes only urban husband-wife families with children present; 1935 includes only urban families (two or more related individuals); 1950 includes urban households; 1972 includes rural and urban households.

f. The 1980 data do not give income for blacks.

g. The 1980 income group was an average of the $20,000 to $30,000 group and $30,000 and over group.

Table 6. *Home and Car Ownership, by Class of Workers, 1918–80*
Percent

Class	1918[a]	1935	1950	1960	1973	1980
Home ownership						
Black	n.a.	19	27	27	38	40
White laborer	19	24	37	43	52	58
White wage earner	24	26	47	53	69	73
White salaried	36	42	54	71	76	80
Car ownership						
Black	n.a.	12	27	42	68	n.a.
White laborer	9	33	49	78	89	n.a.
White wage earner	13	45	68	88	95	n.a.
White salaried	31	76	78	94	97	n.a.

Sources: BLS, Consumer Expenditure Surveys, various years.
n.a. Not available.
a. Automobiles combined with motorcycles and bicycles. Only 6 percent of the sample owned an automobile.

decade, car ownership rose rapidly for all classes. Nevertheless, only 42 percent of black families owned an automobile in 1960, compared with 78 percent of white laborer families and around 90 percent of white wage-earner and salaried families.

1960 to 1973

Between 1960 and 1973 the decline in the relative importance of housework-related expenditures accelerated for white families. At the same time, their family size fell and the participation rate of mothers, particularly those with children under 6, continued its dramatic increase. By 1973 an average of only 29 percent of the white class family budgets was spent on food, clothing, and household operations; and 33 percent of mothers with children under 6 were in the labor force, as were 50 percent of those with children 6–18. Women's work roles had changed sufficiently that the norm was for women to engage in paid labor at least some of the time as well as to maintain their families. The family's income was substantially affected by a wife's work for pay. Nonetheless, a wife's earnings contributed a declining percentage of earned income across class—from around 33 percent in laborer families to around 23 percent in salaried families.[21]

21. Calculated from Bureau of the Census, *Current Population Reports,* series P-60, no. 97, "Consumer Income" (GPO, 1975), tables 39–40. The husband's median earnings were around $7,550 (laborer), $9,800 (wage earner), and $13,500 (salaried), and

Table 7. *Participation Rates by Sex, Age, and Marital Status, 1920–80*

Sex, age, and marital status	1920[a]	1930[a]	1940[b]	1950[b]	1960[b]	1973[b]	1980[b]
Female	22.7	23.6	26.6	33.9	37.8	44.7	51.5
19 and under	28.4	22.8	26.7	41.0	39.4	47.9	52.9
20–24	37.5	41.8	45.6	46.1	46.2	61.2	68.9
25–44	21.7	24.6	30.5	36.4	39.9	51.6	65.5
45–64	16.5	18.0	20.2	33.2	44.3	48.0	50.7
65 and over	7.3	7.3	6.1	9.4	10.8	8.9	8.1
Wives[c]	9.0	11.7	13.8	23.8	30.5	42.2	50.1
With no children	n.a.	n.a.	n.a.	30.3	34.7	42.8	46.0
With children under 6	n.a.	n.a.	n.a.	11.9	18.6	32.7	45.1
With children 6 and over	n.a.	n.a.	n.a.	28.3	39.0	50.1	61.7
Male	84.6	82.1	82.6	86.8	84.0	79.5	77.4
19 and under	51.5	40.1	47.4	66.3	59.4	61.6	60.5
20–24	89.9	88.8	88.1	89.1	90.2	86.8	85.9
25–44	95.6	95.8	94.5	97.1	97.7	96.1	95.3
45–64	90.7	91.0	88.7	92.0	92.0	86.5	82.0
65 and over	55.6	54.0	41.8	45.8	33.1	22.8	19.0
Total participation	54.3	53.2	54.6	59.9	60.2	61.4	63.8

Sources: For 1920, 1930, and 1940, data from U.S. Census; for subsequent years, Bureau of the Census, *Current Population Reports*. Census figures are lower than CPS figures. For example, 1950 female participation rates were 55.1 percent (Census) and 59.9 percent (CPS).

n.a. Not available.
a. Among population aged 14 and over.
b. Among population aged 16 and over.
c. For all married women in 1920 and 1930; for married women with husband present in 1940 and later years. Only children under 18 included.

Within each class, a substantial income gap existed between families with an employed wife and those without, so that classes were no longer characterized by income. A schism was developing between class groups and income groups, depending upon the wife's work status. But this schism, which had been developing over many decades, was probably not as important as the schism between earnings growth and expenditure growth, which was peculiar to this period. Nationally, real disposable per capita income grew 56 percent. However, growth in output and in earnings did not determine expenditure growth across class because of the effect of government income support programs and savings. In 1973 incomes exceeded expenditures for all four classes for the first time in

the wife's median earnings, given the husband's earnings, were $3,709, $3,950, and $4,005 respectively. The 1973 participation rate was fairly constant across class, but black wives still had a substantially higher participation rate than white wives—51 percent compared with 38 percent.

the years studied. Salaried workers families' expenditures were 85 percent of net income; savings had become an important part of their budget. In contrast, laborer families' expenditures were 98 percent of net income.

The shift in income differences between classes was mixed: salaried family income gained relative to wage-earner and laborer family income, while black family income gained slightly relative to laborer family income. However, without government income support programs, which accounted for 12 percent of laborers' income and 15 percent of blacks', the gap between the black and laborer classes would have been larger.[22]

Family size declined for white families and increased for blacks. In 1973 the black class had a larger average family size than all of the three white classes for the first time in any of the survey years. Food and clothing expenditures (per capita) by the white classes continued to fall. There was a large jump in car ownership for blacks and a rise in multiple car ownership for whites: in 1970 one-third of laborer, one-half of wage-earner, and two-thirds of salaried families owned more than one car.[23] White classes also increased their expenditures for housing and personal insurance, which reflected the rise in social security withholding.[24] Blacks' expenditures on food, clothing, and housing remained steady, having reached the minimum levels required for social integration; this allowed them to double their per capita expenditures on transportation.

1973 to 1981

The eight-year period between the last two surveys embraced a time of economic instability, with relatively high unemployment and inflation.

22. Most families (70–80 percent in each class) received some income in this category, which accounted for 9 percent of wage-earner income and 7 percent of salaried income. The categories include income support programs (social security and other retirement income, welfare and public assistance, veterans' compensation and benefits, unemployment insurance, workers' compensation, alimony and other regular support payments, and food stamps) as well as some other minor categories (tax refunds, short-term capital gains). Government transfer programs accounted for 4.0 percent of personal income in 1935, 6.6 percent in 1950, 7.1 percent in 1960, and 9.8 percent in 1970. Bureau of the Census, *Historical Statistics of the United States, Colonial Times to 1970*, pt. 1 (GPO, 1975), pp. 241–42.

23. Bureau of the Census, *Census of Housing, 1970, Metropolitan Housing Characteristics*, vol. 3, pt. 1, tables A-3, A-4.

24. The employee contribution rate to social security rose as follows: 1 percent (1937), 1.5 percent (1950), 3 percent (1960), 5.85 percent (1973), 6.13 percent (1980), and 6.65 percent (1981).

Per capita output increased 12 percent, but real disposable per capita income increased only 4 percent. For the first time since the Depression, the number of earners per family did not rise across classes. The average number of earners fell slightly for wage-earner and salaried families and more noticeably for black families. It increased for laborer families because of a rise in two-earner families and a decline in one-earner families. In contrast, among salaried families the number with two earners increased while those with three earners declined.

At the same time, the total participation rate rose dramatically because of the continued increase in participation by women with children, especially those aged 25–44. Male participation rates, especially for men over 45, continued to fall, as they had over the entire survey period. Compositional shifts in households accounted for the divergent trends in participation rates and earners per family; households of unrelated individuals, especially young workers, were growing in relative importance. The decline in earners per family reflected the fact that older children tended to establish their own households and did not pool their income with their parents. For black families, it also reflected the growth of female-headed families.

There was a shift in income differences between classes in the opposite direction from the two preceding subperiods. Both black and salaried family incomes decreased relative to laborer and wage-earner family incomes, respectively. Real family income fell for all four classes. However, real per capita expenditures rose as family size and additions to assets fell.[25]

Between 1973 and 1981 housing and transportation rose in importance in the family budgets, which continued the trend since 1950 for housing and since 1918 for transportation. Fuel and lighting jumped in relative importance as the price of household fuel tripled over the period. The higher transportation expenditures reflected an increase in multiple car ownership and higher car prices due to government regulation. In 1980 the majority of white families had two or more cars.[26] Housing continued to improve as home ownership rates rose, space per person increased, and the acquisition of air conditioning continued.

25. Since tax data are not available for 1980, only gross expenditure rates (expenditures divided by gross income) can be compared between 1973 and 1980. The gross expenditure rates for 1973 and 1980 were: black 89, 87; laborer, 86, 93; wage earner, 76, 83; and salaried, 72, 74.

26. Bureau of the Census, *Census of Housing, 1980, Metropolitan Housing Characteristics*, *U.S. Summary* (GPO, 1984), tables A-3, A-4.

Table 8. *Family Food Expenditures, by Class of Workers, 1918–80*
1972–73 dollars

Class	1918	1935[a]	1950	1960[b]	1973	1980[c]
Black						
At home	n.a.	1,124	1,363	1,197	1,381	n.a.
Away from home	n.a.	58	210	244	224	n.a.
Per capita	242	296	463	412	424	441
White laborer						
At home	n.a.	1,682	1,329	1,385	1,161	1,015
Away from home	n.a.	105	279	298	329	467
Per capita	274	423	618	581	552	566
White wage earner						
At home	n.a.	1,691	1,703	1,641	1,467	1,205
Away from home	n.a.	131	286	294	428	586
Per capita	297	490	622	583	574	599
White salaried						
At home	n.a.	2,038	1,928	2,123	1,694	1,292
Away from home	n.a.	266	404	531	550	710
Per capita	338	688	686	703	623	663

Source: BLS, Consumer Expenditure Surveys, various years.
a. Includes alcoholic beverages.
b. At home and away from home are for black and white households for laborer, wage earner, and salaried. Per capita is for whites only for these three classes.
c. From CES diary survey, except for per capita, inflated from weekly to annual figures. Blacks and whites are not listed separately. Per capita figures from the interview survey.

Expenditures for food away from home accounted for one-third of the white classes' food expenditures in 1980, compared with slightly less than one-fourth in 1973.[27] If food away from home is assumed to cost twice as much as similar food at home, however, then adjusted per capita food expenditures actually fell between 1973 and 1980.[28] Families were not buying higher-quality food; instead they were paying for the convenience of having meals prepared for them and eaten away from home. Larger food expenditures were now associated with social interaction, including employment, rather than family life.

Summary

The changes in consumption norms that took place between 1918 and 1980 are consistent with the institutional prediction that the labor force

27. Food details for black families are not available, but blacks' expenditures for food away from home lagged behind whites' expenditures. In 1973, only 14 percent of blacks' food expenditures were for food away from home.
28. Adjusted food expenditures would fall even more if food away from home were more realistically assumed to cost more than twice as much as similar food at home.

participation rate of women decreases when consumption becomes more oriented toward expenditures associated with housework (food, clothing, and household operation) and the rate increases when consumption becomes more oriented toward expenditures not associated with housework.

Between 1918 and 1935 the female participation rate increased slowly. Increased expenditures for food and housing expenditures were the major changes in consumption norms. However, changes were also occurring, especially the decline in family size, that would allow the female participation rate to increase during the war-induced recovery. During 1935–50 the participation rate of wives increased dramatically because of the war effort to recruit female workers. Although expenditures for food at home increased, which would dampen female participation, their participation was encouraged by increases in expenditures for transportation and medical care as well as the decrease in family size.

Between 1950 and 1960 the female participation rate continued to rise, but there were still conflicting pulls from shifts in consumption norms, which kept the female labor force participation rate from growing as rapidly as it might have. Large increases in expenditures for transportation, recreation, and housing induced women to work for pay, but the increase in family size induced them to stay at home. This conflict was short-lived, as the birthrate began to fall in the early 1960s, and from 1960 to 1980 there was a major increase in the labor market participation of women, especially mothers. Increased expenditures for transportation, personal insurance, and shelter and decreases in food, clothing, and family size induced women into the labor force. As women's work role encompassed both housework and paid work, urban women's lives became more integrated with the marketplace, just as husbands' lives had during the initial movement from the farm to the city. Economic growth in the United States has meant a more physically mobile and socially active population at all class levels.

Consumption Norms over Time

Overall, money income determines the family's consumption norms, which are the material components of its standard of living. Money income does not, however, measure well-being, since expenditures are also made to provide for comfort and status. Well-being can be determined only by looking at consumption details and evaluating the extent to which the socially defined standards of well-being are met. Since food, housing, and transportation are the most important material components of well-being, both in terms of their direct impact and in terms of their size in the family budget, I focus here on these three items.[29]

Food

Between the two world wars, the family's diet improved dramatically, with real per capita food expenditures more than doubling. Since diets were nutritionally inadequate and monotonous in 1918,[30] the fact that per capita food expenditures grew at the same rate as total per capita expenditures between 1918 and 1935 is not surprising. In addition, improvements in refrigeration and the national transportation system made more types of food available year-round. The relative decline in farm prices during the Depression also made many foods more affordable.

Breakfast and lunch for an average wage-earner family in 1918 consisted mainly of bread, cereal, and home-baked goods; only one daily meal, usually dinner, included a variety of nongrain foods. The quality of these meals thus depended to a large degree upon the wife's baking, which used 7.2 pounds of various types of flours and cornmeal each week. Wives prepared three meals daily for family members, including the meals carried as bag lunches. Only one-third of the families surveyed reported purchasing lunches (including part of lunch) outside the home, and these families averaged 3.4 lunches per week.

The nutritional standards of the period focused primarily on energy needs, because many families had insufficient caloric intake.[31] The caloric content of the average survey diet was more than 10 percent too low for laborer families, sufficient for wage-earner families, and more than 10 percent too high for salaried families. At least one-half of a subsample of the 1918 survey families consumed too few calories for the

29. Although medical care is also a crucial component of well-being, its allocation primarily through an insurance system does not allow its examination with budget data.

30. This analysis of food expenditures and the family diet draws heavily from an unpublished manuscript by the author. Although the daily diet in 1918 was monotonous by modern standards, it was luxurious by preindustrial standards. Seē Fernand Braudel, *The Structures of Everyday Life: The Limits of the Possible* (Harper and Row, 1981), chaps. 2, 3.

31. See Royal Meeker, "Minimum Quantity Budget Necessary to Maintain a Worker's Family of Five in Health and Decency," *Monthly Labor Review*, vol. 10 (June 1920), pp. 1–18.

husband and wife to be engaged in moderately active work. Wage-earner families consumed more than adequate protein but inadequate iron and calcium.[32] Although no information on how calorie deficiencies were spread among family members is available, studies in France and England indicate that the wife reduced her food intake (and sometimes her children's intake) when food supplies were inadequate. Nutritional deficiencies increased down the income scale as grain consumption rose and milk, vegetable, fruit, and meat consumption fell.

By 1935 the diet of the average family with an employed head had improved considerably in meeting caloric needs and providing more diversity as well as more nutrients. The family's food purchases indicate that the amount of baking and food preservation done at home had declined. The diversity and richness provided by the larger grocery budget in 1935 are evident in the larger assortment of fruits and vegetables purchased, in the doubling of the per capita purchase of sugar, and in the appearance of separate listings for soft drinks, bottled salad dressing and mayonnaise, and ready-to-eat cereal.

In 1935 expenditures for food away from home accounted for 7 percent of the wage-earner family's food budget (see table 8). Meals at work accounted for 63 percent and snacks for 17 percent of away-from-home food expenditures. The percentage of wage-earner families reporting expenditures for meals at work rose only slightly to 37 percent. The purchase of food away from home increased sharply with income.

The variety of foods available for lunch and (to a lesser degree) for breakfast had expanded considerably by 1935. The monotony of the large amount of grain products still being consumed was diminished with the addition of more fruits, vegetables, meat, and dairy products. While many families used their earnings to provide greater variety in their diets, they did not necessarily improve their nutrition. At times, cultural norms were in conflict with nutritional standards and inexpensive ways

32. Analysis based upon William F. Ogburn, "A Study of Food Costs in Various Cities," *Monthly Labor Review*, vol. 9 (August 1919), pp. 1–25. Also, niacin deficiency and pellagra were widespread through the South before cornmeal was fortified. Letitia Brewster and Michael F. Jacobson, *The Changing American Diet* (Washington, D.C.: Center for Science in the Public Interest, 1978), pp. 54–55. In this paper, I use National Research Council, Committee on Dietary Allowances, *Recommended Dietary Allowances*, 9th ed. (Washington, D.C.: National Academy of Sciences, 1980) as the benchmark for nutrients other than calories. Since these standards reflect both prevailing wisdom and scientific knowledge, they represent a socially created benchmark that changes over time.

to meet these standards. Three-fourths of the white urban families (ranging from 40 percent in the laborer group to 98 percent in the salaried group) spent enough on food to purchase the "minimum-cost adequate diet" of the Bureau of Home Economics.[33] Actual buying patterns did not follow the recommended diet, so that families consumed too little milk, vegetables, and fruits.[34] The nutritional inadequacies of laborer families and the classes below them reflect budgetary constraints, but among wage-earner families nutritional inadequacies are the result of social norms governing food choice. However, many of the eating habits of the lower-income groups, such as the use in the South of inexpensive leafy greens, sweet potatoes, less expensive cuts of meat, and self-rising flour (containing calcium), were a positive contribution to their nutrition.[35]

Deficient caloric consumption was less serious for families with employed heads in 1935 than in 1918, but many wage-earner families continued to have less than adequate nutrition.[36] For example, even though milk consumption increased by one-fourth between 1918 and 1935, calcium deficiency was still widespread in 1935. Overall, nutritional improvements between 1918 and 1935 resulted in adequate diets for families in the middle-income distribution. However, the bottom 40 percent of the families with incomes below $1,000 still were underfed and suffered serious deficiencies of several nutrients.

By 1948 the diets of most laborer families and even most families of unemployed workers provided sufficient calories.[37] Widespread defi-

33. Calculated from Hazel K. Stiebeling and Medora M. Ward, *Diets at Four Levels of Nutritive Content and Cost*, U.S. Department of Agriculture Circular 296 (GPO, 1933), p. 29. The BHE minimum cost diet was the same in cost as the "emergency level diet" of the Works Progress Administration.

34. Faith M. Williams and Alice C. Hanson, *Money Disbursements of Wage Earners and Clerical Workers, 1934–36: Summary Volume*, Bureau of Labor Statistics Bulletin 638 (GPO, 1941), pp. 72–74, 81–85.

35. The weekly per capita amount needed to provide an inexpensive, adequate diet based upon local food-buying practices ranged from $1.70 for blacks in the South to $2.45 for whites in the North Atlantic. Price differences account for only 4 percent of the variation. See Hazel K. Stiebeling and Esther F. Phipard, *Diets of Families of Employed Wage Earners and Clerical Workers in Cities*, U.S. Department of Agriculture Circular 507 (GPO, 1939), p. 83.

36. Ibid. This nutritional analysis is based on a special food study of 4,000 of the survey families.

37. Details of food purchases were not published from the 1950 (and later) CES. Other food surveys were taken, and the spring 1948 national food survey on urban households is used here. Faith Clark and others, *Food Consumption of Urban Families*

ciencies in categories other than calories (and protein) persisted among families with incomes under $1,000, however. Relative dietary deficiencies by income declined between 1935 and 1948. This decrease primarily reflects a greater equalization of the amounts spent on food per person across classes in 1950 compared with 1935 (see table 8). It is also related to the enrichment of white flour and cornmeal, which became widespread during the war. The enrichment increased the consumption of iron, thiamine, and niacin, and was especially helpful for lower-income families, who ate large amounts of grain products. The wage-earner family's diet continued to grow less reliant on home baking. The diet also continued to become less monotonous as its dependence on grain declined.

Between 1948 and 1965 dietary improvements stopped overall, even though per capita food expenditures increased slightly.[38] As a class characteristic, nutritional deficiencies disappeared by 1950 (except among the very poorest). In the decades following World War II, the types of food eaten at home grew similar across classes. Higher-class families ate more beef and more expensive cuts of meat and more vegetables (other than potatoes) and fruits and replaced some grain products with already baked products. But these changes affected the variety of meals at home and the ease of food preparation more than they affected the nutritional content.

In 1977 the similarity across classes in nutritional intake of food at home included even the poorest class. Poor families' nutrition improved with an increase in real income and with the food stamp program, which had expanded since the mid-1960s. The program's importance in im-

---

in the United States . . . with an Appraisal of Methods of Analysis, U.S. Department of Agriculture Information Bulletin 132 (GPO, 1954). Less than 25 percent of the families in the income groups above $1,000 had insufficient calories. The percentages were calculated on the basis of "nutrition units (physically active man)" compared with the NRC recommended daily allowances (1948 revised).

38. From 1948 to 1955 consumption of thiamine, niacin, protein, and iron rose while consumption of vitamin C fell. Between 1955 and 1965 the national proportion with good diets fell from 60 percent to 50 percent while the proportion with bad diets rose from 15 percent to 21 percent. U.S. Department of Agriculture, Science and Education Administration, *Nutrient Levels in Food Used by Households in the United States, Spring 1977*, Nationwide Food Consumption Survey, 1977–78, Preliminary Report 3, (USDA, 1981); Corinne LeBovitt and others, *Dietary Evaluation of Food Used in Households in the United States*, U.S. Department of Agriculture Household Food Consumption Survey, 1955, Report 16 (GPO, 1961); and *Nutritive Quality of Diets: A Report to the Committee on Agriculture of the U.S. House of Representatives* (Washington, D.C.: U.S. Agricultural Research Service, 1967).

proving the diets of low-income people is underscored by their major nutritional improvements between the 1965 and 1977 surveys.

Although food away from home steadily increased its share of the family's food budget, it lost its sharp class distinction after World War II, when many more people across classes started buying meals at work and meals away from home outside of work and school. Between 1972–73 and 1980–81 the budgetary proportion of food consumed away from home grew almost 5 percent yearly for each white class, so that in 1980 food away from home accounted for one-third of the food budget. Nutritional standards were basically met by laborer families and equalized across class by 1950, with continued improvements made in diversity of foods and ease of preparation, including eating out, after 1950.

Housing

Home ownership rates increased across class and over time. Salaried families were always at least one-third more likely to own a home than laborer families. Laborer and wage-earner families were three times as likely to own a home in 1980 as in 1918, while salaried families were twice as likely (see table 6).

Much of the housing in 1918 was cramped and had inadequate ventilation, lighting, heating, and plumbing. The higher expenditures across class in 1918 were used to buy additional rooms to accommodate larger families and to buy higher-quality housing with more amenities, such as heating, plumbing, electricity, outside windows, and better location. One room per person was considered the standard for adequate housing.[39] Although this standard was met on average by the three white classes, almost one-half of the families fell below the standard.

The quality differences across classes in 1918 are reflected in the percentage of rooms equipped for heating (from 50 percent for laborer to 60 percent for salaried), those with an inside water closet (from 61 percent for laborer to 84 percent for salaried), and those with a bathroom (from 36 percent for laborer to 73 percent for salaried). The most important improvements across class were a private water closet, a bathroom with running hot water, and central heating.

Large differences in energy usage—both amount and type of fuel—

39. William Ogburn, "Rents in Various Cities," *Monthly Labor Review*, vol. 9 (September 1919), pp. 9–30. Overcrowding would be greater in families taking in boarders and lodgers, who have been largely omitted.

existed by class in 1918. Coal, the most widely used fuel, was dirty and difficult to use. Gas and electricity were cleaner, more convenient, and more expensive than coal or wood. On average, salaried families used 16 percent more Btus than wage-earner families—69 percent more electricity, 32 percent more gas, and 14 percent more coal. Wage-earner families used 14 percent more Btus than laborer families—82 percent more electricity, 25 percent more gas, and 11 percent more coal. Gas and electricity became more widely used by 1935 and accounted for around one-half of the fuel budgets, while coal accounted for around one-quarter.[40]

By 1935 housing had improved considerably in terms of plumbing and electricity with the continuing installation of power lines and public sewer and water systems. Now 90 percent of the laborer and 97 percent of the salaried families lived in dwellings with running water, an inside flush toilet, and electric lights. Class differences in the availability of hot running water persisted. The percentage of families living in houses declined by around 20 percent between 1918 and 1935 for the three white classes. The average number of rooms per dwelling remained about the same, however, so that the smaller families in 1935 had fewer people per room.

Home ownership rates rose rapidly for all classes between 1935 and 1950, which meant that housing quality rose even though housing expenditures did not rise. Owner-occupied units have better plumbing and heating facilities and are less likely to be deteriorating or dilapidated. In 1950 almost one-half of wage-earner families and over one-half of salaried families were homeowners (see table 6). A significant proportion of families still did not have full plumbing facilities.[41]

A 60 percent increase in housing expenditures between 1950 and 1960 brought sounder housing and better plumbing facilities. The percentage of dilapidated housing fell by over one-half for all groups; and 90 percent of laborer families, 95 percent of wage-earner families, and 99 percent of salaried families had full plumbing facilities. However, the soundness of housing still varied across class. As plumbing became more universal,

40. Calculated from BLS, *Cost of Living in the United States*; Faith M. Williams and Alice C. Hanson, *Money Disbursements of Wage Earners and Clerical Workers, 1934–36: Summary Volume*, BLS Bulletin 638 (GPO, 1941); and BLS, *Family Expenditures in Selected Cities, 1935–36*, vol. 1: *Housing*, Bulletin 648 (GPO, 1941). Energy conversions from Palmer Cosslett Putnam, *Energy in the Future* (Van Nostrand, 1953).

41. Housing characteristics for 1950, 1960, and 1970 are from census data since the CES does not list housing details for these years.

air conditioning began to vary across class. Some air conditioning, mostly room units, was found in 21 percent of the salaried homes and 10 percent of the laborer homes in 1960.[42]

Between 1960 and 1973 housing expenditures increased relatively more for the lower classes than for the upper classes. By 1973 the majority of laborer families finally owned their homes. Even though the black home ownership rate experienced the largest increase during the time studied, less than 40 percent of black families owned their own homes in 1973. Full plumbing was found in virtually all homes of the three white classes in 1970. Air conditioning still varied across class, with the higher classes more likely to have central units. By 1980 over one-half of the laborer class and two-thirds of the salaried class had air conditioning.[43] Washing machines, dryers, and dishwashers were becoming more widespread, and these amenities also varied by class. Differences in the ownership of a washing machine, an invention that had been available since the beginning of the entire period studied, were less sharp than differences in the ownership of a dishwasher, which had been introduced more recently.

Income increases made sound housing with full plumbing facilities fairly universal across classes by 1960. The housing improvements since 1960 have been in amenities less basic to public health than plumbing facilities and heating. The newer amenities like air conditioning and a dishwasher increase comfort and reduce drudgery, rather than improve health.

Transportation

Although the rise of the automobile did not reflect an improvement in health, the changes that it eventually fostered (such as a decline in the availability and quality of public transportation and the location of new housing in areas with no public transportation) gradually made automobile ownership essential.

Real transportation expenditures tripled from 1918 to 1935 and again from 1935 to 1950. Automobile prices fell dramatically between 1908 and the outbreak of World War I as a result of improved assembly line procedures, including a mechanically driven conveyor chain, and inno-

42. Bureau of the Census, *Census of Housing 1950*, vol. 2, pt. 1, tables B-4–B-7; *Census of Housing 1960*, vol. 2, pt. 1, tables B-3, B-4, B-13.
43. Bureau of the Census, *Census of Housing, 1970*, vol. 2, pt. 1, tables B-3, B-4.

vative marketing and financing strategies. However, only one out of eighteen urban workers had an automobile in 1917–19, while 94 percent of wage-earner families reported expenditures for streetcar fares.[44]

Car prices also fell rapidly during the Depression. Between 1918 and 1935 the number of automobiles registered increased fourfold nationally, and car ownership for the three white classes rose by more than two to three times. In 1935 one-third of the employed laborers, almost one-half of the wage earners, and three-fourths of the salaried workers owned at least one car. Car ownership rates exceeded home ownership rates for the three white classes by 1935 (see table 6). Among black families with employed heads, fewer than one in eight were car owners in 1935. Since ownership of a second car was almost nonexistent, wage-earner families with an auto still used the trolley (82 percent reported trolley fares).

Between 1935 and 1950 car ownership increased by one-half for wage earners and laborers. Nationwide, 59 percent of families owned at least one car in 1950, and car ownership was part of whites' consumption norm, even for laborers. Although blacks' car ownership rate more than doubled between 1935 and 1950, blacks were only half as likely to own a car in 1950 as white laborers. Meanwhile, salaried families were beginning to buy second cars.

Automobile ownership continued to increase rapidly from 1950 to 1960. Ownership rates among the white classes became more equal. Now ownership of more than one car became the major difference among the white classes. These trends continued into the 1970s. Black families began to catch up to laborer families in car ownership rates in 1973. By this time, however, laborer families were beginning to buy second cars. The drive to buy additional vehicles continued throughout the 1970s.

Taxes and Assets

Taxes (income, personal property, and poll) first became noticeable in 1950, when they were 5 to 7 percent of the gross income of the three white classes and 3 percent of the gross income of the black class (see table 5). The tax rate almost doubled between 1950 and 1960 and then rose modestly between 1960 and 1973 for the white classes. However,

44. U.S. Bureau of Labor Statistics, *How American Buying Habits Change* (Department of Labor, 1959), p. 183. The survey results published automobile expenditures with motorcycles and bicycles because they were considered unimportant by themselves, so ownership rates by class are unknown.

the tax rates, especially after 1950, are larger than indicated by the tax measure since social security withholding is listed under personal insurance, although it functions as a tax on earnings. If the real increase in personal insurance after 1950 is counted as a tax, the tax rate was about one-quarter higher in 1960 and two-fifths higher in 1972–73. With this measure, the tax rate more than tripled for the white classes and quadrupled for the black class between 1950 and 1972.

White laborer families had met basic nutritional needs by 1950 and basic housing and transportation needs by 1960. However, while total expenditures approximated net income in 1918, they exceeded net income for the survey years 1935, 1950, and 1960 (see table 5). Only in 1973 did net income finally exceed expenditures. This pattern was also experienced by black and wage-earner families, although wage-earner families had lower ratios of expenditure to net income in both 1918 and 1973. Salaried families had the same pattern as wage-earner families, except that expenditures fell below net income in 1960. Although their real expenditures did not rise significantly between 1960 and 1973, salaried families saved 15 percent of their net incomes in 1973. Greater economic security through savings thus became a new way to distinguish among classes, although all classes' expenditure rates rose in 1980 in the effort to offset declining real incomes.

The Creation and Preservation of Economic Distance

Higher incomes allow the creation of economic distance between classes through different levels of consumption. Established consumption norms define the structure of economic distance. In this section, I examine how the characteristics of economic distance changed with shifts in income differentials and with growth in income levels.

In 1918 economic distance between classes reflected the quality and quantity of food and clothing, the quality of housing, and the number of family members. Higher incomes also provided more economic security since expenditures did not rise as rapidly as income across class. By 1935 transportation had replaced clothing in defining economic distance; food, housing, and transportation accounted for about one-half of the economic distance, while family size became much less important. This pattern of expenditures for food, housing, and transportation, along with family size, continued to form at least one-half of the economic distance from 1950 through 1980. The components of economic distance thus reflected the basics in the family budget.

During periods when economic growth and income differences among classes are not parallel, the areas of the budget adjusted are family size and the perceived need for economic security. Overall, movements in family size across the four classes reinforced trends in income differences up to 1950. Salaried families, especially, seemed able to protect their class position from shifts in relative and absolute incomes. After 1950 the shifts in income differences were less dramatic and family size differences were fairly constant across the white classes. From 1935 to 1981, black family size shifted relative to whites' in a way that offset changes in blacks' relative expenditure growth.

One measurement of economic security is revealed in the spending rate—expenditures divided by net income. This rate has also been affected by shifts in income differences. Since 1935, the spending rate of the laborer class relative to that of the salaried class has steadily increased. The black spending rate relative to the white rates indicates that blacks have less access to credit and less ability to borrow from outside the family. Spending rates rose between 1918 and 1950 for all classes, largely because of the improved availability of credit. After 1950 spending rates fell for the white classes. Blacks' spending rate did not peak until 1960 because it took them longer to gain access to credit. In 1960 the salaried class was at its break-even point (expenditures approximately equal to net income). By 1973 the black and laborer classes were breaking even, and the wage-earner and salaried classes were accumulating assets. With real family incomes no higher in 1980 than in 1973, spending rates rose once again for laborer and wage-earner families and remained steady for black and salaried families. In 1980–81 blacks spent their incomes, while laborers dissaved and salaried families maintained a 10 to 15 percent savings rate.

Families' economic security increased dramatically across all four classes between 1960 and 1973, as the ratio of expenditures to income declined and expenditures for personal insurance increased. These improvements in security reflect the continued growth of income after 1960, when nutrition, housing, and transportation needs had been met. The improved financial security also reflects the need for planned retirement income as life expectancy increased. Between the first survey in 1918–19 and the survey in 1972–73, the expected age at death for 20-year-olds increased five years for white males—from 65.6 to 71.0—and twelve years for white females—from 66.5 to 78.1.[45] White men and women at the beginning of their working lives could expect almost no years of retirement in 1918 and could expect six to thirteen years in 1973. At age 40, white men could expect five years of retirement in 1918 and eight years in 1973. The need for life insurance to provide an income to the family in case of the head's preretirement death diminished dramatically, while the need for retirement income for both spouses increased.

The transformation in work roles for mothers (especially for those with children under 6 years of age) that began in the 1950s and accelerated in the 1960s also allowed families to lower their spending rates. Since childrearing has remained a woman's primary social role and supportive social structures have not been developed sufficiently to allow her work role to be equally important, all but the highest-status women have had to mold their work lives around their family lives, especially while their children are preteens. In addition, the social norm that a woman would share her husband's earnings and retirement income was also transformed through the instability of marriage. With uncertain knowledge about how long their marriages would last, with certain knowledge that their living standard would fall with divorce, and with earnings lower than their husbands', women improved their economic security to the extent that they built up family assets that could be shared upon divorce.

Summary and Policy Implications

The relationships among consumption norms, work roles, and economic growth are complex and evolve over time. Two factors are clear, however. First, within a culture, the level and character of economic development largely determine the role of women as paid workers and as childbearers and child rearers. Second, economic growth in the United States has produced large changes in the work and consumption activities of the family.

Over the decades studied, changes in the consumption norms for food, housing, transportation, and family size had a substantial effect on

45. The expected age at death (if aged 20) for black males increased from 58.4 to 65.7 years and for black females from 57.2 to 73.5 years. See Bureau of the Census, *Historical Statistics of the United States, Colonial Times to 1970,* pt. 1 (GPO, 1975), p. 56; and Bureau of the Census, *Statistical Abstract of the United States, 1976* (GPO, 1976), table 87.

women's work roles. The shifts in social norms allowed, and then required, the participation rates of women to rise. The major improvements in diet, both in terms of nutrition and variety, lessened the family's reliance on the wife's baking. Nutritional improvement ensured that wives obtained enough calories and more iron and calcium. By 1950, after the family's basic food needs had been met, the participation rate of wives began to increase rapidly; further material improvements could come only through the family's increased consumption of market goods and services. Reduced childbearing after 1960 enabled women to devote more years to paid work, while the growth of the service economy created more jobs that were open to women. Entry into paid work gave women greater economic independence, even though few wives earned wages sufficient to support children alone.[46]

Within an institutional world, money income determines a family's material standard of living; social norms determine women's work roles. How economic development affects work roles depends on the importance of money versus other measuring rods in the culture (for example, artistic endeavors and community life). Because money is the primary measure of social position in our society, once wives with older children began increasing their labor force participation in the 1940s and basic needs associated with housework were being met, it became inevitable that most wives would eventually work for pay. Since a wife's earnings raise her family's income, the income distinction between classes is blurred during the transition period when some wives work for pay and some do not. A full-time homemaker cannot use her housework to bridge the economic distance between her family and the family of an employed wife. Each class's expenditure standards shift to include the earnings of both husband and wife.

Given the social emphasis on money income, economic growth created the need for more paid work time for families over the period studied.[47] As food and clothing declined in importance in the family

46. A long line of feminist writers have argued that women need to fulfill both their productive and reproductive powers and that women, as well as men, need to have economic independence. See, for example, Simone de Beauvoir, *The Second Sex*, trans. and ed. H. M. Parshley (Knopf, 1953); and Charlotte Perkins Gilman, *Women and Economics: A Study of the Economic Relation between Men and Women as a Factor in Social Revolution* (Harper and Row, 1966).

47. Overall, the total work time of seventy-one hours (paid and unpaid) for full-time employed urban wives in 1967 (Kathryn E. Walker and Margaret E. Woods, *Time Use: A Measure of Household Production of Family Goods and Services* [Washington, D.C.:

budget; as transportation, recreation, and personal insurance increased in importance; and as the spending rate declined, expenditures that would allow integration into social life and greater financial security became dominant over more basic housework-related ones. Class differences (manifested in economic distance) became more visible as they became centered on transportation and recreation rather than food and family size.

The combination of having basic needs met for most families and of having consumption made more public seems to have increased the desire for inequality across classes since 1973. Now that the basic needs of families with employed husbands have been met, the struggle over income shares no longer necessarily means that one class's comfort and status will come at the expense of another class's well-being. In our culture, growth has resulted in a greater need for paid work, and affluence has intensified the desire for class differences in consumption. This reality is a far cry from the time-honored vision of the Greek philosophers of an affluent, classless society that nurtures the mental, spiritual, and artistic aspects of its members.

By examining actual consumption norms by class and using social standards to measure well-being, the institutional approach I have outlined in this paper allows one to make judgments about the impact of various policies on well-being (as well as on comfort and status) by class. The importance of developing a sound basis for policy formulation and evaluation is particularly evident with respect to women's participation in the labor force. Overall, the rise in women's participation rates can be seen as part of the process of economic development. This movement toward allowing married women in all classes access to paid labor can

---

Center for the Family of the American Home Economics Association, 1976]) was almost as high as the seventy-five (unpaid) housework hours of farm homemakers in 1922 reported by Stanley Lebergott, *The Americans: An Economic Record* (Norton, 1984), p. 490. However, in four studies between 1926 and 1931 urban homemakers were reported to perform only forty-eight to fifty-four hours of housework weekly. Joann Vanek, "Keeping Busy: Time Spent in Housework, United States, 1920–1970" (Ph.D. dissertation, University of Michigan, 1973). Since housework hours increase with the number of children (especially children under 6) and with the opportunity for income-producing activities at home (such as taking in boarders and laundry or selling eggs), a large part of the reduction in housework hours reflected reduced childbirth and changing economic structure. As shown by Tilly and Scott (*Women, Work, and Family*), the increase in paid work hours of urban wives resulted in their work pattern becoming more like preindustrial work patterns, with women doing a combination of paid work and housework throughout their lives (but now spending much less time in childbearing and child rearing.)

be seen as an important improvement in women's position that was achieved after basic material needs were met. However, since our society uses income as its main determinant of well-being and status, there have been no economic forces acting to decrease the standard workweek so that both husbands and wives could spend time maintaining families and raising children. Economic growth, then, has resulted in a substantial increase in urban wives' work time—both paid and unpaid—over the past sixty years even as they have improved their economic and social position. Although economic growth brought women into the labor force through increasing incomes and changing consumption norms, growth itself cannot be expected to further equalize women's position in the labor market vis-à-vis men's, since growth cannot equalize work roles at home. The equalization of work roles at home and in the marketplace will be accomplished only through a long struggle in which government policies, employer practices, and the norms governing behavior within the family are altered.

Comments by Susan B. Carter

It is a pleasure to comment on an extremely provocative study of the impact of economic growth on consumption patterns and the allocation of women's labor between home and market. I have chosen to concentrate my remarks on the analysis of white married women's entry into the paid labor force.

The stylized facts are these: up until the turn of the century (some say until 1940), labor force participation rates of white married women were extremely low.[48] Beginning with World War II and continuing until the present, there has been an extremely rapid increase in women's attachment to the paid labor force at each age, with the largest increases among those aged 25–34.[49] Two questions have been asked regarding this

48. See Elyce J. Rotella, "Women's Labor Force Participation and the Decline of the Family Economy in the United States," *Explorations in Economic History*, vol. 17 (April 1980), pp. 95–117; Martha Norby Fraundorf, "The Labor Force Participation of Turn-of-the-Century Married Women," *Journal of Economic History*, vol. 39 (June 1979), pp. 401–18; and W. Elliot Brownlee, "Household Values, Women's Work, and Economic Growth, 1800–1930," *Journal of Economic History*, vol. 39 (March 1979), pp. 199–209.

49. June A. O'Neill, "A Time-Series Analysis of Women's Labor Force Participation," *American Economic Review*, vol. 71 (May 1981, *Papers and Proceedings, 1980*), pp. 76–80.

pattern: why were participation rates so low at the turn of the century, and why did they rise so rapidly after 1940?

Explanations for women's rapid entry, a pattern that seems all the more remarkable since it coincided with an unprecedented rise in family income, have been based on cross-sectional studies of labor force participation. These studies use Mincer-type models of labor supply decisions in a family context and find the positive effect of the women's own wage swamping the negative effect of other family income.

At first pass, this finding appears to explain women's entry into the paid labor force over a period when men's and women's wages grew at about the same rate. However, careful attempts to use the cross-sectional estimates to predict changes over time have revealed the inadequacy of this approach.

Bowen and Finegan found that their coefficients on family income and job incentive variables (estimated from cross-sectional data on cities in 1960) explained only 25 percent of the actual change in the labor force participation rate of married women between 1948 and 1965.[50] Goldin came to similar conclusions in a study of the labor force participation rates of cohorts of women born between 1865 and 1955. She wrote:

> No generation of young women could have predicted solely from the experiences of their elders what their own work histories would have been. Indeed in 1930 a cohort of twenty-year-old daughters would have been off by a factor of 3.6 in predicting their own participation rates . . . had they simply extrapolated from the experience of their forty-five-year-old mothers.[51]

She added that if they had taken account of differences in educational and fertility experiences they still would have been off by a factor of 2.1.

More recently, O'Neill had more success with a Mincer-type model and a strong time trend in explaining the entry of married women into the paid labor force between 1948 and 1978.[52] Yet even these results are far from a full explanation. We need to know why the coefficients on women's own wages and other family income are so different for men and women and what it is that accounts for the large positive coefficient on the time variable.

In short, we have at best a superficial understanding of the rapid entry of married women into the paid labor force in the post–World II era. Yet

50. William G. Bowen and T. Aldrich Finegan, *The Economics of Labor Force Participation* (Princeton University Press, 1969), p. 208.

51. Claudia Goldin, "The Changing Economic Role of Women: A Quantitative Approach," *Journal of Interdisciplinary History*, vol. 15 (Spring 1983), p. 715.

52. O'Neill, "Time-Series Analysis of Women's Labor Force Participation."

Goldin recently calculated that the process raised GNP by approximately 14 percent—approximately the same as capital deepening,[53] and the process has been linked to so many other social changes it has been termed a revolution.[54] It is against this background that the importance of Brown's innovations should be judged.

Because her argument is complex, it warrants a brief summary. The labor supply decision of married women is situated within a family context. But unlike the Mincer model, in her model decisions within the family are made by reference to class norms rather than idiosyncratic individual taste. Brown's interest is in how such norms change in the process of economic growth. Economic growth affects consumption norms through its rate and the evenness of its distribution across classes.

She presents an extremely interesting and detailed description of the pace and distribution of economic growth and of shifts in consumption expenditures by classes for a number of subperiods between 1918 and 1973. The major finding is that growth patterns in twentieth-century America have been such as to encourage far more expenditure in new ways than imitation of high-class norms, and it was the shift to new consumption bundles that was responsible for women's entry into the paid labor force. The reason is that older consumption bundles, consisting primarily of food, clothing and household operation, could be largely produced by women in their homes, while items in the new consumption bundle—transportation, recreation, and income security—could be obtained by the wife's efforts only if she entered the paid labor force. Thus married women entered the paid labor force out of a desire to maintain class position and to preserve or narrow social distance through consumption.

Brown calls our attention to the irony implied by this finding: women's entry into the paid labor force has come *after* basic necessities have been met. "Growth has resulted in a greater need for paid work, and affluence has intensified the desire for class differences in consumption." She adds, "This reality is a far cry from the time-honored vision of the Greek philosophers of an affluent, classless society that nurtures the mental, spiritual, and artistic aspects of its members."

To determine how plausible this is as an explanation of long-run

53. Claudia Goldin, "The Female Labor Force and American Economic Growth, 1890–1980," in Stanley L. Engerman and Robert Gallman, eds., *Long-Term Factors in American Economic Growth* (University of Chicago Press, 1986).

54. See Ralph E. Smith, ed., *The Subtle Revolution: Women at Work* (Washington, D.C.: Urban Institute, 1979).

changes in married women's labor force participation, we can begin by evaluating the elements of the approach. First, the focus on class norms for consumption patterns and wives' work patterns seems well supported by evidence. Strober's study of strategies used by working and non-working wives to reduce time pressures, for example, found that working and nonworking wives are similar in their purchase and ownership of labor-saving household durables and methods of shopping and meal preparation, holding income and life cycle stage constant.[55] This suggests that class norms have a lot more to do with consumption and labor allocation decisions than do differences in individual circumstances within class.

Second, the notion that consumption patterns are mechanisms for creating and overcoming class distinctions seems well supported and promises to be a way of endogenizing an important source of social change that neoclassical economists have left to the time variable. Recent studies document the role of consumption decisions in affecting class distinctions.[56] In fact, as early as 1899 Veblen argued that consumption of leisure was the quintessential sign of social standing.[57] Middle-class wives' absence from the labor force and upper-class wives' highly ornamental and circumscribed dress and social responsibilities could be understood as efforts to display their husbands' wealth.

However, recalling that Veblen used a similar methodology, but came to diametrically opposite conclusions from Brown as to which uses of time most effectively signal social standing, shows that a fuller description of the economic, social, and cultural context in which the consumption and labor allocation decisions take place is necessary.

For example, in order to understand why transportation was one of the categories in which consumption patterns changed in each of the subperiods studied, we need to know something about the restructuring of urban areas that was occurring over the twentieth century. As Hayden has shown, in the latter half of the nineteenth century growing urbanization and the rise of dense, large cities prompted some social thinkers to speculate that, with thoughtful design, urban environments might

55. Myra H. Strober, "Wives' Labor Force Behavior and Family Consumption Patterns," *American Economic Review*, vol. 67 (February 1977, *Papers and Proceedings, 1976*), pp. 410–17.

56. See, for example, Alison Lurie, *The Language of Clothes* (Random House, 1981); and Paul Fussell, *Class: A Guide through the American Status System* (Summit Books, 1983).

57. Veblen, *Theory of the Leisure Class*.

permit the movement of women into the public sphere and create opportunities for mutually beneficial interactions among classes.[58] Frederick Law Olmstead is the best remembered spokesperson for this movement, but there were others. Beginning in 1869, Metusina Fay Peirce began campaigning for cooperative residential neighborhoods. In the 1870s Frances Willard fought for municipal housekeeping schemes as well as temperance. Jane Addams's social settlement ideas embodied the assumption that urban design could promote equality for women. Charlotte Perkins Gilman devised detailed descriptions of the sort of urban arrangements that would overcome the social isolation and enhance the productivity of women.

This vision was fragmented and momentum was lost in the early twentieth century, Hayden argues, as "dense urban centers of industrial capitalism were succeeded by suburbanized cities of modern capitalism." The changes occurred over several decades in response, in part, to the growing intensity of class conflict, much of which occurred in cities. Hayden quotes businessmen and civic leaders of this period advocating single-family dwellings in order to promote "a conservative point of view in the workingman."[59] A further impetus for single-family dwellings came from corporations, moving out of World War I defense industries into peacetime production, who eyed homemakers as their most attractive market. Several scholars have shown us how the advertising and development of consumer credit by these firms created the surge of spending on household items in the 1920s.[60]

In this literature we have the beginnings of an answer as to how and why the consumption of goods, rather than leisure, came to be the form taken by efforts to maintain or overcome class position. Seeing consumption in a large economic, social, and cultural context also makes us aware that economic growth, even a particular pace and pattern of growth, does not inevitably lead to more intense work effort. Rather,

58. Dolores Hayden, *Redesigning the American Dream: The Future of Housing, Work, and Family Life* (Norton, 1984).

59. Ibid., pp. 32, 33.

60. Heidi I. Hartmann, "Capitalism and Women's Work in the Home, 1900–1930" (Ph.D. dissertation, Yale University, 1974); Barbara Ehrenreich and Deirdre English, *For Her Own Good: 150 Years of Experts' Advice to Women* (Doubleday, 1978); Martha L. Olney, "Towards an Understanding of the Consumer Durables Revolution of the 1920s," paper presented at the 1984 Cliometrics Meeting, Miami University, Oxford, Ohio, April 1984; and Christine E. Bose, Philip L. Bereano, and Mary Malloy, "Household Technology and the Social Construction of Housework," *Technology and Culture*, vol. 25 (January 1984), pp. 53–82.

this result is a product of the specific institutional context in which that growth occurs.

More explicit discussion of institutional content might also shed light on another finding, that family size was the category of consumption most consistently reduced. A way to understand this might be to recognize that family size is the one area of consumption that carries with it an obligation to provide services over a substantial number of years. This implies that child care should be recognized explicitly as a service provided in the home. Moreover, such literature suggests that privately provided child care by the child's own mother remains highly valued by families even as its share in total goods and services consumed by the household shrinks.[61] This suggests to me that family size choices warrant special treatment within the model.

These suggestions for extensions and refinement are motivated by a genuine enthusiasm for the model Brown has developed. I believe that her approach is an effective way to bring together literature from a variety of areas to create a rich understanding of women's entry into the paid labor force.

Comments by Stanley Lebergott

The standard of living, Brown begins, is composed of "well-being, comfort and status together." Economists, then, can offer little on the subsequent discussion. For they notoriously cannot even define two of these three—"comfort" and "status." "Well-being," she urges, should be "judged in practical terms by social norms." Though "social norms" are not defined here, we assume them to be the separate "consumption norms" she reports for blacks, white salaried workers, white craftsmen plus operatives, and white laborers plus service workers.

These norms are simply described as the share of income that each occupation-income "class" spent for items such as food or clothing. Hence by definition each such class achieved its "consumption norms" every year from 1918 to 1980—as successfully in depression as prosperity. Whether this apparatus of norms and classes casts much light on

61. See, for example, Christopher Lasch, *Haven in a Heartless World: The Family Besieged* (Basic Books, 1979); and Edward Shorter, *The Making of the Modern Family* (Basic Books, 1975).

historic changes in family expenditure, and in women's work patterns, is yet to be decided.

The bulk of Brown's paper adapts the Bureau of Labor Statistics consumer expenditure survey data with great care and effort. Yet the BLS data do not conform well to more reliable measures of the changing economy between 1918 and 1980. Hence it may be useful to consider some traditional indicators of economic growth, expenditures, and work (table 9).[62]

Table 9 begins with the all-important, spectacular decline in hours worked by married women—from ninety-four to fifty hours a week. That decline had little to do with women's wages or the labor market. It had much to do with a decrease in large families. As of 1900 one-fourth of all white married women, and 44 percent of all black, typically gave birth to seven or more children in their lifetime. (A fifth of all households had seven or more members.) The enormous decline in those percentages by 1979 strikes one male observer as reflecting millions of personal decisions by individual women. They were concerned about the dangers in giving birth; the onerous and boring tasks required to care for so many children so many years; and the desire to give a better chance to those who were born (that is, Becker's "higher quality" children).

A second major contributor to declining women's work hours came as the percentage of families with boarders fell from 25 percent to 2 percent. It would be odd if those responsible for thus reducing family income from boarders were husbands, or congressmen, or anyone but the same millions of housewives. (Who else cooked and served the meals, cleared and washed the dishes, swept and straightened up?)

These two major changes tended to reduce the shadow price of

62. The first improbable message the survey data apparently report is that median family income (white families?) hardly changed from 1918 to 1935 (table 1). But per capita GNP fell by 24 percent (Simon Kuznets, *Capital in the American Economy: Its Formation and Financing* [Princeton University Press, 1961], pp. 561–62). So great a discrepancy requires some explanation. (1) The 1918 survey intentionally excluded the lower end of the income distribution. It omitted single-person families, slum families, and immigrant families. Moreover, pages of expenditure data contain many wonders. One table asserts that 70 percent of American wage-earner families sent their laundry out and 16 percent had servants. Did wage-earner housewives read *True Confessions* and eat bonbons on wash days? Or was the survey indeed biased? (2) The 1935 survey, though far better, covered only nonrelief families—in a period when millions were on relief. It therefore omitted, as best I can estimate, 22 percent of black families, all of them with incomes below $1,000 (Stanley Lebergott, *The American Economy—Income, Wealth, and Want* [Princeton University Press, 1976], p. 305).

Table 9. *Indicators of Changes in Women's Work, 1900–1979*
Percent unless otherwise indicated

Indicator	1900	1979
Average weekly work (hours)[a]		
All married women	94	50[b]
Homemakers	84	45[b]
Child care		
Married women (45–49) with 7 or more births		
White	27	6
Nonwhite	44	18
Births (per 1,000 women		
aged 15–44)	133	67
Boarder care		
Families with boarders	25	2
Family care		
Food preparation		
Flour baked at home	92	22
Vegetables consumed fresh	96	30
Cleaning		
Homes without running water	76	2
Homes without mechanical		
washing machines	95[c]	30
Memorandum:		
Annual earnings of nonfarm		
employees (1914 dollars)	523	2,229

Sources: Stanley Lebergott, *The Americans: An Economic Record* (Norton, 1984), pp. 193, 380, 488–90, 492; and Lebergott, *The American Economy: Income, Wealth, and Want* (Princeton University Press, 1976), pp. 248–98.
a. Home plus outside work.
b. Data for 1975. The figures for 1979 are probably no higher.
c. Rough approximation.

women's household labor, increasing the relative return from market labor. Nonetheless, women did not increase their labor force participation rates, probably because husbands' incomes concurrently rose. Earnings by husbands gained about as much as earnings of nonfarm wage earners, which more than tripled. (An 82 percent ratio of husband's to family earnings seems to have been one of the great constants in the U.S. economy from 1900 to 1960.)[63]

Few of us would change places with either the typical husband or wife in those decades. One remembers Art Young's cartoon of an exhausted, slatternly figure on a summer day, turning from her coal stove to a bedraggled filthy vision at the door: "Here I've been slaving over a hot stove all day, and you in a nice cool sewer."

63. Stanley Lebergott, "Earnings of Nonfarm Employees in the U.S., 1890–1946," *Journal of the American Statistical Association,* vol. 43 (March 1948), p. 77; and U.S. Bureau of the Census, *Current Population Reports,* series P–60, "Consumer Income," 1947, no. 5, pp. 18, 24; 1950, no. 9, pp. 25, 35; and 1960, no. 37, pp. 26, 42.

But husbands' incomes *did* increase. And that increase was disproportionately used to reduce housework. The factory took over major chores. (1) The 1900 housewife baked half a ton of bread yearly. As home flour consumption subsequently declined, so did housework hours. (2) The 1900 housewife washed most of her vegetables, cut them up, prepared them, and then washed up. By 1979 factories did most of that work. Gourmets confronted by canned or frozen vegetables may have fled to France. But hours of housework declined. (3) The introduction of running water and furnaces in homes proved a boon to companies making pipe and developing cartel tactics. It proved an ever greater boon to women. Who else had hauled all those buckets of water from wells or carried them from spigots in tenement yards? Who else boiled gallons of water regularly for the wash? (4) The shift from the washboard to the mechanical washing machine cut hours no less significantly and increased expenditures.

The above data suggest a different view of women's work experience and family consumption since 1900 than Brown's paper might suggest. Why so?

Brown concludes that "a substantial increase in urban wives' work time (occurred) . . . over the past sixty years." But the sources cited rely on tiny, biased surveys. For the 1920s these surveys disproportionately sampled two groups: women who had domestic servants, and higher-income college graduates.[64] Hildegarde Kneeland, the original sponsor of these studies, adjusted their results for bias. If we follow her lead, the sixty-year rise fails to appear.

The historic review, of course, in no way contradicts Brown's subsequent judgment that "the equalization of work roles at home and in the marketplace will be accomplished only through a long struggle." Economics has no competence to assess when something as ill defined as "work roles in the home" are equalized.

Brown further concludes that "since our society uses income as its main determinant of well-being and status, there have been no economic

---

64. Later studies, under the same Bureau of Human Nutrition and Home Economics auspices, have similar biases. They oversampled women who (a) employed domestic servants, (b) were college graduates, and (c) had higher incomes. For hours worked at the end of the period, Brown refers to a study of housewives in Syracuse as working seventy-one hours. But a national Institute of Survey Research sample for 1975 is more suitable. It shows that U.S. married women in 1975 worked fifty-two hours a week (including home and labor market). See F. Thomas Juster and Frank P. Stafford, eds., *Time, Goods, and Well-Being* (University of Michigan, Survey Research Center–Institute for Social Research, 1985), p. 148.

forces acting to decrease the standard workweek so that both husbands
and wives could spend time maintaining families and raising children.''
John Owen's recent book, and Kendrick's older one, show the standard
workweek declining substantially.[65] And common experience, as well
as time budget studies (by the ISR), shows that "both husbands and
wives could" and do spend time "maintaining families and raising
children.''

A final "summary and policy implication" states that "in our culture,
growth . . . has intensified the desire for class differences in consumption. This reality is a far cry from the time-honored vision of the Greek
philosophers of an affluent, classless society.'' Economists generally
know few Greek philosophers beyond those they met in introductory
philosophy—Aristotle, Plato, and Thales—and these hardly favored a
classless society, or even an affluent one. It is useful to be reminded that
there were others who held different views. And that scholarship beyond
microanalysis may well illuminate our understanding of work roles and
economic growth.

65. John D. Owen, *Working Lives: The American Work Force Since 1920* (Lexington,
Mass.: Lexington Books, 1986); and John W. Kendrick, *Productivity Trends in the
United States* (Princeton University Press for National Bureau of Economic Research,
1961).

HEIDI I. HARTMANN

Internal Labor Markets and Gender: A Case Study of Promotion

THEORIES about internal labor markets, dual labor markets, and labor market segmentation were all developed without regard to gender. Rather the primary motivation behind their development was the place of minorities in the labor market and in the society at large. Michael Piore, coauthor with Peter Doeringer of *Internal Labor Markets and Manpower Analysis*, the seminal work that connected internal labor market analysis with notions of the dual economy, commented:

> The ideas were originally put forward by a group of us who encountered the labor market through participation in the civil rights movement and as advocates for the community based groups that grew up around that movement and President Johnson's War on Poverty. The ideas were an attempt to make sense out of the labor market problems as the people in these communities experienced them (or at least described their experiences) and to describe the labor market as these people saw it.[1]

The appeal of these theories to those concerned about gender differentiation in the labor market and in society is great, however, since they deal with issues of discrimination, restricted mobility, and low pay, all of which have plagued women as well as minorities. A few analysts have assumed that women's situation in the labor market is nearly directly parallel with that of minorities and have sought to demonstrate that

I would like to thank Suzanne Donovan for her most competent assistance in ferreting out problems with the data and in programming regression and other analyses; Barbara Bergmann for making the data set and computer time available; Trisha Hartge for statistical consultation; and helpful friends and staff at the National Academy of Sciences. The opinions expressed in this paper are my own and not those of the National Academy of Sciences.

1. Michael J. Piore, "Labor Market Segmentation: To What Paradigm Does It Belong?" *American Economic Review*, vol. 73 (May 1983, *Papers and Proceedings, 1982*), p. 250.

women work preponderantly in the secondary labor market, which is characterized by instability, high turnover, poor or no promotion prospects, and low pay.[2] Most analysts, however, have noted the division of labor by sex cuts down the middle of all segments of the labor market: sex divides internal labor markets in the primary sector, and even in the secondary sector men and women hold different jobs. Thus there may be no easy identification possible between women and the secondary sector. And women who work in primary labor-type firms in the core sector of the economy often have jobs whose attributes more resemble those of secondary jobs—low pay and limited prospects for advancement.

I offer a brief review of the use of these theories by researchers to understand women's labor market experience, and then present my findings on salary gains and promotion in a large insurance firm with a predominantly female work force. Lastly, I discuss further research on this and similar data bases.

A Review of the Literature

Although theories about internal labor markets and labor market segmentation appeal to those concerned about gender differentiation, a review of the empirical and theoretical literature in this genre is disappointing. Developed without regard to gender, the theories, and the research based on them, provide limited insights into gender differentiation. Yet this general approach, with its emphasis on the qualitative as well as the quantitative experiences of workers, is promising. When combined with feminist theories of gender, it can bring new understanding to the labor market.

Gordon, one of the principal developers of labor market segmentation theory, along with Edwards and Reich, in an empirical analysis of the U.S. labor force finds that women are more likely than men to be secondary workers, much more likely to be subordinate primary workers (this includes many clerical jobs, as well as relatively unskilled but unionized male jobs in the core sector), and much less likely to be independent primary workers (this includes most professional, technical,

2. R. D. Barron and G. M. Norris, "Sexual Divisions and the Dual Labour Market," in Diana Leonard Barker and Sheila Allen, eds., *Dependence and Exploitation in Work and Marriage* (London: Longman, 1976), pp. 47–69.

managerial, and craft jobs).[3] In 1970, 41.8 percent of all women workers, in contrast to 32.5 percent of all male workers, were in the secondary sector. Subordinate primary jobs were held by 40.0 percent of women, compared with 24.8 percent of men; and only 18.2 percent of women were in the independent primary sector, compared with 42.7 percent of men.[4] Gordon and his colleagues have generally noted differences between women and minorities; for example, minorities are more likely to be secondary workers than either white men or women as a group.

Rumberger and Carnoy, in a study of the location and mobility chances of whites and blacks in primary and secondary jobs, and reporting earlier findings from Carnoy, Girling, and Rumberger, concluded that the primary-secondary distinction does not hold up well across sex-race lines.[5] When sectors were defined by occupational and industry characteristics and all workers were located in segments, workers of different races and sexes in the same segments did not experience similar earnings or mobility prospects. For example, blacks and women in primary jobs in the private sector had earnings structures unlike white males in primary jobs, but like white males in secondary jobs. Buchele found that women's earnings are lower than men's in all sectors and concluded that neither orthodox theory nor the labor market segmentation theory explains the male-female earnings gap very well.[6] Jones's research on the Australian labor market confirms the general notion that white males benefit from their status in the primary sector more than other race-sex groups.[7] He argues that the privileged position of relatively unskilled but unionized white males in the subordinate primary sector can be maintained only by social discrimination against women and minority males. This finding is consistent with Freedman's work on sheltering in the

3. David M. Gordon, "Segmentation by the Numbers: Empirical Applications of the Theory of Labor Segmentation" (New School for Social Research, 1982).

4. Ibid., reported in David M. Gordon, Richard Edwards, and Michael Reich, *Segmented Work, Divided Workers: The Historical Transformation of Labor in the United States* (Cambridge University Press, 1982), p. 211.

5. Russell W. Rumberger and Martin Carnoy, "Segmentation in the U.S. Labour Market: Its Effects on the Mobility and Earnings of Whites and Blacks," *Cambridge Journal of Economics*, vol. 4 (June 1980), pp. 117–32; and Martin Carnoy, R. Girling, and Russell W. Rumberger, "Education and Public Sector Employment" (Palo Alto, Calif.: Center for Economic Studies, November 1976).

6. Robert Buchele, "Sex Discrimination and Labour Market Segmentation," in Frank Wilkinson, ed., *The Dynamics of Labour Market Segmentation* (Academic Press, 1981), pp. 211–27.

7. Evan Jones, "Industrial Structure and Labor Force Segmentation," *Review of Radical Political Economics*, vol. 15 (Winter 1983), pp. 24–44.

labor market, in which barriers to entry protect particular groups against competition from others.[8]

Hodson and Kaufman and Lever-Tracy argue that the often conflicting empirical results concerning workers in various sectors are caused by basic problems in the underlying theory.[9] Both suggest that the parallelism between economic segments (core and periphery), labor market segments (primary, including independent and subordinate, and secondary), and worker outcomes (characteristics of workers and working conditions) postulated by the theory just does not and cannot hold. The notion of parallel dualisms is simply too restrictive a concept to analyze real-life labor markets. All the relevant dimensions of employment need not clump together in clearly identifiable segments; instead, jobs and employment opportunities differ along a variety of dimensions. Rather than clear differentiation, either over time or across sectors, reality is characterized by the complex interaction of many factors and many different types of segmentation. Labor market segmentation theory needs to be reconceptualized to take this complexity into account.

With the appearance of Harry Braverman's *Labor and Monopoly Capitalism* in 1974, along with other developments in Marxism, much greater emphasis has been put on the social phenomena of class struggle and what is called the "labor process."[10] The focus is on what actually happens in the workplace: the processes by which managers attempt to control workers and production (often by de-skilling and downgrading jobs, as Braverman argued) and by which workers attempt to maintain or increase control over their working conditions. The quality of worklife, in terms of autonomy and control as well as wages, comes to the fore. Workers and managers interact around these issues every day in factories, stores, and offices. Critical responses to Braverman and Gordon and his colleagues emphasize the role of workers in the process.

8. Marcia K. Freedman and Gretchen Maclachlan, *Labor Markets: Segments and Shelters* (Montclair, N. J.: Allanheld, Osmun and Co., 1976).

9. Randy Hodson and Robert L. Kaufman, "Economic Dualism: A Critical Review," *American Sociological Review*, vol. 47 (December 1982), pp. 727–39; and Constance Lever-Tracy, "The Paradigm Crisis of Dualism: Decay or Regeneration?" *Politics and Society*, vol. 13, no. 1 (1984), pp. 59–89.

10. Harry Braverman, *Labor and Monopoly Capital: The Degradation of Work in the Twentieth Century* (New York: Monthly Review Press, 1974). The work of Edward P. Thompson, particularly *The Making of the English Working Class* (Doubleday, 1964), was particularly important in inspiring an entire generation of historians and social scientists to consider issues of working-class culture, "work culture" (culture on the job), and workers' consciousness.

Workers can be important in altering both conditions within workplaces and the shape of labor markets themselves. Since many adherents of dual labor market theories argue that employers have choices in how they structure their production process, given available technologies and labor supplies, it is likely that actions by workers are also important.

For example, I have argued that sexual divisions in the labor force often resulted from exclusionary actions by male workers who benefited not only by keeping their own wages higher but also by keeping women economically dependent on men, thus assuring household services and male domination.[11]

Phillips and Taylor point out that Braverman's view of the de-skilling process might look entirely different if gender struggle were included.[12] Braverman argues that after managers learn how to de-skill particular labor processes they seek out cheaper labor to perform the new unskilled tasks. Phillips and Taylor argue, in contrast, that the very labeling of jobs as skilled or unskilled is also an object of struggle. This is so particularly between men and women in the workplace, as women seek to have the skills in their jobs recognized and men seek to keep or place women in subordinate positions by devaluing their jobs via labeling and other means. Thus it may be because the jobs are done by women that they are viewed as unskilled and are lower paid, not just that low-wage (low-skill) jobs are created and women are channeled into them. Men and women struggle over how jobs will be defined and labeled as well as who will get to do which jobs. This is particularly obvious with new jobs and those being influenced by technological change. Will physician's assistant be a men's or a women's job? How about keyboarding, word processor equipment repairer, and other computer-related jobs? At what level will these jobs be pegged? Such struggles among women and men, minorities and whites, young and old go on continuously in workplaces. And although economic motives may be important in these struggles, they are surely not the only factor affecting people's consciousness. Culture, tradition, entrenched status hierarchies, and psychological domination all have a role in the workplace.

These directions in labor market theory point toward the importance

---

11. Heidi I. Hartmann, "Capitalism, Patriarchy, and Job Segregation by Sex," in Martha Blaxall and Barbara B. Reagan, eds., *Women and the Workplace: The Implications of Occupational Segregation* (University of Chicago Press, 1976), pp. 137–69.

12. Anne Phillips and Barbara Taylor, "Sex and Skill: Notes towards a Feminist Economics," *Feminist Review*, no. 6 (1980), pp. 79–88.

of considering the processes that structure workplaces and create and maintain differential opportunities as well as the roles workers and managers play in these processes. A brief look at the literature on internal labor markets indicates that just as with labor market segmentation, analysts have begun to notice that the existing models do not fit women's jobs very well.

Much of the early discussion of internal labor markets applied largely to blue-collar jobs traditionally held by men.[13] Whether of a craft or industrial nature, such jobs are thought to have limited ports of entry at the bottom and to provide fairly steady upward mobility through a number of career steps, each of which provides the training and experience necessary to progress to the next. The training for craft jobs was generally organized outside firms (through unions and apprenticeships), and workers might be fairly mobile between firms, while advancement in industrial jobs required entry into a firm at a low level and subsequent firm-specific training.

Both in blue-collar jobs and in their much more likely white-collar jobs, women seem to have limited lines of progression. Very few women's jobs are organized by the apprenticeship system. Even though women's jobs, like men's, are often located in large firms, they seem to be less structured and to provide less clear paths of career progression. Women's jobs are widely held to be dead-end but there is surprisingly little research that confirms or denies this generalization, particularly in white-collar work. This belief seems plausible since lifetime earnings profiles for women are flatter than men's.[14] Studies of the New York State civil service found that women's lines of progression were shorter because their mid-level jobs were less likely to feed into managerial positions than were white males'.[15] In particular, incumbents in women's

13. Peter B. Doeringer and Michael J. Piore, *Internal Labor Markets and Manpower Analysis* (D.C. Heath, 1971).

14. Donald J. Treiman, "The Work Histories of Men and Women: What We Know and What We Need to Find Out," revised version of paper prepared for the 1983 annual meeting of the American Sociological Association.

15. Ronnie Steinberg, "Barriers to Advancement," paper prepared for 1981 Conference on University Barriers to Advancement for Women, University of Pittsburgh; Lois V. Haignere, Cynthia H. Chertos, and Ronnie J. Steinberg, "Managerial Promotions in the Public Sector: The Impact of Eligibility Requirements on Women and Minorities" (State University of New York at Albany, Center for Women in Government, 1982); and Cynthia H. Chertos, "Alternative Routes of Managerial Promotion in New York State: A Research Report" (State University of New York at Albany, Center for Women in Government, 1984).

jobs were often not eligible to take competitive examinations for promotions. In a study of an electrical manufacturing plant, Kelley found
that job ladders (identifiable from sources such as collective bargaining
agreements and interviews with union officials) with predominantly
female incumbents had fewer steps, lower maximum earnings ceilings,
and often lower entry-level wages than did the job ladders with predominantly male incumbents.[16]

As Blau and Jusenius have pointed out, because structured internal
labor markets treat workers as members of groups and tend to treat
workers within these groups consistently, differentiation between women
and men is likely to take the form of segregating women and men into
different jobs, rather than paying them unequally for the same job.[17] In
general, in structured internal labor markets, all individuals in the same
job are likely to be equally paid, except for performance or seniority
differentials. This leaves open the reasons women and men are likely to
be differentiated, but it does suggest that entry-level jobs are likely to be
different for men and women and arranged in different job families so
that segregation will be maintained throughout one's career in the firm.
This is precisely what Kelley found. Beyond that, women's job ladders
may be shorter, and other ways of maintaining differentiation in the firm
may exist. For example, Osterman suggests that in a publishing firm he
studied differential opportunity was maintained by keeping women in
the lowest grade levels of various occupation groups.[18] Institutionally,
that type of differentiation could be aided by placing women in job titles
that differ from related jobs that men hold or possibly by locating them
in different departments.

Such observations suggest that the effects of internal labor markets
differ for men and women, despite their emphasis on consistent rules.
The rules of the game are neutral on their face but disparate in their
impact. The rules may also differ in different parts of the firm. Firms
with otherwise primary-type jobs may arrange substantial portions of
their jobs in secondary ways, where high turnover is essentially encour-

16. Maryellen R. Kelley, "Discrimination in Seniority Systems: A Case Study,"
Industrial and Labor Relations Review, vol. 36 (October 1982), pp. 40–55.

17. Francine D. Blau, *Equal Pay in the Office* (Lexington, Mass.: Lexington Books,
1977); and Francine D. Blau and Carol L. Jusenius, "Economists' Approaches to Sex
Segregation in the Labor Market: An Appraisal," in Blaxall and Reagan, eds., *Women
and the Workplace*, p. 193.

18. Paul Osterman, "Sex Discrimination in Professional Employment: A Case
Study," *Industrial and Labor Relations Review*, vol. 32 (July 1979), pp. 451–64.

aged to keep costs down. This pattern may be more common in women's jobs, such as key punch, telephone, and data entry operators. For example, in a study of predominantly white-collar firms in the Boston area, Osterman found that clerical jobs constituted a secondary system, with many points of entry, high turnover, and low wages, in contrast to computer programming, sales, and management jobs, which were organized along craft or industrial lines.[19]

These observations have led researchers to investigate the prevalence of sex segregation in internal labor markets and the nature of opportunities in predominantly female jobs and job ladders. Research by Bielby and Baron confirms the extremely high degree of sex segregation within firms by job title.[20] In a sample of several hundred establishments in California, over half the establishments were completely segregated by job title—no job title had both male and female workers—and only 20 percent of the firms had segregation indexes of less than 90, meaning that 90 percent of the women or men would have had to change jobs for the job distributions of the sexes to be equal.

In several studies of pay, the effects of sex segregation are estimated using such descriptors of occupation as the proportion of incumbents that is female and objective characteristics of the occupation that might reasonably be supposed to contribute to earnings differentials. For example, in an analysis of occupations from 1970 census data, Treiman and Hartmann found that the female percentage of the occupation had a negative effect on average occupational wages even when they included job characteristics such as substantive complexity, motor skills, physical demands, and unfavorable working conditions, as measured by the *Dictionary of Occupational Titles*.[21] In a study of a large utility, Rosenbaum found that job salaries were affected negatively by the female (and minority) percentages even when such average human capital factors as average tenure and percentage of college graduates were included in the regression analysis.[22] In a study of data from an electrical equipment

19. Paul Osterman, "White-Collar Internal Labor Markets," in Osterman, ed., *Internal Labor Markets* (MIT Press, 1984), pp. 163–89.

20. William T. Bielby and James N. Baron, "A Woman's Place is with Other Women: Sex Segregation within Organizations," in Barbara F. Reskin, ed., *Sex Segregation in the Workplace: Trends, Explanations, Remedies* (Washington, D.C.: National Academy Press, 1984), pp. 27–55.

21. Donald J. Treiman and Heidi I. Hartmann, eds., *Women, Work and Wages: Equal Pay for Jobs of Equal Value* (Washington, D.C.: National Academy Press, 1981), p. 30.

22. James E. Rosenbaum, "Jobs, Job Status, and Women's Gains from Affirmative

manufacturing plant, Kelley found a negative effect on individuals' wages for the female and black percentages, even when other relevant characteristics of the individual's job (such as its entry level and ladder height) were taken into account.[23]

Support for the proposition that something about occupation accounts for sex-based earnings differences can also be found in a review of the literature on earnings differentials among individuals. Earnings regressions that range broadly over many different occupations can rarely explain more than half the gross earnings gap between women and men, even when human capital characteristics are taken into account. When objective occupational characteristics are also included, the explanatory power improves somewhat, but not substantially. Yet if dummy variables are included for each occupation, the gap often shrinks to close to zero. Similarly, if the regression analysis is confined to a narrow occupation (for example, college professor), much more of the gross wage gap between men and women can be accounted for. Thus within occupations sex-based earnings differences can be explained, but between occupations they cannot be (at least not by any reasonable occupational characteristics that have yet been found). One potential inference, then, from the literature to date is that it is the sex composition of the occupation itself that accounts for the earnings differentials: hence the interest in the female percentage as an explanatory variable, and also sources of research support for the controversial remedy of comparable worth.

Yet to conclude that the female percentage is the suspect is not sufficient in itself. Why does this factor have such explanatory power? How are female-dominated occupations structured so as to contribute to their low pay and to women's lesser opportunities?

In an analysis of internal labor markets, it should be possible to incorporate some insights from the current reconceptualization of the labor market segmentation theories. In particular, it should be possible to include consideration of the ongoing ways in which groups of workers struggle with each other and with management around issues of control and working conditions. Shifting boundaries of male and female employment and shifting gender and race composition of jobs, along with changes in relative wage rates, might provide quantitative indicators of

---

Action: Implications for Comparable Worth," in Heidi I. Hartmann, ed., *Comparable Worth: New Directions for Research* (Washington, D.C.: National Academy Press, 1985), pp. 116–36.

23. Kelley, "Discrimination in Seniority Systems."

such struggles. It is also important to remember, as Kelley notes, that the underlying job structure over which workers and management struggle is itself in constant flux.[24] Indeed, conflict can be acted out through altering job structures. Obviously this is an area where qualitative information gained from the actors themselves may be much the best way to learn.

The Internal Labor Market in an Insurance Firm

What one might theoretically like to investigate is, of course, constrained by time, money, and the nature of real-life data sets. I was fortunate to obtain from a colleague a comprehensive data set on a fairly large single establishment of an insurance company. The company had over 5,000 full-time workers at the end of 1981 and had been growing for several years. It is a predominantly female firm; 73 percent of the full-time work force is female, but 40 percent of the managerial, professional, and technical jobs are held by men. Approximately 45 percent of the women and 22 percent of the men are minority group members, nearly all of them black. Black women, like women in general, work disproportionately in the lower-paying occupations. In 1981 white men in this firm earned on average $28,331 per year; minority men earned $19,979; white women earned $18,209; and minority women earned $16,284.

The Data Set

The data available on the firm consist of eight consecutive year-end computerized master files created routinely from data maintained and entered by the personnel office. The files include anyone who had some employment contact with the firm that year: full-time and part-time employees, applicants, retirees, the deceased, job leavers, and those temporarily on leave. Each time an event occurs that affects a worker (a pay increase, promotion, leave, reprimand, training course, or reevaluation), a record of it is made on the worker's master file; fourteen of the previous events are retained on each master file. Copious data on education, previous employment experience, and extracurricular achievements (like Boy Scouts) are available. Each individual's record

24. Maryellen R. Kelley, "Commentary: The Need to Study the Transformation of Job Structures," in Reskin, ed., *Sex Segregation in the Workplace*, pp. 261–64.

on each master file is ten 434-character records long. Moreover, in contrast to the consistency and accuracy of the computerized personnel data Rosenbaum received from a large utility company, these data are characterized by substantial inconsistency, undocumented coding changes, and some undocumented codes.[25] Although a sequence of meaningful events for each employee could be constructed (which would be ideal for tracking career paths and promotions in the firm), I use year-end observations for several years for which consistent data could be constructed. A typical way to handle multiyear data in regression analysis is to pool observations and add dummy control variables for year. I follow that convention here.[26]

A selection of variables from the 1981 master file was used to obtain basic descriptive data about employment in the firm. Promotions were analyzed with the aid of several "match files" that were created by merging pairs of consecutive years of master files and identifying individuals who appeared in both. The resulting match files contain records for individuals with data about both the individuals and their jobs at the end points of both years. These match files are limited to full-time professional, technical, and managerial employees and are available for seven pairs of years. The five match files from 1976–77 through 1980–81 had occupational codes that could be made consistent and were used in the analysis of promotion.

As the literature review in the preceding section notes, occupational segregation by sex or race is likely to be an important determinant of workers' earnings and prospects. Yet in this firm the number of detailed job titles is overwhelming. The 5,000 workers have 2,500 job titles. They also fall into 79 occupational groups identified by the firm. These larger groups are almost certainly too heterogenous to be totally satisfactory for analyzing job ladders and the distribution of male and female workers across jobs, but the job titles are just as obviously too small.[27] In

25. Rosenbaum, "Jobs, Job Status, and Women's Gains from Affirmative Action."
26. The main rationale for pooling the match files to conduct this analysis was to create a sufficiently large data set to be able to identify and analyze differential effects for race-sex groups. Logically each year's data is viewed as a more or less good substitute for additional records in any one year. This procedure, of course, prevents exploiting the potential longitudinal nature of this data set, but time and resources prevented the reorganization of the data files.
27. From observation of a list provided by the company, it seems fairly clear that the 2,500 job titles combine job and department titles, so that reasonably coherent jobs could be developed across departments. For example, "administrative secretary—

describing the work force of the entire firm, I use the 79 larger groups. In analyzing the professional, technical, and managerial employees, I use the 57 broad occupational groups into which they fell, but further differentiate them into 117 subsets by using information about the grade levels employees in the occupation held. The 117 subgroups are called "occ/grades"; each occ/grade spans two grade levels. In this company the professional, technical, and managerial jobs are evaluated and placed in grades by the Hay evaluation system, which attempts to measure such factors as differences in responsibility and job knowledge.[28] Occupations that range across many grade levels are probably aggregations of several different occupations. The occ/grades, in spanning two grade levels, are more homogenous than the broad categories but still represent useful, consistent aggregations of smaller job titles. In some cases a consecutive series of occ/grades exists for a broad occupational group and may represent a job ladder; in other cases the grades within broad occupational groups are not consecutive and probably represent distinct job sets between which little mobility occurs.

The Firm's Labor Market

Indexes of segregation, calculated from data in the 1981 master file, for the sexes and races across occupations, occ/grades, grades, and departments within the firm are shown in table 1. Indexes for this firm are consistent with findings from national data.[29] Sex segregation— whether across occupations, grades, or departments—is more pronounced than race segregation. Job segregation by sex is more pronounced among whites than among minorities, and job segregation by race is more pronounced among men than among women. Of interest is the fact that sex segregation is more pronounced for 21 pay grades than for 117 occ/grades, suggesting that within the 79 occupational groups

accounting" and "administrative secretary—auditing" could reasonably be combined into an administrative secretary job. Again, doing so would require a substantial investment of time.

28. Most clerical jobs are not evaluated by the Hay system and thus do not have grades.

29. Treiman and Hartmann, *Women, Work, and Wages,* pp. 25, 27. The segregation index, or index of dissimilarity, Δ, is given as $\Delta = \Sigma \mid x_i - y_i \mid \div 2$, where x_i is the percentage of one population (for example, men) in the ith category of a classification, and y_i is the percentage of the other population (women) in the ith category. Δ is then the percentage of either population that would have to shift categories to make its distribution exactly equal to that of the other population.

Table 1. *Indexes of Job Segregation, All Workers in Firm, 1981*

Type of segregation	Segregation indexes[a]			
	Across 79 occupations	Across 117 occ/grades[b]	Across 21 grades[b]	Across 49 departments
By sex				
All races	56.0	60.5	66.9	37.7
Among whites	57.7	. . .	. . .	39.8
Among minorities	47.5	. . .	. . .	33.5
By race or ethnicity				
Both sexes	29.9	22.5	27.9	25.6
Among men	36.6	. . .	. . .	24.2
Among women	22.9	. . .	. . .	19.5

a. The percentage of men or women that would have to change jobs for the occupational distribution to be equal between the sexes. See note 29 for calculation.

b. For 1,868 workers whose grade is known; that is, for about ⅗ of those in professional, technical, and managerial occupations, or 54 percent of all men and 28 percent of all women. All other indexes are calculated for the entire full-time work force of 5,191.

there is substantial sex segregation by grade, which is not picked up here because each occ/grade spans two grades. Departments do not appear to be a major way that race or sex segregation occurs, in contrast with many industrial plants, but sex segregation across occupations does vary by department—sales, for example, is the most segregated with an index of 80.4. It is also interesting to note that segregation within this firm is substantially less than in the California firms Bielby and Baron studied;[30] presumably this has to do with the aggregated occupational groups used here (each occupation aggregates thirty job titles on average), compared with the finer job titles used in their analysis.

Tables 2 and 3 display the largest occupations for women and men and for minority women and men. Women work mostly with women. All but three of the top ten women's occupations are predominantly female. In this firm, which is 73 percent female, clerks (77 percent female), supervisors (69 percent), and systems analysts (41 percent) can be viewed as relatively integrated occupations. The men and women have only three of their largest occupations in common, and the men's occupations, from their titles, appear to be closer to the top of the hierarchy, for example, department managers and division directors. Three-fifths of both the men and the women work in these largest occupations. For minorities, too, just three occupations appear in both the lists for women and men. Minority women are 34 percent of the work

30. Bielby and Baron, "A Woman's Place is with Other Women."

Table 2. *Ten Largest Occupations in Firm, for Each Sex, 1981*

Occupation	Number of sex in occupation	Percent of occupation this sex	Number of departments	Number of pay grades	Top pay grade
Women					
Clerk (not elsewhere classified)	492	76.6	19	n.a.	n.a.
Claims processor	340	92.9	5	4	10
Correspondent	276	94.2	7	8	15
Claims auditor	264	96.0	5	6	13
Supervisor	218	69.4	27	9	19
Secretary/steno	218	99.5	35	1	7
Scheduler/utility clerk	176	95.7	13	7	13
Assistant supervisor	168	87.0	10	7	14
Keypunch operator	149	100.0	1	n.a.	n.a.
Systems analyst	109	40.8	14	6	19
Total	2,410ª	83.0	. . .	. . .	. . .
Men					
Systems analyst	158	59.2	14	6	19
Clerk (not elsewhere classified)	150	23.4	21	n.a.	n.a.
Department manager	135	77.6	33	6	22
Accountant/auditor	98	64.9	3	6	18
Supervisor	96	30.6	29	9	19
Sales representative	68	71.6	9	6	19
Division director	56	93.3	32	5	24
Miscellaneous analyst	55	36.9	24	6	18
Computer operator	37	51.4	2	7	15
Coordinator II	32	57.1	18	6	21
Total	885ᵇ	44.7	. . .	. . .	. . .

n.a. Not available.

a. The number of women in these ten occupations represents 63.4 percent of all the women in the firm and 46.4 percent of all employees.

b. The number of men in these ten occupations represents 63.8 percent of all the men in the firm and 17 percent of all employees.

force in this firm, so they are substantially overrepresented in most of these occupations. Key punching is virtually a black female job. Minority men, who are 6 percent of the work force, have their largest representation in technical and professional occupations (accountants/auditors and miscellaneous data processing jobs). Tables 2 and 3 also show that the men's and women's occupations have on average the same number of pay grades (six), so women may not have shorter career ladders per se, but it is particularly striking that 218 women work in a job, secretary/steno, with only one pay grade. It is also striking that the top pay grades in the women's jobs are lower than the top pay grades of the men's jobs;

Table 3. *Ten Largest Occupations in Firm, for Minorities of Each Sex, 1981*

Occupation	Number of sex in occupation	Percent of occupation this sex	Number of pay grades	Top pay grade
Women				
Clerk (not elsewhere classified)	288	44.9	n.a.	n.a.
Claims processor	206	56.3	4	10
Correspondent	149	50.9	8	15
Claims auditor	136	49.5	6	13
Keypunch operator	108	72.5	n.a.	n.a.
Supervisor	91	29.0	9	19
Scheduler/utility clerk	89	48.4	7	13
Secretary/steno	86	39.3	1	7
Assistant supervisor	68	35.2	7	14
Telephone representative	52	48.6	6	13
Total	1,273[a]	46.4	. . .	. . .
Men				
Clerk (not elsewhere classified)	68	10.6	n.a.	n.a.
Systems analyst	24	9.0	6	19
Accountant/auditor	20	13.2	6	18
Supervisor	19	6.1	9	19
Claims processor	12	3.3	4	10
Department manager	11	6.3	6	22
Miscellaneous analyst	11	7.4	6	18
Sales representative	9	9.5	6	19
Miscellaneous electronic data processor	9	18.8	3	13
Computer data entry	9	10.6	n.a.	n.a.
Total	192[b]	8.3	. . .	. . .

n.a. Not available.

a. The number of minority women in these ten occupations represents 71.8 percent of all minority women in the firm and 24.5 percent of all employees.

b. The number of minority men in these ten occupations represents 59.4 percent of all minority men in the firm and 3.7 percent of all employees.

indeed the highest of the top grades in the women's jobs, 19, which is assigned to only two jobs, is the average top grade for the men's jobs.

While tables 1–3 present data taken from the 1981 master file for all workers, table 4 describes professional, managerial, and technical occupations using data from the 1979–80 match file and attempts to capture some of the relationships among important occupational variables, such as earnings, tenure, and sex and race composition. All professional, technical, and managerial occupations that contained more than twenty workers are ranked in order of the mean salary of all incumbents of the occupation. The most striking feature of the table is that almost all the

Table 4. Professional, Managerial, and Technical Employees in Firm, 1979 Year-End[a]

Occupation	Mean salary (dollars)	Total employees	Percent female	Percent minority	Mean salary (women/men)	Mean tenure (women/men)
Executive vice-president	59,231	26	0	0	...	...
Division director	36,915	51	3.9	6.3	0.94	0.64
Department manager	29,714	135	21.5	9.1	0.92	1.00
Coordinator I	29,658	21	19.0	14.3	0.93	1.00
Coordinator II	26,822	46	39.1	11.4	0.95	1.50
Consultant	26,338	28	17.9	14.3	0.94	0.75
Assistant manager	25,562	39	41.0	15.4	0.99	1.70
Sales representative	25,245	77	23.4	12.2	0.89	0.64
Systems analyst	24,320	225	37.8	16.4	0.87	1.29
Accountant/auditor	24,004	121	28.9	19.6	0.92	1.13
Research analyst	23,929	24	50.0	17.4	0.90	1.40
Data analyst	22,869	29	44.8	14.8	0.90	1.50
Miscellaneous analyst	22,731	153	63.4	20.8	0.87	1.00
Supervisor	21,050	285	71.6	35.1	0.86	1.57
Medical review specialist	18,652	47	97.9	51.1	1.24	6.00
Trainer	18,403	27	88.9	40.7	1.11	1.40
Quality analyst	17,262	48	93.8	47.9	0.97	0.54
Miscellaneous data processor	17,109	38	52.6	35.1	0.95	1.60
Account services specialist	17,026	49	100.0	16.3	...	...
Executive secretary	16,646	67	100.0	21.5	...	...
Assistant supervisor	16,249	151	92.1	37.2	1.10	1.60
Miscellaneous analyst	16,189	41	95.1	30.0	1.01	1.75
Other technical	15,944	75	92.0	38.9	1.12	1.75
Correspondent	15,877	236	94.9	56.5	1.04	1.50
Computer operator	15,773	72	44.4	37.1	1.00	1.17
Junior accountant	15,175	45	93.3	29.5	1.13	1.40
Telephone representative	15,073	84	88.1	53.6	1.01	1.50
Claims auditor	14,978	239	96.7	45.8	1.09	1.20
Service worker	12,147	23	26.1	47.8	0.95	0.50

a. Occupations with twenty or fewer incumbents are excluded.

low-paid occupations are disproportionately female, and the better-paid occupations are disproportionately male. The table also reveals that women are paid more than men in the "women's" occupations and less than men in the "men's" occupations, but, as the last column of the table indicates, women are probably paid more than men in the women's occupations because they have substantially more company experience than the men in these same occupations. (It also indicates women have greater seniority than men in several of the men's occupations as well; this suggests, if other qualifications are equal, that discrimination in pay may occur at the upper levels.) In this firm, as in national data, the female percentage of an occupation is negatively correlated with the mean earnings of the occupation's incumbents.

With respect to race, it is fairly striking that minorities, mostly women in these cases, have the "back office" jobs—service workers, technicians, and correspondents (probably word processors). They also have a fair number of supervisor jobs, probably first-line supervision of other minorities. They are notably absent from sales and upper management jobs and particularly from account service specialists, an occupation that requires substantial contact with the public.

Further examination of the occupational data for professional, managerial, and technical employees showed that in the higher-paid occupations promotion was generally less likely for women than men, but was generally more likely in the lower-paid occupations (in which women predominate) than in the higher-paid occupations. Thus a simple correlation between the percentage promoted from an occupation and the female percentage of that occupation would be positive. But since it is likely that in a pyramidal job structure promotion opportunities would become more scarce as one moved up the hierarchy, any association between sex of the incumbent or female percentage of an occupation and promotion possibilities would have to be corrected for the grade level of the job. Promotion is defined as being at the end of year 2 in a job at least one grade level higher than the job held at the end of year 1. It is thus possible to calculate year-to-year promotion rates for women and men for each of the paired-year match files. In general, annual promotion rates were similar for women and men and ranged from 15 to 20 percent across the five years.

To illustrate the usefulness of considering occupation in a study of promotion, examine the following data for all occupations that had incumbents in grade 16 in 1977.

Occupation	Number of incumbents	Percent female	Rank	Percent promoted	Rank
Administrative assistant	9	88.9	1	0.0	11
Personnel specialist	7	85.7	2	14.3	9
Research analyst	9	77.8	3	22.2	6
Miscellaneous analyst	34	70.6	4	17.6	8
Supervisor	9	66.7	5	22.2	6
Assistant manager	6	66.7	6	33.3	3
Mathematician	9	44.4	7	44.4	2
Systems analyst	82	42.7	8	28.0	4
Coordinator II	5	40.0	9	60.0	1
Data analyst	21	38.1	10	14.3	9
Accountant, auditor	47	25.5	11	23.4	5

The colleague who provided the data had analyzed promotions by grade level and found that the transition from grade 16 to grade 17 appeared to be a "bottleneck." I sought to supplement this information by learning something about the occupations that people actually work in and to test in particular whether the sex composition of their occupation affected their promotion prospects or earnings gains.

Few women reached grade 17 and even fewer moved beyond it. In 1981, 77 percent of those in grade 15 were women, roughly proportional to their representation in the firm, but women were only 55 percent of grade 16 (still roughly proportional to their representation in professional, managerial, and technical work). However, they represented only 37 percent of grade 17, and 24 and 23 percent respectively of grades 18 and 19. In the highest grades, 20 through 28, which contained 136 men, women constituted less than 9 percent of the total. How does this bottleneck occur? Are men and women in grade 16 in the same occupations and promoted differentially, or are they in different occupations that provide differential access to promotion?

As the data for promotions from grade 16 in 1977–78 show, the female share of these eleven occupations ranges from 25.5 percent to 88.9 percent. Moreover, the female percentage correlates negatively with the percentage from each occupation that were promoted. With only one exception, the top five occupations ranked according to the female percentage were in the bottom five when ranked by the percentage promoted, and the bottom five in the female percentage were in the top five in the percentage promoted. This preliminary examination for promotion from one grade in one pair of years suggests that the different occupations women and men hold are important determinants of their differential promotion opportunities.

Empirical Analyses

To investigate the effect of sex segregation of occupations on promotion opportunities more generally, I estimated regression equations for professional, managerial, and technical employees in the pooled match files for five pairs of years. Several specifications are reported here. The goal is to determine the net effect of the female percentage on promotion prospects when such factors as education, seniority, and performance level are held constant. In addition to promotion per se, I also estimated determinants of salary growth, another indicator of advancement opportunities. Finally, estimates of earnings determinants for the same data serve as a benchmark of how salaries in this firm are related to job structure, skill requirements, and the race and sex of workers.[31]

Table 5 presents the results of the first set of regressions, in which promotion is the dependent variable. This model essentially replicates one used by Abraham and Medoff to study the effects of an individual's seniority and performance on promotion rates,[32] but this one includes the female and minority percentages for the individual's occupation as an independent variable. Abraham and Medoff argued that in a meritocratic firm, performance variables should be positive and significant, while years of service with the firm would be negatively associated with promotion; that is, at any given grade level, the longer individuals have been in that pay grade the more likely they are to have been passed over for promotion because the best performers have already been promoted. They found that in the nonunion firm they studied, promotion conformed to the meritocratic model.

The first column in table 5 reports results for all professional, managerial, and technical employees for a pool of three paired-year files (computer memory was insufficient to run a logistic equation for all five match files). Race and sex of the individual and the female and minority percentages of the individual's occ/grade (the finer occupational gradations created for this analysis) are included to see how these affect promotion. Abraham and Medoff explicitly excluded women and minorities from their analysis (though the data were apparently available);

31. Tables showing the variables, correlation coefficients, and means and standard deviations are available from the author.

32. Katharine G. Abraham and James L. Medoff, "Length of Service and Promotions in Union and Nonunion Work Groups," *Industrial and Labor Relations Review,* vol. 38 (April 1985), p. 412.

Table 5. *Estimates of Variables Explaining Promotion for Professional, Technical, and Managerial Employees in Firm, 1976–77 to 1980–81*[a]

Variable and summary statistics	All jobs					
	All[b] (1)	White women (2)	Black women (3)	White men (4)	Black men (5)	Grades 16–19[b] (6)
Company tenure (years)	−0.0352* (0.0194)	−0.0608* (0.0312)	−0.0100 (0.0426)	−0.0005 (0.0382)	0.1735 (0.1442)	−0.0108 (0.0398)
Company tenure squared	0.0013* (0.0007)	0.0007 (0.0010)	0.0021 (0.0016)	0.0013 (0.0013)	−0.0093 (0.0081)	0.0024* (0.0012)
Performance evaluation (1 = high)	−0.1502 (0.1710)	−0.5549 (0.3869)	−0.4198 (0.5943)	−0.8216* (0.4480)	0.9889 (1.0404)	0.9201* (0.5386)
Performance evaluation (1 = moderate)	...	−0.4116 (0.3329)	−0.2252 (0.4978)	−0.4440 (0.2822)	−0.2928 (0.9017)	0.3909 (0.3662)
Percent female (occ/grade)	−0.0098‡ (0.0023)	−0.0123‡ (0.0035)	−0.0196‡ (0.0055)	0.0041 (0.0039)	0.0073 (0.0087)	−0.0027 (0.0051)
Percent minority (occ/grade)	0.0224‡ (0.0035)	0.0246‡ (0.0045)	0.0213‡ (0.0076)	0.0092 (0.0082)	−0.0036 (0.0225)	0.0126 (0.0124)

Sex (1 = female)	−0.1049	⋯	⋯	⋯	−0.2625
	(0.1073)	⋯	⋯	⋯	(0.1805)
Race (1 = minority)	−0.3827‡	⋯	⋯	⋯	−0.4502†
	(0.0830)	⋯	⋯	⋯	(0.2214)
Age (years)	0.0707*	0.1212†	0.14501	0.0277	0.0138	−0.0565
	(0.0392)	(0.0563)	(0.1008)	(0.0722)	(0.2144)	(0.0881)
Age squared	−0.0013‡	−0.0016†	−0.0024†	−0.0009	0.0003	−0.0002
	(0.0004)	(0.0006)	(0.0012)	(0.0008)	(0.0025)	(0.0009)
Hay points/grade level	−0.0020‡	−0.0013*	−0.0045‡	−0.0023‡	−0.0052‡	−0.0055‡
	(0.0004)	(0.0008)	(0.0012)	(0.0005)	(0.0019)	(0.0016)
Summary statistics						
Constant	−1.0566	−2.2957	−1.0700	1.4914	−1.7010	4.0025
N	5,353	2,342	1,513	1,874	294	1,382
Percent promoted	20.0	21.0	18.8	18.9	20.7	18.5

* Significant at the 10 percent level.
† Significant at the 5 percent level.
‡ Significant at the 1 percent level.

a. Pooled year-to-year transitions. Maximum likelihood logit procedure; dependent variable = 1 if promoted to higher grade during the year following the year in which the variables were observed, = 0 otherwise. Equations also included variables for experience outside the firm, education, both of these squared, and dummy variables for the years; these variables were rarely significant. Numbers in parentheses are standard errors.

b. For only three year-to-year transitions: 1978–79, 1979–80, and 1980–81.

their data are for one year and, like these, are for professional, technical, and managerial employees. In this regression, data are for three pooled match files and include 5,353 cases. Here total "Hay points" (the total score from the Hay job evaluation system) of the individual's job serve to control for occupational level (since all things being equal, promotion rates are expected to be lower at higher levels), whereas Abraham and Medoff used dummy variables for grade levels. The performance measures used here are similar to those used by Abraham and Medoff, but they also used a measure of potential advancement (highest grade supervisor expects individual to reach) in addition to the standard performance evaluation of high, medium, or low. (Their results show that this measure of potential advancement contributed substantially to the explanation of promotion.) The average rate of promotion, 20 percent, is somewhat higher than it was in the firm studied by Abraham and Medoff.

Although the specification of the model is similar to Abraham and Medoff's, the results are strikingly different; most notably, having an outstanding performance rating, although insignificant, is negatively associated with promotion. Perhaps this is not a meritocratic firm. Tenure inside the firm is negative and significant, however, as one would be led to expect if the firm were meritocratic. The results of one regression, not reported here, showed that the addition of the performance variables moved the coefficient on seniority toward zero, as Abraham and Medoff argued should occur in a meritocratic firm (if it did not move toward zero, they would suspect age discrimination). The seniority coefficient here does not move as far toward zero as theirs, perhaps because the more powerful performance measure (the indicator of potential) is not available here. But the negative sign on the performance variable is disturbing.[33] Are the most able people passed over? Are a lot of able people in dead-end jobs? Perhaps even those with good and outstanding performance evaluations have nowhere to go. Note that, somewhat surprisingly, the effect of age is positive and significant, separately from the effect of seniority. This is also consistent with an "overcrowding" theory that a lot of good people are stuck—in that

33. Dunson also found negative signs on performance evaluation for white males in mid-level jobs in the army and the Department of Defense (although the signs were positive in the air force and the navy). Bruce H. Dunson, "Pay, Experience, and Productivity: The Government-Sector Case," *Journal of Human Resources*, vol. 20 (Winter 1985), pp. 153–60.

situation, a reward for age might make sense as a fairness gesture. Note that the sign on Hay points is negative and statistically significant, as expected, indicating that all other things being equal, the higher in the firm individuals are, the less likely they will be promoted.

Of particular interest in this analysis is the negative sign on the female percentage of the individuals's occ/grade and its significance, as expected. Sex of the individual is negative but insignificant. Race of the individual is negative and highly significant, as one would suspect if there is discrimination based on race; on the other hand, the minority percentage of the occ/grade is positive and significant. Can the combined information from these two variables be interpreted to mean that, all else being equal, white people are promoted out of minority occupations more quickly than others?

Table 5 also shows, in the last column, results for the same three match files for incumbents in jobs in grades 16 to 19 (the mid-range of jobs that appear to constitute the top of the female ladder but the middle of the male ladder). In these jobs the stronger performance variable (evaluation = high) is positive and significant, suggesting a more meritocratic basis for promotion. The female percentage of the individual's occ/grade is still a negative influence, but is not statistically significant. In these higher-level jobs, performance seems to be more important and the female percentage less important than in all jobs. The lack of importance for the female percentage here may stem from the lack of variation in the variables. Above grade 16, few women can be found.

Inspection of the several equations estimated for sex-race groups separately (columns 2–5 of table 5) shows that the strong negative effect for the female percentage occurs for black and white women, rather than men. The same is true for the strong positive effect of the minority percentage. Men's chances for promotion are less affected by the female percentage of their occ/grades, and the effect is positive: the more female the occ/grade, the more likely is promotion for men. White men are the only group for which the coefficient on performance evaluation is significantly negative. For black men, performance evaluation, though insignificant, has a positive sign. The positive and significant age effect is seen to occur largely for white women. The differences in structures apparent from the separate equations for the four sex-race groups are generally statistically significant. Chow tests reveal that the differences in the effect of the female percentage between white women and white men, and between white women and black women, are strongly significant.

It should be noted that little of the variance in promotion chances between individuals is explained by this model (an earlier set of ordinary least squares regressions had very low R^2s). The significance of the exercise lies in confirming an expected negative effect of the female percentage on promotion opportunities, especially for women.

Table 6 presents the results of ordinary least squares regressions with salary growth, rather than promotion possibility, as the dependent variable. The results for all professional, managerial, and technical workers are shown in column 1. Tenure within the firm is negative and significant, suggesting that the more senior one is, the smaller one's salary growth. This is a reasonable expectation. Age is also negative and significant, unlike in the promotion equation. Performance evaluations are positive and strongly significant. Good performance evaluations apparently affect one's salary growth, but not one's promotion possibilities. An individual's race is negative and significant and sex is negative and insignificant, as in the promotion equations. All other things being equal, race discrimination is a strong possibility. The female and minority percentages are, however, positive and strongly significant, in contrast to the promotion equations. The findings in tables 6 and 5, taken together, suggest that people in minority- and female-dominated occupations are disadvantaged with respect to promotion to a higher grade but compensated with salary increases. Since the salary ranges of pay grades overlap, this is not too difficult for the firm to arrange. These findings are similar to those of Killingsworth and Reimers for black civil servants at an army base and of Cassell, Director, and Doctors for white-collar workers in utilities.[34] But, as Killingsworth and Reimers point out, salary growth does not truly compensate for lack of promotion, particularly over the long run.

Some differences among the equations for the four sex-race groups, shown in columns 2–5, stand out. White men are not penalized, in terms of the size of their salary increase, by their seniority. Company tenure is positive, rather than negative, for white men, though its effect is statistically insignificant. The stronger performance evaluation variable is positive but not statistically significant for white men; the other is negative. The importance of the female percentage, strongly positive when all workers are considered together, is more mixed when sex-race groups are considered separately. The lack of significance for black and white men is surprising (the negative sign for black men suggests they may get smaller increases if they are in female-dominated occupations). But the very small positive and statistically insignificant effect for white women is surprising and casts some doubt on the thesis about salary increases as compensation for lack of promotion. For black women, the effect of the female percentage is large, positive, and significant. Thus the effect of the female percentage in the equation for all workers largely stems from the black women. The minority percentage is positive and significant only for white women and men, suggesting they are compensated for being in occupations where they are underrepresented, perhaps because they stand out. Age is strongly negative and significant in all groups.

Column 6 presents results for workers in grades 16 to 19. With respect to promotion, these grades were found to be more meritocratic. The same is true here with respect to salary growth; it is positively and strongly related to performance evaluation. The effects of the female and minority percentages, sex, and race are statistically insignificant. Age still has a strong, negative effect, as do Hay points. This suggests the older and higher up in the firm one gets, the less the salary growth. Hay points for white women are strongly positive and significant; this suggests that if women are promoted to higher grades they may catch up in their salary growth.

For all the equations taken together, variation in salary growth is better explained by the variables for men than for women. The constant terms show how much larger salary growth is for the men than the women. The dummy variables for years of observation were in general significant. These were inflationary years, and the largest salary growth occurred in the last year.

In an alternative approach to identifying the effect of being female, I analyzed five reasonably integrated occupations. These results (not shown here) confirmed the finding that the higher-level occupations (systems analyst, sales representative, and accountant/auditor) are more meritocratic; performance evaluation is always positive and sometimes significant, both for promotion and salary growth. One's race is always

Table 6. Estimates of Variables Explaining Salary Growth for Professional, Technical, and Managerial Employees in Firm, 1976–77 to 1980–81[a]

Variable and summary statistics	All[b] (1)	White women (2)	Black women (3)	White men (4)	Black men (5)	Grades 16–19[b] (6)
		All jobs				
Company tenure (years)[b]	−0.0209† (0.0085)	−0.0308† (0.0123)	−0.0295† (0.0144)	0.0012 (0.0184)	−0.0151‡ (0.0040)	−0.0056† (0.0025)
Company tenure squared[b]	0.0066 (0.0042)	0.0098 (0.0060)	0.0118 (0.0072)	−0.0016 (0.0092)	... ...	... ...
Performance evaluation (1 = high)	0.0222‡ (0.0047)	0.0339‡ (0.0095)	0.0173* (0.0094)	0.0085 (0.0089)	0.0614‡ (0.0162)	0.0479‡ (0.0112)
Performance evaluation (1 = moderate)	0.0131‡ (0.0040)	0.0266‡ (0.0088)	0.0126 (0.0085)	−0.0022 (0.0063)	0.0256* (0.0131)	0.0253‡ (0.0086)
Percent female[b] (occ/grade)	0.0045‡ (0.0012)	0.0005 (0.0031)	0.0062* (0.0035)	0.0029 (0.0018)	−0.0015 (0.0042)	0.0033 (0.0024)
Percent minority[b] (occ/grade)	0.0053‡ (0.0011)	0.0045‡ (0.0016)	0.0014 (0.0032)	0.0056† (0.0023)	0.0052 (0.0064)	0.0015 (0.0028)

Sex (1 = female)	−0.0016	...	...	...	...	0.0004
	(0.0018)	...	...	...	...	(0.0036)
Race (1 = minority)	−0.0028*	...	...	...	...	−0.0045
	(0.0015)	...	...	...	...	(0.0042)
Age (years)^b	−0.0524‡	−0.0432‡	−0.0286‡	−0.0845‡	−0.0351*	−0.0796‡
	(0.0040)	(0.0061)	(0.0064)	(0.0093)	(0.0187)	(0.0104)
Hay points/grade level^b	0.0065‡	0.0115‡	0.0020	−0.0018	−0.0010	−0.0544‡
	(0.0022)	(0.0040)	(0.0038)	(0.0048)	(0.0096)	(0.0143)
Summary statistics						
Constant	0.1885	0.1227	0.0877	0.3699	0.3420	0.6764
R^2	0.274	0.2483	0.3021	0.2951	0.3465	0.299
N	7,350	2,886	1,926	2,166	372	1,878

* Significant at the 10 percent level.
† Significant at the 5 percent level.
‡ Significant at the 1 percent level.
a. Pooled year-to-year transitions. Ordinary least squares analysis; dependent variable = natural logarithm of the ratio of salary in year 2 to salary in year 1. Equations also included variables for experience outside the firm, education, both of these squared, age squared, and dummy variables for the years. Of these variables, only the dummy variables for years were significant. Numbers in parentheses are standard errors.
b. Natural logarithm.

negative, though not significant because the numbers are small. Sales representative is the only occupation that did not have a negative sign on the sex coefficient. For the two lower-level occupations, miscellaneous analyst and supervisor, performance ratings are again negative, suggesting that these tend to be dead-end occupations. With ordinary least squares regressions the amount of variance in promotion that can be explained rose to 10 percent for the systems analysts; and for salary growth, as much as 48 percent was explained for the sales representatives.

The final set of regressions estimates the log of salary for the same pooled data, providing further insight on how job structure, race, and sex are related to outcomes (see table 7). The available independent variables explain 83 to 91 percent of the variance, depending on the model and the population. Tenure with the company, experience outside the company, age, education, and schooling in particular subjects generally contribute positively to earnings in all estimated equations. With the exception of the education variables, these are generally significant across all demographic subgroups. The effect of age, separate from seniority or experience, is positive for all groups but much larger for white men than any other group. Supervisory status is significant and positive for all workers, but not for subgroups considered separately. Hay points are always positive and significant; the higher one's grade, the higher one's salary. Performance evaluation has a negative sign, but only when grade level (Hay points) is not controlled (equation 1a). When grade level is controlled, these variables have the expected positive sign for all workers considered together. Among the demographic subgroups, however, performance evaluation is significantly positive only for white men. The equations for all workers show that individuals' sex and race negatively affect their earnings, but only the race effect is significant.

In equations 1a and 1b, the female percentage is negative when all workers are considered together. In equation 1b, Hay points are added to examine the effect of controlling for grade level. Several studies show that the negative effect that female job occupancy has on salaries is mediated by grade level.[35] When grade level is introduced into the

---

35. Burton G. Malkiel and Judith A. Malkiel, "Male-Female Pay Differentials in Professional Employment," *American Economic Review*, vol. 63 (September 1973), pp. 693–705; Charles N. Halaby, "Sexual Inequality in the Workplace: An Employer-Specific Analysis of Pay Differences," *Social Science Research*, vol. 8 (March 1979), pp. 79–104; Charles N. Halaby, "Job-Specific Sex Differences in Organizational Reward

earnings equations for jobs in Rosenbaum's study, for example, the female percentage becomes much less important. As can be seen, equation 1b yields a similar result, but the female percentage, though smaller, is still significant. This seems somewhat remarkable when nearly all the variance in salary is explained and numerous variables indicative of human capital accumulation are included, as well as grade level. Including the control for grade level generally reduces the size of the coefficients for all variables in the equation.

In contrast to the negative sign on the female percentage for the group as a whole, within the four race-sex groups the effect is positive and significant (except for black men, where it is not significant). This effect apparently also results from the inclusion of the control for grade level (Hay points). In salary equations for these four subgroups that did not include Hay points (not shown here) the effect is strongly negative. Apparently, once grade level is controlled, women (and others) earn a premium for being in a female-dominated job; this interpretation is compatible with the explanation that sees salary as compensation for dead-endedness. The minority percentage, in contrast to the female percentage, is strongly significant and negative for all groups, except black men, where again it is small.

Conclusion and Research Needs

In summary, the descriptive data show considerable segregation by race and sex in this firm, with women and minorities disproportionately in low grades in lower-paying occupations. The data in table 4 suggest that this firm's labor market is bifurcated, with women in the bottom half and men in the top half. It looks as though men start at the middle and move to the top and women start at the bottom and move to the middle. Evidence from the equations about probability of promotion indicates that although promotion in this firm appears to be somewhat meritocratic, a very good performance evaluation decreases one's chance of promotion. This possibly suggests that women in particular hold dead-end, female-dominated jobs. Likewise, the evidence suggests, but is by no means definitive, that women receive some compensation in salary

Attainment: Wage Discrimination vs. Rank Segregation," *Social Forces*, vol. 58 (September 1979), pp. 108–27; and Rosenbaum, "Jobs, Job Status, and Women's Gains from Affirmative Action."

Table 7. Estimates of Variables Explaining Earnings of Professional, Technical, and Managerial Employees in Firm, 1976–1977 to 1980–1981[a]

Variable and summary statistics	All jobs		White women (2)	Black women (3)	White men (4)	Black men (5)
	No Hay points (1a)	Hay points (1b)				
Company tenure (years)	0.0285‡	0.0183‡	0.0201‡	0.0169‡	0.0107‡	0.0247‡
	(0.0008)	(0.0006)	(0.0008)	(0.0011)	(0.0010)	(0.0025)
Company tenure squared	−0.0006‡	−0.0003‡	−0.0004‡	−0.0002‡	−0.0002‡	−0.0008‡
	(0.0000)	(0.0000)	(0.0000)	(0.0000)	(0.0000)	(0.0001)
Outside experience	0.0080‡	0.0044‡	0.0030‡	0.0071‡	0.0008	0.0060†
	(0.0008)	(0.0005)	(0.0010)	(0.0010)	(0.0009)	(0.0024)
Outside experience squared	−0.0001‡	−0.0001†	0.0001	−0.0001‡	0.0000	−0.0002*
	(0.0000)	(0.0000)	(0.0001)	(0.0001)	(0.0000)	(0.0001)
Age (years)	0.0213‡	0.0228†	0.0128‡	0.0132‡	0.0350‡	0.0114†
	(0.0015)	(0.0011)	(0.0014)	(0.0021)	(0.0020)	(0.0052)
Age squared	−0.0002‡	−0.0002‡	−0.0001‡	−0.0002‡	−0.0003‡	−0.0001
	(0.0000)	(0.0000)	(0.0000)	(0.0000)	(0.0000)	(0.0001)
Education dummies						
Completed high school	0.0183	0.0060	0.0370	−0.0203	−0.0173	−0.0170
	(0.0276)	(0.0197)	(0.0257)	(0.0267)	(0.0386)	(0.0431)
Some post-high school	0.0337	0.0149	0.0366	−0.0093	−0.0113	−0.0299
	(0.0278)	(0.0199)	(0.0260)	(0.0270)	(0.0386)	(0.0414)
College degree	0.0900‡	0.0354	0.0416	−0.0367	−0.0002	−0.0126
	(0.0282)	(0.0201)	(0.0267)	(0.0277)	(0.0388)	(0.0419)
Some graduate training	0.1481‡	0.0511†	0.0417	0.0200	−0.0031	0.0618
	(0.0286)	(0.0204)	(0.0280)	(0.0348)	(0.0390)	(0.0422)
Ph.D. degree	0.2073‡	0.0499†	0.1181‡	0.1056	−0.0049	⋯
	(0.0322)	(0.0231)	(0.0399)	(0.0821)	(0.0410)	⋯

Education subject dummies

Business and quantitative[b]	0.0283‡ (0.0050)	0.0196‡ (0.0036)	0.0081 (0.0057)	0.0045 (0.0054)	0.0137† (0.0059)	0.0215† (0.0106)
Law and medical	0.0519‡ (0.0077)	0.0241‡ (0.0055)	0.0199‡ (0.0073)	-0.0137* (0.0082)	0.0011 (0.0111)	-0.0494† (0.0247)
Liberal arts	0.0064 (0.0073)	0.0033 (0.0052)	0.0216‡ (0.0078)	0.0096 (0.0079)	0.0153* (0.0088)	0.0482† (0.0200)
Vocational	-0.0042 (0.0075)	0.0085 (0.0053)	0.0317‡ (0.0062)	0.0044 (0.0073)	0.0821† (0.0383)	0.0189 (0.0332)
Percent female (occ/grade)	-0.0027‡ (0.0001)	-0.0008‡ (0.0001)	0.0007‡ (0.0001)	0.0004‡ (0.0001)	0.0002* (0.0001)	0.0001 (0.0002)
Percent minority (occ/grade)	-0.0038‡ (0.0001)	-0.0024‡ (0.0001)	-0.0012‡ (0.0001)	-0.0014‡ (0.0001)	-0.0019‡ (0.0003)	-0.0003 (0.0004)
Sex (1 = female)	-0.0041 (0.0048)	-0.0034 (0.0034)	⋮	⋮	⋮	⋮
Race (1 = minority)	-0.0202‡ (0.0036)	-0.0191‡ (0.0026)	⋮	⋮	⋮	⋮
Performance evaluation (1 = high)	-0.1673‡ (0.0107)	0.0057 (0.0079)	-0.0006 (0.0122)	-0.0468‡ (0.0175)	0.0282† (0.0125)	-0.0271 (0.0246)
Performance evaluation (1 = moderate)	-0.1491‡ (0.0087)	0.0222‡ (0.0066)	0.0061 (0.0111)	-0.0336‡ (0.0156)	0.0070 (0.0087)	-0.0204 (0.0182)
Supervisory status	0.1075‡ (0.0038)	0.0296‡ (0.0028)	0.0040 (0.0041)	-0.0016 (0.0056)	-0.0069 (0.0045)	-0.0068 (0.0105)
Hay points	⋮	0.0007‡ (0.0000)	0.0015† (0.0001)	0.0017‡ (0.0001)	0.0012‡ (0.0000)	0.0020‡ (0.0001)
Hay points squared	⋮	⋮	-0.0000‡ (0.0000)	-0.0000‡ (0.0000)	-0.0000‡ (0.0000)	-0.0000‡ (0.0000)
Constant	9.4097	8.897	8.7405	8.8382	8.4777	8.687
R^2	.826	.911	.8795	.8580	.9278	.9481
N	7,350	7,350	2,886	1,926	2,166	372

* Significant at the 10 percent level.   † Significant at the 5 percent level.   ‡ Significant at the 1 percent level.

a. Pooled year-to-year transitions. Ordinary least squares regression; dependent variable = natural log of salary. Equation also includes dummy variables years. Numbers in parentheses are standard errors.

b. Includes business, economics and social sciences, mathematics, statistics, computer science, engineering, and actuarial.

growth for the lack of promotion opportunities. Most important, however, the percentage of an occupation that is female is an important
explanatory variable for promotion or salary growth, even when human
capital characteristics of individuals and objective characteristics of the
job (such as grade level and supervisory status) are included in the
models. The sex of the individual, nearly always negative for women,
was rarely significant, but the race of the individual was often strongly
negative.

To the extent women may be discriminated against in this firm, then,
discrimination appears to take the form of their location in female-
dominated occupations. In this sense the internal labor market model
holds: women and men in the same occupations are generally treated
similarly (though not entirely); it's just that they are not usually in the
same occupations. Like the female percentage, the minority percentage
also generally has a significant negative sign, but being a black individual
further decreases one's opportunities. Race of the individual is always
negative and nearly always significant in explaining promotion, salary
growth, or earnings. Hence blacks likely suffer from both a structurally
enforced problem (being in the wrong job) and personal discrimination.
There is also some hint, though it is just a hint, that women and men who
stand out from the crowd tend to do better: white women in a disproportionately minority female occupation, men in women's occupations. For
the most part, women in the predominantly female occupations appear
not to be recognized for their ability or promoted beyond those occupations.

Other than by showing that the percentage of females in one's
occupation has the expected negative effect on promotion possibilities,
no attempt has been made to document differences in career paths. The
analysis supports the view developed in much other recent literature
that occupation is crucially important—above and beyond the characteristics of individuals or the objective requirements of the job.

The preliminary knowledge about starting and ending grades in
occupational chains, and their length, suggests some logical next steps
in analyzing this type of data set. Remaining questions center around
the shape of career ladders and differential occupational assignment by
race and gender. Transition matrices for the same data used here (the
pooled one-year transitions) could be used to identify occupational
destinations and origins; this would allow one to return some of the
institutional flesh to these rather bare-bones models. Other remaining

questions center on some of the anomalies in the results for promotion, such as negative signs on performance ratings. It should be easier to explain promotion probabilities over a longer time period; Dunson was better able to explain the number of promotions over a ten-year period.[36] Data files for individuals could be matched over a larger number of years. More ambitiously, creating event history files from these data, or even stringing together end-of-year observations for individuals, would allow one to determine career paths and "read" the internal labor market rules from the data, again fleshing out the story of what happens to people and what constrains the mobility of women and nonwhites.

Additional questions emerge from the literature review. How have the turfs of women and men workers changed in this firm over time? Have female and male jobs changed their positions in the pay hierarchy, possibly in connection with changes in sex composition? Have promotion possibilities associated with certain jobs changed over time? Some occupations have begun to show change in gender composition in more recent years; for example, more women are now miscellaneous and systems analysts, which appear to lie on the same job ladder and may now be used as transition occupations for women between the bottom and the top jobs. Analysis of such changes in turf would be aided by creating a data set on jobs similar to Rosenbaum's.[37] One could study the changing job structure, the jobs that disappear and are created, their gender and racial composition, and their changing relative wage rates.

Further development of institutional labor market theory could illuminate additional issues of importance in the workplace. The original institutionalists and their modern-day counterparts; Marxists with their understanding of class struggle, work culture, and labor process; and feminists with their understanding of gender struggle and women's aspirations all have a part to play in the development of a more complete understanding of internal labor markets. This is a project that should be shared by sociologists, historians, and others in addition to economists, for sociologists and historians have been studying occupations and workplaces for years, whereas economists have barely yet discovered them. Workplace-based studies could be facilitated if scholars take steps now to share the data that become available. We should also, I think, plan seriously for developing for research purposes an establishment-

36. Dunson, "Pay, Experience, and Productivity."
37. Rosenbaum, "Jobs, Job Status, and Women's Gains from Affirmative Action."

level data base with substantial demographic information about individual employees.

Comments by Paul Osterman

This paper represents the kind of work needed to understand the origins and dynamics of sex discrimination in internal labor markets. By examining a particular firm in detail and attempting to relate her findings to more general theories of internal labor markets, Hartmann moves us forward in this area.

Ultimately, Hartmann is able to generate some provocative results but is not able to explain them fully. I think the reason lies in the incomplete character of theorizing about internal labor markets. Although there has been a great deal of work in the area, it seems fair to say that most of the research has been empirical, not theoretical.[38] With the exception of one major line of work, noted below, our theoretical understanding of internal labor markets still rests on the arguments found in Doeringer and Piore's 1971 book.[39] The model developed there is a somewhat uneasy amalgam of human capital theory, with its emphasis on the role of specific training in generating attachment between firms and workers, and a sociological argument about the roles of custom and work groups in generating norms and rules. Added to this is an implicit emphasis upon the activities of unions in encouraging seniority-based promotion and pay systems.[40]

I characterize this combination of themes as "uneasy" because they rest on a set of arguments that have very different underlying behaviorial foundations. Human capital theory assumes maximizing individualistic behavior, while neither the sociological argument nor many of the union stories make this assumption. Doeringer and Piore are never very clear about how these different arguments come together, and as a conse-

38. Two recent books that contain collections of papers on the subject are Ivar Berg, ed., *Sociological Perspectives on Labor Markets* (Academic Press, 1981); and Paul Osterman, ed., *Internal Labor Markets* (MIT Press, 1984).

39. Doeringer and Piore, *Internal Labor Markets and Manpower Analysis*.

40. For a more explicit argument concerning the role of unions in stimulating internal labor markets, see Sanford M. Jacoby, "The Development of Internal Labor Markets in American Manufacturing Firms," in Osterman, ed., *Internal Labor Markets*, pp. 23–69.

quence their "theory" becomes more a list of considerations than a coherent explanation.

The theory developed by Williamson and others does constitute a more coherent explanation of internal labor markets.[41] In large enterprises, the argument goes, perpetual monitoring of employee activity is difficult and costly. Furthermore, it is very difficult to specify in advance the full range of worker tasks and the desired responses to particular situations that may arise. In addition, workers who become proficient at particular tasks may be tempted to take advantage of their monopoly position to extract special rewards from the firm. Standard economic arrangements—short-term employment contracts and bargaining—are poorly suited to deal with these difficulties since, virtually by definition, they permit individual bargaining and encourage individualistic strategies. Hence internal labor markets establish a set of rules and procedures that reduce the need for monitoring by limiting the incentive to engage in personally advantageous but globally inefficient behavior.

This line of argument clearly contributes useful insights into the advantages, and hence survival, of internal labor markets. The issue, however, is whether this efficiency-based theory provides a satisfactory general explanation of the emergence of internal labor markets and of how they change over time. The problem is that, taken as a whole, this approach runs the risk of seeming tautological. It is equally easy to establish efficiency-limiting aspects of internal labor markets; for example, seniority provisions may prevent the most able from attaining jobs where their talents are best used. More generally, the rules and procedures of internal labor markets limit management discretion and, as recent management attacks on these limitations demonstrate, this can be costly. For proponents of the efficiency-based explanations to prevail, they must assume as a matter of faith (since no data on costs and benefits are available) that the arrangement that prevails is by definition the most efficient. Furthermore, these arguments provide little insight into the historical record: why did internal labor markets emerge when they did, what explains their differential rate of diffusion across firms, and how and why do they change?

The most serious, and interesting, challenge posed to current theories comes from the variety and dynamism of internal labor markets. The

41. Oliver E. Williamson, Michael L. Wachter, and Jeffrey E. Harris, "Understanding the Employment Relation: The Analysis of Idiosyncratic Exchange," *Bell Journal of Economics*, vol. 6 (Spring 1975), pp. 250–78.

image that emerges from most of the literature (and which might be dated to Dunlop's *Industrial Relations Systems*) is static: the stylized facts provided by Doeringer and Piore characterize "mature" systems, and once such a system is in place it is likely to persist. Reality is quite different. A simple consideration of different occupations, such as managers and clerks, quickly leads to the conclusion that the rules governing hiring, promotion, entry from outside the firms, and turnover can vary considerably. Similarly, the increased use of temporary help services, growing employment of part-time workers, and increased insecurity of white-collar employment all are indications that internal labor market rules change.

This variety and change offers researchers an opportunity to generate sufficient empirical variation to study systematically the determinants of internal labor market structure. What motivates firms as they alter their employment systems? What are their goals and the constraints that shape their choices? In my view firms choose among several alternative ways of organizing work.[42] These are alternative internal labor market structures, which I have labeled "employment subsystems." For each of these categories the rules governing hiring, training, pay, and promotion fit together in a logical and coherent way. Viewed in these terms, it is sensible to distinguish three options, which taken together accurately describe virtually all of the occupational configurations we observe. The options may be characterized as industrial, craft, and secondary employment subsystems, terms that are obviously familiar but do not correspond exactly to their conventional usages.

The rules of industrial subsystems in general reflect the stylized facts associated with good blue-collar jobs. Employees enter the firm at a limited number of ports of entry and progress along well-defined job ladders. Wage setting is administered via a series of bureaucratic procedures that, at the minimum, delay and diffuse market forces. Well-defined procedures and company norms govern job security rules. Training typically is on the job and firm-specific. This, plus limited ports of entry, makes interfirm mobility difficult.

An essential point, however, is that the industrial rules or subsystems extend beyond blue-collar work. Managers generally work under industrial rules, as do many technicians and high-level professionals. These work under what might be termed the "salaried" variant of the industrial

42. This view is elaborated upon in Osterman, "Determinants of Firm Choice of Internal Labor Market Structure," *Industrial Relations* (forthcoming).

system (a variant that includes most white-collar work but also blue-collar work in "progressive" firms such as IBM). As in the mainline industrial models, workers spend their careers inside relatively closed (to the outside) job ladders and get much of their training internally. However, job classifications are less precise and the firm has greater freedom to deploy labor as it chooses. In return the firm generally makes implicit, or sometimes explicit, job security pledges.

Craft subsystems are characterized by considerably greater mobility and more loyalty to the skill or profession than to the firm. Craft training typically occurs outside the firm in schools, formal training programs, or apprenticeship programs. More significant, the skills are not very firm-specific and thus provide workers with more market power than under industrial arrangements. As a result of these considerations, these jobs are not embedded in lengthy job ladders, and mobility, far from being penalized, is often rewarded. Several white-collar jobs within firms operate under craft subsystems. At least until recently, computer professionals were highly mobile and rarely stayed at the same firm for more than a few years. There is a strong professional ethos, and loyalty is directed to the profession. In some firms, senior sales people, some on the payroll and others on an incentive system, can also be characterized as craft workers.

The distinction between the craft and industrial subsystems is a matter of industrial relations rules, not of skill level or wage level. Managerial jobs are organized according to an industrial mode, while systems analysts are in a craft setting. Both jobs are highly skilled and well paid. Furthermore, in both jobs workers encounter unexpected situations and function according to a general, rather than situation-specific, set of work principles.

Finally, secondary subsystems contain jobs with few advancement opportunities. They lack career prospects, either within the firm or via interfirm movement. They usually tend to be low skill and poorly paid, but it is more accurate to think of them as lacking clear linkages to future jobs. Examples in so-called primary firms are many clerical workers, mailroom staff, and messengers.

It should already be apparent that my use of the terms "craft," "industrial," and "secondary" differs in significant ways from customary usage. For example, the term "craft workers" traditionally implies a sense of solidarity and self-awareness about the trade. My usage of "craft subsystem" does not imply this attitude. Rather, I am referring largely to portability of skills and sufficiently flexible ports of entry. Similarly, conventional usage of the term "secondary employment" often implies harsh and arbitrary discipline and lack of industrial juris-prudence. However, "secondary subsystems" in large firms are different. Workers are not subject to arbitrary and carpricious personnel systems. Instead there are often some industrial relations rules that extend across all subsystems and are oriented toward procedures and due process.

In choosing from among these alternatives, there are three central goals that firms consider: cost minimization, predictability (with respect to availability of an acceptable labor force at forseeable prices), and flexibility (with respect to internal deployment and staffing levels).[43] Each of these has different implications for the choice of subsystems, and some balancing or weighing of conflicting objectives is necessary. For example, industrial subsystems do well along the dimension of predictability but are frequently inflexible. Four constraints condition which choices are made: physical technology, social technology, the characteristics of the labor force, and government policies. Taken together, the interaction of objectives and constraints leads firms to make choices concerning how to organize work. The choices constitute the internal labor market.

How does this framework enable us to think about sex discrimination? First, it implies that the constraints firms perceive may shift when they can draw upon a large elastic female labor supply. In that circumstance, higher turnover and shorter ladders may be optimal from the firm's perspective. Second, within the category of constraints termed "social technology" are considerations such as power relationships and status maintenance. In this regard one should remember the lesson of sociologists such as Michel Crozier and Alvin Gouldner, who have reminded us that unity of purpose within an organization cannot be assumed and that employment relations may reflect the outcome of power struggles among subgroups.[44] Both these authors had very concrete issues in mind: control over knowledge of production techniques, in the case of Crozier, and work rules, in the case of Gouldner. However, the general point can be extended to include sex-based differences in the organization of work. The empirical sociological literature, particularly ethnographic

43. Again, this analysis is greatly elaborated upon in ibid.
44. Michel Crozier, *The Bureaucratic Phenomenon* (University of Chicago Press, 1964); and Alvin Gouldner, *Patterns of Industrial Bureaucracy* (Free Press, 1954).

studies of particular employment situations, leaves little doubt that status and power issues are relevant in understanding differential structures for male and female jobs and career lines within firms.[45]

In summary, regardless of whether the sketchy analysis presented in this comment is persuasive, the central point is that interpretation of the results developed by Hartmann requires an underlying model of how internal labor markets are structured. The next step, therefore, is to develop a set of case studies similar to that used by Hartmann but in which there is variation in the independent variables that I have suggested influence the choice of internal labor market systems. This will enable us to begin to understand systematically what lies behind these patterns, and I look forward to Hartmann's further work in this area.

Comments by Maryellen R. Kelley

Heidi Hartmann's paper is an ambitious effort to combine a theoretical critique with a case study illustrating her approach for explicitly taking into account gender in a structural analysis of promotions. Each of the paper's two parts could, in my view, be a separate paper. In the first part, she reevaluates the adequacy of structural models of the labor market to explain women's poorer economic status. In the second, drawing on her earlier critique, she shows how sex typing of work roles and race segregation in a large insurance company contribute to inequality of treatment in promotions and earnings. Both theoretically and empirically, this paper makes important contributions to our understanding of the differential treatment afforded women by their employers.

A Feminist Critique of Internal Labor Market Analysis

Though developed to explain, at least in part, how minority men have been denied access to high-paying jobs when working for the same employer as white men, internal labor market analysis seems to hold some promise for the kind of fine-grained investigations of employer

45. For a careful ethnographic study that suggests this point, see Rosabeth M. Kanter, *Men and Women of the Corporation* (Basic Books, 1977); see also Joan Acker and Donald R. Van Houten, "Differential Recruitment and Control: The Sex Structuring of Organizations," *Administrative Science Quarterly*, vol. 19 (June 1974), pp. 152–63.

practices that Hartmann suggests are needed to understand how women and men are treated differently by the same employer. This is a far more common source of inequality than that arising from men's and women's employment in different firms (as posited by labor market segmentation theory). Indeed, in the original presentation of internal labor market theory, Doeringer and Piore explicitly allowed for the possibility of persistent race-segregated structures (most notably in the steel industry and the railroads), but argued that the price of race segregation was a less efficient utilization of human resources within the firm.[46] In their view, internal labor market structures such as career ladders or seniority units (that were not racially discriminatory) were "functional," that is, they served to eliminate competition for jobs between older and younger workers and thus fostered the intergenerational transmission of skills on the job. In a critique of that explanation, Edwards has argued that these bureaucratic structures serve primarily to enhance managerial control over the work force, rather than to develop workers' skills.[47] Workers' loyalty to the firm is reinforced by personnel systems that promise *both* improvements in status (promotions) and higher wages in return for regular service, and consistent, if unexceptional, performance. Hartmann sees both these explanations as inadequate when no attention is paid to gender differences in how these structures affect employment opportunities.

Hartmann provides a much-needed review of that small body of research by economists and sociologists attempting to adapt the internal labor market framework to take into account gender-specific ways in which personnel systems that seem to operate so successfully for men fail to do so for women. She concludes that these efforts provide fairly convincing support for the proposition that sex segregation by jobs and job ladders is a significant factor in explaining the wage differences between men and women in the same firm, independent of individual differences in human capital attributes such as education and years of experience.[48] In relation to this feminist "school" of structuralist theory

46. Doeringer and Piore, *Internal Labor Markets and Manpower Analysis*, pp. 140–45.
47. Richard Edwards, *Contested Terrain: The Transformation of the Workplace in the Twentieth Century* (Basic Books, 1979).
48. Compare Kelley, "Discrimination in Seniority Systems"; Haignere, Chertos, and Steinberg, "Managerial Promotions in the Public Sector"; and Rosenbaum, "Jobs, Job Status, and Women's Gains from Affirmative Action," in Hartmann, ed., *New Directions for Comparable Worth*.

(for which Hartmann is regarded as a leading theorist and sponsor of others' research), her case study is the first to model how the phenomenon of sex and race segregation affects the promotion process for different race and sex groups within the internal labor market of the same firm.

Case Study Results

The results of Hartmann's analysis of promotions and earnings of technical, managerial, and professional employees in a large insurance company show that when women are the most important segment of the work force of such a large, bureaucratically structured organization, the internal labor market does not function as the theory suggests it ought to. Employees whom one would expect to get promoted—those with outstanding performance evaluations—do not have a significantly greater likelihood of being promoted, once the discriminatory effects of race and sex segregation are taken into account. Previous research by others showed that high performance ratings significantly improve an individual's chances of being promoted.[49] Hartmann's analysis suggests that this finding may be spurious, since their models failed to take into account the possibility for systematic bias by the employers against promoting women from highly sex-typed jobs.

Measurement Issues

Within the human capital framework of neoclassical labor economics, there are a set of well-accepted, if imperfect, proxy measures for evaluating an individual's potential productivity, such as years and type of education and years of experience with the firm. For researchers interested in modeling job characteristics and the institutional structures that may limit the wages and promotion opportunities of women and minorities, there are no such standard indicators.

In this case study, the problem of constructing indicators to capture important differences among jobs is made all the more difficult by the large number of job titles used by the company to distinguish very small differences in responsibilities. In the pooled data for five matched pairs of years, Hartmann finds that there are 2,500 different job titles held by 5,000 employees. As Edwards has suggested in his critique of internal

49. Abraham and Medoff, "Length of Service and Promotions in Union and Nonunion Work Groups."

labor market theory, and as my own study of occupational data from a sample of 221 firms showed,[50] employers' job classifications often do not reflect substantial differences in skill content and responsibility. The analyst needs to construct consistent groupings of jobs at a level of aggregation that is not so narrow as to distinguish only trivial differences in job content but is not so broad as to lump together jobs very different in their levels of skills, responsibilities, education, or training requirements.

One solution is to create explicitly arbitrary rules of thumb for grouping jobs together, as Osterman did.[51] Another solution is to devise an objective (and theoretically more well grounded) method, as Hartmann has done, for discounting the tendency of large, bureaucratic organizations to proliferate job titles that reflect very small differences in skills and responsibilities. The construct "occ/grade" can be viewed as an attempt to create new, broader occupational categories than the company's own job titles by combining jobs with closely related skills and responsibilities into the same category. Hartmann's description of how these categories were constructed is not very clear. From my reading, I understand an occ/grade to include only those job titles (of the 2,500) that belong to the same broad occupational group (one of 79) and are only one wage level or pay grade apart. But perhaps I am mistaken. Providing a few examples of the jobs and the span of pay grades that make up an occ/grade would help the reader to understand better this construct and what it measures.

The Importance of Segregation versus Merit in Promotions

The most striking result from Hartmann's analysis of the likelihood of promotions is that, for the individual, a high performance evaluation rating is not a significant, positive predictor of promotion, as previous research has shown. Moreover, her results provide support for the proposition that the sex composition of the individual's position in the internal labor market has a significant negative impact on how rewards (such as promotions) are distributed. Individuals in occ/grades with a

50. Maryellen R. Kelley, "Tasks and Tools: An Inquiry into the Relationship between Tasks, Skills, and Technology with Application to the Machining Labor Process" (Ph.D. dissertation, Sloan School of Management, Massachusetts Institute of Technology, 1984).

51. Osterman, "Sex Discrimination in Professional Employment: A Case Study."

high percentage of women in them are significantly less likely to be promoted than those who are lucky enough to be situated in a less female-intensive job category.

The unexpected finding that individuals in occ/grades with a high percentage of nonwhites have a greater chance of being promoted out of these jobs is puzzling. But when we look at the results for each sex and race group, we find that this holds only for women. In this company, it appears that women of both races are more likely than men of either race to be in jobs with *both* a high percentage of women *and* a high percentage of nonwhites. Perhaps these jobs are low-level positions in the managerial, professional, and technical occupational strata open mainly to women who move up from nonsupervisory positions. Men, by contrast, may start their professional and managerial careers in higher-level positions at this company. Thus one may interpret these results to mean that women, and in particular black women, have to go through more steps in order to move up to the higher-level positions at which men may be just starting their careers.

The number of Hay points of a job is a proxy measure for the individual's position in the company's hierarchy of managerial, professional, and technical jobs. It takes into account the pyramidlike structure of promotion opportunities believed to be characteristic of bureaucratic organizations. The total Hay points for a job are a composite score evaluating the relative level of skills, effort, and responsibility required of that job. The higher the number of Hay points, the higher the position in the occupational hierarchy. The closer one's job is to the top of that hierarchy, the fewer the opportunities for promotion there are likely to be.

Finally, the results for white men seem to show a reversal (not just the absence) of the meritocratic principle of rewarding exceptional performance with promotion. White men with the highest performance evaluation are significantly *less* likely to be promoted than are their poorer-performing colleagues. Perhaps the oft joked-about "Peter principle" is operating for white men in middle-level managerial and professional jobs in this company. Promotion can sometimes be used perversely, not as a reward for good performance, but as a vehicle for removing relatively poorer-performing managers from positions of responsibility. Rather than fire a mediocre manager or force him to resign from the organization, superiors may instead kick him upstairs into an ostensibly higher-status (and presumably better-paying) but dead-end position with less responsibility and fewer opportunities to do damage to the organization.

Structural Factors Affecting Salary Changes

The model for estimating salary growth has the same variables as those used to predict the likelihood of promotions. Unlike the equations for promotions, these show that a high performance evaluation does matter in determining the size of an individual's pay increase for all but white men. That performance ratings don't really matter for white men may reflect their greater ability to bargain as individuals for salary increases because of their status near the top of the hierarchy of managers and professionals in this company (or that the Peter principle is operating here as well).

In Hartmann's view, an individual whose race or sex differs from the majority in the same occ/grade gets a "bonus" from his or her greater visibility. As I interpret her results, the differential effects of location in a highly segregated job seem to hold only for whites, but not for blacks. Both white men and white women receive a significant bonus from being in a job with a high percentage of nonwhites. For black men, there is no significant increase associated with confinement to a highly sex-segregated job with a low percentage of nonwhites. That black women receive a larger salary increase for being in jobs with a high percentage of women cannot be interpreted as showing that black women get a bonus when they stand out by being in jobs filled mostly by white women. Only if the variable for percentage of nonwhites were both negative and significant would I conclude thusly.

Furthermore, I think, Hartmann is simply wrong when she says that the model predicting salary changes explains the experiences of men better than those of women. A comparison of the R^2s for each of the race- and sex-stratified equations shows that white men's salary changes are *not* predicted any better than for black women. Black men's salary changes are best predicted by the model, with all the explanatory power coming from variables measuring individual attributes, such as education and experience, rather than structural factors, such as the degree of race segregation. It seems that only for black men does the merit pay system at this company actually work strictly as it was designed to do.

Estimating the Level of Earnings

The same pooled sample of data from the five matched pairs of years is used to estimate the level of earnings of individuals employed by this company during 1976–81. The use of pooled data in models estimating transitions from one state to another, such as to predict the likelihood of promotions or the size of salary changes, depends on the assumption that promotions and salary changes in one period are independent of those that occur in the next period. But I am puzzled by the use of that sample for the earnings equation. While it seems reasonable to assume that the likelihood of promotion in one year would not affect the likelihood of promotion in a subsequent year, it does not seem reasonable to assume the same relationship between level of earnings from one period to the next, as this pooling of the data implies.

The specification of the earnings equation includes such human capital variables as length of service with the company, years of experience outside the company, and dummy variables for level of education and kind of professional and technical training. In addition to these, Hartmann adds the variables used previously to estimate the effects of race and sex segregation on the wage structure. Performance evaluation measures are included in this model as well, but it is not clear why. These variables have particular theoretical importance in predicting the likelihood of promotions and the size of one's salary increase in a subsequent year. But one's current position and salary level are surely related to the *accumulation* of performance evaluation ratings over time in a firm with a meritocratic promotion process, not necessarily to one's most recent performance evaluation score.

For all workers, there is a significant penalty for being in a job with a high percentage of nonwhites. In the race- and sex-stratified equations, among women of both races and white men there is a significant penalty as the percentage of nonwhites in the same occ/grade rises. Among black men, there is no significant reduction in salary level for being in a more highly race-segregated job.

From Hartmann's previous discussion comparing the sex composition of the ten largest jobs held by men to that of those held by women, we know that for women of both races the mean female percentage of the grades in which they are employed is much higher than it is for men. It seems that men and women are in such different jobs that the negative impact of sex segregation on earnings is only evident *between* the sexes in the results for the pooled sample of all race and sex groups. That overall finding—the higher the degree of sex segregation, the lower the salary level—does not extend to different treatment *within* the different race and sex groups. Women achieve significantly higher earnings (as do white men) as the percentage of women in the same occ/grade rises.

The total Hay points of the job are included in the model predicting earnings as a control for the grade or occupational level. I suggest a different interpretation of the importance of the Hay points variable in this model. Suppose we assume that these scores provide a relatively unbiased estimate of the relative skills and responsibilities for managerial, professional, and technical jobs at this company.[52] If the internal labor market of this company were operating so as to simply exclude women of both races from jobs requiring greater skill and responsibility and to crowd them into jobs that were low skilled or had less responsibility and, as a consequence, were less well paid, one would not expect the female or nonwhite percentages to matter once the degree of skill and responsibility valued by the employer for that job (as measured in Hay points) were taken into account. The only explanation for why job segregation by race and sex continues to matter must be that there are sex and race biases in how this company establishes its wage structure. Once again, by explicitly taking into account gender (and race), Hartmann's analysis reveals another aspect of differential treatment: the undervaluation of the skills and responsibilities exercised by women in highly sex- and race-segregated jobs.

Hartmann does not draw much attention to this result, nor its implications for policy. Affirmative action aims to reduce occupational segregation (and thereby improve women's earnings) by promoting (or hiring) qualified women into higher-paid jobs filled mostly by white men. This policy assumes that the jobs women typically hold are low paid because, compared with so-called men's jobs, they require fewer skills and less responsibility. Neither affirmative action nor the present equal pay policy (based on the Equal Pay Act of 1963) addresses the inequities

52. The Hay system of job analysis that produces these points is typically used by employers to set wages of individual jobs in relation to all other jobs belonging to the same broad occupational group within the firm. It has been used in a number of so-called comparable worth studies as an objective means for uncovering the premiums in earnings afforded men over women that are not attributable to differences in the skills and responsibilities of the different jobs men and women perform.

arising from employer bias in establishing salaries for particular sex- or race-segregated job classifications. Yet Hartmann's results, if they are to be believed, show that jobs with a high percentage of women or non-whites are paid significantly less than less segregated jobs, even when the employer rates the jobs as requiring the same level of skills and responsibility. To remedy this type of discriminatory treatment would require new standards or guidelines for employers to use in establishing unbiased wage-setting practices.

Conclusions

This paper makes important theoretical and empirical contributions to the analysis of gender and internal labor market structures. My major criticism of Hartmann's paper is that, in her presentation of the case study, she provides more than enough description of the phenomenon of job segregation by sex to convince us of its importance in this firm's internal labor market, but less than adequate treatment of the logit and regression models. The significance and implications of her research would have been more apparent had greater care been taken in presenting these empirical results. Of methodical importance are her efforts to capture attributes of the structure of jobs with simple, objective indicators for the degree of job segregation by race and sex and the pyramidlike structure of promotion opportunities. Most important, she has shown that even when women make up the majority of a highly educated technical, managerial, and professional work force, their jobs are under-valued by their employer and the internal labor market fails to operate fairly for them.

MYRA H. STROBER *and* CAROLYN L. ARNOLD

The Dynamics of Occupational Segregation among Bank Tellers

IN RECENT YEARS, occupational segregation by gender has received increasing attention from both social scientists and policymakers.[1] Researchers have pointed to significant connections between occupational segregation and several other policy issues: the female-male wage differential, the feminization of poverty, and the comparable worth debate.

Occupational segregation by gender is a striking aspect of labor markets in all industrialized societies. The majority of women are in occupations that are almost exclusively female, while most men are in

We have received helpful comments on an earlier version of this paper from David Bradford, Susan Carter, Victor Fuchs, Heidi Hartmann, Eleanor Maccoby, Joanne Martin, John Reuyl, Deborah Rhode, and Joan Talbert. None of these, of course, is responsible for the data or interpretations discussed here. This paper is part of a larger study of the dynamics of occupational segregation funded by the Russell Sage Foundation. The analyses and conclusions do not necessarily reflect the views or policies of the Russell Sage Foundation.

1. The first conference on occupational segregation, organized by the Committee on the Status of Women in the Economics Profession (CSWEP) of the American Economics Association, was held at Wellesley College in May 1975. The proceedings of that conference were published first in *Signs: Journal of Women in Culture and Society,* vol. 1 (Spring 1976), and then as a book: Martha Blaxall and Barbara B. Reagan, eds., *Women and the Workplace: The Implications of Occupational Segregation* (University of Chicago Press, 1976). A second conference, organized by the Committee on Women's Employment and Related Social Issues of the National Research Council, was held in Washington, D.C., in May 1982. Those proceedings have now been published: Barbara F. Reskin, ed., *Sex Segregation in the Workplace: Trends, Explanations, Remedies* (Washington, D.C.: National Academy Press, 1984). In June 1984 a conference sponsored by the U.S. Commission on Civil Rights was held in Washington, D.C. Several of the papers for that conference dealt with occupational segregation. See U.S. Commission on Civil Rights, *Comparable Worth: Issue for the 80's,* vols. 1 and 2 (Washington, D.C.: Commission on Civil Rights, 1984).

occupations that are almost entirely male.[2] Although equal employment opportunity legislation and affirmative action orders of the last fifteen years were designed, in part, to reduce occupational segregation, the system of segregation by gender remains entrenched.[3]

Our particular interest in occupational segregation is to gain an

2. In 1980 in the U.S. women were 42 percent of the work force. If one classifies occupations as to their degree of segregation by looking at a 20-percentage-point spread around the female proportion of the work force, an occupation can be termed female dominated or female intensive if 60 percent or more of the workers in that occupation were female in 1980, male intensive or male dominated if less than 20 percent of its incumbents were female in 1980, and neutral if it was 21–59 percent female in 1980. In 1980, of 503 occupational categories, 19 percent were female intensive, 48 percent were male intensive, and 33 percent were neutral. About 63 percent of women in 1980 were employed in female-intensive occupations, about 6 percent in male-intensive occupations, and about 31 percent in neutral occupations. Among men, 8 percent were employed in female-intensive occupations, 53 percent in male-intensive occupations and 39 percent in neutral occupations. See Nancy F. Rytina and Suzanne M. Bianchi, "Occupational Reclassification and Changes in Distribution by Gender," *Monthly Labor Review*, vol. 107 (March 1984), p. 14.

3. There has been some reduction in segregation in the management classification and for young women in professional occupations. See ibid., p. 16; Andrea Beller, "Occupational Segregation by Sex: Determinants and Changes," *Journal of Human Resources*, vol. 17 (Summer 1982), pp. 371–92; and Beller, "Occupational Segregation and the Earnings Gap" in Commission on Civil Rights, *Comparable Worth*, pp. 23–33. However, the index of occupational segregation, ranging on a scale from completely integrated (0.0) to completely segregated (1.0), is today, as it was in 1900, about 0.65; about two-thirds of American men (or women) would have to change their occupations in order to achieve equality in the gender distribution across occupations. See Edward Gross, "Plus Ca Change. . . ? The Sexual Structure of Occupations over Time," *Social Problems*, vol. 16 (Fall 1968), pp. 198–208; Francine D. Blau and Wallace E. Hendricks, "Occupational Segregation by Sex: Trends and Prospects," *Journal of Human Resources*, vol. 14 (Spring 1979), pp. 197–210; and Cynthia B. Lloyd and Beth T. Niemi, *The Economics of Sex Differentials* (Columbia University Press, 1979). O'Neill calculated the index for 1980 at 0.635 using 1980 CPS data for 419 occupations. See June O'Neill, "The Determinants and Wage Effects of Occupational Segregation," Project Report (Washington, D.C.: Urban Institute, 1983), p. 8. Beller computed the index for 262 census occupations and found it declined from 0.683 in 1972 to 0.617 in 1981. Rytina and Bianchi note that between 1970 and 1980 the proportion of women employed in male-intensive occupations did not change. But there were increases in the female share of employment in a few professional and managerial occupations, and the proportion of the female labor force in female-intensive occupations fell. It is not clear how much should be made of the additional numbers of women moving into management positions. Often so-called management positions are in reality upper-level clerical positions with fancy titles (see Beller, "Occupational Segregation and the Earnings Gap"). Additional microlevel work needs to be done to investigate whether women managers are in fact doing the same kinds of jobs as men managers. See William T. Bielby and James N.

understanding of its dynamics. How does occupational segregation operate as a process? How is it "decided" whether an occupation will "belong" to women or to men? What forces keep most occupations gender-typed? How and why do occupations change their gender designation? What happens to the relative pay and status of an occupation when it becomes female?

Most occupations, relatively static in their gender composition, provide little opportunity for studying the dynamics of segregation. Hence researchers must seek out occupations whose gender designations have changed over time or new occupations whose gender designations are not yet decided. However, it is important to note that occupations that begin to change their gender assignments generally become resegregated. When large numbers of women enter a formerly all-male occupation, the occupation often "tips" and becomes virtually all female. This process of occupational resegregation is analogous to the perpetuation of racial segregation of neighborhoods, where the influx of blacks into an all-white area often leads to "white flight" and the eventual reconstitution of the area as an all-black neighborhood.[4] Why does the entry of women into an occupation generally not lead to occupational integration? What would need to change in order to produce successful integration?

This paper seeks to gain insight into some aspects of the dynamics of gender segregation by examining data for bank tellers, an occupation that shifted dramatically from virtually all-male in 1935 to 91 percent female in 1980.[5] Using Strober's theory of occupational segregation as a framework for the analysis, this essay provides a blueprint for studying shifts in the gender designation of an occupation. We examine both qualitative and quantitative data and consider both economic and cultural factors.

Baron, "A Woman's Place is with Other Women: Sex Segregation within Organizations," in Reskin, ed., *Sex Segregation in the Workplace*, pp. 27–55; and Bielby and Baron, "Men and Women at Work: Sex Segregation and Statistical Discrimination," *American Journal of Sociology*, vol. 91 (January 1986), pp. 759–99.

4. See Thomas C. Schelling, "The Process of Residential Segregation: Neighborhood Tipping," in Anthony H. Pascal, ed., *Racial Discrimination in Economic Life* (Lexington, Mass.: Lexington Books, 1972), pp. 157–84.

5. Helen Baker, *Current Policies in Personnel Relations in Banks* (Princeton University, Industrial Relations Section, 1940); and U.S. Bureau of the Census, *Census of Population, 1980, Detailed Population Characteristics: U.S. Summary* (Government Printing Office, 1984), sec. A, table 278.

Strober's Theory of Occupational Segregation

Strober has developed a general theory of occupational segregation.[6] The theory looks at occupational segregation in the absence of legal mandates prohibiting gender discrimination or requiring affirmative action. It also assumes the economic and social mores that existed before the mid-1960s. Thus the theory is discussed using the past tense. This grammatical usage does not imply, however, that all aspects of the patriarchal society described have been relegated to the past; many are still very much alive. The theory discussed here does not yet incorporate the complex interactions among gender, race, and class. At this stage of the theory's development, it reflects the dynamics of occupations filled largely by white middle-class workers.

Before the mid-1960s, how did an occupation become primarily male or female? When a new job came into being, how did employers decide which workers should be offered the job? A simplistic application of profit maximization theory might suggest that employers would offer the job to those with the requisite skills willing to work at the lowest wage. Since women generally were willing to work at wages lower than men's, profit maximization theory might suggest that employers would offer women first choice of employment in new jobs. However, Strober's theory argues that employers gave male workers first choice when new occupations were created. Although some new jobs appeared to be offered first to women, the theory suggests that in such situations employers did not offer them to men first because they already knew that men would not find the new jobs desirable relative to jobs they already held or other new jobs that were available.

Offering men first choice of jobs is not inconsistent with profit maximization; indeed it results from a sophisticated profit maximization that takes into account not simply wage costs, but all relevant costs. An employer considering offering jobs to women before offering them to men would need to consider two types of costs: (1) the costs of incurring the displeasure of existing male workers or customers,[7] and (2) the costs

6. Myra H. Strober, "Toward a General Theory of Occupational Sex Segregation: The Case of Public School Teaching," in Reskin, ed., *Sex Segregation in the Workplace*, pp. 144–56.

7. See Gary S. Becker, *The Economics of Discrimination*, 2d ed. (University of Chicago Press, 1971), chaps. 4, 5.

of incurring the displeasure of family, friends, neighbors, and colleagues for breaking the strong norms of patriarchal gender relations in society.[8]

In a patriarchal society, it is widely assumed that men are the economic providers not only for themselves but for "their" women and children and that men have personal, social, and economic power over women and the services they provide.[9] Thus for an employer to permit a woman to have a job that a man wanted would have violated two fundamental principles of patriarchy: that men are to provide for women, and that men are to have power over women.

Female friends, neighbors, and relatives would have feared the violation of the first principle, that men are to provide for women; it would have undermined their entire system of well-being. The support of patriarchy by many women is often underestimated. Although feminists prefer an economic and social system that eschews both men's support of women and men's power over women, women who have not been trained to provide for their own economic support or who believe (often correctly) that their own efforts in the labor market could never yield the return earned by their fathers or husbands prefer to cede power to men in exchange for their economic support.

Male relatives, friends, neighbors, and colleagues would have feared the violation of the second principle of patriarchy—that men are to have power over women. The subtle and not-so-subtle pressures from both women and other men at home, at church, or at "the club"—heart-to-heart talks, persuasion, jibes, jokes, withdrawal of privileges, loss of prestige, ostracism, and economic retaliation—would have been very costly to errant employers. As a result, because each employer considered it too costly to break the norms of patriarchal relations, male workers continued to get first choice of jobs, even though women might have worked at them for lower wages.

When economists note examples of an effective cartel, even when it is implicit rather than explicit, they are quick to search for a policing mechanism. What, they ask, keeps individuals from breaking away from

8. Strober, "Toward a General Theory," pp. 147–48.
9. See Heidi I. Hartmann, "Capitalism, Patriarchy, and Job Segregation by Sex," in Blaxall and Reagan, eds., *Women and the Workplace,* pp. 137–69; Adrienne Rich, *Of Woman Born: Motherhood as Experience and Institution* (Norton, 1976); Roison McDonough and Rachel Harrison, "Patriarchy and Relations of Production," in Annette Kuhn and Ann Marie Wolpe, eds., *Feminism and Materialism: Women and Modes of Production* (London: Routledge and Kegan Paul, 1978), pp. 11–41; and Zillah R. Eisenstein, *The Radical Future of Liberal Feminism* (New York: Longman, 1981).

the cartel and pursuing self-interest? It is often said that before the civil rights movement race relations in employment in the South were policed by the violence of white supremacists—that southern employers would never hire blacks for jobs that whites wanted, even though it would have been cheaper for an employer to do so, because employers feared the terribly high costs of violent retaliation against their firms, themselves, or their families.

For gender relations there was no policing mechanism equivalent to white supremacist violence. Yet virtually all employers continued to offer male workers first choice of jobs despite the fact that women were available at lower wages. Patriarchy was considered morally correct, admirable, and "natural"—indeed the means by which women were enabled to bear and raise the next generation. Although odious race relations may have required a potential violent external force against employers to keep it in place, patriarchal gender relations did not; each household, each church, each community ensured the perpetuation of the hierarchy of job choice by keeping the costs to the employer of breaking gender norms prohibitively high.

In deciding which jobs to claim for themselves, male workers attempted to maximize their economic gain. They compared the wages, hours, working conditions, and promotion prospects of the new job with those of existing jobs. They may have tried to assess the probability that the job would become and remain male (and therefore more prestigious and high paying). Considering all of these dimensions, if the new job seemed superior to existing jobs, male workers claimed it and moved in; if not, they remained in existing jobs, leaving the new job for women. Thus whether a particular job in a particular labor market was initially male or female was a function of when the job came onto the market and how attractive alternative occupations were for men at the time.

Women, too, made choices, but their choices were more constrained because men were permitted to choose first.[10] By and large, women chose between moving into those jobs that men left for them or working outside of the market in the home. Most white middle-class women chose to marry and hoped that their husbands could and would be able to support them and any children they might bear. If they were widowed

10. Psychologist Eleanor Maccoby suggests that girls learn early that boys and men are permitted to choose first. "It seems to me that part of female socialization must be to learn not to want what men are going to stake out as their territory." (Personal communication, November 15, 1985.)

or their husbands were unable to provide support, they tried to increase family income either by sending sons or daughters to work (in the late nineteenth or early twentieth century) or by entering the labor market themselves (after World War I). When they did seek employment, they often put a premium on jobs that permitted them to continue to carry out their jobs as homemakers.

Unmarried white middle-class women were less constrained than their mothers by family responsibilities but still constrained by the fact that men chose jobs first. Often unmarried women might have wished for the economic independence of a well-paid job; more might have forgone marriage had they been able to pursue a lucrative career. A few did contribute to a very modest breakdown of occupational segregation in the professions. But for the most part, they saw marriage as their most favorable economic alternative. Most chose jobs that marked them as attractive marriage partners; like men, they chose the most economically attractive, although, because their job horizons were relatively short, they placed less emphasis on good promotion possibilities.

Returning to the demand side of the market, how did employers decide the wage rate and working conditions to be assigned to a new job? In the short run, with a particular technology and capital stock, employers estimated the demand for the product or service to be produced and, as the neoclassical theory suggests, estimated the derived demand for labor. Then, based on the existing wage structure of the firm or industry and the wages for similar jobs in the local labor market, employers assigned a wage rate and benefit package to the job and advertised for workers. If "qualified" men showed up—and qualifications were often based on subjective racial and class characteristics as well as on more objective skill criteria—the men were hired.

What happened if an insufficient number of men applied? Employers had several choices: (1) raise the wage rate and try to attract more men or (2) maintain the wage rate, hire those women who applied, and, if necessary, encourage more women to apply.[11] The option exercised depended on how many men were already hired. If a significant number of the positions were already filled by men, employers probably would raise wages and try to attract more men, for employers were unlikely to hire women to fill the remaining jobs in an occupation that men had claimed, even if men hadn't filled all the job vacancies. In the first place,

11. The employer could also attempt to recruit male (or female) immigrant workers or minority workers at the existing wage rate or at a lower wage level.

asking men to work with women in the same job would have lowered the status and possibly decreased the future income of the job by introducing the possibility that the job might become feminized. Thus the men already in the job would have had to be monetarily compensated for working with women. Secondly, there were significant societal taboos about the two sexes working together at the same job. These stemmed in part from the notion that men and women were not considered equal and in part from fears of sexual attraction. (Interestingly, fears about sexual attraction were much more muted when men and women worked together in the usual patriarchal relationships—doctor-nurse, foreman-worker, boss-secretary—than when men and women worked at the same job.)

If some women were hired into a virtually all-male job, it was generally with the explicit or implicit understanding of both employer and employees that they were nonetheless not full members of the "group." A sense of marginality might be conveyed through lower pay, ineligibility for promotion, or ineligibility for membership in the relevant union.

Suppose, however, that few men applied for the new job at the existing wage rate. If an employer believed that an adequate supply of native male labor could be attracted from other industries or other parts of the country, he might raise the wage rate slightly to attract men. He would be more likely to do this if he believed that women were not interested in holding the job (for example, because holding such a job violated existing norms about what employment a woman could hold and still be considered an attractive marriage partner) or if he believed that native men would perform the job significantly better than either women or foreign workers. On the other hand, if financial constraints prevented him from raising wages, and if he thought women could perform the job adequately, he might try to hire women.

If having women perform the job in question violated existing societal norms and few women applied, the employer might engage in a campaign to alter those norms. If the norms would be only moderately violated, the employer's efforts would probably be successful. Norms clearly can be changed, but, except during wartime or times of social revolution, they change fairly slowly. Thus if a job were considered flagrantly unsuitable, ordinary campaigns to alter these norms would not bring forth an adequate supply of women workers of the requisite race or class. In such a situation the employer would begin to recruit workers from abroad or hire native minorities.

If both genders initially took part in an occupation, call it X, eventually one of the two would come to dominate. Only rarely did an occupation remain integrated with respect to gender. Which gender achieved primacy depended on the attractiveness of alternative occupations for men. If, as time went on, X was de-skilled (required lower skills) and wages fell, or if new occupations were created that men found more attractive economically, men moved out of X. On the other hand, if new and existing occupations came to be seen as less attractive economically than X, men might move into X. It was also possible that women might move to other occupations, in which case X might become an occupation for which foreign labor needed to be recruited. In the musical chairs of occupational shifts, there was a clear hierarchy of players: men got first choice of job opportunities. Also, there was considerable interdependence of occupational gender assignments. Whether a particular occupation remained gender typed or changed its gender assignment depended not only on its own wages and working conditions but also on those in alternative occupations.

How was occupational segregation maintained? Once a job was inhabited by one gender or another, it became typed as male or female, and strong forces acted to maintain its gender assignment. When men occupied an occupation, they actively and collectively sought to keep women out, fearing that if women entered they would lower the earnings of the job by accepting lower wage rates or, if paid the same as men, diminish men's sense of superiority and power over women. Although men acted as individual maximizers in choosing their occupations, once they began to work in an occupation and identify with it, they acted collectively to maintain its gender designation. The importance of organizational structures and male "gate-keeping" behavior in keeping women out of male jobs has been elucidated by several scholars.[12]

Most women, for their part, rarely chose to enter a male-typed occupation, fearing sexual harassment or a diminution of their perceived femininity with consequent reduction in their prospects for marriage. When these negative sanctions disappeared, such as during wartime,

12. See Cynthia F. Epstein, *Woman's Place: Options and Limits in Professional Careers* (University of California Press, 1970); Rosabeth M. Kanter, *Men and Women of the Corporation* (Basic Books, 1977); and David L. Bradford, Alice G. Sargent, and Melinda S. Sprague, "Executive Man and Woman: The Issue of Sexuality," in Francine E. Gordon and Myra H. Strober, eds., *Bringing Women into Management* (McGraw-Hill, 1975), pp. 39–58.

women more readily and often enthusiastically entered the higher-paid male occupations. Women may also have been reluctant to enter a male occupation because of the "male culture" that surrounded the occupation.[13] The strength of this culture of course dissipated once there were more women in formerly all-male occupations.

Under what conditions did an occupation change its gender designation? Whenever an occupation became relatively less economically attractive, as compared with jobs with similar educational requirements and occupational prestige, men began to vacate the occupation. For example, if an occupation was restructured so that employees had less autonomy, as happened in teaching in urban schools in the late nineteenth century,[14] or if it provided significantly less status or fewer opportunities for promotion, men often began to leave it. Alternatively, an occupation may have remained constant with respect to job attributes or advancement possibilities, but other occupations requiring similar levels of education and having similar status may have increased their attractiveness. In that situation, too, men might have begun to leave the occupation.

It should be stressed that the maximizing behavior on the part of male workers described here was not pursued with great vigilance. Like most types of decisionmakers, male workers were satisficers rather than scrupulous maximizers. There were numerous forces reinforcing inertia, and the gender designations of jobs changed much less frequently than one would expect from zealous maximizing behavior.

When men began to leave an occupation, employers hired women to fill vacancies. If an occupation was growing rapidly, feminization may have occurred not because men left but rather because new men could not be attracted at existing wage rates. Once an occupation began to shift from all male to partly female, its chances of remaining somewhat integrated depended upon the speed at which men exited and women entered and the percentage of jobs that women held. Below some critical percentage of female employment in an occupation, it may have been possible for an occupation to remain somewhat integrated. Beyond that

13. For an example of the male culture surrounding an occupation, see Sally L. Hacker, "The Culture of Engineering: Women, Workplace, and Machine," *Women's Studies International Quarterly,* vol. 4, no. 3 (1981), pp. 341–53.

14. See David B. Tyack and Myra H. Strober, "Jobs and Gender: A History of the Structuring of Educational Employment by Sex," in Patricia A. Schmuck, W.W. Charters, Jr., and Richard O. Carlson, eds., *Educational Policy and Management: Sex Differentials* (Orlando, Fla.: Academic Press, 1981), pp. 131–52.

critical point, men began to move rapidly out of the occupation, fearing that the occupation would become female and hence reduced in both status and pay. This critical percentage level of female employment may be termed a tipping point. Ironically, it was precisely the expectation that beyond a certain tipping point the job would become female that brought about the fulfillment of that expectation. Exactly what percentage of female employment constituted the tipping point probably varied by occupation and historical period.

The parallels between occupational tipping and neighborhood tipping are striking. Often when whites begin to leave a neighborhood, blacks may begin to move in. If the rate of substitution of blacks for whites is slow, the neighborhood may slowly increase its level of integration. However, at some critical percentage of black ownership (or occupancy), the tipping point, whites begin to fear that their neighborhood will become a black neighborhood and that their property values will fall as a result. They place their homes on the market hoping to beat the decline in property values and, of course, in so doing, contribute to that decline. As in occupational tipping, it is the expectation that the neighborhood will not remain integrated that itself leads to a fulfillment of that expectation.

When neighborhoods tip from white to black, property values often fall. Did the feminization of an occupation similarly result in lower wage rates for that occupation? This is a difficult question to answer because the initial flight of men from an occupation (or failure to increase their numbers in it) stemmed from a decline in the relative attractiveness of the occupation. Thus it is not surprising that in some cross-sectional studies, holding constant education level, experience, job location, and nonpecuniary job characteristics, the higher the percentage of women in an occupation, the lower the wage rate for both women and men in that occupation.[15]

There are two reasons, however, why one might hypothesize that once an occupation became female its relative earnings would decline further. First, the original wage rate, which was set in comparison with existing male wage rates, would become too high in comparison with the

15. For the 1980 CPS data, O'Neill found that a 10 percentage-point increase in the female percentage yielded a 1.5 percent decrease in the wage rate for both men and women (more for white-collar workers, less for blue-collar). Using NLS data for women and men aged 24–34 in 1978, she obtained significantly different results. See O'Neill, "The Determinants and Wage Effects of Occupational Segregation," pp. 34, 74.

wages for other female jobs in the firm. As has been shown in numerous studies, wage rates for jobs fit into a firm's wage structure, and male and female jobs are treated differentially.[16] Over time, as a job became increasingly female, employers would probably lower its wage rate to fit it better into the firm's wage structure. This would be especially true if the job, by virtue of its becoming female, had been taken out of a promotion ladder that led to a still male-dominated managerial position.

Second, the original wage rate would begin to be too high in comparison with the wages in the local labor market for other female jobs that afforded similar status and required similar education levels. Because women were excluded from certain high-paying occupations and crowded into women's occupations,[17] their oversupply to those occupations reduced the wage rate in women's occupations. Thus women's reservation wage was generally lower than men's. Employers would probably lower the wage rate once an occupation became female because they would experience little difficulty attracting sufficient female labor of the requisite quality at the lower rate.

To summarize, employers gave men the right of first refusal when new jobs came into being because to have done otherwise would have been to break the strong norms of patriarchal gender relations in society and incur enormous costs of opprobrium and economic retaliation. Male workers, in deciding which jobs to claim for themselves, attempted to maximize their economic position by comparing the economic package presented by the new job with those of existing jobs. Thus the gender designation of an occupation resulted from the interaction of patriarchy and male workers' utility maximization. If both genders initially took part in an occupation, eventually one of the two came to dominate. Then, once the occupation or job was typed as male or female, strong forces acted to maintain its gender assignment.

Occupations rarely shifted their gender assignments. When they did, the change generally resulted from an alteration in job structure, status, or remuneration that made a particular occupation less attractive to men. Men then began to vacate the occupation and women began to move in.

16. See, for example, Donald J. Treiman and Heidi I. Hartmann, eds., *Women, Work, and Wages: Equal Pay for Jobs of Equal Value* (Washington, D.C.: National Academy Press, 1981).

17. See Barbara R. Bergmann, "Occupational Segregation, Wages and Profits When Employers Discriminate by Race or Sex," *Eastern Economic Journal,* vol. 1 (April-July 1974), pp. 103–10.

After female employment in an occupation reached some critical percentage, men began to move rapidly out of that occupation, fearing that it might become predominantly female and hence reduced in both status and pay. As a result, a job that was once all male would become resegregated as virtually all female. Once an occupation became predominantly female, its relative earnings generally would decline still further.

The Feminization of Bank Telling

In 1935 a Princeton University study reported that none of the fifty banks whose personnel programs it surveyed employed women as bank tellers, despite the fact that all of the banks employed women as clerical workers. The author noted: "Many of the banks' patrons do not have as much confidence in a woman's financial ability as in a man's. This may be a foolish prejudice, but since it is so the bank hesitates to risk business by advancing women to positions where they deal with the public."[18]

During World War II this "foolish prejudice" seemed to dissipate quickly (see cartoon). A wartime study of personnel administration in banking had a separate chapter on women in bank work with the following laudatory comments by various men in bank personnel positions.

> Women are capably filling key positions in all of our internal departments and their performance as tellers is surprisingly satisfactory.
>
> The speed, accuracy and general ability of the girls in the tellers' cages compare favorably with those of the men who formerly occupied these positions.
>
> We now have more women tellers than we have men tellers, and so far as I am concerned there will be no hesitancy on the part of our bank when it comes to putting women tellers all the way down the line.[19]

In 1943 the Bureau of Labor Statistics surveyed 1,312 banks in 144 areas and found that 37 percent of all bank tellers were women.[20] As noted in table 1, this proportion reached 45 percent by 1950. It is likely that by 1945 bank telling had already passed the critical tipping point and was moving rapidly toward resegregation as a female occupation. While

18. Eleanor Davis, *Personnel Programs in Banks* (Princeton University, Industrial Relations Section, 1935), p. 17.

19. American Bankers Association, *Personnel Administration in Wartime Banking* (New York: ABA, 1943), pp. 95, 96, 99.

20. Harold R. Hosea, "Earnings of Bank Employees," *Banking*, vol. 36 (May 1944), p. 28.

"It's been like this
ever since Jones was
drafted"

Source: *Banking*, August 1942, p. 3.

it is not possible to calculate the growth in the employment of bank
tellers between 1940 and 1950 (because the 1940 census included bank
tellers in the broader category of clerical workers), it is clear from the
data in table 1 that employment in bank telling more than doubled
between 1950 and 1960. The number of women employed increased over
the decade by 219 percent, while men's employment grew by only 15
percent. By 1960 women were 69 percent of all bank tellers.

Between 1960 and 1970 employment again almost doubled, and the
occupation became even more feminized. Women's employment increased by 145 percent, and the number of men employed actually
declined, reducing the number of male bank tellers in 1970 to approximately the same as in 1950. By 1970 women were 86 percent of all bank
tellers. Employment in bank telling almost doubled again between 1970
and 1980. Women's employment increased by 109 percent; men's by 25
percent. By 1980 women were 91 percent of all bank tellers.

Explaining the Shift in Gender Assignment

Why did bank telling shift from a male to a female occupation?
Generally this question would be answered by pointing to women's entry
into bank telling during World War II. But Strober's theory suggests that

Table 1. *Changes in Employment, Wages, and Education Level of Bank Tellers, 1950–80*

Item	1950	1960	1970	1980
Total number employed (thousands)[a]	61.7	127.3	251.1	494.9
Number women employed (thousands)[a]	27.7	88.1	216.3	451.5
Number men employed (thousands)[a]	34.1	39.1	34.8	43.4
Percent women employed[a]	45	69	86	91
Female-male salary ratio for bank tellers[b]	76	74	73	78
Salary ratio for women bank tellers/all women wage and salary earners[b]	138	136	114	82
Salary ratio for men bank tellers/all men wage and salary earners[b]	106	91	75	51
Median education level for women bank tellers (years)[c]	12.5	12.5	12.6	12.7
Median education level for all women workers (years)[c]	11.8	12.1	12.3	12.7
Education ratio for women bank tellers/ all women workers	106	103	102	100
Median education level for men bank tellers (years)[c]	12.6	12.7	12.8	13.6
Median education level for all men workers (years)[c]	9.7	11.1	12.3	12.7
Education ratio for men bank tellers/ all men workers	130	114	104	107

Sources: U.S. Bureau of the Census, *U.S. Census of Population, 1950, Special Report: Occupational Characteristics* (Government Printing Office, 1956), tables 1, 10–11, 22; *Census of Population, 1960, Subject Reports: Occupational Characteristics* (GPO, 1963), tables 1, 9–10, 27; *Census of Population, 1970, Subject Report: Occupational Characteristics* (GPO, 1973), tables 1, 5–7, 24, 34; *Census of Population, 1980, Detailed Population Characteristics: U.S. Summary* (GPO, 1984), sec. A, table 278; *Census of Population, 1980, Subject Report: Earnings by Occupation and Education* (GPO, 1984), table 1; educational medians calculated by Paula Vines, Population Division, Bureau of the Census.

a. 1950–60: employees aged 14 and over; 1970–80: 16 and over.

b. 1950–70: ratio is annual median wage and salary income for employed workers; 1980: ratio is annual mean earnings of those who were employed in 1979.

c. Education levels for the experienced labor force, defined as the employed plus the experienced unemployed.

one should look not only at how and why women entered telling, but also how and why men left.

In our view, men with the requisite education left bank telling, or failed to enter it, because they found more lucrative jobs in other occupations. Indeed, we think that during the 1920s and 1930s bank telling was de-skilled and that, if not for the Depression, men might have begun to vacate bank telling sometime in the 1930s. World War II gave women an opportunity to enter the occupation and prove their competence. But the main reason why women remained after the war was that not enough men wanted to fill the growing number of teller positions. After all, during World War I women had also entered bank telling and proved their competence.[21] But their presence in the occupation at that time was short-lived as returning veterans reclaimed their jobs.

A perusal of *Banking,* the journal of the American Bankers Association, for 1941–45 reveals that many of the male bank executives writing about the future of bank telling expected women to quit their jobs when the men returned from the war. Some banks required women to sign agreements that they would work only for the duration in order to ensure that returning servicemen could resume their bank telling jobs. Several writers cautioned that the men would not all return, and that those who returned might not want their old jobs back. They suggested waiting to see how many men wanted the jobs and how many women wanted to quit. A few pointed out that women were better and faster as tellers than men. They argued that since women were working out so well and men would probably look for other jobs, women should be given permanent teller positions. Interestingly, several of the women bank executives writing about this issue assumed that women war workers would remain in banking after the war.[22]

Most occupations that were opened to women during the war were reclaimed by men once hostilities ceased. However, by 1950 women were almost half of all bank tellers. Bank telling was different because men did not reclaim it. Although employers offered bank teller training classes for returning male veterans,[23] apparently men did not apply in large numbers for the growing number of teller jobs.

In 1950 the median educational level of male bank tellers was 12.6 years; the median educational level for the male work force as a whole was 9.7 years, a ratio of 130 percent (see table 1). Yet the salary ratio for men bank tellers versus all men wage and salary earners was only 106 percent. Men moved out or never entered bank telling because they saw greener pastures in other occupations.

The process of change in gender assignment was probably spurred on from the demand side. Women had proved their competence during the war, and employers easily filled their growing number of teller slots with women. The decision to hire women was no doubt made easier by the fact that women were less expensive to employ than were men. As

21. Elizabeth Kemper Adams, *Women Professional Workers* (Macmillan, 1921), pp. 254–66.

22. See *Banking,* vol. 35 (September 1942), pp. 145–53; vol. 35 (February 1943), pp. 41–42; vol. 36 (September 1943), pp. 30–33, 34–36; and vol. 37 (January 1945), p. 30.

23. Ibid., vol. 39 (September 1946), pp. 46–48.

indicated in table 1, in 1950 the female-male salary ratio for bank tellers was 76 percent.

One needs to be careful, however, in espousing a cheapness hypothesis. Historically women have been less expensive to hire than men in virtually every occupation. Yet very few of those occupations have become feminized. It seems likely that although women's willingness to work at bank telling at a lower reservation wage than men assisted the process of feminization, the proximate cause was men's desire to work in alternative occupations.

One way to put the argument is that if not for the availability of women and their proved acceptance by the public, employers would have had to raise wages considerably in order to attract and retain men in an occupation that was growing rapidly. However, it was possible to attract women to the occupation without raising the average salary level. As indicated in table 1, in 1950 the median educational level for women bank tellers was 12.5 years; for all women in the labor force it was 11.8 years, a ratio of 106 percent. Yet the salary ratio for women bank tellers versus all women wage and salary earners was 138 percent. Bank telling was an attractive occupation for women in 1950.

SKILL CHANGES IN BANK TELLING. Did bank telling become less attractive to men in part because the occupation was de-skilled? Braverman and Zimbalist argue that de-skilling, the breaking down of complex jobs into simpler tasks, is often observed in jobs that are taken over by women and minorities (and then, eventually, by machines).[24] To what extent was bank telling de-skilled? When might such de-skilling have occurred? Interpreting the evidence on these matters is complex.

There are several approaches to analyzing the components of job skill and their changes over time. At first, systems of job analysis focused on verbal descriptions of the methods and tasks involved in the job. Since the mid-1950s, job analysis methods have been developed to systematically quantify aspects of tasks or attributes of workers.[25] For the years before 1939 we examined descriptions of teller jobs from various books about banking. The first edition of the *Dictionary of Occupational Titles* (DOT) was published in 1939 by the Department of Labor. For 1939–80

24. Harry Braverman, *Labor and Monopoly Capital* (New York: Monthly Review Press, 1974); and Andrew Zimbalist, ed., *Case Studies on the Labor Process* (New York: Monthly Review Press, 1979).

25. Ernest J. McCormick, *Job Analysis: Methods and Applications* (New York: American Management Association, 1979).

we utilized the DOT's detailed descriptions of the various tasks performed by tellers, looking specifically for how changes in job content, opportunity for promotion, and use of machinery may have affected job tasks. In the third edition of the DOT in 1965, the Department of Labor added quantitative measures of job skill. For 1965 and 1977 we analyzed both verbal and quantitative descriptions.

Comparing the teller job as discussed in a 1922 publication with the 1939 DOT job description leaves one with the impression that tellers in the 1920s had much more responsibility for the money they handled than their counterparts had in 1939. They also seem to have commanded more respect. There were two types of tellers in the 1920s—the paying teller, who cashed checks and paid out money to account holders, and the receiving teller, who accepted checks and money for depositing. The paying teller had much more responsibility: he was in charge of maintaining the legal level of cash in the bank and ensuring that those funds were paid out only to known customers. Paying tellers were considered to have "responsibility of a high order" and the job was seen as "important, complicated, and dignified."[26]

By 1929 banks were starting to combine the paying and receiving functions into one teller job, presumably with the same amount of responsibility as the paying teller. Typical beginning tellers were described as high school graduates having "two or more years of clerical work in a bank" as well as "tact in meeting customers, judgment, reliability, accuracy, and speed,"[27] qualities that would characterize tellers for the next fifty years.

During the 1930s new titles and a new hierarchy of tellers seem to have been established. The 1939 *Dictionary of Occupational Titles* describes twenty-six types of basic Teller I and four types of Head Teller. This hierarchy was mentioned neither in 1922 nor in 1929. The twenty-six categories of tellers refer to the type of accounts and transactions they handled, which varied from loans, trusts, and foreign exchange to simple checking accounts, deposits, and withdrawals. The latter type, called commercial paying and receiving, were more than half of all tellers in 1943 and probably in 1939 as well.[28] The major tasks of the tellers were to receive and pay out checks and cash and to record those transactions. These included verifying the identity of the customer,

26. Glenn G. Munn, *The Paying Teller's Department* (New York: Bankers Publishing Co., 1922), p. 9.

27. Hubert N. Stronck, *Bank Administration* (Rand McNally, 1929), p. 79.

28. Hosea, "Earnings of Bank Employees," p. 28.

judging the validity of any check, and performing the transactions with accuracy, speed, and much respect and courtesy for the customer, all of which had been part of the job since 1922. They used adding machines and sometimes supervised one or more clerks in recording the transactions. At the end of the day they had to add up all their records of payments and deposits and balance them with the cash and checks in their drawer.

The tellers who handled loans were called note tellers, and they seemed to have more discretion than other tellers in that they interviewed customers for loans, accepted loan payments, and handled collateral. Note tellers represented about 14 percent of all tellers in 1943.[29] The head tellers were responsible for providing and protecting the funds the tellers worked with, consolidating daily summary sheets of transactions, and reporting on these transactions and funds to the executives.

The job of the paying and receiving teller described in 1929 had been de-skilled by 1939. Any role that tellers might have had in interviewing customers for loans was now specifically taken over by note tellers. Moreover, by 1939 rank-and-file tellers were specifically supervised by head tellers. With the development of skill hierarchy came pay hierarchy; in the March 1936 *Banking* a salary chart for a typical bank showed note tellers and head tellers with higher salaries than all other types of tellers.[30]

In addition to the development of hierarchies, during the 1930s tellers seem to have experienced some restriction in promotion opportunities. A book on bank personnel policies put the matter delicately: successful tellers were those who were popular with customers, but then they did not develop the "aggressive qualities necessary in a good executive."[31] Chances for a promotion were thus theoretically good but realistically bad, which may have prompted a spate of articles written between 1937 and 1941 by tellers, all of whom were men. One has the impression of a last-gasp attempt to preserve the status of their jobs. "You are, or should be," one of the tellers wrote to other tellers, "a diplomat, a goodwill ambassador, a student of physiognomy, a humorist, a detective." They exhorted one another to do the job better and to become experts on currency.[32]

29. Ibid.; and U.S. Department of Labor, *Dictionary of Occupational Titles*, pt. 1, *Definitions of Titles* (GPO, 1939).
30. *Banking*, vol. 28 (March 1936), p. 26.
31. Davis, *Personnel Programs in Banks*, p. 26.
32. *Banking*, vol. 29 (June 1937), pp. 74–75; vol. 33 (March 1941), p. 24; and vol. 34 (October 1941), p. 23.

World War II provided the necessary jolt that prompted banks to put women into teller positions and to streamline the teller training and teller-customer interactions. However, the titles, content, functions, and qualifications of the teller job do not appear to have changed during the 1940s. It is clear that the amount of on-the-job training required for telling decreased during the war. Before the war it was commonly assumed that five years of on-the-job training was required before one was a skilled teller. But during the war, in order to cope with a huge influx of new employees, including women, high school students, and older men, there was a flurry of attention to training. Teller training was reduced to four to six weeks of full-time study and one month of on-the-job training. Training manuals were developed for formal teller training and for on-the-job reference; and ongoing study groups on banking were set up for all employees.[33]

Some bank managers wrote about simplifying tasks and did de-skill some clerical jobs (and some consciously hired women into the more repetitive jobs). But for tellers, it is not clear how much the job was de-skilled and how much the training process was simply streamlined. Indeed, the whole banking process was examined for improvement in efficiency. During the war years checks were standardized, teller lines were studied for possible moves toward more efficient operation, and new teller machines were introduced that new tellers could learn "with a few hours' practice."[34]

The machines used up to 1944 improved the teller's accuracy in recording and speed in serving customers without taking away any responsibility. The major machines were adding machines, change machines, and machines that sorted, counted, and wrapped coins. By 1948 many of the larger banks also had the new commercial teller machines, which recorded deposits and cash payments on both the customer's receipts and the teller's ledger and added them up. This saved the teller both time and errors.[35]

By the end of the 1940s several themes had emerged about the teller job that would remain for the following several decades. The job mainly

33. Ibid., vol. 35 (September 1942), p. 151; vol. 35 (June 1943), p. 28; and vol. 37 (September 1944), pp. 64–65.
34. Ibid., vol. 34 (February 1942), p. 66; vol. 36 (September 1943), pp. 71–73, 78; and vol. 36 (November 1943), p. 61.
35. Edgar E. Alcorn, *The Bank Teller: His Job and Opportunities* (Cambridge, Mass.: Bankers Publishing Co., 1950).

consisted of serving customers by paying and receiving money and verifying the correct amounts. The main qualities needed in the job were accuracy, speed, and courtesy. The advancement path to and from the job was also well established. In 1948, when more than half of the tellers were still men, the assurance was that banks only placed in teller cages "men of the highest type, whose personality is well adapted to meeting the public, and who have proved their efficiency in other departments of the bank."[36] By 1953 tellers, who were mostly hired with high school degrees, were advanced from the clerical staff. Theoretically, tellers with only high school diplomas could be promoted to officers if they obtained some college or bank industry training.[37]

However, by the 1950s and 1960s it was clear that banks preferred to hire clerical workers (women) with only high school diplomas as tellers and promote them only as far as head teller, and they preferred to hire college graduates (men) into teller jobs as officer trainees, thus producing two different job ladders for women and men.[38] The existence of different job ladders justified different wage rates for men and women tellers, until sex discrimination lawsuits filed under the Equal Pay Act in 1969–70 challenged the separate promotion ladders and pay scales.[39]

The 1950s and the 1960s produced remarkably little change in the Department of Labor's job descriptions of bank tellers. For the 1965 DOT, although some of the twenty-six categories of tellers from the 1939 DOT disappeared or were consolidated into other categories, there was still an equivalent total of twenty-two categories. There were also five rather than four types of head teller. The tasks of all types of tellers remained virtually the same as they had been in 1939. While head tellers remained the most responsible, they neither gained nor lost any status, according to these descriptions.

Another government publication providing descriptions of jobs is the *Occupational Outlook Handbook* (OOH); until 1968 it listed note teller as a job to which a teller could be promoted. By 1968–69, however, only head teller remained as a distinctly higher position than other teller jobs.

Quantitative job rankings of occupational characteristics first ap-

36. Ibid., p. viii.
37. U.S. Department of Labor, Bureau of Labor Statistics, "Employment Outlook in Banking Occupations," Bulletin 1156 (GPO, 1953).
38. Marshall C. Corns, *Organizing Jobs in Banking: The Use of Job Descriptions and Operating Instructions* (Boston: Bankers Publishing Co., 1967).
39. Barbara Allen Babcock and others, *Sex Discrimination and the Law: Cause and Remedies* (Little, Brown, 1975), pp. 440–509.

peared in the 1965 DOT. They ranked complexity of worker function in relation to data, people, and things; training times for general education development and specific vocational preparation; various aptitudes, including verbal and numerical; temperaments; interests; physical demands; and working conditions. Not all of these characteristics were measured for bank tellers and not all were measured in both 1965 and 1977.

On a scale of 0 (high) to 8 (low), tellers in 1965 were ranked 3 on complexity of function in relation to data, 6 in relation to people, and 8 in relation to things. In 1977 the rankings for data and people were the same as for 1965, but the ranking for things increased to 2. In 1965, on a scale in the reverse direction, of 1 (low) to 6 (high) for the general educational development for the job, tellers had a 4 on both numerical and verbal abilities. By 1977 those requirements had declined to a 3 for numerical ability and a 2 for verbal ability. In both years, the job was rated "light" in its physical demands and neither hazardous nor uncomfortable in environmental conditions.

Do the changes in these rankings provide evidence that telling was de-skilled between 1965 and 1977? How are these rankings derived? Are they valid and reliable? An evaluation of the DOT discusses the derivation of the rankings and counsels caution in their interpretation. Job analysis for the DOT is based on a combination of observations and interviews of workers performing a particular job. Although analysts are asked to assign worker trait ratings, including verbal and numerical ability, primarily on the basis of skills or tasks intrinsic to job performance, in most analysts' reports employer hiring requirements "figured prominently in the assignment of these ratings."[40]

The validity of the DOT's ratings of worker functions and traits is subject to question because it is not clear what they are supposed to measure. Moreover, the validity of the educational development scores, including the numerical and verbal components, is questioned because of the high correlations (between 0.7 and 0.9) between them and measures of occupational prestige. Do the verbal and math scores measure the requirements of a job or the job's status?

Some tests of reliability of the rankings found them to be "not very

---

40. Ann R. Miller and others, eds., *Work, Jobs, and Occupations: A Critical Review of the Dictionary of Occupational Titles* (Washington, D.C.: National Academy Press, 1980), p. 133.

high."[41] In addition, there were some important changes between 1965 and 1977 in the procedures for rating jobs, so that a comparison of rankings between those years is particularly difficult. The difference in rankings between 1965 and 1977 on tellers' complexity of function in relation to things should probably be ignored entirely, since the DOT completely revised its ranking on this dimension for all women's jobs in response to allegations of sex bias after the 1965 rankings were published.

It may be that despite the rise in education level of bank tellers over 1950–80, the numerical and verbal abilities of bank tellers actually declined over the period. And indeed employer requirements may have declined as the relative earnings of telling declined. It may be that tellers used to be overqualified for their jobs. A ranking of 4 on numerical ability indicates ability to work with algebra and geometry, abilities that bank tellers probably rarely utilized even when they had them. As relative earnings fell, employers may have sought tellers whose abilities were more in line with the job requirements. Based on the constancy of job description and the availability of adding machines throughout the period, we are inclined to think that the intrinsic numerical and verbal requirements of the job probably remained the same.

The DOT and OOH in the early 1970s showed no changes in the descriptions of worker autonomy or physical conditions from those in the 1960s. However, in the 1974–75 OOH an overview of tellers' work appeared that made the job sound tedious, even though it described what had been the situation since 1939: "Although tellers work independently, their record keeping is closely supervised. They work with detail and are confined to a small work area." Thus, although the tasks remained the same, the perception of them had changed. Somehow the job had lost its status. It had begun to be seen as an entry-level job. According to the 1978 OOH, "for many young people just out of school, working as a teller is their first job. Because the job involves repetitive work with great attention to detail and long periods of time on one's feet, this occupation does not suit some people. The high rate of turnover suggests that after a couple of years' work, many tellers seek other positions."

Despite this attitude toward the job, the OOH kept insisting into the 1980s that outstanding tellers could be promoted to officers if they got college or bank training. However, the way they characterized the job in the early 1980s did not make it sound attractive to people who wanted

41. Ibid., p. 170.

officer positions: "continual communication with customers, repetitive tasks, prolonged standing." The job was the same, the tasks were the same, the promotion ladders were supposedly the same, but the job was not seen in the same way.

Automation could not have affected the content or status of the teller job. Most automation in banks from the 1940s through the 1960s was aimed at mechanizing the processing of checks. While automation cut down on the number of check processing and bookkeeping jobs, it didn't affect the teller job.[42] The teller machine mentioned earlier allowed more accurate and faster work, but it replaced none of the actual tasks. Computer terminals, which allowed tellers to verify checks and retrieve account information, did not become widespread until the mid-1970s. However, while these computers gave tellers more accurate information faster, they still did not replace major teller tasks. Tellers were still responsible for the money and checks they took in and the money they gave out, for recording that information accurately and speedily, and for balancing those records at the end of the day. Automatic teller machines (ATMs), of course, do replace the major tasks, especially the most subjective task: positively identifying a customer. However, as late as the mid-1970s, ATMs were not widespread. In 1974 only 2,000 ATMs were in operation, so it is likely that ATMs had no impact on bank teller jobs until after 1980.[43]

In summary, for reasons other than a change of job content or the introduction of machines, the teller job went from a high-status, albeit clerical, job in 1922 to a low-status clerical job in 1980. If any de-skilling occurred, it seems to have happened before 1939, before women entered the occupation. What could have caused a change of status without an actual change in duties? The answer lies not in what was happening within the teller job, but within the banking industry during this period. It appears that bank telling was not de-skilled, but rather "declassed."

STATUS CHANGES IN BANKING. The Depression and World War II stand between two distinct periods of banking in the United States. Before World War II, banks served almost exclusively to hold the large accounts of corporations and wealthy individuals. Sometime between the 1930s

42. Robert S. Aldom and others, *Automation in Banking* (Rutgers University Press, 1963); and Rose K. Weiner, "Effect of Automation on Employment in Banks," *Occupational Outlook Quarterly*, vol. 6 (December 1962), pp. 9–12.

43. Bureau of Labor Statistics, "Technological Change and Manpower Trends in Six Industries," Bulletin 1817 (GPO, 1974), p. 43.

and the end of World War II, in order to have access to more funds, banks started offering services that would appeal to a larger segment of the population. They introduced "economy checking accounts," which required low or no minimum balances and cost only a small charge per check. Men and women of all incomes began opening these accounts and using checks for the first time. During these years, banks also made available consumer installment loans for such things as automobiles and other household purchases, real estate loans, and small business loans, and they started receiving utility and telephone payments from the public.[44]

All of these activities, as well as World War II itself, set the stage for a huge change in both the number and types of bank clientele and employees. After the war, several important factors converged to create a demand for the exact services the banks were offering. A growing postwar economy gave people money, or the promise of it, to spend, save, or borrow. For both individuals and businesses of all income levels, financial transactions through the banks increased tremendously, and the banks' work loads grew accordingly. Between 1939 and 1952 the number of checking accounts increased from 27 million to 47.1 million.[45] The percentage of people over age 21 with checking accounts increased from 25 percent to over 50 percent in the same period.[46] Most of the increases came after the war.

Banks both responded to and created this demand for customer services by increasing the number of branch offices in cities, suburbs, and factories and by setting up drive-in windows and sidewalk tellers to attract and compete for customers. Consequently, there was an increase in the number of bank employees, including the number and proportion who were tellers. In 1950, bank tellers were 12 percent of all bank employees; by 1980 they were 22 percent.[47]

44. R. David Corwin, *Racial Minorities in Banking: New Workers in the Banking Industry* (New Haven: College and University Press, 1971); and Rose K. Weiner, "Changing Manpower Requirements in Banking," *Monthly Labor Review*, vol. 85 (September 1962), pp. 989–95.

45. Weiner, "Changing Manpower Requirements," p. 989; and Aldom and others, *Automation in Banking*, p. 13.

46. Bureau of Labor Statistics, "Employment Outlook in Banking Occupations"; and David H. McKinley and George L. Leffler, *Your Bank* (Harrisburg, Pa.: Pennsylvania Bankers Association, 1960).

47. Bureau of Labor Statistics, "Employment Outlook in Banking Occupations" and "Technological Change and Manpower Trends in Six Industries"; and Bureau of

Although the bank teller job remained essentially unchanged during this period, these changes in clientele, services, numbers of branches, and numbers of tellers may have affected the way the job was regarded. The change in bank clientele before and after World War II was described "as a shift from class to mass banking," and the changes in banking services were seen as "the retail approach" to banking.[48] Providing the masses with retail bank services gave the teller job less status than providing exclusive financial services to the wealthy, even though tellers were doing the same tasks. The image of the teller job, rather than the tasks associated with it, was probably the main source of the decline in status and wages relative to other white-collar jobs for men and, eventually, for women.

To summarize, bank telling became a female-dominated job long before ATMs. The job description throughout the 1970s, when women were the majority of bank tellers, was very similar to what it had been before World War II, when men dominated the occupation. Very few responsibilities were taken away after 1939. Before 1939, however, when tellers were still all men, much responsibility went from the paying teller to the head teller. Women were allowed into the occupation on trial soon after that, and simultaneously the types of customers and services became much more common and less elite. Women were accepted and filled most of the teller jobs in 1960–80, working for wages lower than most men's but comparable to other women's.

And now the tasks tellers have done for years, whether women or men—checking an account balance and a customer's identification, paying out funds, taking deposits and payments, and recording it all accurately and speedily—are being done by electronic machines, a fate common to de-skilled jobs after they have been inhabited by women or minorities. However, the teller job description did not change for forty years (1939–79). It seems to have maintained its skill and judgment levels right up to the time it was mechanized. What changed was the financial status and gender of the customers, the age and gender of the people doing the job, and, perhaps consequently, the image and the status of the job. This loss of image and status for bank telling was a more

---

the Census, *U.S. Census of Population, 1950: Special Report: Occupation by Industry* (GPO, 1956), table 2, and *1980: Subject Report: Occupation by Industry* (GPO, 1984), table 4.

48. Weiner, "Changing Manpower Requirements"; and Aldom and others, *Automation in Banking.*

important change in the job than any intrinsic de-skilling, of which we can find little evidence during the crucial years when the occupation was tipping from men to women.

Characteristics of the Men in Bank Telling

What were the characteristics of the men who entered or remained in an occupation that was becoming feminized? There are several plausible a priori hypotheses. One might suppose that it would be mostly older men, with poor alternative job opportunities, who would remain in bank telling. In that case, the average age and experience of male bank tellers would have increased over time. Alternatively, one might speculate that it would be mostly younger men who would enter the occupation. Some of these men might have been relatively well educated and planning to use bank telling as a stepping-stone to positions in bank management. In that case, there should be a decrease in the average age of male bank tellers and an increase in the average level of male tellers' educational attainment.

One might also hypothesize that minority men would be more heavily represented in bank telling than in the work force as a whole, if, for example, the more attractive job opportunities in other sectors, to which white men were moving, were not as open to minority men. If there were a queue among men for the more lucrative jobs and minority men were last in that queue, then minority men might have to settle for jobs as bank tellers. In that case one might find that minority men in bank telling were better educated than their white counterparts.

Why, one might ask, would employers hire or retain any men at all for bank telling if on the average they could employ women more cheaply? Employers might have retained older men because they were experienced and therefore "worth" a higher salary or because employers had some allegiance to long-service tellers. Alternatively, employers might have been willing to hire young men and pay them more than they paid women (at least before the equal opportunity laws and orders took effect) because they viewed young men, but not women, as potential management candidates.

Tables 2 and 3 suggest that it was largely young men (aged 16–24) who were responsible for the small net increase in male bank tellers during the postwar period, and that many of these young men left the occupation as they grew older. A comparison of the age distributions of men bank

Table 2. *Distribution of Employed Male Bank Tellers and All Employed Men, by Age, 1950–80*
Percent unless otherwise indicated

Age group	1950		1960		1970		1980		Percent change, 1950–80	
	Tellers	All men	Tellers	All men	Tellers	All men	Tellers	All men	Tellers	All men
16–24[a]	27	15	31	14	37	17	54	19	27	4
25–34	33	24	29	22	28	22	25	28	−8	4
35–44	20	23	13	24	11	21	8	20	−12	−3
45–54	13	19	13	21	9	21	6	17	−7	−2
55–64	5	13	10	14	11	14	5	12	0	−1
65 and over	2	6	3	5	3	4	2	3	0	−3
Median age (years)	30.8	39.6	30.6	40.6	28.3	40.3	28.1	36.2	...	...

Sources: Bureau of the Census, *Census of Population, 1950, Occupational Characteristics*, table 6; *1960*, table 6; *1970*, table 40; *1980, Detailed Population Characteristics, U.S. Summary*, sec. A, table 280.
a. For 1950 and 1960, includes ages 14–15.

tellers over 1950–80 (table 2) shows that the share of total male employment held by young men (16–24) doubled between 1950 and 1980. The share of male employment in the age groups from 25 to 54 fell over the period, while the share of male employment in the group aged 55 and over stayed about the same (with an increase for men aged 55–64 during 1950–70). The median age of male tellers fell by 2.7 years.

For purposes of comparison, table 2 also provides the percentage distribution by age of all employed men for 1950–80. In 1950 the median age of men in bank telling was almost nine years less than that of men in the total labor force. Men aged 16–24 were 27 percent of all male bank tellers but 15 percent of the experienced male work force. In 1980 the difference in the median age of the two groups was about the same as it was in 1950. However, men aged 16–24 were 19 percent of the total male labor force in 1980 but 54 percent of male tellers. Compared with the male experienced work force, bank telling had an increasingly larger proportion of young men.

In table 3 we examine six synthetic cohorts of men bank tellers over 1950–80. Only one male cohort increased its employment in bank telling: those who were 16–19 in 1950 and 25–29 in 1960. For every other male cohort in every other decade, employment in bank telling decreased. That same pattern is shown in a comparison of the three youngest cohorts of male bank tellers over 1970–80.

What about the racial and educational characteristics of the men who

Table 3. *Changes in the Number of Men Employed as Bank Tellers, by Synthetic Age Cohort, 1950–80*

Age cohort				Number of bank tellers[a]			
1950	1960	1970	1980	1950	1960	1970	1980
All cohorts, 1950–80							
16–19	25–29	35–39 }	45–54	870	6,945	2,166 }	
20–24	30–34	40–44 }		8,280	4,602	1,672 }	2,377
25–29 }	35–44	45–54	55–64	7,230 }	5,166	3,268	2,273
30–34 }				3,900 }			
35–44	45–54	55–64	65 and over	6,840	5,209	3,968	995
45–54	55–64	65 and over	. . .	4,410	3,919	694	. . .
Younger cohorts, 1970–80							
. . .	. . .	16–24	25–34	. . .	. . .	13,037	10,819
. . .	. . .	25–34	35–44	. . .	. . .	9,672	3,321
. . .	. . .	35–44	45–54	. . .	. . .	3,838	2,377

Sources: See table 2.

a. Total male bank tellers employed in each of these years: 1950, 34,050; 1960, 39,143; 1970, 34,834; 1980, 43,386. Columns do not add to totals because not all age groups are listed for each year.

remained in or entered this increasingly female occupation? Among the men who were employed in bank telling, were minority men more highly represented than would be expected from their representation in the work force as a whole? Did the men employed in bank telling become better educated over time? Were minority men in bank telling better educated than their white counterparts?

Table 4 presents the age distribution of white, black, Asian-American, and Hispanic men bank tellers in 1980. Of all male bank tellers, 11 percent were black, somewhat more than the percentage of all men employed who were black (8 percent). Similarly, Hispanic men represented 9 percent of all bank tellers, higher than their representation in the employed male labor force (6 percent). There seems to be some support for the hypothesis that minority men were somewhat more attracted to bank telling than were white men, perhaps because minority men were closed out of more lucrative jobs. For both blacks and Hispanics, the age distribution of male bank tellers was quite similar to that of white men, except that the percentage of black and Hispanic men over 55 was less than that of white men over 55. Asian-American men were 3 percent of all male bank tellers in 1980. The Asian-American male age distribution was somewhat different from that of white men, but the number of Asian male bank tellers was so small (1,411) that not too much emphasis should be placed on the differences. In all, one would conclude that the distributions by age of minority male bank tellers were quite similar to those of white males.

Table 4. *Distribution of Employed Male Bank Tellers,*
by Age and Race, 1980

Percent

	Race			
Age group	White	Asian-American	Black	Hispanic
16–19	15	8	17	17
20–24	39	34	41	39
25–34	24	38	27	26
35–44	7	15	9	9
45–54	6	4	5	6
55–64	6	1	1	2
65 and over	3	0	1	*
Ratio of tellers in race to all tellers[a]	82	3	11	9
Ratio of employed workers in race to all employed workers[a]	87	2	8	6

Source: Bureau of the Census, *Census of Population, 1980, Subject Report: Earnings by Occupation and Education,* tables 278, 280.
* Less than 0.5 percent.
a. Total adds to more than 100 because Hispanics can be of any race, and because the category "other races" is not shown.

Table 5. *Distribution of Male Bank Tellers, by Education*
and Race, 1950–80[a]

Percent unless otherwise indicated

Years of school completed	1950	1960		1970			1980			
	All races	All	Nonwhite	All	Black	Hispanic	All	Black	Hispanic	Asian
0–8	6	5	11	2	2	1	2	2	5	*
9–11	12	12	0	9	12	8	7	9	11	5
12	51	48	44	49	56	58	34	38	41	23
13–15	22	27	37	32	25	25	39	42	35	40
16 or more	9	8	7	7	6	7	18	9	9	31
Median (years)	12.6	12.7	n.a.	12.8	12.6	12.7	13.6	13.1	12.8	14.6

Sources: Bureau of the Census, *Census of Population, 1950, Occupational Characteristics,* table 10; *1960,* tables 9, 10; *1970,* tables 5, 6, 7; *1980, Detailed Populational Characteristics, U.S. Summary,* table 282.
n.a. Not available.
* Less than 0.005 percent.
a. Data for 1950–70 refer to experienced tellers, and for 1980, employed tellers.

Table 5 provides information about the distribution by race of years of school completed for male bank tellers during 1950–80. For all male tellers, the median years of education rose slightly over the period, with a large increase between 1970 and 1980. The percentage of men with some college education increased over the decades. This provides further support for the picture that has already emerged: the men in bank telling in the latter part of the period were younger and slightly better educated than their counterparts in 1950.

For black and Hispanic men, in 1970 the median level of education was slightly lower than it was for all men; by 1980 the disparity had grown. Compared with black and Hispanic men, all male bank tellers were more likely to have had some college education. Among these groups, we find no support for the hypothesis that it is better-educated minority men who are likely to enter an occupation that is becoming female. However, this finding does not hold for Asians. In 1980 the census provides for the first time data on education for Asian bank tellers; the median education level of Asian male bank tellers was a full year higher than that of all male bank tellers. This difference reflects a higher proportion of college graduates and those with some college among Asian bank tellers.

Characteristics of the Women in Bank Telling

How do the women employed in bank telling over 1950–80 compare with their male counterparts with respect to age, race, and education? As indicated in table 6, the median age of women bank tellers fell by 1.1 years between 1950 and 1980. Young women (16–24) increased their representation among women bank tellers from 33 percent in 1950 to 40 percent in 1980. (However, in the intervening years the percentage of young women fell.) The proportion of those aged 16–24 among all women bank tellers in 1980 was nonetheless considerably lower than the same proportion among men bank tellers (40 percent versus 54 percent). In the other age groups, women changed their representation only slightly over the thirty-year period. Indeed, given the enormous growth in the number of women bank tellers from 1950–80, it is remarkable that their distribution across the groups aged 25 to 65 and over shifted so little.[49]

49. We have remarked about the relative constancy of employment shares between 1950 and 1980 for women bank tellers in the age groups over 25. In light of the very large increase in women's labor force participation, it is interesting to note the relative constancy of employment shares of the various age groups for all employed women in 1950–80. Women aged 25–34 increased their share by 5 percentage points. Changes in the shares of the other age groups were all smaller. The changes in labor force participation rates across age groups for women were much greater than the changes in the employment shares of the various age groups. See Bureau of the Census, *Census of Population, 1980, General Social and Economic Characteristics: U.S. Summary* (GPO, 1983), table 87.

Table 6. *Distribution of Employed Female Bank Tellers, Female Clerical Workers, and All Employed Women, by Age, 1950–80*
Percent unless otherwise indicated

Age group	1950			1960			1970			1980			Percent change, 1950–80		
	Tellers	Clerical workers	All women	Tellers	Clerical workers	All women	Tellers	Clerical workers	All women	Tellers	Clerical workers[a]	All women	Tellers	Clerical workers	All women
16–24[b]	33	35	23	26	27	19	31	30	23	40	26	24	7	−9	1
25–34	30	26	23	30	21	17	23	18	17	27	28	27	−3	2	4
35–44	20	19	23	24	23	24	22	18	20	16	19	19	−4	0	−2
45–54	13	13	17	14	18	22	17	19	21	11	15	16	−2	2	−1
55–64	3	5	9	5	9	13	6	10	14	5	10	11	2	5	2
65 and over	1	1	3	1	2	4	1	2	4	1	2	3	0	1	0
Median age (years)	29.2	...	36.4	32.8	...	40.4	32.8	...	39.5	28.1	...	34.6	...	...	...

Sources: See table 2.
a. Includes workers in administrative support.
b. For 1950 and 1960, includes ages 14–15.

Table 7. *Changes in the Number of Women Employed as Bank Tellers, by Synthetic Age Cohort, 1950–80*

Age cohort				Number of bank tellers[a]			
1950	1960	1970	1980	1950	1960	1970	1980
All cohorts, 1950–80							
16–19	25–29	35–39 ⎤		1,650	13,823	22,894 ⎤	
20–24	30–34	40–44 ⎦ 45–54		7,500	12,932	24,234 ⎦ 49,972	
25–29 ⎤				5,550 ⎤			
30–34 ⎦ 35–44		45–54	55–64	2,790 ⎦ 21,004		36,697	23,397
35–44	45–54	55–64	65 and over	5,610	11,994	12,601	2,596
45–54	55–64	65 and over	. . .	3,660	4,695	1,644	. . .
Younger cohorts, 1970–80							
. . .	. . .	16–24	25–34	. . .	. . .	68,386	120,905
. . .	. . .	25–34	35–44	. . .	. . .	49,819	72,144
. . .	. . .	35–44	45–54	. . .	. . .	47,129	49,972

Sources: See table 2.

a. Total female bank tellers employed in each of these years: 1950, 27,660; 1960, 88,124; 1970, 216,270; 1980, 451,460. Columns do not add to totals because not all age groups are listed for each year.

Unlike men, women aged 25–54 did not significantly decrease their representation among bank tellers.

In 1980 the proportion of women aged 16–24 in bank telling was much higher than the proportion of women in that age group in clerical work or among all employed women (table 6). On the other hand, women aged 35–64 were less well represented in bank telling than in clerical work or the total work force. In 1950 women aged 16–24 had virtually the same representation in bank telling and clerical work. But between 1950 and 1980 the proportion of women aged 16–24 in telling rose 7 percentage points, while the proportion in that age group in clerical work declined 9 percentage points. Bank telling was clearly attracting a disproportionate share of young women as well as of young men.

This conclusion is confirmed by the synthetic cohort analysis for women, which shows the minimum number of women who were hired in each decade. Table 7 reveals that between 1950 and 1960 employment increased among women in all synthetic cohorts and between 1960 and 1970 among all women except those who were aged 55–64 in 1960 (and most likely retired during the decade). Between 1970 and 1980 employment increased slightly for those who were aged 45–54 in 1980, but decreased for those who were 55 and over in 1980. Employment increased between 1970 and 1980 for all three of the youngest cohorts but the increase was much less for those who were 45–54 in 1980 than for those who were younger than 45 in 1980. These increases show that women of

Table 8. *Distribution of Employed Female Bank Tellers,*
by Age and Race, 1980
Percent

| | | Race | | |
| | | | | |
Age group	White	Asian-American	Black	Hispanic
16–19	11	8	8	14
20–24	29	25	36	39
25–34	25	42	38	30
35–44	16	16	12	11
45–54	12	7	4	5
55–64	6	1	1	1
65 and over	1	0	*	*
Ratio of tellers in race to all tellers[a]	89	2	7	5
Ratio of employed workers in race to all employed workers[a]	85	2	11	5

Sources: See table 4.
* Less than 0.5 percent.
a. Total adds to more than 100 because Hispanics can be of any race, and because the category "other races" is not shown.

all ages were hired between 1950–70, but that between 1970 and 1980 most of the minimum number of new hires were young women under 34.

The racial composition of women bank tellers in 1980 is presented in table 8. Of all women bank tellers, blacks were 7 percent, Hispanics were 5 percent, and Asian-Americans were 2 percent. Hispanics' and Asian-Americans' share of women in bank telling was the same as that among all employed women. Black women's representation in bank telling was below that in the female work force. Compared with whites, black and Hispanic women bank tellers were more likely to be in the younger age groups (under 35), except for blacks aged 16–19.

The educational distribution of all women and minority women bank tellers is shown in table 9. For all women tellers, the median years of education rose slightly over the period. In each year, however, the median level of education of all women bank tellers was less than that of men bank tellers, and women tellers were less likely than men tellers to have some college or a college degree. Unlike men, black women tellers in 1970 and 1980 had a slightly higher median education level than did all women. This may, in part, be a result of the fact that a higher proportion of black women than of all women were in the 20–34 age group. Hispanic women bank tellers, however, had a slightly lower median education

Table 9. *Distribution of Female Bank Tellers, by Education and Race, 1950–80*[a]

Percent unless otherwise indicated

Years of school completed	1950	1960		1970			1980			
	All races	All	Nonwhite	All	Black	Hispanic	All	Black	Hispanic	Asian
0–8	4	2	0	1	1	1	1	1	2	1
9–11	11	12	7	9	12	9	6	7	10	4
12	65	69	52	68	56	72	62	49	57	37
13–15	16	14	29	19	25	16	25	7	27	33
16 or more	4	2	12	2	6	2	5	6	3	24
Median (years)	12.5	12.5	n.a.	12.6	12.7	12.5	12.7	12.9	12.7	13.6

Sources: See table 5.

n.a. Not available.

a. Data for 1950–70 refer to experienced tellers, and for 1980, employed tellers.

level than all women in 1970, but had the same level by 1980. As was the case among men, Asian women bank tellers had a median education level in 1980 almost one full year above that of all women bank tellers.

Effects of the Shift in Gender Assignment on the Earnings Differential

Despite the considerable increase in the size of the bank telling occupation and its increasing female intensity, the female-male salary differential remained remarkably constant at about 74 percent over 1950–70 (see table 1). The relative constancy of the salary ratio is not unique to bank tellers. In our earlier work with computer scientists, programmers, and operators, we found that the female-male salary ratio changed little, even though the occupations grew enormously and their gender compositions changed significantly over 1970–80.[50] Moreover, Gordon's work on the teaching occupation during 1870–1910 showed that although the percentage of women in teaching increased by about 40 percent, the salary differential also remained quite stable.[51]

How might one explain the relative constancy of the salary ratio? The interpretation is complex, for not only is the ratio an outcome of earlier

50. See Myra H. Strober and Carolyn L. Arnold, "Integrated Circuits/Segregated Labor: Women in Computer-Related Occupations and High-Tech Industries," in Heidi I. Hartmann, ed., *Computer Chips and Paper Clips: Technology and Women's Employment,* vol. 2 (Washington, D.C.: National Academy Press, 1987).

51. Audri Gordon, "A Dynamic Analysis of the Sexual Composition of Public School Teaching: 1870 to 1970" (Ph.D. dissertation, Stanford University, 1980).

supply and demand forces in two labor markets (one for women and one for men); it is also a determinant of future supply and demand in those markets.[52] For this essay we analyze the female-male salary ratio only as an outcome variable. We ask, what supply and demand factors changed during each of the decades so that at the end of the decade the salary ratio was just about what it had been at the end of the previous decade?

Women's wage rates may be lower than men's for any of several reasons. On the supply side, women might work fewer hours than men, have less human capital (experience and education) and therefore be less productive, or have fewer alternative employment opportunities and lower wages in alternative occupations and therefore have a lower reservation wage. On the demand side, women might be involved in less-skilled jobs within a job hierarchy or face discrimination. Thus changes in the female-male ratios of any of the following variables would affect the female-male salary ratio: (1) hours worked, (2) experience, (3) education, (4) alternative wage and employment opportunities, or (5) assignments within the teller hierarchy. A change in discrimination would also affect the ratio.

We first sought to determine if one reason for the stability in the earnings ratio was the stability over time in the female-male ratio of mean hours worked. Unfortunately, however, we cannot calculate ratios of mean hours worked for 1950 or 1980. For the ten-year period from 1960 to 70, the female-male ratio of hours worked was constant at 92 percent.[53]

---

52. With respect to teachers, Strober and Lanford attempted to deal with the direction of causality between the percentage of female teachers and the female-male salary ratio in teaching. We hypothesized that before the widespread stereotyping of teaching as a female occupation the salary ratio affected the gender composition of teaching. In later years, we believed, teaching (especially at the primary school level) was defined as a "female occupation," which in turn reduced the supply of men relative to women and caused their relative salary to rise. We therefore argued that the salary ratio caused changes in the percentage of female teachers in the early years (before 1880), whereas in later years the percentage of women in teaching affected the salary ratio. We tested this specification of the causal relationship using two-stage least squares regression. The results were ambiguous; the state-level analyses generally supported our hypotheses, but the county-level data contradicted them. See Myra H. Strober and Audri G. Lanford, "The Feminization of Public School Teaching: Cross-Sectional Analysis, 1850–1880," *Signs: Journal of Women in Culture and Society*, vol. 11 (Winter 1986), pp. 212–35.

53. It should be pointed out that accounting for differences in hours worked does not change the female-male earnings differential very much. For example, in 1979 the

Information about changes in the relative experience of men and women is also difficult to obtain. If we use age as a proxy for experience and assume that the ratios of age to experience remained constant over the period for both men and women, then changes in the relative age structures of women and men should have contributed to an increase in the female-male earnings ratio. The median age of male tellers declined more over the three decades than did the median age of female tellers, and male tellers had a higher proportion of younger workers than did female tellers. Moreover, it is likely that the relationship between age and experience did not remain constant over the period, but rather that as women tellers became younger the ratio of age to experience fell for women. This change would lead us to expect a further contribution to an increase in the female-male earnings ratio. With respect to the relative levels of women's and men's education, we found that the ratio of women's median education level to that of men remained quite stable at about 98 percent over 1950–70 and fell to 93 percent in 1980 (see table 1).

One way of measuring comparative alternative wage opportunities is to look at the female-male earnings ratio for the economy as a whole. This ratio was virtually constant between 1950 and 1980.[54] Another measure of alternative employment opportunities (the relative "crowding" faced by women) is the index of occupational segregation. That index too was quite stable during 1950–80, as discussed earlier.

It is difficult to uncover evidence on changes in the distribution of assignments men and women have held within the teller hierarchy. However, we have found sporadic information on skill and salary hierarchies that may shed some light on the salary differential. There seems to have been a hierarchy of skills among the twenty-six different types of tellers listed in the 1939 DOT from clerical work as a discount teller to interviewing loan applicants as a commercial note teller. The

ratio of mean hourly earnings for bank tellers was 74 percent, not very different from the salary ratio based on mean annual earnings, which was 78 percent. Bureau of the Census, *Census of Population, 1980: Earnings by Occupation and Education* (GPO, 1984), table 1, p. 115.

54. It is important to note that it is the ratio of median annual earnings of full-time, year-round workers that has remained stable. The series measuring the usual weekly earnings of full-time year-round workers shows an increase since 1978 of about 1 percentage point a year in the female-male earnings ratio. The earnings ratio for young people has also been increasing. Francine D. Blau and Marianne A. Ferber, *The Economics of Women, Men, and Work* (Prentice-Hall, 1986), pp. 171, 178.

hierarchy among these types of tellers was reflected in salary differentials. A description of a hypothetical bank in 1936 showed that head tellers and note tellers received much higher salaries than all other tellers, and a survey of 1,312 banks in 1943 showed that note tellers were highest paid for both men and women tellers. There is some evidence that women and men were differentially distributed among this hierarchy of types of tellers. The 1943 survey of banks showed that the percentage of women in telling was highest among all-round tellers (48 percent), the lowest-paid category, and lowest among note tellers (29 percent), the highest-paid category.[55]

By the early 1960s, however, while the number of categories remained almost the same, the extent of salary differences between those categories may have lessened. A salary survey in selected cities in 1960 showed that in three cities—New York, Chicago, and Houston—there was not a consistent salary hierarchy between all tellers, note tellers, and commercial savings tellers; rather, their relative standing varied by city.[56]

In addition, although differences still existed in the percentages of women across teller categories, they were not as sharp. In 1964 women were 72 percent of all bank tellers. They were 66 percent of note tellers and 62 percent of commercial tellers, traditionally the highest-paid categories.[57] As the salary differences between the teller categories shrank, women's representation in each category became closer to their representation in bank telling as a whole. While women's low representation in the higher-paid teller assignments could have contributed to part of the female-male salary differential in the decades during and after the war, by 1960 there was no longer enough hierarchy among tellers to make teller assignment a major variable. Thus a lessening of hierarchy in telling probably acted to decrease the salary differential.

There is some evidence that overt discrimination may have lessened over 1950–80. In 1958 it was still legal to pay women less than men in the same job, and in a survey that year of 130 banks, 23 percent admitted paying women tellers 10 to 30 percent less than men. In addition, banks often put women into downgraded teller jobs—from which physical labor had been removed—and then justified paying lower salaries to the

55. *Banking,* vol. 18 (March 1936), p. 26; and Hosea, "Earnings of Bank Employees."

56. Harry F. Zeman, "Earnings in the Banking Industry, Mid-1960," *Monthly Labor Review,* vol. 84 (January 1961), pp. 37–38.

57. Joseph C. Bush, "Earnings in Banks, November–December 1964," *Monthly Labor Review,* vol. 88 (November 1965), pp. 1331.

women in those jobs.[58] As a result of equal employment opportunity legislation and suits under the Equal Pay Act, some of these practices seem to have lessened.

In summary, we have identified six factors that could affect the female-male salary ratio over time. With respect to the ratio of women's hours worked to men's hours worked, we have inadequate evidence. With respect to relative experience, we think that changes in the age structures of women and men tellers should have contributed to an increase in the earnings ratio. On the other hand, the decline in the ratio of women's education level to men's education level between 1970 and 1980 should have contributed to a decline in the earnings ratio. The ratios of alternative wage and employment opportunities of women to those of men remained constant over the forty-year period and would thus contribute to the constancy of the female-male earnings ratio. We believe the gender distribution of teller assignments became more equal during the postwar period and therefore contributed to an increase in the earnings ratio. We also suspect that some forms of blatant wage discrimination probably lessened between 1950 and 1980; yet the female-male earnings ratio remained constant. In part this may have been a result of inertia—the continued application of "wage norms" for women and men in an occupation or, in other words, the continued existence of subtle discrimination.[59]

Effects of the Shift in Gender Assignment on the Relative Earnings of Tellers

Like the female-male salary ratio, the ratios measuring the relative earnings of bank tellers (the ratio of each sex's earnings as tellers to the

58. *Banking*, vol. 51 (July 1958), p. 128.

59. One type of subtle discrimination may take the form of differential employment patterns for men and women tellers across types of financial institutions. Blau, in a study of clerical occupations across cities, found that even when men and women are employed in the same occupation, women are more likely to be employed in low-wage firms and men in high-wage firms. Francine D. Blau, *Equal Pay in the Office* (Lexington, Mass.: Lexington Books, 1977). Strober and Arnold found a similar kind of segregation in computer occupations. Women programmers, systems analysts, and computer operators were more likely than men to be found in the relatively lower-paying "end-user" industries. Strober and Arnold, "Integrated Circuits/Segregated Labor." Among tellers, it may be that men are more likely to be employed in commercial banks while women are more frequently found in savings and loan institutions or credit unions that pay lower wages. This issue requires further investigation.

average earnings of all wage and salary workers) can be treated as both determinants and outcomes of labor market forces. Thus in our discussion of the origins of the feminization of bank telling we argued that in 1950 men were not particularly interested in going into bank telling because the relative earnings for men were not particularly attractive. In that case, relative earnings were a determinant of supply. However, we now wish to look at relative earnings as an outcome. We ask, what supply and demand factors changed during each of the decades so that at the end of the decade the relative earnings for bank tellers, both men and women, declined?

Table 1 indicates that the salary ratio for women bank tellers declined only slightly between 1950 and 1960. Between 1960 and 1970 it declined 16 percent and between 1970 and 1980 it declined 28 percent. For men bank tellers it declined faster at first and then similarly to the pattern for women: 14 percent between 1950 and 1960, 18 percent from 1960 to 1970, and 32 percent from 1970 to 1980.

Theoretically, several explanations could account for this decline. On the supply side, the relative experience and education of tellers might have declined. On the demand side, the occupation might have become de-skilled. Finally, incorporating both demand and supply factors, the feminization of the occupation per se might have been partially responsible for its decline in relative earnings.

With respect to experience, again using age as a proxy, we find that the ratio of the median age of both women and men bank tellers to that of all employed women and men was fairly stable over 1950–80. The ratio of the median educational level for women tellers to the level for all women in the experienced work force remained relatively constant over time (see table 1). For men, however, the decline was substantial. Thus for women a reduction in relative educational attainment was probably not one of the factors leading to a reduction in relative salaries for tellers; for men it probably was.

We noted in the earlier discussion of possible skill changes in telling that although the job description for tellers did not change over 1950–80, the verbal and numerical scores given by raters to the telling job declined. Although we are not inclined to interpret this decline in ranking as evidence of a change in job content, we think it may indicate a decline in the verbal and numerical skills required by employers when they hired tellers. Rumberger has shown that if one separates employees' levels of schooling into two categories—that required for the job and that not required (surplus)—the returns to surplus schooling are lower than those for required schooling.[60] It may be that the relative earnings of tellers declined in part because as banking was declassed some tellers' education came to be seen as "surplus" by employers and was therefore rewarded at a lower rate than it had been earlier.

To some extent, the feminization of bank telling per se may have contributed to the decline in its relative earnings. Strober's theory is that occupations that became feminized suffered such a decline as employers sought to realign the wage rates of those occupations in accordance with the wage rates for other comparable female jobs within the firm and within the local labor market.

The relative earnings of female tellers also may have declined during the 1970s because at the same time that bank telling became more feminized, the proportion of the female labor force in female-intensive occupations fell.[61] As noted earlier, there is a negative relationship between the female percentage in an occupation and the wage rate for both men and women in that occupation.[62] It is not surprising then that, as bank telling became a more female occupation at the same time that women were less frequently found in female-intensive occupations, the relative earnings of female tellers should decline. It is particularly interesting that the largest decline in relative earnings for women bank tellers was in 1970–80, the same decade in which the proportion of the female work force in female-intensive occupations fell.

In summary, it is likely that the decline in the relative wages of tellers was a result of the decline in the relative education of male tellers, the decline in educational requirements for tellers, the feminization of telling per se, and the decline in the proportion of the female labor force in other female-intensive occupations.

Conclusion

Bank telling is an example of an occupation that changed its gender designation from male to female. As such, it provides the researcher

60. Russell W. Rumberger, "The Impact of Education on Productivity and Earnings," Institute for Research on Educational Finance and Governance, no. 85-A4 (Stanford University, March 1985).

61. Rytina and Bianchi, "Occupational Reclassification and Changes in Distribution by Gender," p. 16.

62. O'Neill, "Determinants and Wage Effects of Occupational Segregation," p. 34.

with an opportunity to explore four significant aspects of the dynamics of occupational segregation: the causes of a shift in gender assignment from male to female; the changes in the demographic characteristics of men and women employed in an occupation that is becoming female intensive; and the effects of female domination of an occupation on the female-male salary ratio and the occupation's relative wages.

The quantitative and qualitative data on the feminization of telling are consistent with Strober's theory of occupational segregation. During World War II women were hired as tellers to fill the positions of men who left for military service. By and large employers did not make permanent job commitments to these women, but waited to see whether men would wish to reclaim their teller positions. After the war, although employers offered classes for returning veterans, few men appeared interested in teller positions. With bank services expanding rapidly, the number of teller jobs grew and employers filled them with women.

Men left bank telling because other occupations became more attractive to them. Indeed, there is some evidence that telling was de-skilled during the 1930s and it may be that, if not for the Depression, men would have left the occupation before World War II. However, between 1945 and 1980, the bank teller position does seem to have experienced declassing. Although the job tasks remained essentially unchanged during this period, the shift from class to mass banking and the change in the age and gender of the tellers substantially decreased the image and status of telling.

As bank telling became more and more female intensive, the age of tellers declined and the earnings of both men and women tellers declined relative to the average earnings of all men and women. Interestingly, however, the female-male salary ratio for tellers remained remarkably stable.

Case studies of shifts in the gender assignment of occupations provide a fascinating window through which to view the determination of employment and wages. The cases illuminate employer and employee motivations, the interactions between labor and product markets, and the intricate relationships among gender, workers' education levels, job content, and job status. At the same time, they offer an opportunity to enrich economic theories and analyses. By examining cultural and institutional as well as economic factors and qualitative as well as quantitative variables, case studies enable the economist to paint a more realistic and useful picture of the operation of labor markets.

Comments by Elyce J. Rotella

Strober and Arnold have taken on what is undoubtedly the central issue in attempting to understand gender in the workplace, that is, the sexual division of labor. Researchers working in the field have long recognized that the sexual division of labor is both the most important and the thorniest puzzle to be solved if we are to understand the female-male wage differential and indeed all other aspects of economic-social-cultural relations between the sexes.

Given the centrality of this issue, it is sad to have to report that we are still stuck for an answer—certainly at least for a simple answer. Indeed, we are at a disadvantage because our training as economists causes us to prefer simple elegant explanations rather than messy, multicausal ones. The complex phenomenon of the sexual division of labor undoubtedly requires a complex, and therefore uncomfortably messy, explanation. Strober and Arnold clearly recognize this complexity and do not shrink from the task. Indeed, they welcome the complexity, saying that "case studies of shifts in the gender assignments of occupations . . . offer an opportunity to enrich economic theories and analyses."

The authors discuss the pervasiveness and relative constancy of occupational segregation in the U.S. labor force (that is, little change in the index of segregation from 1900 to 1980), though they note a decline from 1970 to 1980 in the percentage of women workers employed in female-intensive occupations—those in which women are more than 60 percent of all workers. They also note the constancy (or at best small change) in the overall female-male earnings ratio since 1930. As we well know, the constancy in segregation and the earnings ratio are in marked contrast to the dramatic change in female labor force participation in the same period. Clearly the vast majority of women who joined the labor force went into low-paying female-intensive jobs. Of course, that is too simple. Many women went into jobs that had not always been women's jobs. Some occupations that had been nearly exclusively male were entered by women and became, within a short period, female intensive. So extreme degrees of occupational segregation were preserved, but some occupations changed their stripes. Strober and Arnold examine one such occupation in detail.

The pervasiveness and constancy of extreme sex segregation of occupations begs for a general explanation, and we are offered a general explanation in this paper. Strober's theory of occupational segregation, as put forth here, is a revision of the ideas set out in her 1984 paper. It is a bold undertaking—taking explicit account of the effects on the labor market of the assumptions and institutions of patriarchy. For all its novelty, however, Strober's theory is firmly grounded in the neoclassical choice theoretic model. What the addition of patriarchy does is to fill out the part of the neoclassical model that is usually left vague, that is, tastes. Strober defines patriarchy in terms of two fundamental principles: "that men are to provide for women, and that men are to have power over women." Given these two principles, Strober argues that it follows that employers will always offer jobs to men first and will only hire women for jobs that men have rejected. Since men will take the best jobs for themselves, women will be crowded into the jobs that men do not want and will earn lower wages.

Strober's theory is very much in the spirit of Becker's "taste for discrimination" model. Her discussion of patriarchy provides a rationale for why employers and male workers have a taste for discriminating against women. The well-known problem with the taste for discrimination model is that it predicts the eventual demise of discrimination because employers with lower tastes for discrimination will hire the cheaper workers, earn higher profits, and over time push out the discriminating employers who have higher costs. The same should happen in Strober's model if there is a distribution among employers of adherence to the patriarchal norms. Essentially Strober must be arguing that there is little or no variation among employers in their willingness to adhere to patriarchal norms or that society has the means and the will to enforce these norms on all those who would violate them.

Strober recognizes that her theory begs the question of why profit-maximizing employers would offer jobs to men when women would take them for lower pay. She argues that it is very costly for employers to violate patriarchal norms by offering women something that men want. Pointing out the analogy between this situation and that of cartel members who have an incentive to chisel, she focuses on the policing mechanism necessary to keep individual employers from violating the implicit agreement to favor expensive male workers over cheaper female workers. She asserts that no external policing mechanism was needed to keep employers in line with patriarchal proscriptions because "patriarchy was considered morally correct," and therefore all of society's institutions played a part in imposing high costs on employers who violated patriarchal norms. Certainly this is an area for future historical research. There must have been many employers who experimented with hiring women for jobs that men may have wanted. In every instance where an occupation changed its sex type, there were employers who were the leaders in employing women. The test for Strober's assertion will be found in the historical laboratory. We must see some instances of experimenting employers suffering the costs Strober predicts and being forced to toe the patriarchical line.

Strober's theory does not focus exclusively on the impact of the patriarchal system on the behavior of employers and male workers. She also notes that patriarchy sets up incentives for women to cooperate with sex segregation because women who work in men's jobs will be subject to sexual harassment and will endanger their prospects for marriage.

The authors, using Strober's theory as a framework, provide a detailed examination of an occupation, bank telling, that underwent the sex change operation in the fairly recent past. In 1935 there were almost no women tellers. By 1950, 45 percent of all tellers were women, and the process continued so that by 1980, 91 percent were women. This then was a rapid and nearly complete transformation. The earlier changes in teaching and clerical work had been similarly rapid and complete. There are few hermaphrodite occupations. Once women successfully entered an occupation held mainly by men, that occupation quickly became one held almost exclusively by women. This rapid change in sex type of occupations is likened by the authors to "tipping" of residential neighborhoods undergoing influx of a racial group, with male flight from the changing occupations seen as analogous to white flight from neighborhoods into which minorities are moving.

I have to wonder whether this is a good analogy despite its obvious appeal. In the case of white flight there is often a block-busting realtor who engineers the initial sale, and the rapid exodus of whites is fueled by fear of falling property values and the rush to get out before their wealth is eroded. To really pursue the tipping analogy we should try to identify the block-buster, that is, someone who has an interest in kicking off the process. The only one I can suggest is the employer. However, in Strober's theory the employer is quite passive, offering all jobs to men and hiring only women when men signal their disinterest. The analogy to white flight does not seem to work well either. One might say that the value of men's human capital is threatened by the entry of women, which causes a rapid exodus. But human capital is attached to the individual in a way that physical capital is not. My impression is that the view of male flight has a problem of historical accuracy. In the cases I know best (and bank telling fits this), occupations that underwent sex change were rapidly growing ones. It is not so much that men already employed left the occupations; rather, women entered at a much greater rate than did men. These rapidly growing occupations developed hierarchies in which the already employed men were promoted to the places at the top. It is as if the whites stayed in the neighborhood but moved to the penthouse apartments.

I suggest that a more fruitful analogy is found in the model describing the diffusion of an innovation. The change in the proportion of women in occupations fits well the familiar S-shaped pattern of diffusion. The first, most risk-tolerant firms experiment with the new innovation (women workers). When the experiment is successful, the knowledge of the innovation is quickly transmitted to other firms who adopt it. Eventually only the most backward firms (or those with severe constraints) will not have adopted the new superior technique.

The authors tell us that the doors to bank telling were opened to women during World War II. In a 1935 study of fifty banks there were no women tellers, though many of these banks employed women in clerical positions. By the 1950 census, 45 percent of all tellers were women. These figures, as well as statements by contemporaries, indicate that wartime labor pressures were crucial for lowering that occupational barrier. It is unfortunate that the unavailability of 1940 figures makes it impossible to know what changes, if any, had taken place before the war. Strober and Arnold believe that the stage was set during the 1930s for the eventual movement of women into bank telling. They argue that in that decade the occupation was "de-skilled," which their analysis implies is a precondition for employing women in an occupation.

From Strober and Arnold's description of bank telling in the 1930s, it does appear that a new, more extensive hierarchy of tellers was developed as banks practiced more specialization and division of labor among their employees. It is not clear that this necessarily means that the level of skill declined. The same process took place in clerical work as the occupation grew and more women were hired, but it is not my impression that the level of skill declined. Rather, I have argued that the movement of women into clerical jobs was associated with a change in the skill mix of the jobs from relatively firm specific to firm general. This facilitated the employment of workers who were expected to have a short tenure with the firm. In this paper we learn that training for bank telling declined from five years of on-the-job training before the war to four to six weeks of full-time study and one month of on-the-job training in 1943. This suggests that the job was transformed from one based primarily on firm-specific skills where training had to be done on the job, partly at the expense of the employer, to one using largely general skills that could be acquired quickly and outside the firm if necessary.

Bank telling seems to be one occupation in which consumer discrimination was important in keeping women out. The 1935 study quoted by Strober and Arnold notes the "foolish prejudice" of bank patrons against women in money-handling positions. It would appear that this strong consumer prejudice was overcome rapidly. Undoubtedly the particular pressures of wartime, which forced people to deal with many unusual situations, were important in overcoming these prejudices. It would be very interesting to look more closely at the process. Did banks mount a public relations campaign to get customers to accept women tellers? Did they perhaps suggest that it was the customer's patriotic duty to put up with women in the teller's cage? Did they piggyback on the government's public relations campaign about the acceptability of women working in other nontraditional jobs? If we knew more about this process, might we not also be able to make some judgments about the strength of society's taste for certain patterns of sex-specific behavior and possible ways to change those tastes?

Of course, the entry of women during the war is only part of the story. We must explain why women tellers were not replaced by men at war's end, as was Rosie the Riveter. Strober and Arnold find the answer to this in the expanded opportunities for men in relatively more attractive jobs. Put simply, the women got to keep their jobs because the men didn't want them. In 1950, when the average male teller made only 106 percent of the wage of the average male earner, male tellers had substantially more education than the average male worker. Clearly there were higher returns to male human capital elsewhere. So they left these jobs to women who were happy to get them. Women tellers made 138 percent of the median earnings of all women workers, but had only 6 percent more education. What were bad jobs for men were good jobs for women. So men left (or more correctly did not enter), women came in, and everyone was better off. This part of the story of bank telling is very much in line with Strober's theory, which says that women's jobs are those that men don't want. Those men who did enter bank telling did so only when they were very young, quickly moving out to other jobs, or moving up in the bank hierarchy.

Strober and Arnold find that the wages of both male and female tellers fell relative to the wages of other workers. This is attributed in part to the fact that the educational requirements for tellers fell, which had a negative effect on wages, especially men's. In addition, they offer a unique explanation for the decline in relative earnings and status of tellers—the occupation "experienced declassing." By this they mean that the status (and presumably the pay) of the occupation fell because banks drew a larger share of their customers from the nonelite segments of the population. This is a tantalizing idea, but one that is difficult to accept uncritically. Certainly an alternative explanation is that as bank customers increased and came to include more members of the nonelite segments of society, the services offered by banks increased and became more standardized, allowing for greater specialization and division of labor and the employment of short-tenured workers in jobs with few firm-specific skills.

Overall, this is a very successful paper. The authors ambitiously tackle the difficult task of developing a general theory of occupational segregation that includes fundamental cultural determinants, and they tell a careful and fascinating story of an important occupation that changed its sex type in a way that is supportive of the theory put forward in the paper.

Comments by Lloyd Ulman

These comments are brief, since my own expertise in the field of bank telling has been acquired solely through experience as an infrequent depositor with persistent withdrawal symptoms. I do wish, however, to register enthusiasm for the type of historical case study of which the paper by Strober and Arnold is an interesting and illuminating example, what the authors characterize as "the dynamics of segregation."

Whether the lack of significant representation of women (or of a particular ethnic or religious group) in a particular occupation is the result of exclusion or of preference (aversion) on the part of the absentees is, of course, formally equivalent to the distinction between involuntary unemployment and preference for nonmarket activity. The Keynesian discriminant applies in the former case as well as in the latter: Is there an excess supply of capable and willing entrants in the ranks of those not employed, at the prevailing relative wage? If so, has discrimination operated to exclude them from a particular employment? Discrimination on whose part—employers, employees, or customers? And finally, under what conditions would the termination of effective discrimination be followed by a virtual monopoly of employment by members of the class that had been previously excluded? These are some of the questions raised and addressed in the paper by Strober and Arnold.

The study in detail of an occupation in which a major tilt or reversal of composition by gender has occurred is valuable in part because, in the absence of economically relevant changes in technology, it holds constant those major human capital requirements (prior educational attainment and occupational experience) that have long been regarded as at least proximate causes of exclusion of women from male-dominated occupations. In the case of bank telling, the authors tentatively conclude that de-skilling may have occurred in the 1920s or 1930s, or well before the wartime period when the massive entry of women began. According to data presented in their table 1, moreover, whereas the median educational level for women and men bank tellers was approximately equal in 1950 (at 12½ years), the mean educational level for all male workers was 2.1 years lower than for all female workers. If comparable relationships prevailed before the war, there presumably would have been an ample supply of sufficiently well educated young women to constitute a major part of a then relatively small occupation. The apparent efficiency with which a new force of tellers was trained in a highly syncopated program during the war (a process that occurred in a considerable variety of occupations) also suggests the prior existence of an excess supply of women who were well qualified to absorb the requisite degree of on-the-job training, just as it invites investigation of the hypothesis that the old five-year training program had served as a screening as well as a training device.

In addition, the fact that the 1939 DOT description includes the supervision of clerks as one of the teller's functions suggests that telling could have been made a promotable position that could have been filled by female clerks, especially if the formal educational attainment of the latter did not differ significantly from that of tellers. It is nevertheless possible that this potential source of supply was composed of female clerks who, while able, were not willing to become tellers. It is possible, for example, that female clerks were more averse than men to assuming the higher levels of responsibility associated with telling. Some light might be shed on this point by reference to research in the general area of sex-typed working roles, but, in the absence of explicit evidence of such aversion, one would doubt that women who were already at work in a directly subordinate position would be reluctant to accept promotion to positions for which prior education and current experience had rendered them well qualified.

If, therefore, willing and able female bank employees had been excluded from telling by discriminatory attitudes, among whom did the latter originate? If it originated predominantly among employers, the most important outcome should have been wage discrimination, as ultimately determined (in a partially competitive market) by those employers with the lowest discrimination coefficients. The essay does present evidence of wage discrimination, although only for the postwar period after female entry had begun to occur on a large scale. If, on the other hand, the main discriminatory thrust originated among male employees, the competitive outcome should have been segregation of the sexes by establishments, rather than exclusion from the entire occupation. The authors, however, single out customer prejudice as the prewar culprit, and, as the quotation from a 1935 report makes clear, this type of phenomenon can readily account for occupational exclusion. Moreover (as the quotation implies), the degree of exclusion resulting from this type of discrimination is likely to be an increasing, rather than a decreasing, function of the degree of product market competition, assuming that the distribution of the discrimination coefficients of customers would be decidedly peaked in the case of a pervasive social prejudice. To the extent that such a prejudice was confined to a fallacious presumption of inferior efficiency (''financial ability''), it could theoretically have been dispelled by the action of an enlightened and penny-pinching monopolist in hiring women and giving them the opportunity to demonstrate the falsity of the assumption. Such an opportunity was in fact ultimately provided by the war and the withdrawal of men from the occupational labor force. The huge increase in the employment of women tellers, in both absolute and relative terms, that occurred in the postwar period without any rise in the relative salary of the men suggests that customer bias before the war was based more on the rebuttable presumption of female inefficiency than on some feeling of outraged propriety that could be suspended only for the duration of the emergency. Instead it was the sort of prejudice that the wartime shortage of male labor helped to eradicate.

But while the ending of customer discrimination might have constituted a necessary condition for the expansion of female employment, it does not suffice to explain why the occupation became almost completely feminized. The authors acknowledge the possibility that the persistence or resumption of employee discrimination—which could now take the form of aversion by men to being outnumbered by women in the occupation—may have deterred male reentry. However, as noted above, segregation by establishment could have occurred, especially in an occupation in which total employment increased as greatly as it did in the postwar period. Moreover, it is not obvious that men should have been averse to working with women in a field in which the principal ornaments of machismo used to be the green eyeshade and the sleeve garter.

In any event, Strober and Arnold prefer what economists would regard as a more straightforward explanation in terms of relative and reservation wages—and, in particular, the superior ability of men to find and fill higher-paid jobs in other occupations. It can be hypothesized that by the end of the war, or shortly thereafter, a large excess supply of labor developed, which permitted a great increase in the demand for and employment of bank tellers to be accompanied by a decline in their relative level of occupational pay. The male-female differential within the occupation remained approximately constant, but the salaries of men tellers sank below their reservation wage (approximated by the authors as the average pay of all male wage and salary earners) some three decades before the lower salaries of women tellers fell below their lower reservation wage. This could have helped to account for the gender tilt—the fact that feminization followed female entry. By the same token, feminization should be less likely to occur in higher-paid occupations where initial levels of pay are higher relative to the men's reservation wage. But neither should masculinization occur in such high-level occupations in the absence of discriminatory restraints. Further work by Strober and Arnold should disclose how the probability of occurrence of this phenomenon is related to the relative salary level of the occupation in question as well as to its rate of growth and, of course, the relative reservation wage levels of the two sexes.

LOURDES BENERÍA

Gender and the Dynamics of Subcontracting in Mexico City

THIS PAPER is based on a study of homework and subcontracting carried out in Mexico City during 1981–82. It explores the dynamics of subcontracting from larger to smaller firms, ending at the level of homework, and analyzes the use of gender as a determining factor in the division of labor and employment patterns. Our fieldwork and data collection for the study took place during a period of transition in the Mexican economy from a short three-year recovery during 1979–81 to the crisis that reached a critical point in the summer of 1982.

With a per capita income of $2,270 in 1982, Mexico is included among the upper middle-income countries in the World Bank's classification. Despite the country's uneven development and inequalities in the distribution of resources and income, industrial production grew rapidly during the 1960s and early 1970s but slowed down during 1975–78. This growth took place under strong inflationary pressures that accelerated during the mid-1970s and continued during the vigorous recovery initiated in 1979.[1] These inflationary pressures, together with the sluggish growth of some key industrial sectors due to the priorities given to the oil sector, were at the root of the difficulties that surfaced in the early 1980s.[2] The decrease in oil prices during this period accelerated Mexico's

The research upon which this paper is based was sponsored by the Ford Foundation in Mexico and the Social Science Research Council, and was done in collaboration with Martha Roldán. Many thanks are due to friends and colleagues who commented on previous versions of this paper, particularly Bettina Berch, Nadine Felton, Caren Grown, Jack Hammond, and Michele Naples.

1. The inflation rate, as measured by the consumer price index, reached a peak of 30 percent in 1977. For more information, see World Bank, *Mexico: Development Strategy—Prospects and Problems,* Internal Report no. 3605-ME (World Bank, August 1981).

2. Rolando Cordera and Carlos Tello, *Mexico, La disputa por la nación: perspectivas y opciones del desarrollo* (Mexico City: Siglo Veintiuno Editores, 1981).

159

foreign debt problems; by 1982 this debt had accumulated to over $50 billion, and the debt service represented 29.5 percent of the country's exports.[3] The resulting pressure on key imports of capital equipment and other inputs continued to represent a bottleneck in the country's development. As a result, the recovery of 1979 came to a halt in 1982, which was symbolized by the devaluation of the peso and the freezing of dollar accounts in August of that year.

This study therefore was carried out at a time of transition from a period of growth to one of crisis in Mexico's development. The process of subcontracting and the increase in women's employment analyzed in the paper need to be placed within this larger context. Some subcontracting arrangements were the result of the substitution of domestic production for imports, a need created by import restrictions. Similarly, the shift of production to lower-wage production levels can be seen as a way of dealing with the continuous inflationary pressures. However, subcontracting responds to a complexity of factors that require a more detailed examination, as will be seen below. Although it is not possible to make generalizations about the extent of Mexican subcontracting from our study, most of the firm representatives we consulted believed that it was on the increase.[4]

The main arguments made in the paper are based on two sets of data (see the Appendix) and can be summarized as follows. First, subcontracting implies a process of decentralization of production in search of lower costs, particularly labor costs, by shifting production to labor market segments increasingly closer to the secondary and informal markets. Second, this facilitates the access to a progressively more flexible labor supply, allowing employers to hire labor without rigid contract restrictions. Third, within the sample of firms studied, the proportion of women employed relative to total employment has been increasing. Fourth, the feminization of certain jobs can be linked to both technical and social skills related to gender. Fifth, women workers are preferred because their wages are lower, but also because gender

3. World Bank, *World Development Report 1984* (New York: Oxford University Press, 1984), p. 249.

4. This appeared to be true particularly for the electronics, clothing, metal, and automobile industries. For earlier years, Watanabe found that 54 percent of total payments for vertical subcontracting were concentrated in textiles, clothing, printing, and food processing. Susumu Watanabe, ed., *Technology, Marketing, and Industrialisation: Linkages between Large and Small Enterprises* (New Delhi: Macmillan, 1983), chap. 8.

characteristics are viewed as having an effect on their performance as workers. Sixth, gender characteristics translate themselves into social skills that are used for the assignment of men and women workers to the existing hierarchy of positions within the labor process.

Theoretical Framework

In recent years, the economics of women in the labor market has been the subject of many studies using different models and theoretical perspectives. This paper is based on two assumptions. One is that the classical model of labor markets based on the smooth functioning of competition is not very helpful in explaining the realities of wage determination and labor market conditions in industrialized societies.[5] The other is that neoclassical models of discrimination are not able to explain women's disadvantaged position in the labor market.[6] In particular, there is a great deal of evidence suggesting that wage differentials between men and women cannot be accounted for by human capital factors assumed to affect productivity.[7] Instead, the evidence suggests that job segregation and differences in the characteristics of jobs normally assigned to men and women are important factors in explaining gender inequality in the labor market.[8]

Thus empirical studies tend to support labor market segmentation

5. See, for example, Richard A. Lester, "Shortcomings of Marginal Analysis for Wage-Employment Problems," *American Economic Review,* vol. 36 (March 1946), pp. 63–82; Peter B. Doeringer, "Determinants of the Structure of Industrial Type Labor Markets," *Industrial and Labor Relations Review,* vol. 20 (January 1967), pp. 206–20; and Lester C. Thurow, *Generating Inequality: Mechanisms of Distribution in the U.S. Economy* (Basic Books, 1975).

6. Francine D. Blau and Carol L. Jusenius, "Economists' Approaches to Sex Segregation in the Labor Market: An Appraisal," in Martha Blaxall and Barbara B. Reagan, eds., *Women and the Workplace: The Implications of Occupational Segregation* (University of Chicago Press, 1976), pp. 181–99.

7. Donald J. Treiman and Heidi I. Hartmann, eds., *Women, Work, and Wages: Equal Pay for Jobs of Equal Value* (Washington, D.C.: National Academy Press, 1981).

8. Mary Stevenson, "Women's Wages and Job Segregation," in Richard C. Edwards, Michael Reich, and David M. Gordon, eds., *Labor Market Segmentation* (D.C. Heath, 1975), pp. 243–55; Francine D. Blau, "Sex Segregation of Workers by Enterprise in Clerical Occupations," in Edwards, Reich, and Gordon, eds., *Labor Market Segmentation,* pp. 257–78; and Marianne A. Ferber and Joe L. Spaeth, "Work Characteristics and the Male-Female Earnings Gap," *American Economic Review,* vol. 74 (May 1984, *Papers and Proceedings, 1983*), pp. 260–64.

theory as an alternative model for an understanding of that inequality. Different authors have shown the usefulness of segmentation theory, in its various versions, along these lines.[9] Similarly, the usefulness of this framework will be seen from the analysis in this paper. Yet a segmentation model has its limitations for an analysis of gender in the labor market. As illustrated, for example, by Buchelle's study of job and pay discrimination in the United States, a segmentation model is useful to show that segregation is pervasive or that women are paid much less than men; yet the study concludes that "none of the variables and parameters that these theories point to really explains why" this is so.[10]

Segmentation theory offers more a *description* than an *explanation* of women's labor market conditions. The analysis does have a gender (and a racial) dimension. Yet gender (and race) are not an integral part of the theory; describing *where* women are located in the labor market and under what conditions does not necessarily explain *why*. Why do women tend to be located in the lower echelons of the labor hierarchy regardless of whether it is the primary or secondary market? What are the general characteristics of the jobs that result in this employment pattern? What are the factors determining the high proportion of women in the segment of homework? These are the types of questions that a description of women's location in the labor market cannot answer.

To be sure, part of the work on segmentation has moved beyond this description; this is the case with the analysis, particularly that by Edwards, of the connection between workers' characteristics and habits on the one hand and the behavioral rules governing different tasks and segments on the other.[11] Yet the analysis of segmentation by gender has continued to be mostly descriptive. Other authors, while using a model of market segmentation, have moved it in a direction that is more promising in terms of answering these questions. One example is provided by Rubery and Wilkinson, who, while analyzing industrial homework as a segment of the labor market, have emphasized the need

9. Blau and Jusenius, "Economists' Approaches to Sex Segregation in the Labor Market"; and Heidi Hartmann, "Capitalism, Patriarchy, and Job Segregation by Sex," in Blaxall and Reagan, eds., *Women and the Workplace,* pp. 137–70.

10. Robert Buchele, "Sex Discrimination and Labour Market Segmentation," in Frank Wilkinson, ed., *The Dynamics of Labour Market Segmentation* (Academic Press, 1981), p. 223.

11. Richard C. Edwards, "The Social Relations of Production in the Firm and Labor Market Structure," in Edwards, Reich, and Gordon, eds., *Labor Market Segmentation,* pp. 3–26.

to focus on the specific structure of female labor supply—a dimension that has been neglected by segmentation theorists.[12] From a different perspective, Ferber and Spaeth have found that a group of characteristics involving control over job-related resources—including the work of others, organizational policies, and monetary resources—together with structural determinants, "have important wage effects over and above the effects of human capital."[13] The authors view their findings as consistent with the dual labor market theory. Yet they move beyond it by providing a more general explanation, rather than a description, of women's labor market conditions. Finally, recent work on segmentation illustrates a change in the discussion "from an emphasis on explaining a fairly stable structure of pay and job inequalities towards an analysis of dynamic changes in labour market structure."[14]

This paper will make use of a segmentation model as it applies to the different subcontracting levels and to job segregation within firms. However, the analysis will be complemented with more specific questions regarding the division of labor and women's employment within firms. In exploring these questions, I will borrow from the theoretical perspective that has been called the labor process approach, rooted in Braverman's work and the literature that has followed, some of which has incorporated more specific gender dimensions in the analysis.[15]

A basic premise in this approach is the view that the capitalist labor process—the organization of production and its corresponding division of labor—tends to be hierarchical, not because it necessarily increases productive efficiency but because, first, it facilitates management control from the top down, and, second, it lowers the wage bill by a process of skill differentiation, de-skilling, and cheapening of less-skilled work. Braverman has described this principle, first elucidated by Charles Babbage in 1832, as "fundamental to the evolution of the division of labor in capitalist society." "Dividing the craft cheapens its individual

12. Jill Rubery and Frank Wilkinson, "Outwork and Segmented Labour Markets," in Wilkinson, ed., *The Dynamics of Labour Market Segmentation*, pp. 115–32.

13. Ferber and Spaeth, "Work Characteristics," p. 261.

14. Wilkinson, *The Dynamics of Labour Market Segmentation*, p. viii.

15. Harry Braverman, *Labor and Monopoly Capital: The Degradation of Work in the Twentieth Century* (New York: Monthly Review Press, 1974); Brighton Labour Process Group, "The Capitalist Labour Process," *Capital and Class*, no. 1 (Spring 1977), pp. 3–26; Tony Elger, "Valorisation and 'Deskilling': A Critique of Braverman," *Capital and Class*, vol. 7 (Spring 1979), pp. 58–99; and Anne Phillips and Barbara Taylor, "Sex and Skill: Notes towards a Feminist Economics," *Feminist Review*, no. 6 (1980), pp. 79–88.

parts" and "gives expression not to a technical aspect of the division of labor, but to its social aspect."[16] That is, fragmentation of tasks and dissociation of labor (a social process) lowers labor costs regardless of its productivity (an economic and technical process).

This implies that the production process cannot be adequately understood only as a system of technical relations without reference to social relations. Therefore an analysis of labor allocation and its corresponding wage structure needs to take both into consideration. The labor process literature has emphasized, for example, that the combination of technological factors and relations of production under capitalism has led to (1) the separation between manual and intellectual labor; (2) a hierarchical control of production through the establishment of a labor hierarchy; and (3) a fragmentation of the work process and de-skilling of labor, or the loss of workers' skills, with the introduction of machinery.[17] A basic point made by Braverman concerns the tendency for information, knowledge, planning, and control of production to be concentrated in the hands of a relatively small minority. At the same time, workers involved in the execution of orders are deprived of any significant degree of control and comprehension of the overall labor process: hence the tendency toward degradation of work under capitalism. Thus, for Braverman, the principles of scientific management espoused by Frederick Taylor are but the expression of a fundamental tendency of capitalist production.

For the purpose of this paper, the advantages provided by this approach are that (1) it focuses on the core of capital-labor relations and therefore on the root of changes in the firm's structure of production and the division of labor; (2) it shifts the analysis from the external market to the labor structure within the firm; (3) it allows in-depth scrutiny of the division of labor in terms of skill requirements and the criteria used to allocate individual workers to specific tasks; and (4) it views the concept of skill not only in relation to a given productive capacity but also as a possible social construct related to a hierarchy of jobs and wages. Finally, in an aspect not taken up in this paper, it can illuminate questions regarding what type of technology is introduced in the workplace.

16. Braverman, *Labor and Monopoly Capital*, pp. 80–81.
17. Braverman refers to de-skilling to describe, for example, the process by which automation and the use of machinery in modern production made craft skills obsolete, thereby requiring a lower level of skill on the part of workers. This loss of skill, he argues, is accompanied by a loss of general knowledge and control over the labor process.

Thus a given position will require a certain array of both technical and social skills on the part of the individual worker who fills it. A large category of positions, particularly those involved with the execution of tasks, appears to involve very little in the way of technical skills, but does involve a very definite set of social skills, such as "rules orientation."[18] These are acquired through a long process of socialization in which factors such as those related to social background, education, race, and gender play a determining role. Social skills, therefore, acquire an economic significance when used for the assignment of workers to given positions. In addition, as Thurow and others have argued, most cognitive job skills, general or specific, are acquired through on-the-job training rather than through formal schooling, as is normally assumed.[19] To the extent that this is so, social skills will also affect on-the-job training.

Subcontracting Links

Mexico's industrialization process offers an example of dependent development in which the role of multinational capital and external financial aid has been very significant.[20] In particular, a high proportion of Mexico's industrial development and international capital is concentrated in Mexico City.[21] A close look at subcontracting processes provides a window into this dependency. For example, although in our sample only eleven firms (16.4 percent) were multinational, over 69 percent of the remaining firms subcontracted from them. However, the proportion of multinational links was underrepresented in the sample because access to the largest firms became very difficult in some cases, particularly within the automobile industry.

Subcontracting also provides a window into a process of decentralization of production parallel to that observed in other countries and on

18. Edwards, "The Social Relations of Production," p. 11.
19. Thurow, *Generating Inequality*, p. 78.
20. It has been estimated that more than one-third of Mexico's industrial production is provided by multinational firms, particularly from the United States. This proportion reaches 40 percent and 60 percent for production of capital equipment and consumer durables, respectively. Cordera and Tello, *Mexico: La disputa por la nación*.
21. For an analysis of the effects of Mexico City's growth on its labor markets and demographic factors, see Brígida García, Humberto Muñoz, and Orlandina de Oliveira, *Hogares y trabajadores en la ciudad de Mexico* (Mexico City: El Colegio de Mexico/ UNAM, 1982).

a world scale.[22] The type of subcontracting encountered was predominantly of a vertical type (in Mexican Spanish, *maquila*), which consists of production carried out for other firms under very specific contract arrangements that include the provision of the raw materials used. (Homework constitutes the last level of subcontracting or, as it is called in Mexico, *maquila domestica*). For the most part, it affects labor-intensive tasks resulting from fragmenting the production process while subcontracting out parts of it to more specialized units.

Table 3 in the Appendix shows the distribution of the firms in the sample by industry and size. The shift of production from larger to smaller firms may involve as few as two levels and, in our sample, a maximum of four.[23] Figure 1 describes a typical subcontracting chain of four levels; production is subcontracted from a large firm to increasingly smaller ones—the last level being the homework distributed, in this case, by a workshop operating illegally from the basement of the owner's home. Employment at the last two levels is occasional and follows the patterns found in the informal sector. Workers in firm C were paid a minimum wage without fringe benefits. However, our estimates show that homeworkers, working always with piece wages, received an average wage equivalent to less than one-third (30.2 percent) of the legal minimum. The ratio of average monthly wages (not including fringe benefits) for unskilled workers engaged in the production of electronic

22. Folker Fröbel, Jürgen Heinrichs, and Otto Kreye, *The New International Division of Labour: Structural Unemployment in Industrialised Countries and Industrialisation in Developing Countries* (Cambridge University Press, 1980); Gioacchino Garofoli, ed., *Ristrutturazione industriale e territorio* (Milan: Franco Angeli, 1978); and Garofoli, "Sviluppo regionale e ristrutturazione industriale: Il modello italiano degli anni '70," paper presented at symposium on "Reflexiones en torno a la economia de los paises mediterraneos desarrollados," Sitges, Spain, September 1983; Fergus Murray, "The Decentralisation of Production—The Decline of the Mass-Collective Worker?" *Capital and Class*, vol. 19 (Spring 1983), pp. 74–99; and Watanabe, *Technology, Marketing, and Industrialisation*.

23. Other researchers have argued that, in Mexico, subcontracting stops at the level of medium-sized firms. Watanabe, for example, has argued that instead of generating a pyramidlike shape as in the case of Japan (with a large number of small firms at the base of the pyramid), Mexican subcontracting resembles a diamond cut, with few small-sized firms engaged in it. (Watanabe, *Technology, Marketing, and Industrialisation*.) Our research, on the other hand, indicates that the pyramid shape can also be found in the case of Mexico, particularly when underground units of production are taken into consideration. A more detailed analysis of this issue is included in Lourdes Benería and Martha Roldán, *The Crossroads of Class and Gender: Industrial Homework, Subcontracting, and Household Dynamics in Mexico City* (University of Chicago Press, 1987), chap. 3.

Figure 1. *Typical Subcontracting Chain*

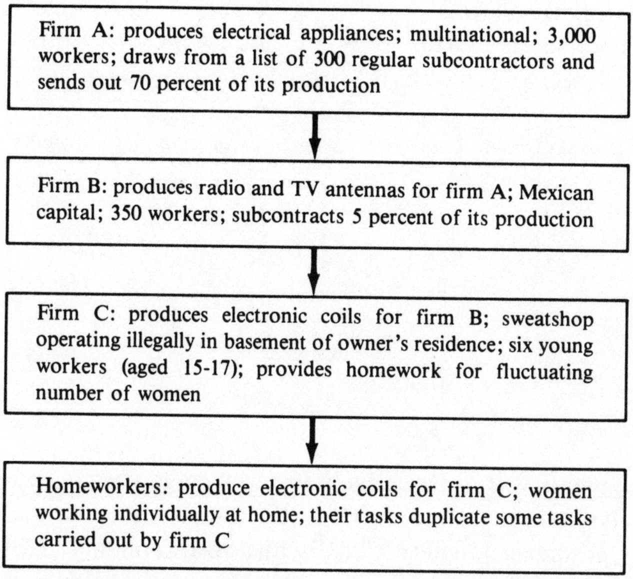

```
┌──────────────────────────────────────────────────────────┐
│ Firm A: produces electrical appliances; multinational; 3,000 │
│ workers; draws from a list of 300 regular subcontractors and │
│ sends out 70 percent of its production                       │
└──────────────────────────────────────────────────────────┘
                            │
                            ▼
┌──────────────────────────────────────────────────────────┐
│ Firm B: produces radio and TV antennas for firm A; Mexican   │
│ capital; 350 workers; subcontracts 5 percent of its production │
└──────────────────────────────────────────────────────────┘
                            │
                            ▼
┌──────────────────────────────────────────────────────────┐
│ Firm C: produces electronic coils for firm B; sweatshop      │
│ operating illegally in basement of owner's residence; six young │
│ workers (aged 15-17); provides homework for fluctuating       │
│ number of women                                              │
└──────────────────────────────────────────────────────────┘
                            │
                            ▼
┌──────────────────────────────────────────────────────────┐
│ Homeworkers: produce electronic coils for firm C; women      │
│ working individually at home; their tasks duplicate some tasks │
│ carried out by firm C                                        │
└──────────────────────────────────────────────────────────┘
```

coils between firm A and homework was estimated to be 6.75:1 (corresponding to chain A in table 1). This ratio typifies the wage disparities encountered between different subcontracting levels; chains B and C in table 1 further illustrate these wage scales—in this case, for two chains in the cosmetics industry of three and two production levels, respectively.

The lowering of labor costs was the most frequent reason given by firms for subcontracting (79 percent of the cases). However, other reasons were mentioned, such as (1) savings in installation of capital equipment (75 percent of the cases); (2) allowing the firm to separate and send out the production of simple tasks (72 percent); (3) avoidance of labor problems (41 percent);[24] (4) avoidance of a larger firm requiring additional financial and organizational resources (33 percent);[25] and (5) dealing with cyclical or unstable production (21 percent).

In any case, subcontracting can be seen as a shift of production to

24. In particular, small firms of close to twenty workers were concerned with unionization of their work force, given that this is the limit set by Mexican law, beyond which unionization is required.

25. This was mentioned by relatively small firms operating on the basis of family business and by firms expressing concern over the economic crisis facing Mexico at the time of our fieldwork.

Table 1. *Average Monthly Wages for Manual Workers,*
by Subcontracting Level, 1981
Wages in 1981 Mexican pesos (23 = $1)

Subcontracting level	Chain A Wages	Chain B Number of workers	Wages	Chain C Number of workers	Wages
1	12,000	2,500	11,000	2,500	11,000
2	8,500	50	5,880	20[a]	3,000
3	5,880	5[b]	1,776	c	. . .
4	1,776	. . .	. . .	. . .	. . .
Wage ratio between highest and lowest levels	6.75:1	. . .	6.19:1	. . .	3.67:1

a. Underground workshop.
b. Homework.
c. No homework in this chain.

labor market fragments with progressively lower average wages. At a given boundary, it also represents a shift from the formal to the informal sector or to underground economic activity, with a corresponding sharp drop in wages, disappearance of fringe benefits, and intensification of the factors normally associated with the secondary labor market, such as unstable work and poor working conditions. The boundaries between the two sectors are often fuzzy; while homework is always an underground activity, many workshops and small units operate on the borderline—with, for example, a legal storefront that pays taxes and minimum wages and an underground "backyard" that does not. However, the linkages between the sectors are direct and clear, a fact that contradicts the notion of a dual economy with separate and independent sectors.[26]

Despite the separate production and labor market segments, the overall picture emerging from a close observation of subcontracting links is that of a hierarchy of interconnected units of production. The great bulk of subcontracting in the sample ultimately depended on multinational firms—except in the garment, food, textile, and some of the metal-sector industries, in which subcontracting is initiated by Mexican capital. This dependency can be observed through the monopsonistic power enjoyed by large firms, which generates an intense competition among small subcontractors to obtain production contracts from them.

26. For an elaboration of this point, see Benería and Roldán, *The Crossroads of Class and Gender,* chap. 4.

This in turn has its effects on other dimensions of this hierarchy. In addition to differences in wage rates, disparities between firms at different subcontracting levels exist regarding other factors, such as working conditions, access to financial and other resources, level of technology, and work stability. Working conditions—evaluated in terms of services available to workers, light, working space, safety measures, and temperature level—deteriorate as one moves down the subcontracting pyramid. Similarly, work stability diminishes at the lower levels of subcontracting; while restrictions against firing workers in Mexico are rather severe, they are quite meaningless in the informal sector, particularly for underground activities. In addition, smaller firms make frequent use of a law that allows them to hire workers for a twenty-eight-day contract, after which employment can be terminated.

Finally, this hierarchy of firms increases the range of options available to those that send production out. Subcontracting amounts to having more choices regarding the location of production and its corresponding division of labor. In particular, it expands the mechanisms for meeting the firm's demand for labor and the conditions under which labor is hired, thus giving the firm access to a more elastic labor supply.

Theoretically, it should be noted that most analyses (orthodox and nonorthodox) of productive and labor market hierarchies have concentrated on hierarchies *within* the firm. To some extent, segmentation theory is an exception, since the different segments are related to a hierarchy of wages and labor market conditions. Yet segmentation analysis focuses more on the noncompetitiveness created by the existence of compartmentalized market segments than on the connections *among* firms with the corresponding hierarchy at the macro level suggested by my analysis.

The Dynamics of Women's Employment

There is growing evidence that the latest phase in the internationalization of capital, which has taken place since the mid-1960s, has resulted in the employment of a high proportion of women.[27] A high concentration of women workers can be found not only in the more traditional "women's industries" such as garments and textiles; women are also

27. Fröbel, Heinrichs, and Kreye, *The New International Division of Labour.*

employed increasingly in the electrical or electronics, metal, and chemical industries.[28] Most studies have called particular attention to the concentration of women workers in free-trade zones and in areas with a heavy concentration of foreign investment, such as the U.S.-Mexican border.

One question is the extent to which the trend toward an increase in female employment can also be observed in an industrial center, such as Mexico City, that is more oriented toward a national market, where national capital plays an important role and coexists alongside multinational investment. A subsequent question deals with the factors affecting the employment of women and the role played by gender in differentiating men and women workers.

Within our sample of firms, the proportion of women employed was, on average, higher among those with less than one hundred workers than among the larger firms (see figure 2). That is, the smaller firms tend to be more "feminized"; this feminization was practically complete for homework.[29] The apparent exception to this trend in the sample was for firms above 1,000 workers. However, the proportion of women in this case is very likely to be overestimated because the sample does not include some of the largest firms in the automobile and metal sectors that were at the top levels of the subcontracting pyramid;[30] the low proportion of women employed in these industries would have lowered the figures for the group of firms above 999 workers. The relative number of women employed therefore increases as employment becomes progressively less formal and more labor intensive. The data in table 2, on the other hand, show that over 40 percent of the firms reported a tendency to employ a higher proportion of women during the three preceding years or under current plans at the time of the fieldwork. The trend toward an increase in female employment was found particularly among firms whose work force was 30 percent or more female. In some firms,

28. Helen I. Safa, "Runaway Shops and Female Employment: The Search for Cheap Labor," *Signs: Journal of Women in Culture and Society,* vol. 7 (Winter 1981), pp. 418–33; Diane Elson and Ruth Pearson, "The Subordination of Women and the Internationalization of Factory Production," in Kate Young, Carol Wolkowitz, and Roslyn McCullagh, eds., *Of Marriage and the Market: Women's Subordination in International Perspective* (London: CSE Books, 1981); and June Nash and Maria Patricia Fernández-Kelly, eds., *Women, Men, and the International Division of Labor* (Albany: State University of New York Press, 1983).

29. During our fieldwork, we encountered only two exceptions of male homeworkers.

30. As stated earlier, this was due to difficulties in obtaining data from these firms.

Figure 2. *Proportion of Women Workers, by Firm Size*

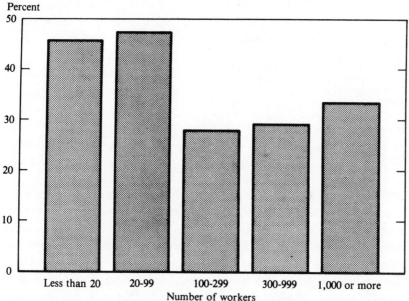

the feminization of the work force was taking place at a rapid pace. To illustrate, the proportion of women workers in a firm of fifty workers producing and assembling plastic goods under subcontracting arrangements shifted from 25 percent to 75 percent in the period of one year. This change was parallel to the restructuring of the labor process with the introduction of more automatic machines and a moving line for assembly work. The manager expressed optimism about the employment of women. As he noted, the trend was new; it was also pointed out by other observers.[31]

It is interesting to note that this trend toward the increased employment of women was also found in industries that previously had employed very few women. For example, a metal firm (a previous multinational now controlled by Mexican capital) shifted from zero to 20 percent female employment in a period of three years. The shift took place after a series of tests that showed women to have higher productivity than men. They were found to be particularly more productive in assembly tasks that required "a high degree of concentration, patience, and

31. See, for example, the June 1981 newsletter *Panorama Económico*, published by Bancomer, one of the largest Mexican banks.

Table 2. *Increases in Female Employment*[a]

Percent of women in firm's work force	Number of firms	Number of workers employed	Percent of firms reporting increase in proportion of women employed[b]
10 percent or less	12	2,892	23.5
10–29	9	2,154	33.3
30–49	12	4,639	42.8
50 or more	26	4,085	51.8

a. For firms that registered an increase in the proportion of women employed between the summer of 1981 and that of 1982, the table refers to the figures given in 1982.
b. During the three years before the interview or under plans at the time.

physical 'immobility' for long periods of time," according to the firm's representative. Women were clustered in the tasks where they replaced men. Women were also found to be more productive in some types of supervisory work, such as quality control. In this case, however, management decided against replacing men with women because "men did not take well the directives coming from women in positions of quality control." Another example was that of a manufacturer of electrical equipment with ambitious plans for expansion as a result of joint ventures with an Italian multinational: after employing no women (other than clerical personnel), the firm had plans to begin hiring them, particularly in a new plant of 600 workers. One year after the first interview, the old plant (of over 100 workers) did not yet employ women as production workers, but the new plant had a 40 percent female work force.

Several related issues require further investigation. If women's employment is increasing, what factors affect this trend and what types of jobs are women filling? To begin with the last question, it is useful to distinguish among three types of job categories. In the first, women replace men without any change in the nature of the job. To illustrate, in a cosmetics multinational of 2,500 workers, women have been replacing men in accounting, sales, and middle-management tasks; for most of these jobs, there appears to be no change in the job content and degree of responsibility associated with it. However, in some cases, a subtle distinction has been introduced when the same job is subject to a redistribution of supervisory tasks. In this case, a new supervisor is appointed to oversee the jobs that become "feminized," thus decreasing the relative responsibility and ranking of the job.

Second, there are instances in which the nature of the job changes mostly through the introduction of new technology or the restructuring of the labor process, or both. The introduction of automatic plastic injection machines to replace manual machines is often accompanied by putting the machine under the care of women—a job that had been male. In the same way, the introduction of a moving line or a conveyor in the assembling of consumer durables is for many firms an opportunity to replace men with women. In both cases, there is a degree of de-skilling taking place (see below) even when it is not accompanied with a lower wage.

Third, there are jobs that are defined as female jobs from the outset; this has been the case in the more traditional female industries, such as garment and textiles, but can also be observed in the new industries, such as electronics. In these instances, the increase in the employment of women is due to the dynamics of subcontracting rather than to their substituting for men.

In all three cases, the question of why women are hired needs to be investigated further. Given that hiring can be observed in traditional as well as nontraditional women's tasks, a general conceptualization of the reasons behind the increase in women's employment is necessary. There are several types of factors behind this increase, which can be classified within two main categories: lower wages for women and assumed characteristics of women workers.

Lower Wages

Given the same productivity, lower wages for women may be the result of wage discrimination or of occupational segregation. In our study, wage discrimination, or unequal pay for equal work, was difficult to detect because interviewees (mostly middle-to-top management, other professionals and technicians, or heads of workshops and owners of small firms) would not report it. However, there were indirect indications of its existence. To illustrate, an executive from the personnel department of a large cosmetics firm pointed out that "for each job, there is a minimum and a maximum salary—depending upon seniority, productivity, and other factors. Women tend toward the minimum and men toward the maximum; women, in particular, see their salary as a complement to family income and accept lower pay." Similar situations were detected in other firms, affecting young women workers in particular. However, the extent of this type of discrimination can not be systematically documented from the data.

Contrary to the difficulties encountered in the reporting of wage discrimination, the clustering of women in specific jobs with relatively low pay was widespread and commonly reported because, in this case, firms tend to see the lower pay as justifiable and related to a variety of reasons—the jobs' requirements of lower skill and less physical strength were the most commonly given. For example, a large firm producing electrical appliances had women clustered in the assembling of parts for the production of irons, fans, and radio and TV sets. Women assembled parts and the finished body of irons, and both men and women assembled fans, although performing different tasks. Radios and TV sets had women assembling the minute parts—coils, and wires attached to the screen, for example—while men concentrated on the final stages of assembling. Similarly, the assembling of larger electrical appliances, such as refrigerators and washing machines, was entirely men's work. Women mostly worked sitting down and within very limited and crowded spaces, while men's working areas were spacious and allowed physical mobility. Although it was all assembly work, the clustering of tasks by gender was associated with lower pay for women.

This type of wage differential was prevalent in firms where women and men were segregated in clusters performing different jobs. It was consistently justified by pointing out that men's tasks required greater physical strength and mechanical knowledge. Yet, when asked why they hired women for assembly work (and for other tasks), employers stressed women's "greater dexterity" and "manual ability" (see below). These characteristics, while clearly recognized as skills, were not seen as deserving the same reward as physical strength and mechanical ability.

Lower wages for women are also associated with part-time or intermittent full-time employment, both of which are more prevalent at the lower levels of subcontracting. Homework is the most prominent example of highly unstable and mostly part-time work; it also consistently represents the lowest-paid work. The estimated average wage for a forty-eight-hour week was 444 pesos, which amounted to less than one-third of the minimum wage. However, homeworkers usually do not work the equivalent of a full-time job; the average reported was twenty-four hours a week. For garment homeworkers (the best paid) the average wage was 1,010 pesos, about 69 percent of the legal minimum. On the other hand, temporary full-time work was common in the case of small subcontractors who either made use of a law allowing twenty-eight-day contracts (at minimum wage levels) or were operating underground (at wages below the minimum). Women workers were prevalent in both cases.[32]

To sum up, the increase in female employment associated with lower women's wages can take place particularly through three types of changes: the shifting of production to lower subcontracting levels or labor market segments; the restructuring of the production process and changes in the nature of jobs that lead to a redefinition of new job clusters as female; and defining tasks as female in new industries, such as electronic coil making. All three were at work in our sample of subcontracting and offer the most plausible explanation for the increase in women's employment.

Assumed Characteristics of Workers

When asked about the reasons for hiring women, firm representatives hardly mentioned lower wages. Instead, they referred to specific qualities of women as workers. The table below shows the breakdown of the most frequent answers to the question ''what advantages do you see in hiring women?''

Reported characteristics of women workers	Percent of firms
Reliability and work stability	47.4
Careful manual work	27.8
Discipline and patience	21.4
Ability to follow orders	15.9
Productivity	4.5
Less troublesome	3.8

Each of these answers needs some clarification. First, the most common example of reliability given was women's lower rate of absenteeism, particularly on Mondays when absenteeism among male workers is very high due to weekend drunkenness: a minority of employers mentioned a rate as high as 30 percent, but the problem was mentioned in many cases. In the electronics industry, turnover rates were also

32. To illustrate, a small subcontractor working for the pharmaceutical and cosmetics industries listed thirty to sixty workers as the oscillating number of employees working according to the availability of contracts. The average age of workers was 20 and women represented 80 percent of the firm's work force; according to the firm's manager, ''young women are ideal for short-term employment.''

reported to be lower among women.[33] Some employers mentioned that single mothers are among their "best workers" because their responsibility as head of a household implies that they cannot rely on anybody else for family subsistence (even when they may rely on the extended family for child care).

Second, more careful manual work mostly referred to the handling of objects: when assembly work is involved, women are said to have more patience and greater dexterity in handling meticulous work and small parts. This is of course the traditional nimble-fingers argument, which was alive and well in our sample of respondents as well as elsewhere in Mexico; the June 1981 Bancomer newsletter affirms (with no evidence given) that women's "dexterity in both hands is 75 percent greater than men's."[34] This is argued in relation to women's assembly work in the electronics industry in Mexico, where 80 percent of the work force is female, and is written in the spirit of a new discovery of the advantages of hiring women workers.

Third, with regard to discipline, patience, and ability to follow orders, the answers given clustered around two types of examples. One was that women are more able than men to sit for long periods of time without becoming restless. The other was that women tend to be less mechanical and, unlike men, do not touch the machines when they break down. This implies that, by relinquishing mechanical knowledge to a supervisor, control over the machine and the labor process becomes more centralized. This example suggests that, in this case, there is an element of de-skilling in the process of substituting women for men: the new worker is preferred because she does not exercise the same degree of mechanical control over the machine. Therefore a process of centralization of knowledge is taking place very much along the lines described by Braverman. The feminization of these types of tasks results both from technical factors and from the social characteristics of women as workers.

Fourth, although the proportion of firms that mentioned women's higher productivity is small, this answer is of particular interest in terms of breaking stereotypes regarding women as workers. It can also explain the cases in which the replacement of men with women did not imply, according to the firm, a lower wage.

Finally, women were said to be less troublesome than men in raising

33. Bancomer, *Panorama Económico*, June 1981.
34. Ibid.

demands about working conditions and in involvement with union activity. Although only a few employers mentioned this factor, the information gathered is likely to have been biased because questions dealing with unions were usually a source of tension in the interview. In any case, this factor, together with women's discipline and tendency to follow orders, has much in common with the stereotype of women as "submissive and docile workers." This raises the question as to whether these are actual or perceived characteristics.

Gender Traits and Women's Employment

The characteristics of women workers listed above reflect the use of common stereotypes about women, or gender traits acquired through their socialization or gender formation—ranging from learning to work with "nimble fingers" by sewing and embroidering at home to being socialized to please and serve, follow orders, work in reduced spaces, and accept subordinate positions. The important question here is how and for what purpose gender traits can be used in the workplace. Thus the reasons reported by firms for hiring women fall into three categories.

First, to the extent that these reasons refer to a source of increased productivity, they provide an argument based on economic rationality. That is, women are hired because they are perceived to be more efficient; firms' answers mention productivity directly or in a mediated form such as "work stability" or "careful manual work." Second, to the extent that the reasons are about perceptions of women as more patient and disciplined, less troublesome, and better able to follow orders, they support easier management control. This is particularly important when more centralized controls are introduced—such as with moving lines— and when mechanical skills become more concentrated in a few supervisory positions while other tasks are subject to de-skilling. Third, these reasons can provide a rationalization for placing women in specific jobs and female clusters. In a hierarchical organization of production, criteria need to be designed to assign workers to the different echelons of the labor structure. While skill criteria such as educational credentials, experience, and seniority are accepted criteria, use of gender (and race) is viewed as discriminatory unless it is justified by some form of rationalization; this is the function that gender traits can play. Thus reported characteristics such as "reliability," "careful manual work," and "discipline" can be used to provide a rationale for the firm to allocate women to electronic assembly work and men to (better-paid) assembly of large electrical appliances.[35] Similarly, the predominance of women in industrial homework responds to their concentration in household activities and child care, a role also resulting from a social construction of gender.[36]

All this implies that gender traits can be translated into *actual skills*—as with women's garment work, for which they are trained by doing similar tasks at home. On the other hand, gender traits may be merely *perceived* or falsely *assumed* without corresponding to any actual differential skill between men and women. Thus the assumption that women are more disciplined or less troublesome workers may be an example of a perceived trait; as other authors have argued, docility may be a mirage that can disappear when authoritarian structures break down.[37] In the same way, women may raise fewer demands for wage increases if they perceive themselves as secondary wage earners.

Finally, given that gender traits are not natural or universal but socially acquired, they can be used as an ideological tool working in opposite directions: what justifies calling a given task or occupation "female" under specific circumstances may change over time or across cultures and economic conditions—as history has shown repeatedly.[38]

35. The following quote from an economist working in the sales section of a home appliances firm of 250 workers provides a poignant summary of the use of gender in the workplace: "Women are at lower levels in production and are paid less because employers understand that their wages are for their individual needs whereas a man has to cover more expenses, particularly if he is married. There are few women who can move beyond the level of unskilled work; a woman has the burden of her children and has no time to get an education so as to be promoted. For promotion we look for men. It is assumed that women are dependent, even if only from a psychological point of view. Given that she has no time to educate and advance herself, she knows that she cannot aspire to more. Women's opportunity to distinguish themselves depends also on their beauty; a beautiful young woman working on a conveyor line might become a secretary because of her looks. A young woman better prepared but less beautiful will find that promotion more difficult and she will have to compensate by greater efficiency on the job. In men we only look for efficiency and loyalty."

36. For a more detailed analysis of the concentration of women in industrial homework, see Benería and Roldán, *The Crossroads of Class and Gender,* chap. 4.

37. Noeleen Heyser, "From Rural Subsistence to an Industrial Peripheral Work Force," in Lourdes Benería, ed., *Women and Development: The Sexual Division of Labor in Rural Societies: A Study* (Praeger, 1982), pp. 179–202.

38. Along the U.S.-Mexican border, assembly plants have begun to employ men in a clear shift from previous practices. This has been attributed to a rising labor demand but also to a deliberate policy to employ men because, according to the president of

A remaining question in this analysis has to do with why an increase in women's employment was taking place in this particular period in Mexican development. Although it is not possible to generalize from this study, it points toward three types of factors. One is the trickle-down effect of the increasing employment of women by multinational firms, as mentioned earlier. An emulating mechanism seems to be at work once some specific tasks and occupations have been filled by women in the larger and more modernized firms. This is parallel to a second factor that affects both demand and supply, namely, a change in attitude toward greater acceptance of women's participation in the labor market. Men and women alike spoke of this as representing a profound change in Mexican society.[39] Finally, a third factor is related to the need to tap new sources of cheap labor—as done through subcontracting—at a time of economic crisis and intense international competition in labor-intensive production.

Concluding Comments

It can be argued that the shift of production toward more informal and underground units gives the economic system a great deal of flexibility in expanding and contracting the productive capacity of the small business sector. For this reason, different authors have suggested that, given the high proportion of active labor in the informal sector in third world countries, this flexibility might be important in building an infrastructure of small firms that would provide a basis for growth. The most positive contribution of this sector is that it stimulates the development of small businesses that are more adaptable to the economic conditions prevalent in these countries, and it creates the basis for

---

the Association of the Border Assembly Plants, the area had become a "matriarchy." The policy objective is to increase the proportion of male workers to 60 percent by the end of the decade. See Richard J. Meislin, "Mexican Border Plants Beginning to Hire Men," *New York Times*, March 19, 1984. Although this objective may be difficult to reach, it illustrates the imposition of ideology over labor market trends.

39. This is not to say that the more traditional attitudes have totally disappeared; 5 percent of the homeworkers in our sample reported that their main reason for doing homework was the husband's opposition to their working outside of the home.

fostering and channeling entrepreneurial skills and developing other productive forces.[40]

However, there are limits to this optimistic view. At least for the small businesses associated with subcontracting, a dynamic development of this sector is highly dependent on the large firms in which it originates; it will be self-sustaining only to the extent that the general development of the country is. In addition, the small businesses' permanence in the market is constantly threatened by the competition of larger firms and the tendency toward economic concentration. From labor's perspective, this form of decentralized production implies a recomposition of the industrial working class toward the more marginal workers, with important gender dimensions, and in a way that intensifies labor's weaknesses rather than its strength. In fact, the development of this sector is built precisely on labor's low pay and general vulnerability.

Other implications can be derived from this paper. At the theoretical level, it suggests that a close analysis of changes in the labor process is useful to understand the dynamics of segmentation and women's employment. In particular, and in order to search for an explanation rather than a description of women's location in the labor hierarchy, this analysis needs to focus on how gender is used as an allocative factor in the division of labor—not only within the firm but across firms throughout subcontracting chains or market segments. That is, the dynamics of employment result from a combination of technical and social relations in which gender plays an important role.

In terms of policies dealing with gender inequality in the workplace, the analysis in this paper suggests two directions. One is related to the question of how skills are defined and workers assigned to specific tasks. By what criteria are some skills ranked as being superior to others? Why is it that women's jobs are defined in such a way that they tend to be placed at the bottom of skill hierarchies and below male jobs? Why is "physical strength" associated with wages higher than those associated

40. For example, a portion of the literature on the informal sector has taken this position. See Hans W. Singer, "Dualism Revisited: A New Approach to the Problems of the Dual Society in Developing Countries," *Journal of Development Studies,* vol. 7 (October 1970), pp. 60–75; and International Labour Office, *Employment, Incomes and Equality: A Strategy for Increasing Productive Employment in Kenya* (Geneva: Imprimeries Populaires, 1972). As pointed out by Doeringer in his comments below, secondary labor markets "may foster generic strengths" such as "the ability to mobilize informal sources of credit, the development of a flexible reserve production capacity, and the potential for import substitutions. . . ."

with "manual dexterity" in assembly work? Assuming a large supply of labor in both types of skills—an assumption that is probably realistic for Mexico City—it seems reasonable to argue that the wage differential is not due to supply factors but to the ranking of skills. The need to question the criteria behind this ranking—very much along the lines of comparable worth principles—becomes obvious. In addition, it is also important to question whether men and women do not have (or cannot acquire) the physical strength or the manual dexterity attributed to the opposite sex.

A second direction for policy derives from questioning the necessity of a hierarchical organization of production. Comparable worth policies assume a given hierarchy in the structure of production. Yet there are political and economic reasons for not taking it as a given. The political reasons derive from questioning the capital-labor relation and aim either at eliminating or reducing the corresponding hierarchical organization of production. This requires institutional changes toward cooperative and more democratic forms of production. Women are likely to benefit from a flattening of the labor pyramid because it would reduce the need to use gender traits as a rationalizing factor in the division of labor. To the extent that there is a political and a social aspect to productivity, as has been argued by many authors,[41] there are also economic reasons for not taking this hierarchy as a given. If this assumption is correct, productive arrangements that increase workers' control among medium-sized and small business and subcontractors could provide an avenue to increase their productivity and wages. This would represent an alternative that would have the advantages of a decentralized and flexible sector without the negative aspects for labor outlined above.

Appendix

The analysis in this paper is based on two sets of data, one from a series of formal in-depth interviews with 140 women homeworkers, and the other from interviews with managers, technicians, or other representatives of 76 firms of different size and sectors engaged in subcontracting.

41. See, for example, Samuel Bowles, David M. Gordon, and Thomas E. Weisskopf, *Beyond the Waste Land: A Democratic Alternative to Economic Decline* (Anchor Press/Doubleday, 1983); and Michele I. Naples, "The Unraveling of the Union-Capital Truce in the U.S. Industrial Productivity Crisis," *Review of Radical Political Economics*, vol. 18 (Spring–Summer 1986), pp. 110–31.

Table 3. *Mexican Firms in Sample, by Industry and Number of Workers*

| | Number of workers in firm | | | | | |
Industry	19 or less	20–99	100–299	300–999	1,000 or more	Total	Percent of total
Electrical/electronics	3	2	2	3	0	10	14.9
Consumer durables	1	0	1	3	5	10	14.9
Cosmetics	1	2	0	2	1	6	8.9
Plastics	6	9	2	0	0	17	25.4
Metal	2	3	0	3	0	8	11.9
Garment/textiles	5	1	0	0	1	7	10.5
Other[a]	5	3	0	0	1	9	13.4
Total	23	20	5	11	8	67	99.9
Percent of total	34.3	29.8	7.5	16.4	12.0	100.0	

a. Glass, toys, and decoration of glass and plastic containers.

Whenever possible, the interviews included visits to the site of production—repeated, for some firms, during the summers of 1981 and 1982.

Sequentially, the interviews with homeworkers took place first. A random process of selection for our sample was not possible, given the scant information about the universe of homework in Mexico City. (Although there are no laws against homework in Mexico, it is de facto an underground operation because legal requirements of minimum wages and payments of fringe benefits and taxes are not met.) We located the homeworkers by inquiring in neighborhood locations such as markets, shops, and health centers in different neighborhoods in Mexico City. Once a homeworker was located, she often provided a lead to others. We have therefore a nonprobability, purposive sample.

Similarly, information about the firms visited was obtained by following subcontracting links—normally starting at the level of homework, jobber, or workshop. An effort was made to concentrate on nontraditional types of industrial homework rather than the more traditional garment work; the type of tasks included in the sample ranged from assembly work for several industries (28.6 percent of the cases), to plastic polishing (27.1 percent), textile finishing (11.4 percent), packing (5.7 percent), and others (including a proportion of 11.4 percent of garment work that was included mostly for comparative purposes since it had been studied by other researchers and was better known.)[42]

42. See, for example, José Antonio Alonso, "The Domestic Seamstresses of

Comments by Alice H. Amsden

The subject of Benería's paper is homework and subcontracting in Mexico City in 1981–82 and the use of gender as a determining factor in the division of labor and employment patterns. The object of the paper, however, is to explore "the dynamics of subcontracting from larger to smaller firms." The reader would have benefited if Benería had stated from the outset the questions she wished to address. Instead, the author begins with a summary of her six main arguments. These are: First, subcontracting implies a process of decentralization of production in search of lower costs. Second, subcontracting facilitates access by employers to a labor supply that is unprotected by legislation. Third, within the sample of firms studied, women's share of total employment has been rising. Fourth, the feminization of certain jobs can be linked to both technical and social skills related to gender. Fifth, women workers are preferred because their wages are lower and gender characteristics are viewed as having an effect on their performance as workers. Sixth, gender characteristics translate themselves into social skills that are used for job assignment in the existing job hierarchy.

These arguments do not exist at the same level of abstraction. The first three are more or less factual, whereas the last three qualify as hypotheses. The last three are very interesting and are the focus of much of the paper. Since they were introduced as arguments, however, it would have been helpful if they had been treated as such.

The author proceeds to her theoretical framework and states that her paper is based on two assumptions: the classical model of labor markets based on smooth functioning of competition is unhelpful in explaining labor market conditions in industrializing societies, and the neoclassical models of discrimination are not able to explain women's disadvantaged position. Instead, empirical studies (with references, incidentally, to only industrialized societies) tend to support labor market segmentation theory as an alternative model for understanding inequality. The author notes, quite correctly, that segmentation theory is more descriptive than analytical. It fails to answer the "whys," like "why do women tend to be located in the lower echelons of the labor hierarchy regardless of

Nezahualcoyotl: A Case Study of Feminine Overexploitation in a Marginal Urban Area'' (Ph.D. dissertation, New York University, 1979).

whether it is the primary or secondary market?'' This, in effect, is the question that Benería addresses with respect to subcontracting in Mexico City. But she does not say so. Instead, she says that her essay "will make use of a segmentation model as it applies to the different subcontracting levels and to job segregation within firms.'' However, after this reference her essay makes no use of the segmentation model and we hear nothing more of it. Benería could have presented her insights more sharply had she made some attempt to tie together her discussions of theory and subcontracting. It would also have been interesting for the reader to have had a discussion of the large segmentation literature related to developing countries.

Benería's arguments are based on two sets of data, one from a series of formal in-depth interviews with 140 women homeworkers, and the other from interviews with managers, technicians, or other representatives of 76 firms of different size and sectors engaged in subcontracting. The author uses these data to show that feminization of employment is high and probably rising, particularly among smaller subcontractors. This leads to the question of the role played by gender in differentiating men and women workers in the subcontracting process.

According to Benería, feminization of employment is on the rise because women are paid less than men (either because of crowding or unequal pay for equal work). Additionally, they are hired because they are perceived, rightly or wrongly, to be better than men because they are more dexterous, or docile, or diligent, for example. Why, if they are perceived as being better, are they paid less? She answers the question by posing another one: "The important question here is how and for what purpose gender traits can be used in the workplace.'' Her answer seems to be that their purpose is to help employers make job assignments:

> In a hierarchial organization of production, criteria need to be designed to assign workers to the different echelons of the labor structure. While skill criteria such as educational credentials, experience, and seniority are viewed as rational, use of gender (and race) is viewed as discriminatory unless it is justified by some form of rationalization; this is the function that gender traits can play. Thus, reported characteristics such as "reliability,'' "careful manual work,'' and "discipline'' can be used to provide a rationale for the firm to allocate women to electronic assembly work and men to (better-paid) assembly of large electrical appliances.

Benería seems to be arguing that in a hierarchical organization, when a job becomes available and a job applicant appears at the door, gender traits serve to rationalize the assignment of women to lower-paying jobs.

Without such rationalization, hierarchical firms would have to admit to practicing discrimination.

This strikes me as an argument for an advanced country. It suggests that discrimination was unacceptable behavior in Mexico City in 1981–82. Why not simply test a hypothesis to the effect that subcontracting the world over tends to be crushingly competitive and is likely to have been especially so in profit-torn Mexico in the early 1980s? Under the circumstances, women workers are preferred to either machines or men because they are cheaper and, by comparison with men, are perceived as being more docile and dexterous. In the face of an unlimited supply of such labor (an assumption of classical rather than either neoclassical or segmented labor market theory), the purpose of gender traits is to act as a global signaling device to firms about where to locate their plants. The inferred supply and demand relationships, rooted in deep and long-standing sexism, are what drive subcontracting internationally.

Comments by Peter B. Doeringer

This paper presents interesting and original research on the changing structure of production between large firms and subcontractors in Mexican manufacturing industries and on the changing gender mix in manufacturing. It attempts to place this research into a "labor process–labor control" framework to show how "secondary" labor markets emerge. The empirical findings, however, show that more traditional economic explanations—factor costs, productivity, and efficiency—are the main motivations behind the restructuring of production and the employment of women.[43]

Turning to the more detailed research findings, the major contribution is the documentation of Mexico's elaborate, multitiered subcontract

43. In an earlier version of this paper, a stronger case for the labor process–labor control thesis was offered by the author when she concluded that the organization of market production closely parallels that of family economic production. The subordinate role of women with respect to their attitudes, status, and work assignment in the family appears to carry over into the labor market. It is therefore not surprising that considerations of efficiency, taking family organization and structure as given, appear to govern the labor market. This line of argument points to the importance of historical analysis in the search for "explanations" of gender effects. In particular, the historical study of how production in the "family" economy developed, and how it interacted over time with the "factory" economy, would be most fruitful.

system—the *maquila*. Benería's study provides an unusual window into the way in which the formal sector in manufacturing tapers off into the informal sector. These vertical subcontracting linkages are often assumed to occur in developing countries, but are rarely documented. She further finds that the proportion of women employed is inversely related to the size of firm and the complexity of tasks. Each lower tier of subcontracting has simpler jobs and a higher fraction of female labor.

The most interesting questions raised by these findings relate to the larger role of subcontracting in the Mexican economy. What are the determinants of the *maquila* system? Does it arise out of the structure, the rate of growth, or the variability of demand? Does the regulation of the labor market or the pattern of social insurance coverage have an effect? Is the *maquila* system tied to earlier developments in Mexico's cottage industry?

The example of Mexico also contributes to a growing body of international research suggesting substantial differences among countries in the way subcontracting is organized. In Italy, for example, it has been argued that many small metalworking shops have acquired the most advanced technologies and are now at the forefront of innovation and highly skilled production. In Japan, the ability of the subcontracting system to respond rapidly to changing demand appears to reduce the reliance of large firms on inventories of parts and components. Do these international differences in subcontracting arrangements affect economic performance; do they affect inequality; and what do they argue for the changing mix between formal- and informal-sector employment in the course of economic development? While not directly answering these questions, Benería's research adds one more fragment of evidence to support the view that there is considerable discretion over how work and production are organized, both domestically and internationally, under similar technologies.

The paper does reveal clues about how jobs that were once performed primarily by males become feminized. Observing such gender transitions in the labor market highlights the devices used by employers to bring about changes in gender staffing and pay patterns. Often the substitution of female and male labor was associated with a dramatic alteration in production practices—the establishment of a new plant, the introduction of a new technology, or the redesign of work methods or job content. This suggests the possibility that a change in the gender identity of work is most easily accomplished when it is linked to, and arguably caused by, some other production change.

It also suggests that the timing of such changes needs to be understood. The advantages of using lower-cost and more productive female labor in place of male labor must have been available for a long time in the Mexican economy. What triggered the recent move to employ females? The paper is not definitive on the factors that shaped and activated the specific set of changes selected. Was it the growth rate of the Mexican economy, more intense international competition, or a "tipping" phenomenon caused by male workers vacating certain jobs?

In industrialized countries, the types of secondary labor market jobs described by Benería often have negative connotations because of their implications for productivity, inequality, and discrimination. It is less certain that this conclusion applies with equal force to developing countries, where the placement of work into the secondary labor market may contribute to the production infrastructure. It may foster generic strengths in the small-enterprise sector that may aid economic growth: the ability to mobilize informal sources of credit, the development of a flexible reserve production capacity, and the potential for import substitution arising from the use of second-hand equipment and used intermediate inputs.

The implications of these secondary jobs for inequality are also uncertain. The pairing of feminization of employment with a growing reliance upon subcontracting means more jobs for women, but lower pay for the work performed. The *maquila* system results in the incidence of aggregate economic instability being transferred from larger businesses to family firms and small businesses. It also increases the dependence of small enterprises on the large-enterprise sector. One result is that instability in manufacturing demand disproportionately affects the jobs and income of the lowest-paid workers. Partially offsetting this vulnerability, however, is the access such workers have to family and kinship systems that can help to cushion such shocks.

Benería concludes that gender and the hierarchial organization of work are the villains in the *maquila* system. Policies to implement comparable work principles and provide more egalitarian work organization should therefore be considered. The empirical basis for these conclusions, however, is unclear.

The most significant unanswered question raised by this essay, however, is whether feminine-based growth in the subcontracting sector will perpetuate low pay and economic segregation in female labor markets long after its economic rationale has diminished. The experience of the industrialized world suggests it is generally difficult to remove gender differences in pay and employment once they have been built into the structure of the economy.

RICHARD B. FREEMAN *and* JONATHAN S. LEONARD

Union Maids:
Unions and the Female Work Force

WHILE unions could prosper with only limited organization of women when males dominated the labor force, in the 1980s and the foreseeable future, women will constitute close to half of the work force, making organization of women a key element in any revival of unionism in the United States.

Women have traditionally been less likely than men to be organized into trade unions. In 1956, for example, just 15 percent of female workers were union members, compared with 31 percent of male workers. Despite union policies designed to reduce wage differentials across plants and personal differentials within plants, which should produce a greater union premium for women than for men, estimates of union wage effects by sex have found no clear pattern of differentials between men and women. Some unions, notably in construction, have often been charged with restricting or discouraging women from entering their trades.

How have women fared in unions in recent years? Are women becoming more organized? What explains the traditionally low proportion of women in unions? Do unions help or hamper efforts to improve the economic position of women within organized plants? Are they a positive intervening force in equal opportunity and legal efforts to advance women's rights in the workplace?

Organization of Female Workers

The literature on unionization has long found that women tend to have lower rates of organization than men, while at the same time finding

The research reported here is part of the National Bureau of Economic Research's research program in labor studies. Any opinions expressed are those of the authors and not of the NBER.

little or no difference in desires for organization between unorganized workers by sex. As noted by Fiorito and Greer, however, with rare exception there have been no empirical studies of unionization of special groups such as public-sector or white-collar employees, who constitute the key to our analysis of female unionism.[1]

We have examined three indicators of the receptiveness of women to unionization: (1) the proportion of women who are organized; (2) the success of unions in National Labor Relations Board (NLRB) representation elections in female-intensive units; (3) answers to opinion poll questions about willingness to vote for unions in elections or desires for unions at one's workplace.

Table 1 presents the relevant data on the organization of female and male workers and the percentage of union workers who are women. In 1984, 15 percent of female workers were unionized, compared with 24 percent of male workers. This differential, while large, represents a marked change from earlier decades. Although the proportion of male workers in unions has fallen since the mid-1950s, the proportion of female workers has actually risen, reducing the gap in unionization rates. In conjunction with the rising proportion of females in the work force, this has increased the female proportion of union members from 19 percent in 1956 to 36 percent in 1984.

Disaggregation of the work force into public and private employers and into white-collar and blue-collar jobs shows that the increase in female unionization is a public-sector, white-collar phenomenon. From 1973 to 1984 the proportion of females organized in the public sector almost doubled, to attain near equality with the proportion of males organized in that sector. Part of the rise for both groups in the public sector represents the change in the role of associations in public employment, as groups such as the National Education Association have become increasingly involved in collective bargaining. The Current Population Survey expanded its question about union membership to include employee associations in 1977 as a reflection of that changing role. While raising the proportion of respondents indicating union membership in the public sector, the change had only a modest effect on the female proportion of unionists.[2] In the private sector, by contrast, the proportion

1. See Jack Fiorito and Charles Greer, "Determinants of U.S. Unionism: Past Research and Future Needs," *Industrial Relations,* vol. 21 (Winter 1982), pp. 1–32, especially p. 15.

2. Our tabulations show that in the public sector 31.6 percent of men were organized

Table 1. *Union Membership of Workers, by Sex and Type of Employment, Selected Years, 1956–84*

Percent

Item	1956[a]	1966[a]	1973[a]	1980[b]	1983[b]	1984[b]
Union membership						
Total work force						
Female	14.9	12.6	14.7	16.9	16.3	15.0
Male	31.0	29.7	32.0	30.1	25.5	23.8
Public sector						
Female	n.a.	n.a.	17.1	32.2	36.6	33.2
Male	n.a.	n.a.	27.9	39.7	38.5	37.7
Private sector						
Female	n.a.	n.a.	14.1	12.6	10.9	10.4
Male	n.a.	n.a.	32.8	28.3	22.8	21.2
White collar						
Female	n.a.	n.a.	10.4	14.9	15.0	13.7
Male	n.a.	n.a.	14.4	17.2	15.6	12.1
Blue collar						
Female	n.a.	n.a.	22.3	21.3	19.1	18.2
Male	n.a.	n.a.	42.8	38.9	33.1	32.8
Female share of union members						
Total work force	18.5	19.3	23.7	30.8	34.9	35.7
Public sector	n.a.	n.a.	36.1	46.8	49.3	48.5
Private sector	n.a.	n.a.	21.1	24.7	27.8	28.2
White collar	n.a.	n.a.	44.9	53.9	56.7	60.9
Blue collar	n.a.	n.a.	17.1	18.6	20.4	19.4

Sources: Data for 1956–66 from Linda H. LeGrande, "Women in Labor Organizations: Their Ranks Are Increasing," *Monthly Labor Review*, vol. 101 (August 1978), pp. 8–14. These data are from the Bureau of Labor Statistics' Survey of Unions. Data for 1973–84 tabulated from Current Population Survey, May of each year. These data are from reports of households and they exclude agricultural and private household workers.

n.a. Not available.

a. Limited to union membership.

b. Includes union and employee association membership.

of women organized fell by 25 percent, which was smaller than the nearly 40 percent drop in organization among men, but still marked. Women are as organized as men among white-collar workers, but less organized than men among blue-collar workers. Because of female concentration in white-collar jobs, however, women constitute 61 percent of white-collar unionists. Among the most important white-collar public-sector unions with large female representation are the education unions (National Education Association, American Federation of Teachers); the

in 1976, compared with 38.0 percent in 1977, and 21.2 percent of women were organized in 1976, compared with 28.4 percent in 1977. The female proportion of public-sector employees rose from 40.6 percent to 43.9 percent between the two years.

Table 2. *Estimates of the Effect of Being Female on the Probability of Union Membership*

	Effects	
Equation	1973[a]	1983[b]
With female as sole factor	−0.17	−0.09
	(0.004)	(0.007)
With other demographic controls	−0.15	−0.07
	(0.004)	(0.007)
With industry and occupation controls	−0.06	−0.02
	(0.005)	(0.008)

Source: Based on linear probability regression analysis of Current Population Survey data, May 1973 and May 1983. Numbers in parentheses are standard errors.
a. Sample size in 1973 was 35,479.
b. Sample size in 1983 was 11,212; the CPS union question was administered to only part of the overall sample.

American Federation of State, County, and Municipal Employees; and the nursing associations.

The decline in male-female differences in unionization is explored further in table 2, which records the results of a linear probability equation for the effect of being female on union status, first without and then with controls for demographic factors and occupation and industry. We estimated the following equation:

$$(1) \qquad UNION = a + b\,FEMALE + \Sigma_i c_i X_i + d_i.$$

where

X_i is the relevant control variable;

UNION is a variable that takes on the value of 1 if yes and 0 if no;

FEMALE is a variable that takes on the value of 1 if yes and 0 if no.

The decline in the female coefficients from −0.17 to −0.09 corroborates the picture given in table 1. With the addition of a full set of controls, the coefficient of being female falls by two-thirds in both years, producing a four-point difference in unionization between men and women in similar sectors and jobs in 1983. More complex analyses, taking account of the size of firm, job tenure, and fringe benefits for the intermediate year 1977, show that over 80 percent of the male-female unionization differential is due to workplace differences rather than any less desire for unionization among women.[3]

3. Richard B. Freeman and James L. Medoff, *What Do Unions Do?* (Basic Books, 1984), p. 28. Also see Joseph R. Antos, Wesley Mellow, and Mark Chandler, "Sex Differences in Union Membership," *Industrial and Labor Relations Review*, vol. 33 (January 1980), pp. 162–69.

Consistent with this, evidence on the desire for unionization from the Michigan Quality of Work Survey shows greater preference for unions among women. In 1977, 41 percent of women workers who were not union members (compared with 27 percent of men) said they would vote for unions if an NLRB representation election were held at their place of work.[4] Interpretation of these data is, however, somewhat complicated. Since more men are organized, one might expect on the margin a smaller proportion of men than women to want unions, even if all men and women had the same desire for unions. An analysis of the desire for unions shows that after taking account of the proportion of the two groups organized there is no indication of a pure "taste" differential for unionism by sex.[5] Detailed investigation of the attitudes of women toward unions, using the 1984 AFL-CIO Harris Poll, shows that only among nonunion public-sector white-collar workers do women have a greater belief than men in the ability of unions to benefit them. Among nonunion blue-collar private-sector workers, the two sexes have similar views—a result consistent with empirical evidence of actual union effects.[6]

Finally, evidence on union success in NLRB election campaigns reveals that unions do roughly as well in female-intensive sectors as in male-intensive sectors or slightly better. In a survey of more than 200 organizing campaigns that culminated in an NLRB election, the AFL-CIO Department of Organization and Field Services found that unions won 50 percent of campaigns in which women made up 75 percent or more of the work force (largely in health care service); they won only 40 percent of campaigns in which women made up less than 50 percent of the work force (largely in manufacturing).[7] While multiple regression analyses of the success rate show no pure "female" effect, the fact that women are concentrated in the few sectors where there is union growth implies a continued rise in the female proportion of unionists. Further evidence that women have become more receptive to unionization over

4. Freeman and Medoff, *What Do Unions Do?* p. 29.

5. Henry S. Farber, "The Determination of the Union Status of Workers," National Bureau of Economic Research Working Paper 1006 (Cambridge, Mass.: NBER, October 1982).

6. Linda F. Blash, "Can Women Save the Unions?: The Interrelationship between Trade Unions and Women" (Senior thesis, Harvard University, 1985).

7. AFL-CIO Department of Organization and Field Services, *AFL-CIO Organizer Survey* (April 1, 1984), p. 18.

Table 3. *Union Membership of Workers in California, by Sex and Type of Employment, Selected Years, 1961–79*
Percent

Item	1961	1971	1979
Total work force			
Female	26	24	19
Male	51	46	32
Public sector			
Female	35	38	35
Male	62	60	50
Manufacturing			
Female	35	32	22
Male	42	42	28
Trade			
Female	13	12	12
Male	24	22	17
Services			
Female	11	11	7
Male	11	9	5
Utility and transportation			
Female	47	49	48
Male	81	76	65

Source: California Department of Industrial Relations, "Union Labor in California," 1961, 1971, 1979.

time is found in an analysis of the effect of the female percentage on NLRB representation election outcomes.[8]

Table 3 turns from national data to figures for California, where the Department of Industrial Relations has gathered unionization figures from unions comparable to the now discontinued Bureau of Labor Statistics national series. The figures show that organization has declined among men and women in the private sector and among men in the public sector, but the proportion of women organized in the public sector has remained roughly constant. Most organized workers in California were in associations that did not bargain collectively in 1961 but were doing so by 1981, so the public-sector figures underestimate the rise in effective

8. Blash, "Can Women Save the Unions?" Regressing the log of the ratio of workers won by unions in NLRB elections to employment across industries and time (with various controls) for 1914–81, she finds the following coefficients and standard errors: on the female percentage in the industry: -0.32 (0.08), and on the interaction of women and time: 0.03 (0.01). This implies that unions did markedly worse in female-intensive industries in the earlier period but better in the latter, since the positive interaction dominates the negative main effect by the end of the period.

unionization there.[9] As a result of the changing unionization of men and women, the percentage of union (association) workers who are female rose from about a quarter to nearly a third.

All told, the evidence for the most recent years shows a striking change in unionization among women; together with data on preferences and voting, this indicates that women will no longer be one of the least unionized demographic groups in the United States. The new unionization of women is, however, quite different from traditional unionization of men. It is white-collar, public-sector unionism, and as such is limited to one segment of the overall work force. As yet, outside of health care and a few selected private-sector industries, there has been no breakthrough in unionization of women in the private sector.

What Unions Do to Female Wages and Employment

How harmful or helpful have unions been to the wage and employment interests of women workers? In the political sphere, the AFL-CIO has often joined with women's groups and others in coalitions to press for certain types of legislation. In the workplace, the situation has been more complex, with some unions having policies that help female workers and others having policies that are harmful. To determine the impact of unionism on female wages and employment, we have examined two sets of data: national Current Population Survey statistics on the usual hourly earnings of women and men, and data on employment in California manufacturing establishments. Our findings on wages overturn the traditional conclusion that unionism has similar effects on female and male wages. Our findings on employment reject the notion that women fare more poorly in unionized settings because of discrimination or seniority rules, which are thought to benefit men more than women because men are more likely to have greater seniority. Finally, we have examined the role of unions as an intervening institution in affirmative action and found no significant union effect on the success of affirmative action in altering female employment.

9. California introduced a collective bargaining law for teachers and a meet and confer law for state and local workers in the period.

Table 4. *Summary of Studies of Union Wage Effects, by Sex*

Data set[a]	Mean estimates of union effect[b]
Survey	
Current Population Survey (25)	0
Survey of Economic Opportunity (11)	−0.02
Michigan Panel Survey of Income Dynamics (8)	0.01
Year	
1967 (12)	−0.02
1969–71 (8)	0.03
1973–76 (17)	0.01
1976–79 (11)	0

Source: H. Gregg Lewis, *Union Relative Wage Effects: A Survey* (University of Chicago Press, 1986), chap. 7. These calculations give the log differential in union effects in the various studies.
a. Numbers in parentheses are number of studies.
b. Estimates show effect on males minus effect on females.

The Wage Evidence

In his recent summary of evidence on the differential effect of unionism, Lewis surveyed forty-eight studies dealing with the impact of unions on female and male wages and concluded that in 1967–79 "the numerical magnitude of the difference [in estimated union effects on men and women] is close to zero."[10] Table 4 presents a summary of the data that lead Lewis to this conclusion.

The problem with the studies cited by Lewis is not that they have erred in their regression models, but that they have ignored the public sector, where women unionists predominate, and they have focused on all workers or blue-collar workers, rather than on white-collar workers, where women are organized. Given our findings that female unionization is a public-sector, white-collar phenomenon, this is obviously not the appropriate way to determine what unions do to female wages. Accordingly, we have analyzed the effect of unions on female and male earnings by the sector and nature of work, using the standard log-linear earnings function.

Table 5 presents our basic results. For the private sector our results differ marginally from the studies cited by Lewis, revealing a modestly

10. H. Gregg Lewis, *Union Relative Wage Effects: A Survey* (University of Chicago Press, 1986), chap. 7.

Table 5. *Estimates of the Effect of Unionism on Average Hourly Earnings of Male and Female Workers, by Type of Employment, 1973 and 1983*[a]

Type of employment	1973		1983	
	Male	Female	Male	Female
Private sector	0.19	0.17	0.18	0.14
	(0.01)	(0.01)	(0.01)	(0.02)
N	19,444	12,106	5,892	4,888
Public sector	0.12	0.13	0.06	0.09
	(0.02)	(0.02)	(0.02)	(0.02)
N	3,804	3,564	1,276	1,352
White collar	0.08	0.15	0.07	0.12
	(0.01)	(0.01)	(0.02)	(0.02)
N	8,725	9,962	3,093	4,365
Blue collar	0.23	0.19	0.22	0.17
	(0.01)	(0.01)	(0.01)	(0.03)
N	14,223	5,708	4,075	1,875

Source: Calculated from May 1973 and May 1983 Current Population Survey tapes.

a. Based on mulivariate regressions, which include dummy variables for education, age, race, region, one-digit occupation, and two-digit industry. Sample excludes agricultural and private household workers. Numbers in parentheses are standard errors.

greater union effect on the wages of men than women. In the public sector, however, we find the opposite, with unions raising female wages more than male wages in 1983, though not in 1973.[11] The white-collar–blue-collar decomposition in table 5 shows a more dramatic picture, with unions raising the wages of blue-collar male workers more than the wages of female workers, but raising the wages of white-collar females more than those of white-collar males.[12] Because the May 1983 CPS tape has a relatively small sample size, any firm conclusion about the differential effects of unionism on the wages of male and female workers in these categories requires further investigation. Accordingly, we have also looked at the effect of unionism on wages by sex, type of work, and sector in the annual 1984 CPS tape, which contains roughly six times as many observations (see table 6). The regression results based on the annual data suggest that both type of work and sector affect the union differential by sex: we obtain notably *greater* union effects on female pay for all categories except blue-collar workers in the private sector.

11. Sharon P. Smith, *Equal Pay in the Public Sector: Fact or Fantasy* (Princeton University Press, 1977), p. 124, also reports a larger effect on the wages of women than of men among public-sector employees.

12. Joseph R. Antos, "Union Effects on White Collar Compensation," *Industrial and Labor Relations Review*, vol. 36 (April 1983), pp. 461–79, also reports a bigger effect for women than men among white-collar workers.

Table 6. *Estimates of the Effect of Unionism on Average Hourly Earnings of Male and Female Workers, by Type of Employment, 1984*[a]

Type of employment	Female	Male	Difference
Private sector			
White collar	0.18	0.12	0.06
	(0.01)	(0.01)	...
N	41,319	30,029	...
Blue collar	0.24	0.26	−0.02
	(0.01)	(0.00)	...
N	20,600	44,853	...
Public sector			
White collar	0.11	0.04	0.07
	(0.01)	(0.01)	...
N	13,595	8,688	...
Blue collar	0.18	0.14	0.04
	(0.02)	(0.01)	...
N	2,665	6,403	...

Source: Calculated using the same model as in table 5. Data come from the full twelve months of Current Population Survey tapes.

a. Agricultural and private household workers excluded. Numbers in parentheses are standard errors.

Our results do not, however, imply that unionization reduces the male-female pay gap in the economy as a whole. The effect of unions on the economywide gap depends not only on the union impact on wages within groups, but also on the proportion of men and women organized in these groups. If, as is the case, male unionists are concentrated in the sector with the greatest union premium (blue-collar, private-sector workers), then unionism could raise their wage in the economy as a whole more than it raises the wage of women, thus exacerbating the male-female pay gap.

We estimate the impact of unionization on the overall male-female pay gap by taking weighted averages of the figures in table 6 to obtain average union effects on the wage bill for each sex, assuming no spillover effects:

$$(2) \qquad \Delta W_i = \sum_j \alpha_{ij} \Delta W_{ij}$$

where

ΔW_{ij} = average percentage-point effect of unionism on wages for the ith sex in jth sector.

α_{ij} = ratio of union workers of ith sex in sector j to total workers of ith sex.

In our data tabulated from the 1984 CPS, α_{ij}, the proportions of workers unionized, by sex, sector, and type of employment, are:

Type of employment	Female	Male
Private-sector white-collar	3.7	2.0
Private-sector blue-collar	4.6	15.8
Public-sector white-collar	6.0	3.2
Public-sector blue-collar	0.7	2.8
Total	15.0	23.8

Solving equation 2 shows that unionism has an insubstantial effect on the overall male-female pay gap: the average union wage effects in 1983, ΔW_i, are 0.052 for males and 0.026 for females. Among union members, the average union wage effect is slightly lower for women (0.17) than for men (0.22). Considering that a greater proportion of men than women are union members, this implies that unions raise male wages slightly more than those of females.

The Employment Evidence

Turning to employment, we have examined the effect of unionism on turnover and employment growth in the private sector and on the impact of affirmative action in California establishments. Our findings on employment are consistent with those on wages; we find that unions have similar effects on women and men and do not impair the workings of affirmative action in altering employment patterns.

Table 7 summarizes the results of an analysis of the effect of unions on turnover and growth of employment by sex and ethnic group. The estimates are based on regressions that relate the specified turnover variables for each group to a measure of whether a plant is covered by collective bargaining and a host of other control variables. As can be seen, the principal finding is that unions have no statistically significant effect on turnover or employment share growth across demographic groups. Indeed, the only marginally significant impact is for union plants to promote blacks more than other groups. In particular, there is no significant evidence here that union seniority rules have worked to the detriment of minorities or females.

To examine the effects of unionism on the ability of affirmative action to increase female employment, we have analyzed the effect of contract compliance and contract review on the growth of the female share of the

Table 7. *Estimates of the Effect of Unionism on Turnover and Employment Growth, by Sex and Race, 1974–80*[a]

Sex and race	Growth of employment share	New hires rate	Promotion rate	Termination rate
White females	0.000	−0.021	0.004	−0.011
	(0.003)	(0.029)	(0.009)	(0.018)
White males	0.003	−0.021	−0.008	−0.004
	(0.003)	(0.018)	(0.013)	(0.026)
Hispanic females	−0.001	0.023	0.005	−0.001
	(0.002)	(0.070)	(0.025)	(0.049)
Hispanic males	−0.003	0.016	0.018	0.002
	(0.002)	(0.032)	(0.015)	(0.028)
Black females	−0.000	0.103	0.055	0.069
	(0.001)	(0.123)	(0.031)	(0.098)
Black males	0.001	0.119	0.057	0.056
	(0.001)	(0.109)	(0.035)	(0.068)

Source: Estimated from California establishment data set, as described in Jonathan S. Leonard, "Unions, Turnover, and Employment Variations" in David Lipsky and David Lewin, eds., *Advances in Industrial Relations* (Greenwich, Conn.: JAI Press, forthcoming).

a. All equations include seventeen industry dummies, five region dummies, and seven year dummies, and variates for growth rate of total employment during year of observation; proportion of blue-collar (craft, operatives, labor, service) workers in previous year's work force; total establishment employment and its square; and an indicator for whether the establishment was part of a multiestablishment company. Sample size = 558 establishments for new hires, promotions, and terminations, 693 establishments for employment share. Numbers in parentheses are standard errors.

work force in union and nonunion establishments in California. The test is based on a sample of 1,273 California establishments described in Leonard.[13] The results of this calculation, given in table 8, show no significant union effect. Indeed, these data indicate that in California the white and black female share of employment (but not the Hispanic share) grew more in unionized than in nonunion plants in 1974–80. While some might hold union plants to a higher standard, whatever unions did at

13. These are log-odd estimates weighted by the establishments' total blue-collar employment. A given group's 1980 employment share is regressed on 1974 employment share, two- or three-digit SIC industry, SMSA, establishment size and growth, proportion that are craft workers, and a control for whether the establishment was part of a multiplant corporation. Of particular interest here, controls are also included for whether the establishment was part of a federal contractor company obligated to pursue affirmative action under Executive Order 11246, whether the establishment experienced an affirmative action compliance review between 1974 and 1980, and the interactions of contractor and review status with union status. Our test of the intervening role of unions on affirmative action for females is whether the interaction terms in the female equations are significant. See Jonathan S. Leonard, *The Impact of Affirmative Action* (National Bureau of Economic Research and University of California–Berkeley, Institute for Industrial Relations and School of Business Administration, 1983).

Table 8. *Estimates of Interactions between Unions and Affirmative Action*[a]

Independent variable	White males	Black males	Hispanic males	White females	Black females	Hispanic females
1. Union (U)	−0.231	3.04	−4.97	1.11	0.41	−1.34
	−0.010	0.506	−0.260	0.107	0.147	−0.127
	(0.101)	(0.135)	(0.115)	(0.155)	(0.154)	(0.173)
2. Contract (C)	5.61	1.57	−2.20	0.97	0.58	−0.76
	0.242	0.261	−0.115	0.093	0.207	−0.072
	(0.070)	(0.094)	(0.080)	(0.108)	(0.107)	(0.120)
3. Review (R)	1.83	1.56	0.038	1.13	0.62	0.77
	0.079	0.260	0.0020	0.109	0.223	0.073
	(0.063)	(0.085)	(0.072)	(0.097)	(0.097)	(0.108)
4. $U \times C$	2.39	−1.97	4.34	−0.080	−0.16	−1.44
	0.103	−0.328	0.227	−0.008	−0.058	−0.136
	(0.112)	(0.150)	(0.128)	(0.172)	(0.171)	(0.192)
5. $U \times R$	−3.67	−0.25	1.20	0.104	−0.42	−0.95
	−0.158	−0.042	0.063	0.010	−0.151	−0.090
	(0.081)	(0.108)	(0.092)	(0.125)	(0.124)	(0.138)

Evaluation

Estimated net impact of contract on employment share
In nonunion plants

(row 2)	0.056	0.016	−0.022	0.010	0.006	−0.008

In union plants

(row 2 + row 4)	0.080	−0.004	0.021	0.009	0.004	−0.022

Estimated net impact of review on employment share
In nonunion plants

(row 3)	0.018	0.016	0.004	0.011	0.006	0.008

In union plants

(row 3 + row 5)	−0.018	0.013	0.012	0.012	0.002	−0.002

Source: Estimated from California establishment data, as described in Jonathan S. Leonard, "The Effect of Unions on the Employment of Blacks, Hispanics, and Women," *Industrial and Labor Relations Review*, vol. 39 (October 1985), p. 129.

a. The dependent variable is the logarithm of $P/(1 - P)$, where P is share of 1980 blue-collar employment. The first line is 100 "*dP/dX*" evaluated at mean P. The second is the coefficient from the log-odd equation. The third is the standard error. All equations include twenty industry and five region dummies along with controls for establishment size, growth, and structure, and 1974 employment share.

workplaces in the private sector during this period did not deter female employment or the operation of affirmative action.

Conclusion: The Puzzle

The evidence given here suggests that unions have done well for women in general and have done better for women than for men in the public sector, but not in the private sector. Why the difference? At this stage of our research we cannot provide a definite answer. Since, as we have seen, unionization reduces male-female wage gaps in the public sector among blue-collar as well as white-collar labor, we believe the answer does not lie in differences in the types of workers organized by sex in the public sector.

Indeed, in one sense the puzzle of our results (and of the earlier work cited by Lewis) is why the union wage premium is not greater for blue-collar women in the private sector, given policies such as standardization of rates, promotion by seniority, and explicit antidiscrimination clauses in contracts.

There are three possible explanations:

1. That blue-collar women work in different industries than blue-collar men—in apparel and garments rather than autos and steel—and that union power is less in the predominantly female industries, counterbalancing any tendency to reduce male-female differentials at workplaces.

2. That blue-collar women are so occupationally segregated from blue-collar men that it is the effect of unions on occupational differentials (which varies greatly), rather than on personal differentials, that dominates the statistics.

3. That, despite explicit wage policies, unions are unable to alter male-female pay differentials at given workplaces.

The first of these hypotheses suggests analyses of union effects on wage differentials within detailed industries and of the relation between the level of pay by industry and employment of male and female unionists at industry levels more detailed than those held fixed in our calculations. The second suggests analysis of occupational segregation and wages within specific sectors. The third suggests investigation of gaps between expressed and actual union policies in the private sector.

Unions and Comparable Worth

Despite equal pay legislation, equal employment opportunity, and affirmative action, women in the United States continue to earn noticeably less than men even after account is taken of differences in human capital, measured by years of work experience, tenure, and education. The table on page 203 shows the average hourly earnings of women as a percentage of those of men. As can be seen, other countries did a much better job in improving the relative earnings of women in the 1970s:[14]

14. Organization for Economic Cooperation and Development, "The Role of Women

	1970	*1981–82*	*Change*
Australia	65	86	21
Sweden	80	90	10
United Kingdom	60	70	10
Italy	74	84	10
West Germany	69	73	4
United States	62	65	3

The doctrine of comparable worth—equal pay for comparable work—can be seen as an historical outgrowth of the confrontation of the movement for equal employment by women with the fact that most women workers are concentrated in female-dominated occupations beyond the purview of the Equal Pay Act of 1963. As an active federal policy, pay equity for women can be traced back at least as far as the War Labor Board of World War II. The board and its agents commonly adjudicated wage disputes and altered inequitable wage schedules within plants and soon developed the principle that within a plant men and women in different jobs that required the same skill, effort, and responsibility deserved equal pay.[15] With the easing of wartime pressures, direct federal intervention in wage setting declined, as did the prominence of women in traditionally male jobs in manufacturing. The issue of pay equity for women was not again the direct object of federal policy until passage of the Equal Pay Act in 1963 as an amendment to the Fair Labor Standards Act. The Equal Pay Act is chiefly of interest because of a curious history in which it has threatened, through the Bennett amendment to the Civil Rights Act of 1964, to hobble the application of title VII of the Civil Rights Act to gender wage discrimination cases (see below). While the Equal Pay Act provides administrative requirements

---

in the Economy, Women and Their Integration in the Economy," Working Paper, May 3, 1984, p. 76; and *Statistical Abstract of the United States, 1984* (Government Printing Office, 1983), p. 434, table 716.

15. See General Order 16, November 24, 1942, 24 *War Labor Board Report* (BNA), xii, which authorized "adjustments which equalize the wage or salary rates paid to males for comparable quality and quantity of work on the same or similar operation." In practice a more restrictive equal work policy may have prevailed. In *Rotary Cut Box Industry,* 12 *War Labor Board Report* (1944), the board states, "this doctrine is not to be invoked to abolish wage differentials between jobs which have historically been performed by women entirely and jobs which have been recognized in the industry as jobs limited for the most part to men." As Gabin argues, this distinction may have been shaped by the expectation that men would replace women in the traditionally male jobs after the war. Nancy Gabin, "Women Workers and the UAW in the Post-World War II Period: 1945–54," *Labor History*, vol. 21 (Winter 1979–80), pp. 5–30.

and remedies that are often preferable to those of title VII to plaintiffs, its application is limited to equal pay for equal—not comparable—work.[16]

This limitation to cases of equal work is a crucial one because of occupational segregation—the concentration of most women in female-intensive jobs or in solely female jobs where the Equal Pay Act cannot be applied. Madden states that "the main employment disadvantage of women is their unfavorable occupational distribution," and Oaxaca concludes that "unequal pay for equal work does not account for very much of the male-female wage differential. Rather it is the concentration of women in lower paying jobs that produces such large differentials."[17] Clearly, the importance of occupational segregation in determining the wage gap depends on how narrowly occupations are defined. Nevertheless, to achieve pay equal to that of men, women essentially have had two avenues open: achieve the same jobs as men, or gain pay equal to that of men in comparable jobs.

In attempting to use unions as a vehicle to gain traditionally male-dominated jobs, women have legal recourse to both title VII and to the National Labor Relations Act (NLRA). The courts have long held that along with the right of exclusive representation unions must also bear the responsibility of fair representation.[18] While the Supreme Court has held that a union may not circumscribe an employee's opportunity to seek relief under title VII, it has also held that subgroups of employees (such as minorities or females) cannot circumvent their elected representatives to engage in direct bargaining with their employer over issues

16. The basic prohibition states: "No employer having employees subject to any provisions of this section shall discriminate . . . between employees on the basis of sex by paying wages to employees . . . at a rate less than the rate at which he pays wages to employees of the opposite sex . . . for equal work on jobs the performance of which requires equal skill, effort, and responsibility, and which are performed under similar working conditions, except where such payment is made pursuant to (i) a seniority system; (ii) a merit system; (iii) a system which measures earnings by quantity or quality of production; or (iv) a differential based on any other factor other than sex." The Equal Pay Act also forbids unions "to cause or attempt to cause . . . an employer to discriminate" (29 U.S.C. 206d), although unions' monetary liability is unclear. See *Denicola* v. *G. C. Murphy Co.*, 562 F. 2d 889 (3d Cir. 1977); and *Northwest Airlines* v. *Transport Workers Union*, 451 U.S. 77, 67 L.Ed.2d 750 (1981).

17. Janice Fanning Madden, *The Economics of Sex Distribution* (Lexington, Mass.: Lexington Books, 1973); and Ronald Oaxaca, "Male-Female Wage Differentials in Urban Labor Markets," *International Economic Review*, vol. 14 (October 1973), p. 708.

18. See, for example, the cases of *Steele* v. *Louisville and Nashville R. R. Co.*, 323 U.S. 192 (1944); and *Vaca* v. *Sipes*, 368 U.S. 171 (1967).

of employment discrimination.[19] Justice Douglas, in dissent, argued that this judgment made union members prisoners of the union, but that may well be one cost of maintaining a system of collective bargaining.[20] Furthermore, the walls of the "prison" are not impervious, because individuals maintain the right to bring suit under title VII.

Moreover, the union itself has a duty not to discriminate in its own practices and may be liable for employer discrimination engaged in under a collective bargaining contract.[21] In a 1966 case, the courts held that a union implicated in discrimination with an employer under a collectively bargained agreement must propose specific contractual provisions to prohibit discrimination.[22] The elimination of race or sex discrimination is a mandatory subject of bargaining, so an employer is subject to bad faith bargaining charges if he refuses to bargain with the union in this area.[23] These rights and responsibilities under NLRA law have profound implications that are slowly developing in decisions of the NLRB and the courts. Perhaps of greatest import, recent decisions under the NLRA have established legal tools that unions are in a unique position to use to uncover and eliminate discrimination. The International Union of Electrical, Radio and Machine Workers (IUE), represented by Winn Newman, led in many of these pathbreaking cases. One established that the employer, as part of the duty to bargain, must tell an inquiring union the race and gender breakdown of all its employees and its promotions.[24] Knowledge is power. In this case the union has access to knowledge that is generally denied to an individual worker. This is a key to understanding the confluence of interests of feminists and unionists. Newman and Vonhof have outlined the uses to which such knowledge may be put:

> The union may use the data to negotiate a new collective bargaining agreement, to administer an existing agreement, or to protect the rights of its members

19. *Alexander* v. *Gardner-Denver Co.*, 423 U.S. 1058 (1976); and *Emporium Capwell Co.* v. *Western Addition Community Organization*, 423 U.S. 1014 (1975).

20. See *J. I. Case* v. *NLRB*, 321 U.S. 332 (1944); and *Mallinckrodt Chemical Works*, 162 NLRB Dec. (CCH) 387 (1966).

21. See *Handy Andy* v. *New*, NLRB Dec. (CCH) 17,938 (1977); and *NLRB* v. *Mansion House Center Management Corp.* 473 F. 2d 471 (1973).

22. *Local No. 12, United Rubber Workers* v. *NLRB*, 368 F. 2d 12, 24–25 (5th Cir. 1966). The extent of union liability and responsibility in such cases is open to question. See David Offen Simon, "Union Liability under Title VII for Employer Discrimination," *Georgetown Law Journal*, vol. 68 (April 1980), pp. 959–87; and "Union Liability for Employer Discrimination," *Harvard Law Review*, vol. 93 (February 1980), pp. 702–24.

23. *Farmers' Cooperative Compress*, 396 U.S. 903 (1969).

24. *Westinghouse Electric Corp.*, 239 NLRB Dec. (CCH) 106 (1978).

by filing complaints of discrimination with government agencies or courts. Armed with such information and ability to obtain additional information from their members and their knowledge of past company practices, *unions stand in an excellent position to identify discrimination which may otherwise have gone unrecognized* by affected 'employees. Unions also are able to inform affected workers about their rights and to assist them in bringing complaints before the proper authorities. Moreover, as several courts have recognized, unions can contribute immeasurably to the effectiveness of fair employment litigation through their ability to offer financial support, knowledge of the plant, technical expertise, and moral support to plantiffs who are union members.[25]

Indeed, one of the most notable recent developments in industrial relations is that women have developed a wider appreciation of the usefulness of collective bargaining, while at the same time many unions have increasingly acknowledged the importance of women.[26] This confluence of interests holds with particular strength in the female-intensive public sector, where fears of male backlash may be reduced.

Joyce Miller, president of the Coalition of Labor Union Women (CLUW), has stated, "We in the labor movement know that the fastest way for women to gain economic equality is to join a union. Women join unions for the same reasons men do: better pay, better benefits and job security."[27] The drive by women for pay equity finds a remarkable echo within certain unions, particularly the IUE and the American Federation of State, County and Municipal Employees (AFSCME). These are not always the unions with the greatest proportion or largest number of women members, but they are the unions that appear to be in closest alignment with CLUW's goals. For example, the IUE has stated the case plainly:

Hiring more female and minority organizers is good for affirmative action. It is also good for unions and good for organizing. The increasing number of women entering the work force means that today's biggest organizing potential is among women and minorities. If unions are to succeed in their current organizing efforts, it is critical to have more women and minorities as

25. Winn Newman and Jeanne M. Vonhof, "'Separate but Equal'—Job Segregation and Pay Equity in the Wake of Gunther," *University of Illinois Law Review*, vol. 1981, no. 2, p. 319 (emphasis added).

26. Women are still rarely found among the top leadership of national unions. In 1982 sixteen labor organizations apparently were led by women. Most of these were small public-sector unions.

27. *CLUW News*, vol. 8 (July–August 1982), p. 1.

organizers. This is not only morally right, but it complies with the IUE's policy calling for greater participation of women and minorities in the union.[28]

It is worth considering why Newman and Vonhof can conclude that "both sides of the pay equity debate, consequently, agree that immediate initiatives will not come from the government, but from private plaintiffs and labor unions."[29] The answer turns on the development of and prospects for comparable worth under title VII law.

Union Pay Equity Suits under Title VII Law

It is not surprising, in light of the position of unions outlined above, that unions have been in the forefront of pay equity suits under title VII and comparable suits. The first pay equity lawsuit under title VII was probably that filed by the IUE in the early 1970s, which resulted in back pay awards through a 1977 out-of-court settlement.[30] Success in such cases was severely limited, however, because several courts held that the application of title VII to gender wage discrimination cases was limited to the restrictive equal work standard of the Equal Pay Act.

Title VII makes it an unlawful employment practice for an employer "to discriminate against any individual with respect to his compensation, terms, conditions, or privileges of employment, because of such individual's . . . sex." The Bennett amendment to title VII, however, provides:

It shall not be an unlawful employment practice under this title for any employer to differentiate upon the basis of sex in determining the amount of the wages or compensation paid or to be paid to employees of such employer if such differentiation is authorized by the provisions of section 6(d) of the Fair Labor Standards Act of 1938, as amended (29 U.S.C. 206(d)).[31]

Some courts had interpreted this to mean that in the case of gender wage discrimination, the Equal Pay Act, by way of the Bennett amendment, would swallow title VII and eliminate the application of title VII to cases of nonequal work where the Equal Pay Act does not apply. This

28. *Proceedings,* 19th Constitutional Convention, IUE, p. 61.
29. Newman and Vonhof, " 'Separate but Equal,' " p. 317. The emphasis here is not on channeling all pay equity energies into collective bargaining, but rather into collective bargaining in conjunction with the threat of title VII litigation. As Newman and Wilson state, "The IUE has recognized that discrimination will generally not be corrected at the bargaining table, at least not without using the law for support." Winn Newman and Carole W. Wilson, "The Union Role in Affirmative Action," *Labor Law Journal,* vol. 32 (June 1981), p. 324.
30. *Rinehard* v. *Westinghouse Electric Corp.,* No. 70-537 (N.D. Ohio 1979).
31. Civil Rights Act of 1964, 42 U.S.C. 2000e-2 (1978).

theory was rejected by the Supreme Court in 1981 in its important *Gunther* decision.[32] However, it is important to realize that while *Gunther* did not slam shut the door to comparable worth claims under title VII, it opened the door only a crack, and it took great pains to disavow being a decision on comparable worth.

> We do not decide in this case how sex-based wage discrimination litigation under title VII should be structured. . . . Respondents' claim is not based on the controversial conception of "comparable worth." . . . Rather respondents seek to prove, by direct evidence, that their wages were depressed because of intentional sex discrimination, consisting of setting the wage scale for female guards, but not for male guards, at a level lower than its own survey of outside markets and the worth of the jobs warranted.[33]

The courts have been reluctant to become enmeshed in wage setting, although there are limits beyond which employers become liable. On the one hand, *IUE* v. *Westinghouse* held, in a case involving different jobs, that deliberately discriminatory wage classifications and segregated jobs are illegal. As Judge Higginbotham put it, "The statutory issue here is whether Congress intended Westinghouse to willfully discriminate against women in a way in which it could not discriminate against . . . any other group protected by the Act."[34] On the other hand, as Judge Rehnquist noted in his dissent, the *Gunther* decision left untouched lower court decisions against the doctrine of comparable worth in two other cases.[35]

32. *County of Washington* v. *Gunther*, 452 U.S. 161 (1981).

33. To appreciate the narrowness of the *Gunther* decision, consider the following extract: "Petitioner argues strenuously that the approach of the Court of Appeals places 'the pay structure of virtually every employer and the entire economy . . . at risk and subject to scrutiny by the federal courts.' . . . Respondents contend that the County of Washington evaluated the worth of their jobs; that the county determined that they should be paid approximately 95% as much as the male correctional officers; that it paid them only about 70% as much, while paying the male officers the full evaluated worth of their jobs; and that the failure of the county to pay respondents the full evaluated worth of their jobs can be proven to be attributable to intentional sex discrimination. Thus, respondents' suit does not require a court to make its own subjective assessment of the value of the male and female guard jobs. . . . We do not decide in this case the precise contours of lawsuits challenging sex discrimination under title VII. It is sufficient to note that respondents' claims of discriminatory undercompensation are not barred . . . merely because respondents do not perform work equal to that of male jail guards." Michael J. Zimmer, Charles A. Sullivan, and Richard F. Richards, *Cases and Materials on Employment Discrimination* (Little, Brown, 1982), pp. 608–16.

34. *IUE* v. *Westinghouse*, Lab. Rel. Rep. (BNA), 28 Fair Empl. Prac. Cas. (BNA) 588 (1980).

35. *Lemons* v. *City and County of Denver*, 620 F. 2d 228 (10th Cir. 1980); and *Christensen* v. *Iowa*, 563 F. 2d 353 (8th Cir. 1977).

In addition, a post-*Gunther* decision refused to engage in a direct comparison of overlapping but unequal jobs.[36] At the same time, the Equal Employment Opportunity Commission (EEOC) has yet to pursue a comparable worth charge, take a public position, or issue guidelines. At best, the prospects for pursuing gender wage discrimination charges in unequal jobs are unclear.

The recent celebrated decision in *AFSCME* v. *State of Washington,* while heralded as a comparable worth case, may be seen as falling within the narrower confines of *Gunther*: the employer had studied salaries, determined the worth of somewhat different jobs held by women and men, yet had continued to pay a lower wage in proportion to worth for the "women's" jobs. In fact, Justice Tanner called it a straightforward "failure to pay" case. In his opinion, the court was not required to make a subjective assessment as to the comparable worth of the jobs involved, because the state had already done so: "The state has failed to rectify an acknowledged discriminatory disparity in compensation."[37] To some extent, management tied its own noose in these cases. In reaction to the Washington decision, one state legislator thought that states might be "hesitant to conduct studies and collect the data that could then be used against the state in a lawsuit." The AFSCME, on the other hand, hoped that public employers would be willing to negotiate, rather than meet in court. Eleanor Norton, of the National Council of the Future of Women in the Work Place and former EEOC chair, has stated that success in the public sector is discouraging job evaluation studies by private-sector employers. Where management has not tied itself to a comparable worth study, the courts have left it unclear just how far, or in what manner, gender wage discrimination cases may proceed.

There is one major sector in which management has commonly tied itself to formal job evaluation schemes, in which women make up a substantial proportion of the employees, and in which unions have made substantial organizing gains in recent years. These three factors are not unrelated. A leading title VII defense lawyer, Bruce Nelson, has stated that "public employers seem to be more vulnerable to the equity argument than private employers" and that "if I were going to prove this legal theory [of comparable worth], I would sue municipalities all

36. *Plemer* v. *Parsons-Gilbane,* 713 F. 2d 1127 (5th Cir. 1983).
37. Bureau of National Affairs, *Daily Labor Reporter,* December 15, 1983, pp. D-8, 9.

the time."[38] These public-sector employers are particularly vulnerable because they are typically committed to both a merit pay system and a public obligation to perform job evaluation studies in defense of their pay system.[39] In addition, they typically employ large numbers of women and have recently been opened to unionization.

The AFSCME, along with a few other unions, has been quick to seize the initiative in such cases, both in the courts and, with less public fanfare but perhaps greater results, at the bargaining table. The first strike mainly over comparable worth issues was by the AFSCME in San José, California, in 1981. This has been followed by negotiated pay equity adjustments and litigation in a growing number of state and local governments. At the state level, the AFSCME and other unions have pressed for comparable worth studies, followed by wage schedule adjustments in the course of collective bargaining. At least eighteen states, including Minnesota, California, Illinois, Iowa, Maine, Maryland, Kansas, New York, Oregon, and West Virginia, have come under such pressure. The state level of government has become quite important in this area. Alaska, Arkansas, Georgia, Idaho, Kentucky, Maine, Maryland, Massachusetts, Nebraska, North Dakota, Oklahoma, Oregon, South Dakota, Tennessee, and West Virginia are among the states that have adopted legislation prohibiting *all* employers from paying women less than men for comparable work, and California, Minnesota, Montana, and Washington have passed such legislation covering only state government employees.[40] Part of the future effects of a national policy of comparable worth could presumably be judged from the current experience of these states.

In pursuing this course, the challenge women face is reminiscent of the "gilded ghetto" dilemma urban blacks faced in the 1960s. Then, with

38. Bruce Nelson, quoted in Winn Newman, "Pay Equity: An Emerging Labor Issue," *Industrial Relations Research Association, Proceedings of the 34th Annual Meeting,* December 1981, p. 171.

39. Of the 226 comparable worth charges pending before the Equal Employment Opportunity Commission as of June 1982, 218 were against municipalities, according to the statement of Clarence Thomas, EEOC chairman, in *Pay Equity: Equal Pay for Work of Comparable Value,* Hearings before the House Committee on Post Office and Civil Service, 97 Cong. 2 sess. (GPO, 1982), pp. 374, 393.

40. Gary R. Siniscalco and Cynthia L. Remmers, "Comparable Worth in the Aftermath of AFSCME v. State of Washington," *Employee Relations Law Journal,* vol. 10 (Summer 1984), pp. 6–29; and Siniscalco and Remmers, "Nonjudicial Developments in Comparable Worth," *Employee Relations Law Journal,* vol. 10 (Autumn 1984), pp. 222–40.

some resignation in the face of great difficulties in achieving residential integration, attention turned instead toward improving conditions in the ghetto, which in turn reduced the incentive to leave the ghetto. In the face of difficulties and delays in applying title VII and affirmative action to achieve occupational integration by gender, attention has shifted toward improving conditions in the clerical and service "ghetto." But, as Phyllis Wallace has noted, "In the final analysis the shifting of women workers out of the female-dominated occupations to the higher-paying jobs in the predominantly male occupations would tend to raise wages for women. An adjustment of wages in the predominantly female occupations (sex-segregated) may be difficult to achieve."[41]

Given the changing political climate and the prospect of a more conservative cast to the Supreme Court, a number of women's groups have seen that there is an existing alternative to fighting for comparable worth in the U.S. Congress or under title VII in the courts. That alternative is collective bargaining. It has long been established under the NLRA that unions may, in the course of collective bargaining, set wages without any legally required reference to market wages or to any external standard whatsoever. Where there are enough current or potential women union members, many unions, which have always had at their core some notion of pay equity, will pursue equal pay for comparable worth in collective bargaining. They may have little choice if they are to continue to succeed in the only sector in which they have made substantial organizing gains in recent years, the public sector.

What Comparable Worth May Do

Assume that comparable worth does indeed succeed in changing the structure of pay by occupation through court decisions or collective bargaining. Will it prove to be an economic whirlwind "costing untold millions" or will it prove to be a fruitful remedy to longstanding male-female pay inequity? Most economists, it is safe to say, would bet on the whirlwind, expecting an exogenous change in the structure of pay to produce great loss of jobs and economic misery in affected sectors. As empiricists, we are hesitant to predict the future. The implementation of comparable worth in Australia may provide a useful example. It was the

41. Phyllis A. Wallace, ed., *Women in the Workplace* (Boston: Auburn House, 1982).

main reason for the dramatic twenty-one-point increase in the female-male pay ratio there from 1970 to 1981. Contrary to the fears of many, Australian women have not been disemployed in larger numbers, nor has the Australian economy suffered great dislocation.[42] Recent estimates of what comparable worth might do to the U.S. occupational wage structure suggest a surprisingly modest decline in male-female wage differentials, which should "soothe the fears of comparable worth opponents who view it as the worst idea since minimum wage legislation."[43]

Conclusion

In past decades unions, like the rest of labor market actors, could treat women workers cursorily, as secondary labor with no strong attachment to the workplace. Except for a few limited industries and occupations, the role of women in the workplace was not critical to unions' success. The situation in the 1980s is quite different.

According to our analysis:

1. Women have come to be an increasingly large proportion of the unionized work force and are critical in the one area in which unions have recently succeeded—the public sector.

2. In the public sector and in white-collar occupations where women unionists are concentrated, unions raise women's wages more than they raise the wages of men.

3. In the private sector, unions have essentially the same effect on women in wages, turnover, and employment and do not deter affirmative action programs to raise female employment.

4. Comparable worth presents a rare confluence of interests of unions in search of members (particularly in the public sector) and women in search of higher wages, and it will likely continue to be used by both, especially within the confines of collective bargaining.

42. See Robert G. Gregory and Robert C. Duncan, "Segmented Labor Market Theories and the Australian Experience of Equal Pay for Women," *Journal of Post Keynesian Economics,* vol. 3 (Spring 1981), pp. 403–28.

43. George Johnson and Gary Solan, "Pay Differences between Women's and Men's Jobs: The Empirical Foundations of Comparable Worth Legislation," National Bureau of Economic Research Working Paper 1472 (Cambridge, Mass.: NBER, September 1984). For larger estimates see Robert Buchele and Mark Aldrich, "How Much Difference Would Comparable Worth Make?" *Industrial Relations,* vol. 24 (Spring 1985), pp. 222–33.

Comments by Elaine Sorensen

Freeman and Leonard present a substantive empirical investigation into the effects of unionism on male and female earnings and employment. In certain instances, however, the study does not provide the fuller discussion of the issues warranted by their findings. For example, past studies have suggested that women and men receive similar wage premiums from unionization, but these analyses have focused upon the private sector and blue-collar occupations. Freeman and Leonard correct this oversight by including the public sector in their analysis and distinguishing between white- and blue-collar occupations. After integrating these new factors, they find that women receive a higher union wage premium in white-collar jobs and in the public sector. However, the authors do not provide an explanation of these results. They discuss the egalitarian goals and policies of private-sector unions in other parts of the paper. Do public-sector unions pursue these same policies, and are these policies producing this differential premium or are they caused by other forces?

In contrast to their findings for the public and white-collar sectors, Freeman and Leonard find that men and women receive similar union wage premiums in the private sector. However, most private-sector unions have pursued, through collective bargaining, wage policies that appear to reduce intra-industry wage inequality. Such wage solidarity could conceivably help female workers more than male workers since women are generally employed in lower-paid occupations than men. Why doesn't this differential union wage premium exist for female workers as it apparently does for black workers? Freeman and Leonard offer some suggestions as to why these differences occur, but additional research is needed to answer these questions more definitively.

The authors tend to overstate their case with regard to the impact of unionization on male and female employment levels. Freeman and Leonard conclude that unionization does not have a differential impact on the amount of male and female employment. However, one difficulty with this conclusion is that their analysis is limited only to the 1970s. They are able to determine that during this period unions were neutral with regard to sexual differences in hiring, promotion, and termination rates, and that unions did not inhibit female employment growth. They also found that unionization did not reduce the effective operation of affirmative action programs. While this analysis supports the view that unions did not exacerbate sexual employment differentials during this period, it is silent concerning unionization's pre-1974 impact. If unionization did contribute to prior sexual employment differentials, then those differentials have continued to persist.

Furthermore, many analysts would have expected unions to reduce sexual employment differentials because unions establish formal rules and procedures that reduce the employer's ability to make arbitrary and possibly discriminatory decisions against women. For example, seniority is an important promotional criterion for promotion in union establishments, whereas a supervisor's judgment is often given more weight in nonunion firms. Given that prejudice can influence judgment, one might expect that women would fare better in a union shop. On the other hand, some studies have found that seniority inhibits promotional opportunities for women in union establishments because women are hired into different occupations than men and these female-dominated occupations have extremely short promotional ladders. According to Freeman and Leonard's findings, unionization does not affect the promotional opportunities of women in either a negative or positive manner. These are rather surprising results; thus a further examination is needed to explain this finding.

Any analysis of the salient issues concerning unions and women workers should include a discussion of comparable worth. In their discussion of this topic, Freeman and Leonard point out that, despite equal pay and equal employment opportunity legislation, American women continue to earn considerably less than men even after correcting for human capital differences. They cite other work that suggests that the reason these legislative initiatives have had such limited success in reducing wage differentials between women and men is the severe sexual segregation of occupations that persists in the labor force. They provide a brief legal history of the pay equity issue and a brief overview of the state comparable worth initiatives. Also discussed is organized labor's increasingly prominent role in comparable worth fights and the growing use of collective bargaining as a means of achieving pay equity. They predict that the judicial or contractual implementation of comparable worth would have the favorable result of reducing the male-female wage differential without generating serious negative impacts on the national economy.

This assessment is somewhat controversial, given the concern that some other economists have expressed regarding the pay equity issue. Some have argued that employer discrimination, the central issue pay equity seeks to address, is not the major factor contributing to the sexual earnings gap. Instead, less work experience and higher turnover are the main reasons women continue to earn less than men. It is suggested that as women increase their work experience the earnings gap will disappear. In this instance, pay equity solutions would attack a nonexistent problem and could actually make women worse off by generating allocative distortions in the labor market. However, most empirical work finds that at most half of the earnings gap can be potentially eliminated by increased work effort among women. The other half is unexplained by human capital differences between women and men and consequently will not disappear with greater female attachment to the workplace. Comparable worth initiatives are attempting to eliminate this unexplained portion of the wage gap.

Others have argued that the enforcement of existing equal pay and equal employment opportunity laws is sufficient to eliminate economic discrimination against women. While these laws have had some favorable impact, thus far they have been unable to reduce the earnings disparity between women and men primarily because of the persistence of occupational segregation. Unfortunately, it is predicted that the degree of occupational segregation will continue to decline only slightly during the 1980s, suggesting that existing laws will not result in substantially smaller wage differentials in the near future.

Finally, others predict that implementing comparable worth will cause considerable economic distortions by interfering with efficient market forces. In particular, it is predicted that comparable worth will actually have the negative unintended effect of reducing female employment opportunities. However, as Freeman and Leonard note, other countries have already implemented various forms of pay equity legislation without dire consequences for their economies or female workers. In fact, it has been reported that the portion of total earnings going directly to female workers has dramatically increased in some countries implementing comparable worth legislation, strongly suggesting that women as a whole have gained from these policies. Additional research is obviously needed to estimate the effects of implementing comparable worth within the American context. I hope Freeman and Leonard will continue to cast their analytical eyes on this and other issues in this area.

Comparable worth is an idea that apparently has widespread and growing support—not only among female workers, as evinced by the Yale University strike by clerical and technical employees and public opinion surveys reported by the *Harvard Business Review*— but among the general public as well. Pay equity could also be the issue American trade unions have been searching for to bolster their attenuated ranks with new members from the sectors of the economy that have so far been union resistant.

KAREN C. HOLDEN *and* W. LEE HANSEN

Part-Time Work, Full-Time Work, and Occupational Segregation

THE PROPORTION of the work force employed part time has increased since 1954, when data on this group of workers were first gathered. The increase has been attributed to the growing proportion of women and students who work, to the effect of work disincentives created by retirement and other income transfer programs, and to the shift in employment toward industries where part-time work is concentrated.[1] Part-time opportunities greatly expand the work options of women who are unable or unwilling to work full time and simultaneously meet their household and child-rearing obligations. At the same time, because many part-time jobs are in occupations dominated by women, part-time employment may reinforce women's traditional work roles and also offset their employment gains in male-dominated occupations.

While other studies have explored trends in the occupational concentration of men and women over this period, none have examined the occupational concentration of women and men who work part time. We are interested in finding out how female occupational segregation has been affected by the mix of part- and full-time workers. Thus we explore the occupational distribution of part- and full-time jobs to determine whether increases in part-time work and the different occupational distribution of male and female part-time workers have retarded or exaggerated the reported decline in occupational segregation for the total work force.

The computations for this paper were supported by Center Grant HD-05876 from the National Institute of Child Health and Human Development to the Center for Demography and Ecology at the University of Wisconsin, Madison. Daniel Myers provided valuable assistance in the data analysis.

1. William V. Deutermann, Jr., and Scott Campbell Brown, "Voluntary Part-time Workers: A Growing Part of the Labor Force," *Monthly Labor Review*, vol. 101 (June 1978), p. 3.

Occupational Segregation among Part-Timers and Full-Timers

The traditional analysis of occupational segregation begins with the position stated by Beller:

> If more than half the population is denied access to 60 percent of the occupations, being crowded into a few at lower earnings, equality of opportunity does not exist. But if women freely choose to enter only a third of all occupations and those occupations pay less, then women's lower earnings may not be a fundamental social problem. The major issue is whether the dramatic differences in the occupational distributions of the sexes result from different choices made by each, given equal opportunities, or from unequal opportunities to make similar choices.[2]

The concentration of women workers in a small number of occupations is well documented. According to Current Population Survey data, in 1981 over 65 percent of female employees worked in twelve out of forty-four occupations (at the two-digit SIC level). Only 13 percent of male employees worked in these same twelve occupations. In fact, over half of all male workers were employed in twenty-five occupational groups characterized by disproportionately high ratios of males to females. These occupational groups also tend to be more remunerative, as measured by wages paid during the survey week.[3] This evidence indicates that female occupations persist, and that women have had relatively minor success in penetrating what have come to be known as traditionally male occupations. To illustrate the extremes (again, using two-digit groupings), in 1981 only 3.2 percent of engineers, 1.2 percent of carpenters, and 0.2 percent of auto mechanics were women, compared with 98.2 percent of stenographers and secretaries, 87.0 percent of bookkeepers, and 87.3 percent of health service workers other than physicians and dentists.

Several recent studies indicate that occupational segregation has diminished over time, with an acceleration of the decline during the 1970s. To the extent that occupational integration of women accelerated during the 1970s, it proceeded most rapidly in the so-called male occupations—those in which women were employed at levels far below

2. Andrea H. Beller, "Occupational Segregation by Sex: Determinants and Changes," *Journal of Human Resources*, vol. 17 (Summer 1982), p. 372.

3. These figures are for workers aged 25–59 only. See below for a discussion of occupational groupings.

their share of the total labor force. Entry of women into managerial and professional occupations was particularly strong.[4] Nevertheless, although measured occupational segregation has fallen, it appears that the traditionally male occupations remain bastions of male employment.

To know why occupational segregation persists despite some erosion in recent years has led researchers to ask what roles choice and sex discrimination play in determining occupational selection by women. Polachek argues that occupational segregation is largely a result of rational economic choices by women who choose jobs based on their own expectations about employment continuity during their working life.[5] By contrast, Beller and England find little support in their empirical work for this human capital rationale for occupational segregation.[6] Beller argues that the timing of the reduction in occupational segregation is consistent with the view that federal equal employment laws reduced discriminatory barriers to female employment. But whether the reduction can be attributed entirely to the change in the legal environment remains unclear.

Curiously, the same degree of attention has not been given to how occupational segregation shapes and in turn is shaped by decisions of women to work part time rather than full time.[7] This lack of attention

4. Andrea H. Beller, "Trends in Occupational Segregation by Sex and Race, 1960–1981," in Barbara F. Reskin, ed., *Sex Segregation in the Workplace: Trends, Explanations, Remedies* (Washington, D.C.: National Academy Press, 1984), pp. 13–14, 19; Nancy F. Rytina and Suzanne M. Bianchi, "Occupational Reclassification and Changes in Distribution by Gender," *Monthly Labor Review*, vol. 107 (March 1984), p. 14; and Gregory Williams, "The Changing U.S. Labor Force and Occupational Differentiation by Sex," *Demography*, vol. 16 (February 1979), pp. 73–87.

5. Solomon William Polachek, "Occupational Segregation among Women: Theory, Evidence, and a Prognosis," in Cynthia B. Lloyd, Emily S. Andrews, and Curtis L. Gilroy, eds., *Women in the Labor Market* (Columbia University Press, 1979), p. 138.

6. Beller, "Occupational Segregation by Sex," pp. 385, 387; and Paula England, "The Failure of Human Capital Theory to Explain Occupational Sex Segregation," *Journal of Human Resources*, vol. 17 (Summer 1982), p. 358.

7. This is not to say that part-time work has been entirely ignored in the literature. It is a component of any labor supply study of hours of work. Sylvia Lazos Terry, "Involuntary Part-Time Work: New Information from the CPS," *Monthly Labor Review*, vol. 104 (February 1981), pp. 70–74, and Carol Leon and Robert W. Bednarzik, "A Profile of Women on Part-time Schedules," *Monthly Labor Review*, vol. 101 (October 1978), pp. 3–12, are examples of more descriptive studies of part-time work. What is lacking is the explicit attention to full-time and part-time status in discussions of trends in occupational segregation. A recent exception is Mary Corcoran, Greg J. Duncan, and Michael Ponza, "Work Experience, Job Segregation, and Wages," in Reskin, ed., *Sex Segregation in the Workplace*, pp. 171–91, who study the relationship between job

Table 1. *Nonagricultural Work Force, by Full-Time and Part-Time Work and by Sex, 1971–81*[a]

Numbers in millions

Year and sex	Full-time work[b]		Part-time work	
	Number	Percent	Number	Percent
1971	59.4	83.2	12.0	16.8
Male	39.8	90.2	4.3	9.7
Female	19.6	71.8	7.7	28.2
1981	74.3	81.4	17.0	18.6
Male	46.0	88.8	5.8	11.2
Female	28.3	71.6	11.2	28.4

Source: U.S. Department of Labor, Bureau of Labor Statistics, *Handbook of Labor Statistics* (Government Printing Office, 1984), tables 19, 20.

a. Aged 16 and over.

b. Includes persons who usually work full time but worked part time at the time of the survey because of temporary noneconomic reasons.

may be due in part to the conventional view that part-time employment is technologically constrained to particular occupations and that therefore both men and women wishing to work part time are similarly limited in their job choices. We investigate the truth of this assumption here. Even though part-time working males are not occupationally distributed like full-time male workers, it does not necessarily follow that they are distributed like part-time female workers.

We attempt to weave together the two strands of research on occupational segregation and the characteristics of part-time versus full-time workers. We do this by disaggregating the work force into full-time and part-time job holders and observing how occupational segregation in these two job groups has contributed to the measured level of and change in occupational segregation for the total work force. The size of the part-time work force suggests that this disaggregation might be important. In 1971, 17 percent of the nonagricultural work force aged 16 and over worked fewer than thirty-five hours a week (see table 1). This was true for 28 percent of all females and 10 percent of all males. By 1981, 19 percent of the work force was employed part time. But this growth was due largely to the far greater increase in the absolute size of the female nonagricultural work force and the resulting increase in the number of

---

segregation and labor force variables predicted by human capital theory to determine the former. They include years of part-time work in male- and female-dominated jobs and find that the wage consequences for women of part-time work do not differ from those of labor force withdrawal. That study does not look specifically at job segregation of part-time work.

female part-time workers by more than 3.5 million, compared with a 1.5 million increase for male part-timers. The percentages of the work force employed part time remained stable: 28 percent of all females and 11 percent of males. The distribution of these millions of new part-time workers among occupations affects both changes in measured occupational segregation and the conclusions that can be drawn about changes in job opportunities for women workers over this decade.

The measured level of occupational segregation for all workers may be an artifact of the different distribution of women and men between part- and full-time jobs. For instance, if particular occupations are more amenable to flexible hours of work, both women and men who prefer shorter hours of work should be similarly concentrated in these few occupations. However, if more women than men want to work part time, these "part-time" occupations will be female-dominated even though female and male part-time workers are treated exactly alike. This should result in a high level of measured occupational segregation for the total work force but little real occupational segregation within either the full-time or part-time labor force.

On the other hand, if separate occupational segregation indexes for part-time and full-time workers show considerable segregation by sex within both groups, this would suggest that women's stronger preference for part-time work is not a sufficient, or even a major, explanation for occupational segregation within the total work force. Indeed, the true level and trend in job segregation may be obscured by the typical aggregation of full-time and part-time workers when segregation indexes are calculated. We provide two examples of how this may occur.

First, if women are barred from the more lucrative full-time jobs held by males in some occupations, employers in these occupations may respond to women's demand for work by structuring more part-time jobs for women while retaining higher-paying jobs for full-time male workers. If employers in male-dominated occupations are more likely to respond this way, it might appear that there are reductions in occupational segregation for the total labor force despite little actual improvement in the ability of women to compete with men in the full-time job market.

Second, because part-time jobs tend to be in female-dominated occupations, the continuing rise in the number of women seeking part-time work may conceal important changes in full-time work opportunities for women. Even though full-time female workers may be desegregating male-dominated occupations, these trends would be partially offset by the number of women filling the growing part-time positions in female-dominated occupations.

Data and Definitions

For our investigation we use data on employment from the March Current Population Surveys (CPS) for 1971, 1981, and, to a lesser degree, 1976. The years 1971 and 1981 cover the period over which the decline in occupational segregation accelerated.

The March CPS classifies workers by the total number of hours worked during the reference week. The fact that the focus is on hours worked, rather than hours worked in a particular job, leads to some ambiguity. People working fewer than thirty-five hours a week are more clearly employed in part-time jobs although a few may have more than one part-time job. Those working more than thirty-five hours, however, may in fact hold two or more jobs, neither or only one of which is full time. This means that the regular monthly labor force survey underestimates the number of part-time jobs held by workers. Only in the periodic surveys of dual job holders is it possible to identify the total number of part-time jobs held.

Another and more important shortcoming is that the census classifications do not easily distinguish between workers who hold "regular" or "permanent" part-time jobs and those with full-time jobs. The CPS does ask why workers work fewer than thirty-five hours, and we use these reasons to group workers into two groups: those who hold a job that is usually part time and those who hold a job that is usually full time. This distinction differs from those made by the CPS between "voluntary" and "involuntary" reasons and between "economic" and "noneconomic" reasons for why people are currently working part time. Our distinction is aimed at discovering whether women and men who typically work part time are assigned to different jobs. Therefore, we want to distinguish part-time jobs—chosen voluntarily or not—from jobs that have had a short-term reduction in hours for whatever reason.

Figure 1 provides a graphic explanation of our classification system. We define holders of full-time jobs as those who currently work thirty-five hours or more, as well as those who say they usually work that much but are currently on a shorter work schedule because of temporary

Figure 1. *Classification of Workers by Full-Time and Part-Time Jobs and by Reasons for Part-Time Work*

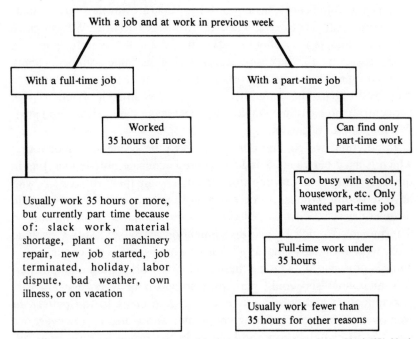

Source: U.S. Department of Commerce, Bureau of the Census, *Current Population Survey*, March 1971, March 1981.

reductions in hours.[8] This category includes cases in which labor demand has been reduced, workers who have just been hired or terminated, and those with various other reasons for not working full time during the survey week.[9]

Our group of part-time job holders includes four subgroups. The first group includes those who state that they can find only part-time work. The second includes those who are too busy with school and housework to take a full-time job or those wanting only part-time work. A third group is persons who regard themselves as full-time workers even though

8. Though part-time workers are asked if they usually work thirty-five hours or more, we do not know how many "full-time workers" usually work part time. Thus full-time jobs may be overestimated by those who had their hours of work increased temporarily during the survey reference week.

9. A small group of workers who usually work full time are not doing so for unspecified reasons. We cannot classify these, but do include them in labor force totals.

they work fewer than thirty-five hours a week.[10] The last group consists of those who usually work a short week for other unspecified reasons.

This study does not consider or try to separate out those individuals who work only part of a year, whether full time or part time. We recognize that some people may choose between working full time for part of a year or part time for the entire year, and that the same arguments apply to separating out part-year workers from full-time workers. But since reasons for part-year employment are more difficult to define, we concentrate on part-time employment and leave the more general analysis for another occasion.

In addition, we confine our attention to the prime-age labor force, which is aged between 25 and 59. There is considerable job shifting in the early years of labor force attachment. To help focus on workers who have settled into the labor force in a more permanent way, we exclude those under age 25. At the older ages, occupational distribution may be determined as much by age discrimination as by sex, so we exclude those workers aged 60 and above. This is not to say that the occupational choices or constraints facing these excluded workers are unimportant. A similar analysis would perhaps distinguish between age and sex discrimination among older workers or give clues to the pattern of employer preferences in hiring young men and women. However, our intent is to examine how job holders in the prime working ages are distributed across occupational categories.

The Index of Occupational Segregation

We use the 1970 three-digit occupational codes provided in the 1971, 1976, and 1981 surveys to maximize the measure of occupational segregation.[11] We use two measures of occupational segregation in this paper. The index of segregation indicates the proportion of women in

10. Janice Neipert Hedges and Stephen J. Gallogly, "Full and Part-time: A Review of Definitions," *Monthly Labor Review*, vol. 100 (March 1977), p. 23, find that the demographic characteristics of these workers resemble voluntary part-time workers more closely than full-time workers.

11. The fineness of the occupational classification affects the degree of occupational segregation measured. Our use of data for about 500 occupations will show more occupational segregation than the 12 or 44 occupational classifications also given by the CPS, because of the offsetting effect within these broader categories of male- and female-labeled occupations.

Table 2. *Indexes of Occupational Segregation by Sex, for Full-Time and Part-Time Job Holders, 1971–81*[a]

Status of job holder	Actual index[b]			Standardized index[c]		
	1971	1981	Percent change	1971	1981	Percent change
Full-time	69.0	61.8	−7.2	69.0	62.0	−7.0
Part-time	77.6	66.1	−11.5	77.6	68.7	−9.0
Total work force	70.6	63.4	−7.2	70.6	63.8	−6.8

Source: Authors' calculations based on March CPS public data files for 1971 and 1981.
a. Includes only workers aged 25–59.
b. The percentage of women in the labor force that would have to change occupations to achieve equal distribution by sex (see footnote 11).
c. Same as previous index but controlled for size of each three-digit (SIC) occupation.

the labor force group that would have to switch occupations in order to be distributed like male workers.[12] In addition, we label occupations as "male," "female," or "integrated"; this shows, in greater detail than is possible with a summary measure, how the distribution of females and males across occupational groups contributes to changes in the index of segregation. We will first discuss changes in the index of occupational segregation.

Changes, 1971–81

Occupational segregation diminished consistently, albeit slowly, over the decade of the 1970s. In 1971, 71 percent of the female (or male) labor force would have had to change occupations in order to have an equal distribution of workers for both sexes (table 2). By 1981, this figure had dropped to 63 percent. This improvement was accomplished by reduced occupational segregation in both full-time and part-time employment.

What is surprising is the higher degree of occupational segregation among part-time job holders. Recall that part-time job holders exclude those whose jobs are usually full time but are currently on reduced schedules because of temporary economic fluctuations. This definition should reduce the effect on the part-time index of men working reduced hours because of economic slowdowns or temporary material shortages.

---

12. The index is defined as $I(t) = \frac{1}{2} \sum_i |m(i,t) - f(i,t)|$, where $m(i,t)$ is the percentage of all males in the labor force at time t that are employed in occupation i, and $f(i,t)$ is the same percentage for females in occupation i. We calculate indexes $I(t)$ for all workers, and for those in part-time and full-time jobs separately. See Otis Dudley Duncan and Beverly Duncan, "A Methodological Analysis of Segregation Indexes," *American Sociological Review*, vol. 20 (April 1955), pp. 210–17.

Thus the index for part-time job holders suggests the differential hiring by sex. For whatever reasons, men and women with part-time jobs end up in quite different occupations.

Changes due to Sex Mix

Reductions in the index of segregation can be due either to changes in the male-female composition of individual occupations or to the more rapid growth of male-dominated occupations.[13] While both forces may indicate growing opportunities for women, only the former change indicates a long-term improvement in the way employers treat female job seekers compared with males.

To separate out the importance of changes in sex composition within occupations from changes due to employment growth, we calculate an index standardized by the size of each occupation in 1971 (table 2).[14] Changes in this index reflect changes in the sex mix of each occupation; differences between the unstandardized and standardized indexes are due to different rates of employment growth between 1971 and 1981 in male- and female-dominated occupations. The standardized index falls somewhat less than does the unstandardized. The very small difference between the two indexes for full-time workers indicates that the sex mix within occupations was the major factor in the decline in occupational segregation. On the other hand, the effect of standardization is larger for part-time jobs. This suggests that in part-time jobs the effect of growth in employment has been more important in opening up opportunities for women in male-dominated occupations than has been true for the full-time work force. At the same time, the change in occupational segregation due to the sex mix has also been greater for part-time than for full-time job holders (-9.0 versus -7.0).

These data show that the overall level of occupational segregation was slightly higher because of greater occupational segregation among workers in part-time jobs; change over time was not affected. The decline in occupational segregation of part-time jobs was due both to changes in the sex mix of part-time jobs within occupations and the growth of

13. Francine D. Blau and Wallace E. Hendricks, "Occupational Segregation by Sex: Trends and Prospects," *Journal of Human Resources*, vol. 14 (Spring 1979), pp. 197–210; and Beller, "Trends in Occupational Segregation," p. 19.

14. A third factor is an interaction term that is arbitrarily assigned to the occupational size component in our standardization.

Table 3. *Index of Occupational Segregation by Job Type, for Males and Females, 1971–81*[a]

Sex	1971	1981	Percent change
Male	43.7	42.4	−1.3
Female	41.6	37.3	−4.3

Source: Authors' calculations based on March CPS public data files for 1971 and 1981.

a. The percentage of part-time job holders that would have had to change occupations to achieve equal distribution by sex (see footnote 15). Includes only workers aged 25–59.

occupations in which part-time work had a more favorable sex mix in 1971. This contrasts with full-time work, in which occupational growth contributed little to the reduction in segregation.

Despite considerable occupational segregation in part-time work, male part-time workers are apparently not treated like male full-time workers, and within the female work force part- and full-time workers are not treated equally. Table 3 presents unstandardized occupational segregation indexes that indicate separately for each sex the degree of occupational segregation between full- and part-time job holders.[15] In 1971, for part-time job holders, almost 44 percent of males and 42 percent of females would have had to change occupations in order to achieve equal occupational distribution by sex with their full-time counterparts. By 1981 there was only a small decline in the index among male workers, but a somewhat larger decline for females. We conclude that even though male and female part-time workers are assigned different jobs, they are similarly disadvantaged relative to full-time workers of their sex. While male part-time workers are differently distributed than are male full-time workers (table 3), they are also likely to work in different occupations than part-time female workers.

Changes by Age

It is important to indicate the effect of restricting our analysis to workers aged 25–59, rather than all workers. The inclusion of workers of all ages somewhat reduces the decline in occupational segregation for the total work force between 1971 and 1981. When we include younger

15. This index is defined as: $I(t) = \frac{1}{2} \sum_i |ft(i,t) - pt(i,t)|$, where $ft(i,t)$ is the percentage of the full-time work force at time t that is employed in occupation i, and $pt(i,t)$ is the percentage of the part-time work force in occupation i at time t. We calculate separate indexes for male and female workers.

and older workers, the overall measure of occupational segregation falls. This is consistent with our hypothesis that when job seekers are relatively young or old, employers are less likely to assign jobs on the basis of gender than they are in the case of prime-age workers. Why this is so deserves attention but will not be pursued in this essay. We also investigated which age group among the excluded age groups most affects both our total and full-time measures. Full-time workers aged 16–19 and those 65 or older seem to experience greater occupational equality between the sexes. The index for 1971 changes little when only those aged 20–24 and 16–64 are included. However, the part-time index is substantially reduced when those aged 20–24 are included. We suspect this indicates the relatively equal treatment of part-time men and women in the age bracket in which most would be attending college.

Changes by Occupation

To gain a clearer picture of the occupations of part-time job holders by sex and the direction of occupational changes accounting for the drop in occupational segregation over the 1970s, table 4 shows the distribution of males and females by occupation in 1981. These numbers merely clarify conclusions drawn above. Table 2 shows that female part-time workers are distributed differently than male part-time workers. Table 4 shows, for example, that employment in crafts accounts for some of this: only 1.7 percent of female part-time workers are in that occupation, compared with 16.5 percent of male part-time workers. Further, table 3 shows that among males part-time and full-time workers are differently distributed, and table 4 shows that this is a result in part of the lower percentage of male part-time workers than full-time workers in crafts (16 versus 23 percent). Similarly, among females the different distribution of part-time and full-time workers is largely a result of the larger percentage of part-timers in sales and services.

The distribution of workers across occupations by sex and job status reveals an enormous variation in sex ratios by occupation (table 5). Of relevance to our discussion is the variation in sex ratios even when workers in part-time jobs are distinguished from those on permanent full-time schedules. Only 30 percent of part-time craft workers are females, while 95 percent of part-time clerical workers and 99 percent of private household workers are women. Though the percentage of part-time workers who are female is always greater than the percentage of

Table 4. *Distribution of Full-Time and Part-Time Job Holders, by Occupation and Sex, 1981*[a]

Percent

	Males			Females		
Occupation	Full-time jobs	Part-time jobs	All jobs	Full-time jobs	Part-time jobs	All jobs
Professional and technical	18.4	24.1	18.5	20.8	17.2	19.9
Managerial and administrative (nonfarm)	18.1	10.6	17.8	9.8	4.5	8.6
Sales	5.9	5.2	5.9	4.3	9.7	5.5
Clerical	5.7	6.4	5.7	35.8	30.8	34.3
Crafts	22.9	16.5	22.6	2.1	1.7	2.0
Operators (except transportation)	10.2	7.6	10.1	11.7	4.3	10.0
Transportation equipment operators	5.4	5.6	5.5	0.6	1.4	0.8
Nonfarm laborers	4.2	8.0	4.4	1.0	0.9	1.0
Private household	*	*	*	1.1	4.3	1.7
All other services	6.4	12.7	6.6	12.3	23.7	15.4
Farmers and farm managers	2.0	1.2	2.0	0.2	0.5	0.3
Farm laborers and foremen	0.8	2.0	0.9	0.5	0.9	0.5
Total	100.0	100.0	100.0	100.0	100.0	100.0

Source: March 1981 CPS public data files.
* Less than 0.1 percent.
a. Includes only workers aged 25–59.

female full-time workers, the variation across occupations in this ratio is large and results in the high level of occupational segregation in part-time jobs reported earlier.

Changes by Cohort

While occupational segregation may have declined for all age groups combined, women in different age groups may not have shared equally in the growing opportunities for part-time and full-time jobs in male-dominated occupations. In addition, it is important to know whether the gains for any single cohort of women were maintained, increased, or eroded as they aged over the decade. It is conceivable that occupational segregation declined over time only because each new group of young labor market entrants faced fewer barriers to entry into male-dominated jobs while the barriers remained unchanged for workers already in the market. On the other hand, it may be that as older, experienced cohorts

Table 5. *Percentage of Full-Time and Part-Time Job Holders Who Are Female, by Occupation, 1981*[a]

Occupation	Full-time jobs	Part-time jobs	All jobs
Professional and technical	39.0	81.0	43.5
Managerial and administrative (nonfarm)	23.3	64.7	25.5
Sales	29.0	88.8	40.0
Clerical	78.0	95.4	81.1
Crafts	5.0	30.3	5.9
Operators (except transportation)	39.4	70.8	41.2
Transportation equipment operators	5.5	52.5	9.8
Nonfarm laborers	11.5	50.5	13.7
Private household	95.8	99.3	98.0
All other services	52.1	88.9	62.4
Farmers and farm managers	6.3	65.0	10.1
Farm laborers and foremen	22.5	65.5	29.5
All occupations	36.0	82.2	41.6

Source: March 1981 CPS public data files.
a. Includes only workers aged 25–59.

changed jobs and were promoted, their gains in job integration exceeded those of new entrants.

To sort out how occupational segregation changed over time for each birth cohort, we calculate an unstandardized index of occupational segregation for each age group in 1971, 1976, and 1981 and show the absolute change in that index for each cohort over the ten-year period (table 6). For full-time job holders, it is clear that reduced occupational segregation for each new group of young workers contributed to the overall decline in segregation between 1971 and 1981. At the same time, as each cohort aged, except for those who were 45–54 in 1971, the occupational segregation index declined. Changes in occupational segregation for part-time job holders were less uniform. Between 1971 and 1976 the index increased for some cohorts and declined for others, but between 1971 and 1981 the index fell for all those aged 30 and older in 1971.

It is difficult to conclude with any confidence what decisions are being made by employers and employees that would account for differences in changes in the index of segregation across cohorts and type of job held. It is apparent that over the 1970s the acceleration in the decline in that index was a result not only of increased job opportunities for younger women, but also of older women moving into less female-dominated occupations. On the other hand, an interesting age-related phenomenon is apparent for part-time job holders. Occupational segregation is relatively low at younger ages and rises sharply as women move into their thirties. This is evident both from the difference for each year between women aged 25–29 and those in the next five-year age group and from the increase with age in the occupational segregation of the cohorts aged 20–29 in 1971. Perhaps when women's job attachments are increasingly conditioned by child-care responsibilities, both they and employers are less agreeable to part-time employment in male-dominated occupations; as women move out of their thirties, occupational segregation declines among part-time job holders and continues to do so for all older cohorts. At all ages, however, occupational segregation among part-time job holders remains considerably higher than among full-time job holders. For full-time workers, occupational segregation declines over time as each cohort ages.

The cohort data reinforce our earlier findings and conclusions. Female part-time job holders of all ages experience far higher occupational segregation than do full-time job holders. While female part-time job holders may face more severe labor market constraints in job choice than women willing to work full time, it is clear that the sex of these part-time workers is as important in determining their employment as it is for other workers. Even part-time jobs may be allocated to men and women differently; the decision to work part time is not sufficient to explain the measured occupational segregation for the total work force since this decision may in fact subject workers to even greater than average discrimination on account of sex.

Sex-Labeled Occupations and the Distribution of Jobs

The second measure of occupational segregation we use is the distribution of males and females working in part- and full-time jobs among occupations labeled "male," "female," or "integrated."

In identifying occupations as male, female, or integrated, we choose as our identifying criteria a deviation of 10 percentage points from the mean percentage of regular full-time jobs held by women. We choose full-time work as our reference group because we believe that this is the concept of employment lying behind efforts to open up equal opportu-

Table 6. Index of Occupational Segregation by Sex, for Age Cohorts among Full-Time and Part-Time Job Holders, 1971, 1976, and 1981[a]

Age cohort			Full-time job holders				Part-time job holders			
1971	1976	1981	1971	1976	1981	Change, 1971–81	1971	1976	1981	Change, 1971–81
15–19	20–24	25–59	...	...	61.1	...	...	...	67.7	...
20–24	25–29	30–34	...	66.6	61.5	...	...	66.8	76.4	...
25–29	30–34	35–39	71.0	66.8	64.7	−6.3	67.3	81.7	77.5	9.8
30–34	35–39	40–44	73.0	68.6	65.5	−7.6	92.4	85.1	83.3	−9.1
35–39	40–44	45–49	74.0	70.0	66.1	−7.9	82.8	92.4	80.8	−2.0
40–44	45–49	50–54	70.5	70.2	67.3	−3.2	88.8	87.1	78.1	−10.7
45–49	50–54	55–59	69.5	69.2	69.6	0.1	90.8	87.8	84.3	−6.5
50–54	55–59	60–64	72.0	73.4	...	...	85.2	85.4	...	...
55–59	60–64	65–69	71.5	...	...	...	79.6	...	...	...

Source: Authors' calculations based on March CPS public data files for 1971, 1976, and 1981.
a. Includes only workers aged 25–29.

Table 7. *Female Job Holders in Sex-Labeled Occupational Groups, by Job Type, 1971–81*
Percent

Type of occupation[a]	Type of job					
	Full-time		Part-time		All jobs	
	1971	1981	1971	1981	1971	1981
Male-labeled	5.1	10.8	31.3	38.1	6.0	12.1
Female-labeled	75.1	76.7	96.1	94.1	79.8	80.7
Integrated	25.8	35.9	68.3	74.5	28.4	39.3
All occupations	30.2	36.3	84.6	82.4	36.2	42.1

Source: Authors' calculations based on March CPS public data files for 1971 and 1981.
a. Labeled according to the deviation in 1971 from the mean percentage of regular full-time jobs held by women.

nities for women. The 10 percentage-point deviation lies between the 5 percentage-point figure used by Beller and the 20 percentage-point figure used by Rytina and Bianchi.[16] No strong theoretical reason exists for choosing any particular percentage-point cutoff. We consider the 5 percentage-point cutoff as quite restrictive, particularly in view of our use of comparable CPS data that have larger statistical errors than census data. This smaller deviation probably tends to overestimate female occupational segregation. On the other hand, the 20 percentage-point deviation seems rather conservative, and in our study it would lead to the labeling of occupations as "male" only if fewer than 10 percent of all employees are female. We believe this range is too wide and it leads to an underestimate of female and male occupational segregation.

The use of this measure does not provide additional information on the degree of occupational segregation; we use it here to indicate the types of occupational shifts that led to reduced occupational concentration of both part-time and full-time workers. Occupations are labeled by their 1971 ratio of females to males. Thus we show shifts over the decade in the percentage of the work force that is female for a constant group of occupations (table 7).

We begin by comparing the data in this table with the previous reported declines in the index of occupational segregation shown in table 2. The index of occupational segregation for all job holders declined from 70.6 to 63.4. This was the net result of the increased hiring of women into both male-labeled and integrated occupations and little

16. Beller, "Trends in Occupational Segregation," p. 18; and Rytina and Bianchi, "Occupational Reclassification," p. 14.

change in the percentage of the work force that was female in already heavily female occupations. Similar changes for full-time job holders and part-time job holders contributed to this overall change.

Women doubled their share of full-time jobs in male-dominated industries: their share of full-time jobs in the integrated sector also increased substantially. This growth was only slightly offset by the increase in the percentage of women among full-time job holders in female-dominated occupations. Changes in the part-time job sector consistently contributed to the more rapid decrease in the segregation index for part-time job holders: females both reduced their share of part-time jobs in female-dominated occupations and increased their share of jobs in the other two groups.

Explanations

What explains the relatively small decline in female occupational segregation over the 1970s, when the potential for change was apparently so great because of the exceptionally large number and percentage of female entrants into the labor force?

A variety of explanations come to mind. We can classify them into several different categories, including differences in the relative growth of opportunities for employment in gender-labeled occupations, changes in the relative qualifications of females, preferences of females for different types of occupations, and lingering discrimination against females. We also discuss below changes in institutional arrangements that might alter opportunities for women to seek jobs or affect the kinds of jobs they seek.

To the extent that larger numbers of women than men entered the labor force in the 1970s, and to the degree that employment opportunities expanded rapidly in male-dominated occupations, we would have expected to see sizable increases in the percentages of women in male-dominated occupations. This would apply with particular force to women working full time. On the other hand, because part-time employment has typically been concentrated in female occupations and these occupations also expanded rapidly, we would have expected part-time female workers to move in large numbers into traditional occupations.

These expectations do not agree with what happened. We calculate that between 1971 and 1981 male-dominated occupations grew by only 23.1 percent, while female occupations grew by 38.0 percent and integrated occupations expanded by 31.0 percent. Thus opportunities expanded more slowly in occupations where entry would have contributed most to reducing occupational segregation. This explains why overall occupational growth failed to contribute to greater integration of the work force (as indicated by the small difference between the standardized and unstandardized indexes in table 2). Nevertheless, the percentage of women working full time in male-dominated occupations doubled, but this was offset somewhat by the increase in the percentage of full-time females in female-dominated occupations (table 7). The only bright spot is the large-scale movement of women into integrated occupations: their share rose to 36 percent. In short, the pattern of employment growth impeded substantial gains for women.

What about changes in women's qualifications? Obviously, the increasing number of women obtaining college degrees and other types of training enhanced their ability to move into male-dominated occupations. This is particularly the case for highly visible occupations in the professional and managerial fields where employers have been under greater pressure to hire women.

Less can be said with certainty about preferences. It does seem obvious that women became increasingly likely to devote a substantial part of their lives to working and responded by changing their attitudes and aspirations about work and careers.

The degree to which employer prejudice limits the occupational choices of women remains unclear because direct evidence of discriminatory practices is difficult, if not impossible, to locate. However, the persistence of occupational segregation by sex at relatively high levels in full- and part-time jobs, despite the changing characteristics of the female labor force, suggests that sex discrimination still plays a role.

We conclude that it is not possible to assign weights to these explanations. It is evident that far more needs to be done to facilitate the entry of women into male-dominated occupations. Occupational segregation persists among full-time workers, and the occupational segregation of part-time workers suggests that segregation of males and females may be a more pervasive norm than often thought.

One might expect occupational integration to be constrained by the early job choices of now-older working women. Yet the cohort data show that as they aged, women moved, however slowly, into male-dominated occupations. Among older cohorts this change was substantial for women holding part-time jobs.

Increasing Part-Time Work Option Programs

We can only speculate about how programs to stimulate part-time work options—such as flextime or work sharing—might affect occupational segregation, since our data do not lend themselves well to this type of analysis. In addition, we have little information on the extent to which women in particular sex-labeled occupations move from part-time to full-time jobs in those or other occupational groups. We can only guess at how the creation of part-time options in particular types of occupations would reduce occupational segregation.

If only "traditional" part-time work options are fashioned in response to women's greater demand for work, two developments are likely. One is greater integration of the part-time (and therefore total) work force in traditional occupations as both men and women discover these options to be attractive. The other is greater integration as the percentage of part-time female workers (and of all female workers) rises in nontraditional occupations. In neither case would there be an increase in women's opportunities in more lucrative full-time work. On the other hand, full-time jobs in male-dominated occupations are increasingly held by women, and so are part-time jobs. It is not clear whether these trends reinforce each other, or whether the latter is a sign of employers' reluctance to accommodate demands for full-time work. Table 7 showed that women's share of part-time jobs in nontraditional occupations increased during the 1970s. If these women subsequently gain access to full-time positions, this process of institutional change would accelerate occupational integration of full-time workers. However, if women in part-time jobs are barred from moving into full-time positions, new programs need to focus on developing full-time work options in male occupations. Perhaps institutional arrangements such as flextime, job sharing, and affirmative action will be effective in expanding integration if they are focused on those occupations in which male part-time workers seem to have a comparative advantage. It appears, however, that most of these arrangements are being developed in the female occupations and hence will do relatively little to ease the problem of occupational segregation. Thus there is considerable need to expand employment opportunities for women in male occupations in part-time as well as full-time jobs.

Summary

We have attempted to identify separate trends in occupational segregation for full-time and part-time workers. Because three-quarters of all women workers aged 25–59 hold full-time jobs, it is understandable that changes in occupational segregation for all women reflect this fact.

To enable us to focus on part-time versus full-time job holders, we defined part-time workers as those who are employed at jobs that are usually part time. These are not all voluntary part-time workers since those who could find only part-time work are included in this category. We took this approach because of our interest in how part-time *jobs* are allocated across groups of occupations and between men and women.

Occupational segregation was persistently high over the 1971–81 period, though it fell steadily due primarily to the changing sex mix within each occupation for both full-time and part-time jobs. The result was that females more than doubled their share (though from a small mean of only 5 percent of all workers) in those occupations that were predominantly male in 1971.

Occupational segregation by sex was higher for part-time jobs than for full-time jobs, suggesting that males and females, even if both work part time, are not treated the same in the labor market. Whether because of personal or employer preferences, differences in work experience, or demographic characteristics, men and women are assigned to different types of part-time jobs. However, the index of occupational segregation declined more over the decade for the part-time than the full-time work force, in part because trends in all three types of occupational groups (male, female, and integrated occupations) were conducive to the greater integration of this group. In addition, the cohort data suggest that declines in occupational segregation are due to the fact that both young women workers and prime-age women workers become less likely over time to enter or remain in sex-segregated part-time work.

Nevertheless, the 1981 data give us a picture of continued occupational segregation. Persistently male occupations continue to employ relatively few women, and they continue to prefer male workers even as part-time workers. Labor force growth continues to be concentrated for each sex in its respectively dominated occupational groupings. Though there is a cause for optimism in the growth of males in female occupations and of females in male occupations, important constraints remain that limit the ability of *both* full-time and part-time working females to penetrate male occupations.

Comments by Francine D. Blau

The Holden and Hansen paper uses data from the Current Population Survey to study the relationship of part-time and full-time employment patterns to occupational segregation. The neglect of this topic in the literature on sex differentials is surprising. A common view would be that since traditionally female jobs provide greater opportunities for part-time employment, women's larger propensity for part-time work would be a factor contributing to occupational segregation by sex. Thus it would be logical to net out the impact of part-time workers in examining both the extent of occupational segregation at a point in time and trends in its magnitude over time. The Holden and Hansen paper, which focuses upon prime-age workers (25–59), sheds considerable light on these and other issues and goes a long way toward closing this gap in the literature. I would like to highlight some of their more interesting findings and suggest some fruitful directions for future research.

Holden and Hansen find that in both the years they examine, 1971 and 1981, the degree of occupational segregation is somewhat lower among full-time workers than among the total work force (including part-time workers). Perhaps more interesting than this finding itself are the reasons for it. First, it is probably true, as expected, that female part-time workers are more heavily concentrated in predominantly female jobs than their full-time counterparts. Unfortunately, Holden and Hansen do not provide information on this directly. But they do show that female part-time and full-time workers are differentially distributed across occupations and that the former are more likely to be employed in sales and service jobs and less likely to work as managers, craftsmen, and operatives. While female part-time workers are also less likely than full-time workers to be clerical workers, the inference that they are more likely to be in female jobs is probably correct (but nonetheless should be verified).

Second, and more surprisingly, they find that in both years there was a higher degree of occupational segregation by sex among part-time than among full-time job holders. The authors, understandably, put considerable emphasis on this finding. Again, the conventional wisdom would attribute some of the observed occupational segregation to women's preference for part-time employment and the greater opportunities for such jobs in the female sector. While this may indeed be true, Holden and Hansen have shown that such segregation is of great magnitude even between men and women who have similarly restricted hours. This is the case even though male part-time workers are unfavorably distributed across occupations relative to male full-time workers, being less likely to hold managerial or craft jobs and more likely to be in labor or service occupations.

While so-called involuntary part-time workers are included in Holden and Hansen's definition of part time, they correctly argue that their focus is on "those who hold a job that is usually part time." For like reasons they include among full-time job holders those persons whose jobs are usually full time but are on reduced schedules due to temporary economic fluctuations. Thus the higher segregation index among part-time workers would not be due to the inclusion of men in traditionally male blue-collar jobs who generally work full time but are temporarily on short hours.

A second set of findings from the Holden and Hansen study relates to trends in the degree of occupational segregation over time. Here the most important result is that, although inclusion of part-time workers raises the segregation index at a point in time, the reduction in the degree of segregation between 1971 and 1981 is the same regardless of whether or not part-time workers are included. There are two reasons for this. First, in the age group considered, there was no change in the proportion of women working part time (28 percent) and little change in the proportion of men (from 10 to 11 percent). Second, the degree of sex segregation declined among both full-time and part-time workers, with a greater decline for the latter group. Further, the occupational distribution for part-time workers of both sexes drew closer to that of their full-time counterparts, particularly that of women.

While, as the authors note, occupational segregation remained substantial in 1981 for both full-time and part-time workers, the signs of progress for part-time workers that they do find are encouraging. The male-female pay gap is likely to be reduced not only by more women working full time over longer portions of the life cycle, but also by a reduction in the economic disabilities associated with part-time work for women. Holden and Hansen's findings provide grounds for cautious optimism that the latter is beginning to occur.

Holden and Hansen also examine changes in the degree of segregation by age. Among both part-time and full-time workers they generally find declines in occupational segregation for each age group over 1971–81. Among full-time workers the largest decline was for the group aged 25–29 (from 71.0 in 1971 to 61.1 in 1981). Among part-time workers the largest drop was for the group aged 30–34 (from 92.4 to 76.4). Further research to determine the reasons for this difference in age patterns would be of interest.

Holden and Hansen further consider trends for birth cohorts over the period. In this regard, it seems to me they need to be a lot more cautious in interpreting their results. It must be recalled that such synthetic cohorts, formed with cross-sectional data, do not necessarily contain the same individuals over time. When one considers the total labor force, it is still quite interesting to see how such birth cohorts of women fare relative to their male counterparts, even though there will have been some turnover in the labor force group. However, in examining part-time and full-time workers separately, the exercise becomes less meaningful: not only is there labor force turnover, but also movement of individuals between the two categories of part-time and full-time employment. However, I do believe that through their effort to use the data in this fashion, Holden and Hansen have implicitly identified an excellent direction for future research on this topic. It would be extremely interesting to use longitudinal data to learn more about the relationship of part-time employment to occupational segregation. In this way one could not only identify a stable group of part-time and full-time workers, but also explicitly trace the consequences of movements into and out of part-time status for the jobs women hold.

Comments by David Stern

Holden and Hansen have unearthed some interesting clues about the nature and causes of occupational segregation by sex. Females are more concentrated than males in low-paid occupations, and part-time jobs are also concentrated in low-paid occupations. Should the fact that more women than men work part time therefore be interpreted as a by-product of women's segregation into less desirable occupations? Likewise, should the higher proportion of females who work part time even within better-paid occupations be interpreted as a sign that employers are merely practicing a more subtle form of discrimination by relegating women to part-time positions within these more desirable occupations?

Holden and Hansen suggest this as a possible interpretation. They also suggest an alternative view, that women are more likely than men to *seek* part-time work. Given the concentration of part-time jobs in low-paid occupations, this interpretation implies that the concentration of female workers in these occupations is a by-product of their preference for part-time work. Holden and Hansen are explicitly agnostic on the extent to which females take part-time work by choice. However, both their own data and some additional evidence, which I will describe, can support the conclusion that discrimination by employers plays a smaller role than women's own choices—but those choices are constrained by the division of labor in households. I will discuss the evidence, then comment on some implications.

Evidence from Holden and Hansen

The most obvious evidence that women who hold part-time jobs have chosen to do so was reported in a previous version of Holden's and Hansen's essay. In both 1971 and 1981 more than 70 percent of females in part-time jobs indicated to the Current Population Survey interviewers that they did not want full-time work. However, it is possible that this response was given because the jobs available to these women were unattractive and poorly paid. If better jobs were available, they might want to work full time. This interpretation could be tested by comparing the responses of women working part time in well-paid, high-status occupations with those working part time in poorly paid, menial jobs. Are the part-time lawyers more likely than the part-time waitresses to say they would prefer full-time work?

Other evidence developed by Holden and Hansen raises doubts about the importance of direct discrimination by employers in assigning women to part-time jobs. Their table 2 shows more segregation by sex in part-time jobs than in full-time jobs in both 1971 and 1981. If employers were restricting women to part-time jobs in order to bar them from full participation in predominantly male fields, why would jobs in these fields be more available to women working full time than to women working part time?

As a method of discrimination, restricting women to part-time work would be expensive for employers, due to the large quasi-fixed costs of hiring, training, and certain fringe benefits. The growing importance of these costs appears to have led employers generally to assign more overtime and to *deter* creation of more part-time jobs.[17] Therefore, the fact that a larger proportion of female than male workers continues to work part time seems less likely to result from constraints imposed by employers than from women's own choices about how much time to spend in paid work. Employers who discriminate against women presumably can find cheaper ways to do so than assigning women to part-time work.

However, in addition to constraints imposed by employers, women's choices about spending time in paid work are limited by their household responsibilities. These responsibilities constrain women more than men. More women than men are single heads of households with children. In households with two adults, women usually do more of the housework and child care. Decisions in the market for paid labor are not made in a vacuum; they are made together with choices about division of labor in households. If males took more responsibility for household work, more females might choose to seek full-time work for pay.

Evidence from a Survey of Work Time Preferences

Additional information about workers' preferred combinations of earnings and work time and the influence of spouses' work status is available from a 1978 national survey conducted by Louis Harris for the National Commission on Employment Policy.[18] The sample of 614 male and 341 female adult workers was interviewed at home. Respondents were given several sets of hypothetical choices. One set offered reduced work time, with current earnings reduced by the same proportion. The proportion by which work time and pay could both be reduced ranged from zero to one-half. The range of choices was presented five times,

17. Ronald E. Ehrenberg and Paul L. Schumann, "Longer Hours or More Jobs?" (Cornell University, New York State School of Industrial and Labor Relations, 1982).

18. U.S. Department of Labor, Employment and Training Administration, "Exchanging Earnings for Leisure: Findings of an Exploratory National Survey on Work Time Preferences," R&D Monograph 79 (Government Printing Office, 1980).

each time in terms of a different method of reducing work time. The five methods were: shorter workdays, shorter workweeks, more vacation, an extended leave every seventh year (a sabbatical), and earlier retirement. Respondents were asked how much they would like their work time to be reduced by each method, if their annual pay were reduced by the same proportion as their work time.

Results are summarized in table 8. A substantial minority of workers stated some interest in having their time and pay reduced by each of the methods. The more popular methods are vacations and sabbaticals, which would give extended periods of time off, rather than a few minutes or hours each day or week. These responses indicate that preferences about "part time" depend on how the time is arranged. One person might want a 10 percent reduction in time and pay if the extra time off came in a big piece, while another might want it in small pieces.

The report on this survey also indicates a calculation of the *maximum* reduction in work time and pay each respondent would want: 59 percent of respondents would prefer some reduction of work time and pay by at least one of the five methods. This is true even though only a minority would prefer a reduction of work time and pay by any one of the methods considered separately.

Female respondents stated a preference for larger reductions of work time and pay than male respondents did, although more of the females already work part time. (The survey found that workers currently employed fewer than forty hours per week expressed more interest in further reductions of work time and pay than those currently working forty or more hours a week.) This result again suggests that part-time work is not something foisted on females by employers.

Though the evidence seems to suggest that a lack of full-time job openings is *not* the main reason why more women than men work part time, women's preferences—and men's—are affected by the household division of labor. Table 9 shows the percentages of men and women who expressed interest in some amount of work time and pay reduction, by each of the five methods. Here one can see a striking asymmetry. While the proportions of unmarried men and women who would prefer some reduction of work time and pay are very similar, the proportions differ substantially between men and women whose spouses work full time. Men whose wives work full time for pay are *less* interested in reducing their own work time and pay, while women with full-time working husbands are *more* interested in reducing their own work time and pay.

Table 8. *Employed Men's and Women's Preferences for Reduced Work Time and Pay, by Sex*

Percent

Sex and type of reduction	Reduction in time and pay (percent)										
	0	2	5	10	12	15	20	30	33	40	50
Men											
Workday	79	8	5	..	5	..	..	1	..	..	2
Workweek	76	10	..	8	..	..	4	..	..	1	2
Vacation	61	20	9	6	..	..	2	..	2	..	..
Sabbatical	62	22	7	5	..	4	..	..	..	..	..
Retirement	66	17	7	6	..	..	3	..	..	..	..
Women											
Workday	74	10	6	..	6	..	..	3	..	..	1
Workweek	70	14	..	7	..	..	6	..	..	1	1
Vacation	52	29	8	7	..	..	2	..	2	..	..
Sabbatical	51	29	9	5	..	6	..	..	..	..	..
Retirement	61	18	10	5	..	..	6	..	..	..	..

Source: U.S. Department of Labor, Employment and Training Administration, "Exchanging Earnings for Leisure: Findings of an Exploratory National Survey on Work Time Preference," R&D Monograph 79 (Government Printing Office, 1980).

Table 9. *Employed Men's and Women's Preferences for Reduced Work Time and Pay, by Work Status of Spouse*

Percent

Sex and status of spouse	Type of reduction				
	Workday	Workweek	Vacation	Sabbatical	Retirement
Men					
Not married	25	33	50	48	35
Wife working full time	18	21	37	37	32
Wife working part time	23	29	45	42	36
Wife keeping house	19	19	29	29	30
Women					
Not married	23	24	45	50	36
Husband working full time	29	37	55	53	44

Source: U.S. Department of Labor, Employment and Training Administration, "Exchanging Earnings for Leisure."

How to interpret this asymmetry? A standard income effect could explain why women with working husbands want more time off—but why does the same effect not operate on men with working wives? Comparing men whose wives work full or part time makes it appear that the income effect is actually working backwards: those whose wives are presumably bringing in *less* cash income are *more* likely to want to buy additional time off for themselves. To make matters even more complicated, men whose wives are full-time homemakers *do* seem to comply with the standard income effect: they express the least interest in buying extra time off.

We might just dismiss the data: leave surveys to the sociologists. But these responses, while hypothetical, are consistent with the observed fact that more women than men work part time. The evident pattern is that in two-earner households women are more likely than men to want reduced work and pay. Presumably this frees them to take care of household responsibilities. But unless women have some comparative advantage in doing housework, it is hard to explain this in terms of simple economic principles.

Conclusion

To understand the role of part-time work in perpetuating occupational segregation by sex, one has to consider the division of labor in households. In two-earner households it is the women rather than the men who seek part-time work. This presumably benefits the household, but at some cost to the women's careers. Part-time workers are at a disadvantage in competing for positions that offer more rewards but require more commitment. Once the husband's market wage exceeds the wife's, the division of labor can be rationalized on economic grounds. If the couple become separated or divorced after having children, the mother usually takes custody, and household responsibilities become an even greater impediment to career advancement.

BARBARA R. BERGMANN *and* MARK D. ROBERTS

Income for the Single Parent:
Child Support, Work, and Welfare

THE NUMBER of children living with only one parent is growing rapidly. About one-fifth of all children in the United States are in this situation, most of them living with their mothers.[1] There are three possible sources of economic sustenance for these families: paid work for the mother, child support and alimony payments from the father, and government benefits such as welfare, food stamps, and medicaid. None of these, separately or in combination, can currently be relied on to keep single mothers out of poverty; thus almost one-half of such families do live in poverty.[2]

One method of improving the economic condition of single mothers and their children is to improve the level of child support payments and the reliability with which they are received. Federal legislation to encourage more stringent enforcement of child support payments was enacted in 1985. A 1981 survey showed that about one-half of all single-parent families with court-ordered child support awards were receiving all payments owed to them (see figure 1).

Improved child support enforcement would undoubtedly go some way toward relieving poverty and reducing welfare costs. However, even strict enforcement of current awards would go only part of the way toward solving the poverty problem among single mothers. Many of

1. U.S. Bureau of the Census, *Current Population Reports,* series P-20, no. 399, "Marital Status and Living Arrangements: March 1984" (Government Printing Office, 1985), table D, p. 4. For an excellent general review of the issues relating to single mothers and their children, see Heather L. Ross and Isabel V. Sawhill, *Time of Transition: The Growth of Families Headed by Women* (Washington, D.C.: Urban Institute, 1975).

2. Bureau of the Census, *Current Population Reports,* series P-60, no. 145, "Money Income and Poverty Status of Families and Persons in the United States: 1983" (GPO, 1984), table 18, p. 28.

Figure 1. *Status of Child Support Awards, 1981*[a]

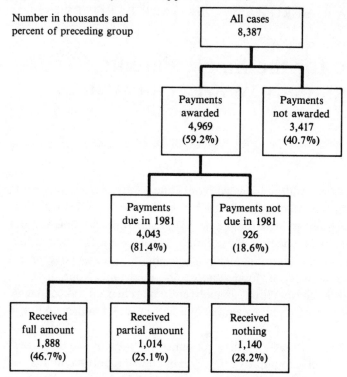

Number in thousands and
percent of preceding group

All cases
8,387

Payments
awarded
4,969
(59.2%)

Payments
not awarded
3,417
(40.7%)

Payments
due in 1981
4,043
(81.4%)

Payments not
due in 1981
926
(18.6%)

Received
full amount
1,888
(46.7%)

Received
partial amount
1,014
(25.1%)

Received
nothing
1,140
(28.2%)

Source: U.S. Department of Commerce, Bureau of the Census, *Current Population Reports*, series P-23, no. 124, "Child Support and Alimony: 1981" (Government Printing Office, 1983), table A, p. 2.
a. Child support payments from an absent father for women with their own children under 21 present in the house.

them have very low awards (the mean payment in 1981 was $2,106); and, as shown in figure 1, about 40 percent have no awards at all.

In this essay we explore the effects for single-parent families of improvement in the delivery of child support payments and in the number and level of awards. We estimate the extent to which such improvements, if strictly administered, would raise the income and at the same time reduce the welfare costs for this group of families.

A 1979 U.S. Census survey of single mothers allows us to compare the work effort, wage income, and welfare recipiency of single-parent families with various levels of child support.[3] The data support the idea that mothers who get child support payments have a greater incentive to take

3. Bureau of the Census, *Current Population Survey, March–April 1979 Match File: Tape Technical Documentation* (Washington, D.C.: Bureau of the Census, undated).

employment than do mothers who get no child support. These extra work efforts raise the income for at least some families to a level that makes them independent of welfare. In a subset of cases the combination of wages and child support pushes the family income above the poverty line.

This work-incentive effect of child support payments on single-parent families' financial status depends on the mother's knowledge that the child support payments have been established and her belief that they will continue after she takes a job and ceases receiving welfare. This is why the institutional arrangements for child support enforcement are important to the outcome of any reform of the enforcement system.[4]

We demonstrate that the improved collection of currently owed child support payments will cause some reduction in welfare costs, but only a minor reduction in the poverty problem. Universal awards at higher levels would make inroads on poverty. However, the child support awards that would suffice to eliminate poverty would be considerably larger than present ones and might be considered unreasonably burdensome on the absent fathers. For single mothers and their children to live at a decent standard without welfare support, they will need access to better-paying jobs than are now available, as well as reliably collected child support at reasonable levels.

The Economic Situation of the Single Mother

The choices facing the single mother who is receiving little or no child support are bleak. If she chooses not to work for pay and to depend on public assistance, she is promised food, a roof over her head, and medical care for herself and her children, but in most cases she will live at a level below the poverty line.[5] Some single mothers do remarry, but a majority do not.[6]

Once on the welfare rolls, there is a strong disincentive to take any

4. Mark D. Roberts, "Child Support, Welfare, and Single Parents" (Ph.D. dissertation, University of Maryland, 1983), pp. 22–37.

5. For examples of how the states actually apply need standards, see U.S. Department of Health and Human Services, Social Security Administration, Office of Family Assistance, *Characteristics of State Plans for Aid to Families with Dependent Children* (GPO, 1980).

6. Of mothers in 1982 reporting children living with them whose fathers were absent from the household, 26 percent were currently married to some other man. (See Bureau of the Census, *Current Population Reports*, series P-23, no. 124, "Child Support and Alimony: 1981" (GPO, 1983), table B, p. 3.

job except one that has a relatively high wage, because taking a job involves the following consequences:[7]

1. The partial or complete loss of cash welfare benefits.

2. The loss of medicaid benefits, food stamps, and other in-kind benefits collected by people on welfare.

3. The need to find child care, possibly expensive and of suspect quality.

4. Work-related expenses for transportation and appropriate clothing.

5. The hardship, extra effort, or boredom entailed by the job and the loss of leisure.

6. Difficulty in getting back on the welfare rolls if the job is lost.

A single mother on welfare with no child support will presumably compare the advantages and disadvantages (in terms of pay and working conditions) of each possible job she might have with the advantages and disadvantages of her current condition. Only jobs whose advantages outweigh the disadvantageous consequences listed above would be acceptable.

If single parents were all white men, they would be more likely to obtain such jobs. Most of them would be self-supporting and above the poverty line. In reality, of course, most single parents are women and many are black or Hispanic, so they are affected by race and sex discrimination in employment. A considerable proportion of the single mothers would not currently be able to get a job whose wages, benefits, and working conditions would outweigh the advantages of staying on welfare. In fact, the 1979 census survey showed that 44.6 percent of the single mothers living alone with their children were on welfare.

Child support payments—at least those the recipient believes will continue reliably whether or not she goes off welfare and takes a job— can be thought of as changing the trade-off between self-support and welfare. Figure 2 contrasts the choices faced by the welfare mother who gets no child support payments with the choices open to the welfare mother for whom child support payments are established. The welfare mother without child support has the alternative of working, but in many cases the wage she might expect is not a great deal larger than the welfare benefits she would lose. However, suppose that a substantial child

---

7. U.S. Department of Health and Human Services, Social Security Administration, Office of Family Assistance, *Compilation of Regulations Published in Code of Federal Regulations Subtitle B—Department of Health and Human Services: Chapter II—Office of Family Assistance (Assistance Program)* (GPO, 1982), sec. 233.20.

Figure 2. *How Child Support Payments Increase the Incentive to be Employed*

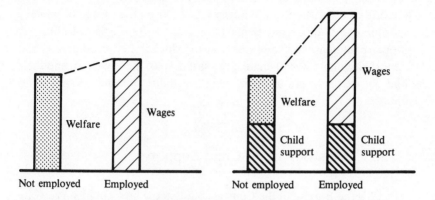

support payment is established and that the payments can be counted on to continue if the mother were to become employed. The rules governing welfare require that her welfare benefits be reduced almost dollar for dollar to take account of the child support payments. So as long as she continues to get welfare payments, her income is little different from what it was before the child support payments were established. Her marginal tax rate is also unchanged.

However, a welfare mother contemplating a move to independence is considering a considerable jump in earnings, not a marginal change. Welfare mothers, who need their wits about them to survive, are probably smart enough not to confine their attention to the tax on the first dollar of wage income, when what they are contemplating is a jump in earnings of considerably more than one dollar. To a welfare mother the prospect of a job plus the assured collection of substantial child support is bound to look better than the offer of the identical job and no award (see figure 2). Therefore the mother with the award, in making a comparison between staying on welfare (and essentially getting no benefit from the child support award) and taking that job plus the award, is more likely to choose the job and leave welfare than is the mother who has the same job in prospect but no award.

If a single mother were initially receiving no child support and then started to receive it on a reliable basis, some jobs that would have been unacceptable to her would become acceptable. This suggests that single mothers receiving child support would work in higher proportions than single mothers not receiving any, allowing for the influence of such factors as education. The census data support that hypothesis.

The focus of this essay is, of course, the economic situation of mothers who bring up children apart from their fathers. However, the economic situation of the fathers is obviously a concern in the design of policies regarding child support payments that will most often be made by fathers. After an examination of the extent to which higher, better-enforced child support payments would change the situation of these women and their children, we shall turn to the issue of the ability of fathers to pay child support.

The Census Survey of Child Support

In 1979 the Bureau of the Census conducted a household survey of a sample of 3,557 mothers who had children living with them whose fathers were not currently members of the household. These mothers were asked questions concerning child support payments and alimony payments owed to them and received by them in 1978.

The same group of mothers responded to questions about labor force participation, wage income, welfare recipiency, and marital status. For each household member, information was collected about the person's education, age, race, and income. The survey thus presents us with a source of information that we can use to explore the nature of the relationships between child support, work, and welfare.[8]

We have concentrated our statistical analysis on those mothers in the sample who were the only adults in their households and lived alone with their children (1,262 out of 3,557). These mothers are not living with a second husband or with a friend or relatives who might be providing income to the household.

The Census Bureau survey shows that in 1978 there were 2.5 million families of the type we are focusing on here—single mothers living with their children, with no other adult in the household. They average about two children a family. Almost half of these families were on welfare at some time during the year, and about the same percentage had incomes for that year that put them below the poverty line.

8. Bureau of the Census, *Current Population Reports*, series P-23, no. 112, "Child Support and Alimony: 1978" (GPO, 1981), pp. 1–12.

About one in two of these single mothers had no child support awards from the absent father of the children. This means that they had failed to go through a court procedure that would have resulted in an official order that the father make periodic payments for the children's support. Of those who did have awards, the average amount was $1,999 a year, of which $1,404 was reported as collected, on average.

While providing a great deal of relevant information about single mothers, the survey is by no means perfect for our purposes.[9] Given its limitations, we have thought it best to distinguish sharply in our analysis between single mothers who were independent over the entire course of 1978, and all of the rest of the sample of single mothers. We define a single mother as independent over the course of the year if she had no welfare payments whatever and worked at least three-quarters time during the year.

The census data were used to measure the influence of factors that might be conducive to single mothers' independence, thus defined. We were particularly interested in the influence of child support on work behavior and hence on independence. We then went on to ask how many more single mothers might have been independent if existing child support awards had been more faithfully collected and how many more might be independent if child support awards were more universal and at higher levels. We also estimated what independent mothers would earn on average, given their characteristics. We were then able to go on and estimate the proportion of single mothers who would remain in poverty under various regimes of child support collection.

The Relationship between Child Support and Independence

Our estimate of the effect of child support on independence appears under equation 1 in table 1. The probability of independence is increased

9. Ibid., pp. 41–45, 53–57. The answers the respondents made to questions about family composition, ages of children, and presence of other adults in the household refer to the two-month period from March to April 1979. The answers concerning child support, welfare, and wage and nonwage income refer to the twelve-month period of calendar 1978. During the course of a year, a person's status may change several times. A person may be a married homemaker part of the year, a working single parent for part, and a welfare client for the rest. Thus we are unable to distinguish whether part-year participation in the labor force is due to low incentive over the whole year or to a change in marital status or child support recipiency during the year.

Table 1. *Estimates of Variables Explaining Independence of Women, Earnings of Independent Women, and Child Support*[a]

Variable and summary statistics	Mean value	Equations		
		Independence of women[b] (1)	Earnings of independent women[c] (2)	Child support due[d] (3)
Child support received		0.179E-3	. . .	. . .
(dollars a year)	1,203.7	(2.9)	. . .	. . .
Child support received		−0.137E-7	. . .	. . .
squared	. . .	(−2.6)	. . .	. . .
Education (years)	11.9	0.284	1,387	132.2
		(8.5)	(5.5)	(5.3)
Has children under 6		−0.750	−979.6	. . .
(1 = yes; 0 = no)	0.45	(−4.9)	(−3.6)	. . .
Has 2 children		. . .	. . .	688.5
(1 = yes; 0 = no)	0.37	. . .	. . .	(5.6)
Has 3 children		. . .	. . .	1,121.8
(1 = yes; 0 = no)	0.13	. . .	. . .	(6.4)
Has 4 children		. . .	. . .	1,120.1
(1 = yes; 0 = no)	0.07	. . .	. . .	(5.0)
Race				
(1 = white;		0.543	2,313	. . .
0 = nonwhite)	0.68	(3.7)	(3.0)	. . .
Age (years)	32.5	0.376E-2	70.6	. . .
		(0.4)	(2.4)	. . .
Summary statistics				
Lambda[e]	. . .	. . .	6,514	. . .
		. . .	(2.9)	. . .
Intercept	. . .	−4.12	−16,597	−101.5
N	. . .	1,228	497	659
R^2	. . .	(LR = 211)	0.157	0.114

a. Numbers in parentheses are *t*-statistics.
b. Logit. Mean value is 0.404 (1 = independent; 0 = not).
c. Ordinary least squares. Mean value is $9,789 a year.
d. Ordinary least squares. Mean value is $1,999 a year.
e. Corrected for curtailed sample. See James J. Heckman, "Sample Selection Bias as a Specification Error," *Econometrica*, vol. 47 (January 1979), pp. 153–61.

with greater education and age and with being white; it appears to decrease with having children under 6. These variables have an effect on independence because they influence the kind of job a single mother has a chance of getting. Child support appears to have a positive, although modest, influence on the probability that a single mother will be independent.[10]

10. Fathers may have reduced their child support payments to any of the mothers who achieved high earnings. If this is an important effect, then we may be underestimating the positive effect of child support on independence.

The effect of improved child support on independence for single mothers depends on their situation. Equation 1 suggests that a white high school graduate whose youngest child is older than 6 has a 49 percent likelihood of being independent with no child support, a 57 percent chance with $2,000 in total child support, and a 59 percent chance with $3,000 in total child support. A white high school graduate with one or more children under 6 is estimated to have a 31 percent likelihood of independence with no child support and a 38 percent likelihood with total child support of $2,000. For a nonwhite woman, again a high school graduate whose youngest child is over 6, we estimate a 36 percent chance of independence with no child support and a 43 percent chance with total child support of $2,000. The lower probability that a nonwhite woman will be independent, compared with a white woman with similar characteristics, is due to the nonwhite's lower chance of getting a well-paid job.

We next made a direct estimate of how certain characteristics affect the salary a woman can expect to get if she chooses independence, as defined above. Our estimates of these effects are shown in table 1 under equation 2. A mother's wage in 1978 is estimated as depending on her education (increasing by $1,387 for each additional year of education), whether she had children under 6 (decreasing $979 if she did), her race (increasing $2,313 if she was white), and her age (increasing $70.60 per year of age). As an illustration of the wages equation 2 suggests these mothers can hope for, a 25-year-old nonwhite woman who was a high school graduate and had one or more children under 6 is estimated to have earned on average about $7,600 in 1978. For a mother having children under 6, child care problems may reduce the hours the mother can work and make jobs at certain locations unacceptable, thus reducing her wages.

The third equation in table 1 estimates the relationship between the size of the child support payment awarded and the number of children in the family fathered by the payee. An additional variable, the mother's education, was put in as a proxy for the father's education and hence his wage.[11] This equation is useful in one of the simulations described below.

11. See Andrea H. Beller and John W. Graham, "Variations in the Economic Well-Being of Divorced Women and Their Children: The Role of Child Support Income," in Martin David and Timothy Smeeding, eds., *Horizontal Equity, Uncertainty, and Economic Well-Being,* Studies in Income and Wealth, vol. 50 (University of Chicago Press for National Bureau of Economic Research, 1985). See also Bureau of the Census, "Child Support and Alimony: 1978," p. 4.

Simulating the Effect of Various Reforms

We used the relationships discussed in the last section to estimate how improved collection of current child support awards would affect family income, welfare costs, and the proportion of single mothers in poverty. We assumed that the collection of child support payments had improved enough so that each mother received (from the father or from some public fund set up to replace contributions not forthcoming from fathers) precisely what she told the Census Bureau was owed to her.

These estimates were made by simulating the effect of this reform, as follows:

1. Using the data for individual mothers, we assigned to each mother a child support payment equal to the amount she reported owed to her. For those mothers with no award or those who reported they were getting all they were owed, this represented no change. We assumed that those who had suffered from delinquent payments received 100 percent of their periodic payments in 1978. No arrears were assumed to be paid.

2. Using equation 1 in table 1, we estimated the probability that each mother in the data file was independent, based on her newly recalculated child support and her other characteristics. On this basis we assigned each mother a status of independent or not.[12]

3. For those mothers assigned a status of independent, welfare was dropped to zero. For those not so assigned, welfare receipts were reduced dollar for dollar by the increase in child support, if any.

4. For those mothers assigned an independent status, equation 2 was used to estimate the wage income they earned.

5. Finally, the newly simulated family income was compared with the poverty borderline to see whether the family was or was not in poverty under the proposed policy.

The results of these operations are the estimates shown in table 2 under the heading "Collect all currently owed." We estimate that if all child support currently owed were actually collected, child support paid would rise from $3.1 billion to $3.9 billion. Welfare expenses would drop

12. For example, assume a mother's probability of independence was estimated by equation 1 as 60 percent, based on her characteristics. She would be assigned a status of independent if a random number drawn from a uniform distribution was between 0.0 and 0.6 and of not independent if the random number drawn was between 0.6 and 1.0.

Table 2. *Estimates of Effect of Various Child Support Schemes, 1979*

Item	Actual child support level	Collect all currently owed	Assign all mothers awards		
			At current level	At $1,800 per child	At $3,600 per child
Welfare expenditures (billions of dollars)	3.1	2.8	1.4	1.0	0.4
Child support paid (billions of dollars)	3.1	3.9	6.2	9.4	18.8
Average family income (dollars)	7,899	8,117	8,851	10,060	13,654
Average child support per family (dollars)	1,228	1,548	2,469	3,742	7,483
Average income per person (dollars)	2,566	2,636	2,875	3,268	4,435
Average earnings per family (dollars)	4,919	4,919	5,286	5,414	5,599
Single mothers on welfare (thousands)	1,119	1,051	750	421	92
Percent of total	44.6	41.9	29.9	16.8	3.7
Families in poverty (thousands)	1,100	1,070	902	633	150
Percent of total	43.9	42.7	36.0	25.2	6.0
"Independent" families (thousands)	995	995	1,125	1,163	1,194

somewhat less, from $3.1 billion to $2.8 billion, because some of the increase in child support payments would go to mothers not on welfare. The increase in the number of mothers who would be independent and the decrease in the number of mothers in poverty would be negligible, according to our calculations.

The next simulation performed was an estimate of the effect of getting awards for the single mothers who do not have them. Every mother in the data base who was without an award was provided with one, at a level equal to the average of existing awards. We assumed that, like existing awards, they were larger the more children involved and were positively related to the level of the father's income. In making this simulation, we used equation 3 in table 1, which estimates current average awards based on number of children and the education of the mother. As noted above, the latter variable was the best proxy we had for the education of the father and hence his income.

Steps 1 through 5 were repeated, except that in step 1 those mothers who had zero awards were assigned awards based on equation 3. Again, the assumption was that these awards would be paid by the father or through some public fund. The results of this simulation are shown in the third column in table 2, "Assign all mothers awards and collect at current level."

This case turns out to represent a considerable improvement over the actual situation and shows that the attempt to get awards for mothers without them would have a significant effect. Welfare expenditures are reduced by half and child support received is doubled. This set of policy measures is estimated to reduce welfare recipiency from 44.6 to 29.9 percent. Poverty is reduced, but the effect is less dramatic, from 43.9 to 36.0 percent. Although this degree of improvement is not negligible, it is very far from a solution to the problem of poverty among single mothers and their children.

Given that better enforcement and additional awards at current levels leave so many of these families in poverty, we performed some additional simulations that give an idea of what could be accomplished if the level of awards were increased. In these latter simulations, we continued to assume that each mother had an award and collected all of it without fail.

We chose a level of award of $1,800 per year, equivalent to slightly under $5 a day per child, and assumed that each mother got exactly that. This level appears to be about 50 percent higher than the average level these mothers reported having been awarded. We estimate this level of awards would cut welfare budgets by two-thirds and reduce the proportion of mothers in poverty from 43.9 percent to 25.2 percent. Part of the reduction in poverty would be due to an increase of nearly 20 percent in the number of mothers estimated to be independent, because of the increased incentive to do paid work.

In a final simulation, we doubled the amount of child support assumed to be infallibly received to $3,600 per child. This assumption forces welfare payments down to 13 percent of their actual levels. It represents about a threefold increase in the average levels of awards from their actual levels and pushes family income up to $13,654.

Increasing the support level from $1,800 to $3,600 per child does little to stimulate further the entry of mothers into the labor force as full-time workers, according to our estimates. Equation 1 in table 1 suggests that as awards grow, the increase in motivation to work slacks off. The simulated drop in the poverty rate from 25.2 percent to 6.0 percent when awards go from $1,800 per child to $3,600 is almost entirely due to the direct effect of the increased child support on the family budget, as little additional labor force participation is estimated to occur. When awards rise above $1,800 per child a year, there is relatively little additional loss of welfare dollars, because at the $1,800 level 83 percent of the mothers are off welfare and have no welfare dollars to lose.

The Ability of Absent Fathers to Pay

The data set used for the simulations described above was based on questions put by the Census Bureau to mothers raising children apart from the children's fathers. That survey provided no usable information on the financial condition of the fathers of these children, because many of the mothers did not have the knowledge to provide it. A separate survey by the Census Bureau designed to obtain information directly from a sample of absent fathers proved to be considerably biased. Many of the men who had fathered children currently living apart from them did not declare those children to the census enumerator.[13]

Another set of data, deriving from the Panel Study of Income Dynamics (PSID), conducted by the Institute for Social Research at the University of Michigan, has information about the financial conditions of absent fathers, as well as information about the households of the mothers with whom the children live. Two studies have recently been completed using these data.[14] The PSID sample of absent fathers on which both of these studies are based is quite small (187 men). A more serious problem is that the sample excludes cases in which the absent father was never married to the mother of his children. (The degree to which this causes the PSID sample to be unrepresentative can be gauged by the fact that 20 percent of the mothers of children with absent fathers interviewed by the Census Bureau in 1982 described themselves as

13. See Andrew Cherlin, Jeanne Griffith, and James McCarthy, "A Note on Maritally-Disrupted Men's Reports of Child Support in the June 1980 Current Population Survey," *Demography*, vol. 20 (August 1983), pp. 385–89.

14. Martha S. Hill, "PSID Analysis of Matched Pairs of Ex-Spouses: The Relation of Economic Resources and New Family Obligations to Child Support Payments" (University of Michigan, Institute for Social Research, November 1984); and Ron Haskins and others, "Estimates of National Child Support Collections Potential and the Income Security of Female-Headed Families" (University of North Carolina–Chapel Hill, Bush Institute for Child and Family Policy, April 1985).

Table 3. *Annual Child Support Payments under Wisconsin Standard, by Absent Father's Income Group and Number of Children, 1980*[a]

Dollars unless otherwise indicated

Father's income quintile[b]	Mean income quintile[b]	Number of children			
		1	2	3	4 or more
		Payments			
First (0–6,300)	3,480	592[c]	870[c]	1,009[c]	1,079[c]
Second (6,301–12,210)	9,228	1,569	2,307	2,676[c]	2,861[c]
Third (12,211–18,630)	15,296	2,600	3,824	4,436[c]	4,742[c]
Fourth (18,631–25,375)	21,998	3,740	5,500	6,379	6,819[c]
Fifth (25,376 and over)	40,004	6,801	10,001	11,601	12,401
	Percent in quintile	Percent of fathers			
First (0–6,300)	15.2	1.5	4.6	4.1	5.1
Second (6,301–12,210)	18.3	3.1	6.6	3.6	5.1
Third (12,211–18,630)	27.4	5.6	11.7	3.1	7.1
Fourth (18,631–25,375)	16.8	2.0	8.7	3.6	2.6
Fifth (25,376 and over)	22.3	4.6	10.6	3.6	3.6
Total	100.0	16.8	42.2	18.0	23.5

Source: Distribution of fathers and fathers' mean incomes from Ron Haskins and others, "Estimates of National Child Support Collections Potential and the Income Security of Female-Headed Families" (University of North Carolina–Chapel Hill, Bush Institute for Child and Family Policy, April 1985), tables 4 and 5, pp. 17, 19.

a. The Wisconsin standard calls for an absent father to pay 17 percent of his gross income for one child not living with him, 25 percent for two, 29 percent for three, and 31 percent for four or more.

b. Income quintiles and mean income determined by 1,930 fathers in the Panel Study of Income Dynamics.

c. Payments lower than $1,800 per child.

"never married.")[15] Nevertheless, the PSID data do provide a look at the group of fathers most likely to have gone through the divorce courts and to have been ordered to make child support payments. Only 4.1 percent of the absent fathers in the PSID sample were in a state of poverty.[16]

Table 3 shows the distribution of absent fathers in the PSID data base by income group and by numbers of children. The table also gives the annual child support obligations that the fathers would have had under

15. Bureau of the Census, "Child Support and Alimony: 1981," table B, p. 3. An additional 19 percent described themselves as "separated."

16. Hill, "PSID Analysis of Matched Pairs of Ex-Spouses," table 5, p. 42.

Table 4. *Child Support Payments by Previously Married Fathers as a Percentage of the Wisconsin Standard, 1980*
Dollars unless otherwise indicated

Fathers' income quintile	Fathers' mean income	Average Wisconsin standard child support payment	Percent of standard actually paid
First	3,480	950	3
Second	9,228	2,408	9
Third	15,296	3,881	22
Fourth	21,998	5,682	20
Fifth	40,004	9,987	46

Source: Haskins and others, "Estimates of National Child Support," table 8, p. 25; and authors' calculations.

the "Wisconsin Percent of Income Standard," a child support award system that calls for the father to pay 17 percent of his gross income for one child not living with him, 25 percent for two children, 29 percent for three children, and 31 percent for four or more children. These values represent amounts that attorneys, social work professionals, and legislators in Wisconsin have agreed on as fair and affordable. The Wisconsin standard provides less than $1,800 per child in 46 percent of all cases. Given that the PSID sample underrepresents unwed mothers, while the census sample on which our simulation was based does include them, we can say that somewhat fewer than half of the fathers of children in the census sample would have been required to pay $1,800 per child under the Wisconsin standard. It must be emphasized, however, that collectively the fathers in the PSID sample are actually paying far less than called for by the Wisconsin standard through a combination of low awards and noncompliance. Even fathers in the highest income group actually pay less than half of what would be called for under the Wisconsin standard (see table 4).

Another piece of evidence about absent fathers is found in data concerning the incomes of fathers involved in the caseload of the North Carolina Office of Child Support Enforcement. This agency tends to concentrate on fathers with children on aid to families with dependent children (AFDC), so the fathers involved in the agency's cases proved to have far lower incomes on average than those represented in the PSID data set. For a period of four quarters starting in the last quarter of 1983, the fathers of children on AFDC had incomes of $9,512, and fathers of children not currently on AFDC had average incomes of $10,095.[17]

17. Haskins and others, "Estimates of National Child Support," p. 47.

The information we have about the ability of absent fathers to pay is clearly inadequate, based as it is on small and incomplete samples. The evidence we do have, however, points to very low payments on the part of many fathers who are commonly judged to have the ability to pay considerably more. On the other hand, widely agreed-upon standards of child support awards, based on the father's income, would provide only about half of all mothers with $1,800 a child and a very small proportion with as much as $3,600 a child. This in turn suggests that the replacement of welfare by a system of payments similar to child support financed partly by payments from fathers and partly from the public purse is an alternative that should be studied. Otherwise, the goal of eliminating the poverty suffered by single mothers and their children cannot be reached.

Gary Burtless has suggested that there is a drawback to the pursuit of biological fathers for child support payments: better delivery of child support payments might reduce the incentive of single mothers to remarry. Those who are inclined to agree that this is a worthy and telling argument against child support enforcement might contemplate their own frame of mind if they were forced to consider marrying someone with whom they would not wish to be closely involved were it not for the money.

Conclusion

Our results suggest that merely improving the enforcement of currently existing child support awards would not have a large effect on welfare expenditures or on the proportion of single mothers in poverty. However, increasing the number of women who have awards and ensuring that they are faithfully paid by the father or from a public fund would cut poverty incidence by one-fourth. The net savings in public funds would depend on the extent to which the child support money could be extracted from fathers.

To eliminate poverty among single mothers solely by ensuring the delivery of child support would require universal awards at levels two to three times those currently being made. At these levels the fathers' ability to pay becomes problematic in many cases.[18]

18. For further discussion of the sharing of the burden of child support between noncohabiting parents, see Barbara R. Bergmann, "The Share of Women and Men in

Thus better child support, even if strictly administered, cannot by itself be realistically expected to solve the problem of poverty for single mothers and their children. While stricter enforcement should undoubtedly be pursued, other sources of income are needed for single mothers. The most obvious road to better income for them is access to better jobs than those to which they are now restricted. Effective programs, including training, job creation, and affirmative action, are needed to get single mothers into relatively well-paid jobs, which few of them now hold. The availability of such jobs would be an incentive to welfare recipients to become self-supporting, and the pay, along with reliably delivered child support at reasonable and sustainable levels, would provide for them and their children at levels above the poverty line.

Comments by Gary Burtless

Among female-headed families in which children are present, the incidence of poverty is appalling. In 1985, the most recent year for which we have statistics, more than 45 percent of these families had money incomes below the poverty line. Even including the value of in-kind transfer payments, the poverty rate of these families exceeded 35 percent.

The most important reason for the high poverty rate among single-parent families is the lack of wage earnings available to them. Many single women with child-rearing responsibilities find it difficult to earn enough money on their own to provide a comfortable life for themselves and their children. Especially for mothers of very young children, it may be difficult to cope simultaneously with the responsibilities of child care and full-time work. If the family is to be supported with wage earnings, the source of the earnings must often be the absent father.

Bergmann and Roberts consider the effect of raising the child support contributions of absent fathers. According to census statistics cited in the paper, only 60 percent of single mothers were awarded court-ordered child support payments in 1981. The level of court-ordered payments was quite low—only $2,100 per year—and only 47 percent of court-

---

the Economic Support of Children," *Human Rights Quarterly*, vol. 3 (Spring 1981), pp. 103–12. See also Barbara R. Bergmann, "Setting Appropriate Levels of Child Support Payments," in Judith Cassetty, ed., *The Parental Child-Support Obligation: Research, Practice, and Social Policy* (Lexington, Mass.: Lexington Books, 1983), pp. 115–18.

ordered payments were fully paid. (An additional 25 percent of payments were partially paid.) By implication there is a great deal of room for improvement, both in requiring that fathers make some effort to support their children and in enforcing court-ordered levels of support.

The emphasis in this paper is on the relationship between child support payments, dependence on welfare, and wage income of the single mother. The authors consider a mother to be "independent" if she receives no welfare payments and works at least nine months out of a year. There is an obvious inverse relation between welfare payments and child support, and this inverse relation is built into the welfare benefit formula. Hence, increased child support directly contributes to the independence of welfare mothers under the definition used in this paper.

The authors also believe that replacing welfare with child support will act as an incentive for the single mother to work. Their reasoning is straightforward. The welfare benefit formula contains a high marginal tax on earnings. Child support payments have no explicit or implicit tax on earnings. If the mother's earnings rise by one dollar her child support payment will continue undiminished.

The authors' analysis is correct if a single mother's combined welfare, food stamp, and medicaid benefits are *entirely* replaced by a child support payment of equivalent cash value. Otherwise, I think the conclusion is much less obvious. Suppose a mother and her two children receive the equivalent of $7,300 per year in welfare, food stamp, and medicaid benefits. (This is a reasonable estimate for a nonworking mother in Maryland.) A court orders the absent father to pay $3,000 in child support. (Again, this is about average, given the statistics in the paper.) An honest mother is financially no better off after the award of child support than she was before. After reporting the $3,000 award to the welfare office, her AFDC benefit is reduced by almost the entire amount of the award. The composition, but not the amount, of her income is changed. If she decides to begin working, her marginal dollar of wages will still be taxed at a 100 percent rate. In this illustrative example, the mother faces an identical marginal incentive to work before and after the child support award. Her nonwage income is unchanged, and her marginal tax rate is still 100 percent.

This example also illustrates why there is no particular inducement for some single mothers to press for court-ordered child support payments. They and their children would be better off if they received irregular gifts or money payments from the absent father rather than regular cash support. The former are much more difficult to trace and may not have to be reported to the welfare office.

It is also conceivable that child support payments may act as a work disincentive, contrary to the suggestion in the paper. If the level of child support is sufficiently high, a mother with child care responsibilities might reasonably decline to work and instead devote full attention to rearing her children. I would therefore argue that the effect of child support payments on the work effort of single mothers is much more ambiguous than indicated in the paper. Whether an additional $1,000 in child support raises or lowers the expected earnings of the mother depends on her particular circumstances and her preferences for market versus home work.

Turning from the authors' model to their empirical estimates, I have a few comments. The second set of results gives the authors' estimate of an earnings function for independent mothers. The authors interpret their results as showing an independent woman's earnings potential if she turns her back on welfare and relies instead on earnings. The equation is apparently estimated using the selection correction technique proposed by James Heckman. However, the reader is not informed about either the specification or estimation of the first-stage selection equation that makes it possible to use Heckman's technique in this application.

In my opinion, the authors have made two critical errors in estimating their earnings function. First, they have apparently excluded a large proportion of working single mothers from their estimation sample. These women are excluded because they were at least partly dependent on welfare or because they worked fewer than nine months a year. Those are not good reasons to ignore the wage information available for the excluded women. Earnings equations typically explain a depressingly small fraction of variance in the earnings distribution. The earnings equation in this paper is no exception. We know far more about the potential earnings of working women as a result of observing their actual wage rates than we can learn from observing earnings of women who work year-round and don't collect welfare.

The second error is to estimate an annual earnings function rather than a wage rate equation. Earnings are determined by both wage rate and annual hours of work. I am skeptical that receipt of child support or welfare significantly affects a woman's market wage rate. Both, however, should affect annual hours worked. To make a significant contribution to economic knowledge, the paper should explain how child support and welfare jointly explain the annual work effort of single mothers.

Instead, the paper tries to explain how child support affects economic independence, as that term is narrowly defined by the authors. The first equation gives the authors' estimate of this independence function. The reduced-form specification is very simple. The authors enter age, race, education, and a dummy variable indicating the presence or absence of children younger than 6. The amount of child support received is entered in quadratic form. For unexplained reasons, the equation excludes variables representing the market work and welfare income opportunities available to mothers. Market work opportunities could be indicated with the woman's market wage rate (or an equivalent proxy variable) and some representation of the local area unemployment rate. The welfare income potential could be crudely represented by the welfare guarantee level available in the state (or group of states) in which the woman resides. In view of the exclusion of these crucial variables, it is hard to take the results of the equation very seriously.

The last estimated equation shows the dependence of child support awards on the education of the mother and the number of children in the family. Although the equation is estimated by excluding mothers who have no court-ordered awards, for some reason the authors do not apply the Heckman selection correction procedure to control for the effects of this sample exclusion.

The last section of the paper contains simulation results based upon the equations just described. The simulations show the predicted amount of support collected, the impact of these support awards on the independence, earnings, and welfare benefits of single women, and the net effect of the awards on family income. In view of the serious statistical problems in the paper, I don't think we can place very much faith in these simulation results.

The authors conclude that 100 percent collection of present child support awards would have only a slight effect on welfare outlays and poverty. One can hardly quarrel with this conclusion. A very high fraction of awards is presently collected, at least partially, so an increase in collection rates will not markedly affect the incomes of most families. Assigning child support to *all* families would have a much larger impact. Again, this result is hardly surprising: only 60 percent of single mothers are presently assigned a child support award. Nonetheless, even this reform would leave a large fraction of single-parent families below the poverty line. The authors argue that to significantly reduce poverty, child support awards must be substantially raised. I think this is true, but my acceptance of the conclusion does not depend on the simulation results in this paper.

It seems to me there is a curious omission in this paper. The authors' major focus is on the independence of single mothers rather than the net welfare of both mothers and their children. Hence the authors are interested in mechanisms that make mothers independent of the welfare system—reliable child support and a healthy level of wage earnings. While I certainly don't disagree with these objectives, one method of attaining them is never mentioned in this paper—marriage or remarriage of the single mother.

According to statistics compiled in the Panel Survey of Income Dynamics, marriage is the most efficacious method of providing income to both mother and children. Women who become widowed, divorced, or separated have a high poverty rate. Women in that situation who marry or remarry have a poverty rate that is no different than that of other two-parent families.[19] If the goal of policy is to provide nonwelfare income to single mothers and their children, one cannot overlook the potential gains arising from marriage and remarriage.

In considering the impact of increased child support, the authors have overlooked its potential effect on marriage and remarriage rates. It is conceivable that women receiving generous child support awards may be less inclined to marry or remarry, probably for good reasons. For one thing, the new marriage might weaken their financial claim on the absent father—if not legally, then socially. This question cannot be examined with the sample of women used in the Bergmann-Roberts study, which is restricted to single mothers.

To examine seriously the impact of child support on welfare payments, earned income, and the financial resources available to raise children, economists will have to consider its effect on the marriage patterns as well as the labor force participation of single mothers. In my opinion, this paper does not do a convincing job in studying even the latter question.

19. Greg J. Duncan and James N. Morgan, *Five Thousand American Families: Patterns of Economic Progress*, vol. 4 (University of Michigan, Institute for Social Research, 1976), pp. 20–22.

Comments by Isabel V. Sawhill

Bergmann and Roberts estimate how various child support reforms might directly and indirectly improve the welfare of female-headed families. The direct effects stem from the additional resources presumed to be provided by absent parents to the children in these families under various specified reforms, while the indirect effects stem from a hypothesized increase in work effort among female heads in response to the lower rates of benefit reduction associated with private support, as opposed to public support.

The paper is analytically lean, its results are clearly presented, and its policy implications are very strong: private transfers are a very effective antidote to both poverty and welfare dependency. If every child living with a single mother received $1,800 per year from the absent parent, the poverty rate for this group would drop from 44 to 25 percent and the welfare dependency rate would drop from 45 to 17 percent. Other studies have come to similar conclusions.[20] Let me raise the following two-part question: should we believe these results, and if we do, what is preventing us from achieving them in practice?

With respect to the credibility of the results, my major concern is with the paper's assumption that providing a mother with more child support will increase the probability that she will work her way off welfare. Although there is some positive correlation between the amount of child support received and what Bergmann and Roberts call the probability of being independent (that is, working at least three-fourths of the year and receiving no welfare), I suspect that this result reflects the common influence (on both work behavior and receipt of child support) of some variables omitted from, or incompletely measured in, their equation 1. An example would be socioeconomic status.[21] Thus, unless there is a strong a priori reason for the positive coefficient that shows up in the

20. See, for example, Isabel V. Sawhill, "Developing Normative Standards for Child-Support Payments," in Judith Cassetty, ed., *The Parental Child-Support Obligation: Research, Practice, and Social Policy* (Lexington, Mass.: Lexington Books, 1983).

21. In earlier work, we found that family income before divorce or separation was significantly related to amount of child support received, even after controlling for fathers' earnings. See Nancy M. Gordon, Carol A. Jones, and Isabel V. Sawhill, "The Determinants of Child Support Payments," Urban Institute Working Paper 992-05 (Washington, D.C.: Urban Institute, June 1978).

regression equation, I am inclined to be skeptical about its significance. Bergmann and Roberts's a priori argument is that child support reduces incentives to work far less than welfare so a substitution of one for the other will lead to greater work effort. But there are at least two reasons for questioning this hypothesis. First, fathers may tend to reduce their support as the mother's income rises. Indeed, my own view is that this is the way the system *should* work, and I have constructed formulas for child support awards that take both the mother's and father's income into account. Second, and more important, there is little evidence that the high marginal tax rates associated with the current welfare system have much, if any, negative impact on work behavior.[22] In light of this, we probably shouldn't assume that replacing public with private transfers will lead to significantly greater work effort. If it does increase work effort, it may be because monthly checks from absent parents are less secure than monthly checks from the government—not because of differences in marginal tax rates.

Finally, if we are going to worry about incentives, we should also look at the effects on child support payments of rules which—until recently—reduced welfare benefits by a dollar for every dollar of child support received. Legislation passed in 1984 permits the first $50 of child support to be disregarded in calculating AFDC benefits, and this provision should increase incentives for absent parents to provide support.

To summarize my major point so far, Bergmann and Roberts's estimate that 20 percent more mothers would achieve "independence" because of the diminished disincentive to do paid work under a more generous child support regime is probably too optimistic. Another factor that may lend an upward bias to their estimates of the reduction in poverty and welfare dependency associated with higher child support payments is their use of equation 3 (table 1) to estimate child support awards for those who don't now have them. It was unclear to me why they went to the expense and trouble to correct for sample selection bias in equation 2 and not in equation 3. Perhaps it is because equation 3 is weakly specified to begin with, as they acknowledge.

I now want to say something about the policy implications of this paper and what they suggest about priorities for future research. Bergmann and Roberts show that stricter enforcement of the existing child

22. For a recent review of the evidence, see Robert Moffitt, "Evaluating the Effects of Changes in AFDC: Methodological Issues and Challenges," *Journal of Policy Analysis and Management,* vol. 4 (Summer 1985), pp. 537–53.

support system would have a small payoff relative to increasing the number of mothers with awards or increasing the generosity of these awards. This is an important finding. But it leads us back to all of the thorny questions related to the father's ability to pay. At one level, these are normative issues that some of us have been debating for a number of years. I have tended to favor an income-sharing approach—that is, awards should be based on each parent's ability to contribute to the support of the children. Bergmann has tended to favor a cost-sharing approach—that is, awards should be based on the costs of raising a child. The current system is a compromise between these two sets of principles, but tilts toward the cost-sharing model. As I understand it, Bergmann's preference for the cost-sharing approach is based on the assumption that it is not realistic to assume much higher contributions from fathers and that such contributions might discourage mothers from working. What would help to resolve or clarify this debate is more evidence on two issues. First, how burdensome are current child support payments for the payees? And second, do such payments discourage mothers from working? On the first issue, my own past research suggests that most fathers contribute about 15 percent of their after-tax earnings (measured at the time of divorce) to child support. (Those fathers with very low incomes pay a little more than this.)[23] Other evidence, cited by Bergmann and Roberts, points in the same direction, but all studies to date have been based on very small and incomplete samples. As for the mother's work effort, I am not convinced that more generous child support would undermine it, but perhaps we should investigate this further as well.

Bergmann and Roberts have written a very stimulating and useful paper. I hope that they and others will continue to investigate these issues.

23. See Gordon, Jones, and Sawhill, "The Determinants of Child Support Payments," p. 21.

CHARLES BROWN *and* SHIRLEY J. WILCHER

Sex-based Employment Quotas in Sweden

SWEDEN'S national commitment to equality between the sexes in working life has fostered the development of a wide range of national labor market programs designed to effectuate this goal. One of these programs is the sex-based employment quota component of the Swedish regional development assistance program, which targets private employers in the underdeveloped areas of Sweden. It provides capital subsidies and other forms of assistance to firms that reserve for each sex at least 40 percent of the additional jobs created with this aid. Thus, unlike anything used to promote equal employment opportunity in the United States, this program sets the same hiring levels for both men and women.

The National Women's Law Center initially undertook a study of the Swedish program in 1981 to learn information that could be used to improve the design of U.S. programs addressing problems of sex discrimination in employment and to examine the Swedish experience of setting equal goals for both women and men instead of for the traditionally underrepresented groups.[1]

We would like to express our appreciation to the German Marshall Fund of the United States for underwriting this research project and to the computer science center of the University of Maryland for additional computer support. We are also grateful to Annika Baude, consultant to this project; Vera Hirsch and Ted Westermark, formerly of the National Labor Market Board (AMS) and currently with the National Industrial Board (SIND), who met with us and provided the data used to analyze the quota program; and Berit Rollén, former head of division of the AMS and currently undersecretary of the Ministry of Labor, who availed to us the resources of the AMS. Lastly, we thank Jeanne Rosen, who translated Swedish language documents, and Theresa Butler, Francine Cromwell, Rowena Holt, Jodi Lipson, and Chuck Perov.

1. However, the data we analyzed included few cases in which meeting the quota required that men be hired, so our analysis will focus primarily on the impact of the quota in promoting employment opportunities for women.

271

Of course, there are many differences between labor markets in Sweden and those in the United States. Sweden's workers are overwhelmingly unionized, and its unions have a larger formal role in government equality activities. The Swedish government takes a more active role in training workers after they end their formal schooling, and the reputation of these programs among employers is more positive. These training programs have attempted, with some success, to increase the number of women in traditionally male occupations. Other indications of greater government involvement in the labor market are the requirement that all vacancies be listed with the Employment Office and the wider acceptance of relief work when unemployment rates are high. Finally, antidiscrimination laws are more recent and place greater burdens on the plaintiff in Sweden than in the United States.

These differences—and the limited scale of the development assistance—would make nonsense of any attempt to attribute differences in the labor market position of women in the two countries to the quota requirement, but that is not our reason for studying the quota. Rather, our goal is to study the Swedish quota in its own context, to see whether it suggests lessons that might be applied in the United States. The detailed rules associated with the quota make it feasible to isolate its impact more readily than would be true for other labor market programs.

The Regional Development Assistance Program

In the early 1900s Sweden experienced a sharp industrial shift that resulted in a concentration of industries into large units and the closure of factories in smaller areas. At the same time, agricultural labor demand diminished. Consequently, the labor market became centered in Stockholm, Göteborg, and Malmö.[2]

The regional development assistance program was created in 1965 in order to induce industries to return and settle in underemployed areas. It was reasoned that assistance from the state would not only create more jobs in areas of high unemployment and underemployment, but would also make possible a more diversified labor market.[3] To this end,

2. Briefing by representatives of the Industrial Location Division, National Labor Market Board (AMS), May 19, 1981.

3. *Bilaga 13 till statsverkspropositionen 1974* (Stockholm: Arbetsmarknadsdepartmentet, 1974) [*Appendix to the Budget and Finance Bill* (Stockholm: Ministry of Labor, 1974)], pp. 180–82.

Sweden was divided into newly created zones with varying types and amounts of aid. During the 1970s, regional aid expenditures grew gradually from about Skr 400 million to Skr 500 million in fiscal year 1978–79. They increased to Skr 775.8 million in fiscal year 1979–80.[4]

Legislative Origins of the Sex-based Employment Quota

Partly as a result of various labor market and tax measures adopted by the Swedish government, increasing numbers of women entered the labor force in the 1960s and 1970s. Despite this increased participation, a lack of public transportation and child care, the existence of negative attitudes toward female employees, and the influence of the tradition of the man as the family breadwinner all contributed to limit working women's available options and potential employment status. In 1973 the Advisory Council on Equality between Men and Women recommended that location assistance, including training subsidies, be conditioned on the availability for each sex of no less than 40 percent of the total number of training positions in a company. The National Labor Market Board (AMS) could grant exemptions; for example, priority for new jobs might be given to those who had recently lost their jobs as a result of the displacement of an old company.[5] The council proposed that companies be required to specify their recruitment plans when they submitted an application for assistance, which would include what jobs were to be made available and what hiring opportunities were to be extended to both men and women. Such a recruitment plan was to be the product of a cooperative effort on the part of the company, the County Labor Board, and the unions. Further, the council suggested that the County Labor Board be responsible for continuously monitoring the companies during hiring to ensure that the approved plans were followed.[6] The bill incorporating the council's recommendations was passed by Parliament in 1974.

4. National Labor Market Board, "Regional Aid 1979–80," p. 1. During the 1970s, the exchange rate fluctuated between four and five Skr per dollar. Beginning in 1981, the number of Skr per dollar increased more or less continuously, reaching more than eight in 1984.

5. *Bilaga 13 till statsverkspropositionen* (Ministry of Labor, *Appendix*), pp. 48–50. Responsibility for administering the quota was reassigned from the AMS to the National Industrial Board (SIND) in 1982.

6. Ibid.

Types of Regional Development Assistance

The Swedish regional development assistance program provides aid in the form of location aid, introduction (new employment) grants, special assistance, and transport subsidies. Until 1982 the program also provided training grants.

The largest component of regional development assistance is location aid, which is given to support new capital investment in manufacturing and in a few related industries. Location aid takes two forms—depreciation loans or grants and regular location loans or grants.

Depreciation loans or grants are initially given to enterprises as loans. If a firm receiving such aid complies with all of the requirements, including the sex quota, 30 percent of the loan is forgiven after the first year, 20 percent in the second year, and 10 percent each year thereafter. The regular loans are offered on more attractive terms than firms in these areas would otherwise have to pay. The maturity of the loan is fixed according to the economic life of the assets, with a maximum of twenty years. Repayment may be postponed for up to five years.[7] Together, depreciation loans or grants and normal loans may finance up to 70 percent of the cost of buildings and machinery.

Regional development assistance also includes introduction (employment) subsidies. A company that increases employment in a development area may qualify for annual grants based on the number of person-years by which its labor force exceeds the company's peak work force during the three-year period before its first grant.

In fiscal year 1979–80 the total amounts of regional development aid expended were: Skr 158 million for depreciation loans, Skr 9.9 million for training subsidies, and Skr 20–30 million for employment expansion aid.[8] In fiscal year 1983–84 Skr 571.2 million was paid for location grants or loans and Skr 17 million for employment expansion aid.[9]

A firm interested in location aid for new investment in the eligible areas makes an application with the county administration. The local Labor Market Board and the Employment Office are then consulted.

---

7. Ibid.
8. AMS, *Regional Aid,* p. 3. The Skr 20–30 million is our estimate, based on the fact that Skr 10 million was given to firms for 633 jobs begun in 1979 and that subsidies (of unstated amounts) were given for 1,120 jobs begun in 1977 and 1978. Ibid.
9. Briefing by Ted Westermark and Vera Hirsch, National Industrial Board (SIND), August 22, 1984. Between 1979 and 1983 prices in Sweden rose by about 50 percent.

Small projects are approved by the county administration, and large projects are forwarded to the Industry Board for approval. Approximately two-thirds of approved projects are approved at the county administration level.[10] Approval is based on the economic merits of the project, as well as the conformity of planned recruitment with the sex quota.

How the Sex Quota Works

The quota requires that 40 percent of the new employment from a project be reserved for each sex. The amount of effort needed to meet such a quota depends on various definitional details (as well as the firm's previous policies and labor market conditions). Five of these details are particularly important:

1. Employment is measured in workers—not in person-years or full-time equivalents—in administering depreciation loans or grants and regular location loans.[11] Thus two half-time workers would count as two workers, rather than one, in meeting the quota. Since women are more likely to work part time than men, measuring the quota in workers makes it easier for firms to reach their quota of women than would a 40 percent quota for full-time equivalents. In industrial occupations such as "textiles and sewing work" and "workshop, building, metal, and precision mechanics," the proportion of women working part time is less than for the economy as a whole, but it is by no means negligible—39 and 27 percent, respectively.[12] There appear to be no comparable statistics for aided firms, although part-time work was not significant in the firms we visited.

2. The establishment at which the additional investment occurs is the focus of the quota. Employment at unaided establishments of the firm is not subject to the quota.

3. When the location aid is applied for, the firm indicates its current level of employment by sex at the plant to be aided and the number of

10. Ibid.
11. Employment is measured in full-time equivalents in administering the employment-increase support. AMS briefing, May 19, 1981.
12. *Jämställdhet på arbetsmarknaden: Statistik* (Solna, Sweden: Arbetsmarknadsstyrelsen, 1980) *[Equality in the Labour Market: Statistics* (Solna, Sweden: National Labor Market Board, 1980)], p. 10.

extra men and women it intends to hire if the application is approved. At least 40 percent of that planned increase must be men (which is rarely the issue) and at least 40 percent must be women. If the actual increase in employment is less than or equal to that which was planned, then 40 percent of the net increase in employment must be female.

A few examples will illustrate how the net increase in employment is carried out. A plant that started with 100 employees, 12 of whom were women, and expanded its total employment by exactly the 10 workers estimated at the time of application would have to employ 16 women (the 12 originally employed plus 40 percent of the 10 additional employees) to meet the quota. If business conditions were less favorable than had been anticipated, and the firm expanded employment from 100 to only 105, the firm would have to employ 14 women (12 plus 40 percent of the net increase of 5). Since the quota applies to net increases in employment, not new hires, if the establishment with a net increase of 5 workers, of whom 2 were women, also replaced 5 men who quit with 5 men, it would still meet the quota. Women would make up 40 percent of its net increase in employment, although only 2 out of 10 of its new hires. Alternatively, if 5 women quit, the firm would have to replace those 5 with women and hire 2 additional women to meet the quota. Thus 7 out of 10 new hires would have to be women. As these examples illustrate, whether a net-increase quota is more restrictive than a new-hire quota depends on the turnover rates of men and women, as well as the proportion of the initial work force that is female.[13]

4. If a firm's actual employment increase exceeds that estimated in applying for aid, employment of women need increase by only 40 percent of the *planned* employment increase. Thus a firm that planned to hire ten workers in its recruitment plan, but in fact hired twenty, would be required to hire only four women to meet the quota.[14] The importance of this interpretation has been limited in recent years by unfavorable

13. *Kommentar till uppfoljning av föroksverksamnet med könskvotering perioden 1974–07–1–1976–06–30* (Solna, Sweden: Arbetsmarknadsstyrelsen, 1977) [*Comments on the Follow-up Report on Sex Quotas for the Period July 1, 1974 to June 30, 1976* (Solna, Sweden: National Labor Market Board, 1977)], pp. 2–3.

14. AMS briefing, May 19, 1981. It might seem that this provides an important incentive to understate the planned employment increase in order to minimize the number of women who must be hired. However, the proportion of location aid that takes the form of the more attractive depreciation loans depends on the planned increase in new employment. Therefore underestimating the true employment increase would significantly reduce the value of the subsidy received for the investment.

business conditions, which reduce the likelihood that firms will exceed their planned employment increase.

5. While the establishment specifies the types of occupations of the workers of each sex who would be hired at the time of application, this occupational distribution has no role in determining whether the quota has been met.[15] If the firm can create a sufficient number of new positions that are traditional for women, it need not place any women in nontraditional jobs to fulfill the quota.

Exemptions

Exemptions to the quota can be given either at the time the project is approved (preliminary determination) or when the last portion of the aid is paid out (final determination). Exemptions can be given for several reasons. First, projects with planned increases of three or fewer workers are exempt. Second, projects that reopen a plant closed due to bankruptcy are required by law to reemploy the workers from the closed plant. This reemployment is determined by the sex composition of the formerly employed workers, and the quota does not apply. Third, exemptions can be given if too few women (or men) are available for the type of work required by the project. The views of the local government officials are important in determining whether the asserted unavailability is true. In the period from July 1975 to September 1980, one-third (533 of 1,635) of all projects were exempt because projected employment increases were for three workers or fewer. Of the remaining projects, more than a third (383 of 1,102) were exempt for other reasons.[16]

Policy on the timing of exemptions has changed since 1974. Initially exemptions were granted at the preliminary determination when unavailability was found to be a serious problem. Now, however, exemptions are rarely given at this stage. The firm is forced to try to meet the quota, and an exemption is not given until those efforts have proven unsuccessful.[17]

Sanctions

An establishment that fails to meet its quota is subject to sanctions. For example, its depreciation loan may be converted to a regular loan.

15. Ibid.
16. Ibid.
17. Ibid.

A significant minority of aided projects are sanctioned.[18] However, these sanctions almost always lead to the establishment's agreeing to abide by the quota, so that little money is recovered for the national treasury through sanctions.[19]

Comparison with U.S. Experience

The sex-based quota component of the Swedish regional development assistance program and the U.S. affirmative action scheme embodied in Executive Order 11246 constitute alternative numerically oriented approaches to increasing female participation in private-sector development.[20] There are two important differences in the contexts of the two programs that have important implications for their operation.

First, the U.S. contract compliance program functions on a much larger scale than the Swedish program. In 1984 the regulations of the Office of Federal Contract Compliance Programs (OFCCP) affected more than 115,000 nonconstruction and 108,000 construction establishments.[21] Coverage of the executive order includes all facilities of a contractor, regardless of whether they are being used in the performance of a particular contract.[22] The OFCCP regulations therefore covered 26 percent of the U.S. labor force (114 million) in 1984.[23] In comparison, the number of Swedish companies receiving location grants and loans and therefore covered by the quota totaled 358 in 1983–84, and the planned increase in employment covered by the quota totaled 2,095 people, 0.05 percent of the Swedish labor market in that year.[24]

18. Apparently, data about the frequency of sanctions are not tabulated. When we asked for a *rough* estimate of this frequency, we received estimates of 10 to 20 percent. AMS briefing, May 19, 1981; interview with Hirsch and Westermark, AMS, May 19, 1981.

19. Interview with Hirsch and Westermark, AMS, June 4, 1981.

20. 3 C.F.R. 339 (1964–65 Comp.); 3 C.F.R. 684 (1966–70 Comp.); and 3 C.F.R. 803 (1966–70 Comp.).

21. Telephone interview with Dale Barone, Division of Program Analysis and Review, OFCCP, October 5, 1984.

22. See 41 C.F.R. secs. 60-1.40 and 60-4.6 (1986).

23. Telephone interview with Rick Devens, Office of Employment and Unemployment Statistics, U.S. Bureau of Labor Statistics, October 5, 1984.

24. Letter from Vera Hirsch, National Industrial Board (SIND) to Shirley Wilcher, NWLC, September 25, 1984; and telephone interview with Britta Cronquist, Embassy of Sweden, Washington, D.C., October 9, 1984.

Second, under the Swedish system, government agencies are much more closely involved in the day-to-day operations of the labor market. In particular, government-provided training is more extensive (and seems to enjoy a better reputation with employers), and Swedish employers must notify the Employment Office of all job vacancies.

Enforcement Mechanisms

A fundamental difference between the Swedish program and the U.S. program is the method of securing enforcement of the quota or goals. The agency that administers the Swedish program secures compliance by means of the exemptions process: all companies that determine that they cannot meet the quota must seek exemptions from the county labor boards, or, in some cases, from SIND. At this point, the agencies can investigate and either accept or reject the employers' requests, triggering the sanctions process in the case of intransigent employers.[25] SIND also monitors annually the retention of employees up to five years after the final disbursements are made. Under the U.S. program, the OFCCP attempts to assure compliance by means of compliance reviews initiated by the agency and by agency investigations of complaints of discrimination filed by individuals or organizations. Because the number of federal contractors is so large, the agency conducts its compliance reviews selectively, with relatively little chance of any firm's being reviewed in any given year.[26] The OFCCP's stated policy is to review the contractor establishments that are the largest, offer the best earning opportunities, and show less employment of women (and minorities), the assumption being that these firms would yield the greatest number of opportunities for employment and advancement. In practice, it appears that such targeting has often not been achieved.[27]

25. The transfer of oversight and administration of the regional development assistance program from AMS to SIND in 1982, and the enlargement of the authority for approving projects by the County Labor Boards, may have an effect on the intensity of enforcement of the quota (that is, the number of exemptions granted or sanctions imposed). We were informed in our most recent visit to Sweden that SIND's agenda is less employment-focused than is AMS's. Hence the quota may not be as high a priority matter as it was.

26. Charles Brown, "The Federal Attack on Labor Market Discrimination: The Mouse that Roared?" in Ronald G. Ehrenberg, ed., *Research in Labor Economics*, vol. 5 (Greenwich, Conn.: JAI Press, 1982), p. 39.

27. Office of Federal Contract Compliance Programs, "Review of the Effect of

The enforcement process under the Swedish program is enhanced by the involvement of the Employment Office, which not only refers candidates for the jobs in question but also, with the use of "equality personnel," conducts a follow-up of the applicants' success or failure in securing jobs under the quota. Moreover, if the employer requests an exemption from the quota requirement on the grounds of unavailability, the Employment Office is consulted to confirm or reject the employer's assertion that the requisite number of candidates cannot be found. Although the U.S. Job Training Partnership Act program (JTPA) calls for linkages between private industry and employment or training programs, the history of U.S. employment and training policy leads us to conclude that, unless additional changes are made, it is unlikely that local employment and training agencies in the United States will be as actively involved with the OFCCP in enforcing the executive order's requirement as is the Employment Office under the Swedish program.

Swedish Quotas versus U.S. Goals

Given the availability of exemptions under the Swedish sex quota program and the frequency with which the exemptions are accorded, the quota requirement, as applied, has many similarities to the goals requirement of the U.S. executive order program. Moreover, the conditions for obtaining an exemption reflect principles similar to those needed to demonstrate a "good faith effort" in meeting one's goal in the United States.[28]

Closely connected with the issue of what constitutes a good faith effort by employers in both the Swedish and U.S. systems is the issue of availability, how it is determined, and what constitutes a qualified labor pool. Under the Swedish system, government agencies are much more closely involved in the daily operations of the labor market. Thus determinations of the availability of the requisite work force can be based substantially on the judgment of government officials who are personally familiar with the local labor market. In the United States, however, availability is primarily determined on the basis of calculations

---

Executive Order 11246 and the Federal Contract Compliance Program on the Employment Opportunities of Minorities and Women'' (January 1983), p. 33; and Jonathan S. Leonard, "Affirmative Action as Earnings Redistribution: The Targeting of Compliance Reviews," *Journal of Labor Economics*, vol. 3 (July 1985), pp. 363–84.

28. 41 C.F.R. sec. 60-2.12 (1986).

of the number of workers by occupation or education in the relevant geographical area.

The distinction between qualified and unqualified employees or applicants for employment is unclear, both in the Swedish and U.S. program rules and practices. In Sweden, employers have few formal qualifications except experience; subjective factors such as reputation in the community, a particular employee's behavior, and perceived interest in performing the work in question were often mentioned as criteria for an acceptable (qualified) applicant for employment. Moreover, the level and quality of education and work experience, although objective factors, could be applied inconsistently without incurring legal sanctions.

The OFCCP regulations require employers to consider, among other things, the availability of women having the requisite skills in the immediate labor area and in an area in which a contractor can reasonably recruit; the availability of women seeking employment in the labor or recruitment area of the contractor; and the availability of promotable and transferable female employees within the contractors' organizations.[29] Thus the OFCCP regulations provide guidance as to the labor pool from which available workers may be drawn. However, the regulations are not specific about the acceptable criteria for determining whether an employee is qualified and therefore available, or about what constitutes the requisite skills, for any particular position in which minorities and women are underutilized. It is not clear whether the final determination of the criteria for requisite skills is left up to the employer or is otherwise governed by the executive order.

It should be noted, however, that U.S. law prohibits discrimination in employment on the basis of sex for contractors and noncontractors alike.[30] Notwithstanding employers' subjective or objective criteria for hiring or promotion, their hiring or promotion practices cannot have an adverse, discriminatory impact on members of one particular sex. Swedish law also prohibits employment discrimination on the basis of sex, and in the public sector, which is governed by the Swedish constitution, the law expressly requires that appointments be based only on "material qualifications," including merit and aptitude.[31]

29. 41 C.F.R. sec. 60-2.11(b) (2) (1986).

30. See U.S. Commission on Civil Rights, *Affirmative Action in the 1980s: Dismantling the Process of Discrimination: A Proposed Statement of the U.S. Commission on Civil Rights* (The Commission, 1981).

31. See Anita Dahlberg, *The Equality Act* (Swedish Center for Working Life, 1982),

Linkage to Job Training Programs

Job training provides a pool of available personnel under both the Swedish program and the U.S. affirmative action program. The linkage between their antidiscrimination programs and job training programs is a fundamental distinction between the two countries' approaches.

The Swedish system requires employers applying for regional development assistance to submit recruitment plans to the local employment offices. These plans are currently submitted during the early stages of the application process, instead of later during the actual hiring. Thus the employment offices are able to contact the employers concerning their employment needs and to recruit and train personnel, if needed, in time for the hiring process. Employers are encouraged to make use of the employment offices' resources, but may also recruit and hire personnel from other sources.

In the United States, as in Sweden, no mandatory linkage exists between the contract compliance program and any government-sponsored or privately operated training program, although contractors are required to list job opportunities with the U.S. Employment Service under the federal contractor job listing program.[32] In 1979 the Employment Training Administration (ETA) established a policy of linkage between the OFCCP and the ETA-funded delivery agents in order to place the economically disadvantaged and "covered group" clients in private-sector jobs.[33] This policy did not require that the ETA-funded delivery agents be the exclusive source of referrals. If a contractor could convince the OFCCP that alternative organizations could better meet its recruitment and promotion needs, rather than ETA sources, linkage was not implemented. The status of this linkage policy, given the demise of the CETA program and the incipient stage of the JTPA, is unclear.

In the Swedish system, the broader role for training programs and the

---

p. 155. The Act concerning Equality between Women and Men at Work, SFS 1980:412 (1980), prohibits employment discrimination on the basis of sex in individual cases where the complainant has better material qualifications for the work than another who is hired or promoted to the position at issue. Ibid., p. 162. The act, which governs both the public and private sectors, does not provide for class complaints of discrimination, however.

32. See U.S. Department of Labor, Field Memorandum no. 250-79 (April 25, 1979), p. 4.

33. Covered groups included women, minorities, disabled workers, and Vietnam-era and disabled veterans.

involvement of the local employment offices in the enforcement process leads to tighter linkages. Additionally, regional development aid is typically provided to firms that are expanding and looking for new (perhaps newly trained) workers. In the United States, on the other hand, federal contracts finance continued employment for existing workers as well as new employment. Thus the association of federal contractors with governmental training and referral agencies may be relatively weaker under the U.S. program even if governmental involvement in the labor market is held constant.

Due Process and Judicial Review

Lastly, a contrast between the two countries' programs is that the U.S. program accords due process rights to the contractor sanctioned by the federal agency and the right of injured parties (beneficiaries of the program) to file individual and class complaints of discrimination.[34] The provision of such rights is rooted in U.S. constitutional requirements. There are no similar constitutionally based rights in the Swedish program, although an employer may apply for reconsideration of sanctioning by the Industrial Board. There is no right to judicial review.

Conclusion

Of the several aspects of the Swedish sex-based quota program that distinguish it from the U.S. affirmative action model, the most noteworthy are the enforcement mechanism and the employment-training linkages. It is these two factors U.S. policymakers should closely examine in developing ways to enhance existing affirmative action programs.

The Swedish enforcement mechanism is noteworthy, not only because of its virtually universal application, but also because it is in fact used and employers apparently perceive that it is used. Enforcement is clearly the key to any program that seeks to alter age-old barriers to equal employment opportunity, and the Swedish program represents an excellent example of this truism. Linkage with employment-training programs that may assist the employer in locating and placing qualified personnel is important because availability is a primary element in the implementation of any affirmative action-type program.

34. 41 C.F.R. secs. 60-1(B), 60-30 (1983).

Effect of the Quota on Female Employment

Despite a significant number of exemptions, employment of women has apparently increased appreciably at establishments receiving regional development assistance in Sweden. From July 1974, when the quota became effective, through September 1980, 33 percent of the aided projects received general exemptions (planned increases of three or less) and 23 percent received other exemptions.[35] Thus only 44 percent of the projects were subject to the 40 percent quota. For these projects, women were expected to account for 45 percent of new employment.[36] Combining the exempt and nonexempt projects, the planned increase in female employment was 36 percent of the total. By 1979–80, 44 percent of the planned increases for all aided projects were going to women.[37]

The apparent increase in planned employment of women between the early years of the program and 1979–80 (and later) may reflect the changed approach to exemptions noted earlier. At the beginning of the quota, exemptions were granted at preliminary determination and were reflected in planned recruitment. More recently, such exemptions have been delayed until attempts are actually made to meet the quota. This means that few of the eventual exemptions will be reflected in the recruitment plans for the year of approval.

The key questions, however, are to what extent are the recruitment plans fulfilled, and to what extent do the fulfilled quotas represent outcomes that would not have occurred without the quota provision? Available information suggests that firms have, on average, fulfilled their recruitment plans, especially for location aid. Women represented 35 percent of the additional employment by projects granted regional development aid in the first two years of the quota; women's share of employment in these establishments increased from 19 to 21 percent. Among firms receiving location aid, the female share of increased

35. AMS briefing, May 19, 1981.
36. The excess over 40 percent represented both projects for which the 40 percent minimum for men was binding and projects for which the planned female share "voluntarily" exceeded 40 percent.
37. AMS, *Regional Aid*, table A. Women's share of planned increases has declined somewhat since 1979–80, however. In 1981–82, 40 percent of the planned increases were women; in 1982–83, 34 percent; in 1983–84, 40 percent. A representative of SIND explained that in 1982–83 one large plant received a relatively large portion of regional aid as well as an exemption from the quota.

employment was 41 percent. Among a sample of projects receiving location aid in the first thirty-nine months of the quota, women constituted 47 percent of the increase. In projects receiving location aid in the first four years of the quota, the share of women in total employment rose from 16 to 21 percent.[38]

If anything, these statistics point to a relatively high level of female hiring. In the first two years of the program, one-fourth (67 of 265) of the projects receiving location aid were granted exemptions, yet together the exempt and nonexempt projects managed to exceed the 40 percent quota.

The question remains, however, of how much of this expanded employment is due to the quota. It must be assumed that many expanding firms would have hired some women even without the quota. Thus only the female employment above that which would have occurred without the quota represents the impact of the program.

In an experimental science, determining the effect of some treatment is relatively straightforward. If a group of mice is randomly divided into two cages and those in one cage are fed a suspected carcinogen, a difference in the incidence of tumors between the residents of the two cages is a sensible estimate of the effect of the substance on mice.

Few governmental policies can be evaluated so simply. Those individuals or firms who are eligible for the program differ from those who are not in a systematic rather than random way, and those who choose to participate are also likely to differ from those who do not. Thus a control group is lacking to demonstrate what would have happened to the participants if they had not participated in the program.

Evaluation of the Swedish sex quota program falls into this category. Eligible establishments differ geographically and industrially from those that are not eligible, and participating establishments are expanding, while those that are eligible but do not take advantage of the subsidy are not growing. Thus there is no simple comparison of participant and nonparticipant establishments that will provide a reliable way of determining the program's impact. Any such comparisons will be subject to doubts about whether it was the sex quota program or other differences between participants and nonparticipants that caused the difference.

Given these limitations, we chose to judge the impact of the quota by

38. *Siffror om män och kvinnor* (Stockholm: SAF/PTK nämnden för jämställdhet i arbetslivet, 1979) [*Men and Women: Key Figures* (Stockholm: SAF/PTK Committee for Equality at Work, 1979)], pp. 212, 214.

looking for evidence that firms that met their quota *just* did so. The premise here is: if the quota is really forcing firms to do what they would not otherwise do, they should react by meeting rather than exceeding the quota.[39] On this approach, firms that hired women to meet, but not exceed, their quota are behaving in a manner which suggests that the quota is really increasing their employment of women.

We attempted to determine what each of the firms we visited would have done had location assistance not included a quota requirement. One firm that produced textile products represented the atypical case in which the 40 percent quota on male hiring was binding. It met the quota by hiring two men in the packing department, which in this industry appeared to be a traditionally male job; the firm said it would have done this with or without the quota. At two other plants (one manufactured steel-reinforced cement products and the other assembled aluminum products), it was clear that the quota had made a difference. The first had fulfilled its recruitment plan despite the manager's view that the current share of female workers (25 percent) was relatively high considering the heaviness of the work. The second also fulfilled its plan despite the fact that 95 percent of the applicants (and, in the proprietor's opinion, the seven best applicants) were men. Interestingly, both hired exactly the number of women called for by the quota. A similar view was expressed by an engineering firm that had not yet begun filling its new positions: the quota required the management to prefer "less-qualified" women. The fifth plant provided a more complicated picture. The proprietor said that increased availability of trained women, in particular those from the training centers, was responsible for his hiring women, and that he would have done so without the quota. We learned later that he was required to hire an additional half-time woman employee to avoid sanctions.

Another bit of evidence suggesting that the quotas have had some positive impact is the experience with sanctions discussed above. A nontrivial minority of firms are sanctioned for failing to meet the quota, and they uniformly respond by satisfying the enforcement authorities. Whether this means meeting the quota or doing as well as can be expected given that "too many" men have already been hired is unclear, but some positive response seems to be the rule for these firms.

39. This idea has received considerable attention in estimating the effect of minimum wage laws in the United States. See Orley Ashenfelter and Robert S. Smith, "Compliance with the Minimum Wage Law," *Journal of Political Economy*, vol. 87 (April 1979), pp. 333–50.

Data from Individually Aided Projects

Because the available statistical evidence seemed inconclusive on several issues, we requested and received project-level data from the files of the AMS.[40] For each of 180 projects approved in 1976, we have data on total and female employment at the time the project was approved and at the end of 1979 and 1980. Out of 155 projects in the data file with complete information, 37 had general exemptions (planned increases of three or less); 14 had other exemptions under which no increase in female employment was required; and 26 had zero or negative employment growth.[41] Thus 78 projects were subject to the quota.

This tabulation should give a sense of the importance of two of the factors that limit the impact of the quota. General exemptions apply to about 20 percent of the projects, though to an obviously smaller proportion of employment growth.[42] Nearly another 20 percent would be unaffected due to lack of employment growth. The latter statement is only approximate, since a project could have originally had employment growth subject to the quota and then fallen back by 1979. We also looked into the exemptions apart from the general ones. While we have no direct information on exemptions, we do have data on planned increases in total and female employment. If the plans called for females to account for less than 40 percent of the total increase, we can infer an exemption for women. This would reflect exemptions at the preliminary determination only, but we were told that this was when most exemptions were given for projects of this vintage. In any case, we found 14 out of the 155 projects had complete exemptions and another 15 had partial exemptions.

For those plants with positive employment increases between 1976 and 1979, we cross-tabulated the change in female employment and the change in total employment.[43] Increases in total employment were

---

40. We thank Ted Westermark and Vera Hirsch of AMS (now SIND) for providing the data.

41. We excluded from the total of 180 projects 25 where female employment in 1979 was unavailable or employment changes were implausible.

42. Throughout this discussion, we assume that missing data is randomly missing, because we know of no reason why it should be missing in any systematic way. For example, if planned-increase data were often not listed for firms with general exemptions, then we would obviously understate the relative frequency of such exemptions.

43. A few plants had several projects between 1976 and 1979. Since we wanted to be able to characterize plants unambiguously according to whether they had achieved their net employment increase, multiproject plants posed a problem. (They might have

categorized as less than planned, equal to planned, or greater than planned. Increases either one more or one less than planned were grouped with those equal to planned. Similarly, increases in female employment were categorized as less than, equal to, or greater than required by the quota. For plants that had increased total employment, required increases in female employment were calculated as 40 percent of planned employment growth, less exemptions, times the ratio of actual employment growth to planned employment growth. The resulting cross-tabulation is presented below.

	Increase in female employment			
Increase in total employment	Less than required	Equal to required	Greater than required	Total
Less than planned	3	14	12	29
Equal to planned	4	8	1	13
Greater than planned	6	14	16	36
Total	13	36	29	78

About one-sixth of the plants failed to meet their quota. However, one-half (thirty-six out of seventy-eight) *just* met their required level of female increase. This is what we would expect if the quota was forcing some plants to hire more women than they would ordinarily do. Nearly as many firms exceeded the requirement as met it, which suggests that they probably were not forced to expand their hiring of females by the quota. Exceeding the quota is somewhat more common among plants that expanded employment more than they had planned. Firms that do so are required to increase female employment by only 40 percent of planned growth in total employment. For a project that considerably exceeds the planned increase, the quota may require no more female hires than would have occurred anyway. The tendency for such firms to exceed required increases of women supports this argument.

Our analysis of the projects approved in 1976 suggests two conclusions. First, the quota requirement does have an effect on some firms. The tendency for plants to just meet their quota would not be expected if the quota was having no impact on their hiring. Second, several features of the quota limit its impact. Exempting projects with planned

---

fulfilled the employment gain planned in the first project, but not the second.) Our solution was to analyze actual employment at the time of approval of the second project instead of the 1979 data in these cases.

increases of three or fewer workers and effectively exempting firms that do not experience employment increases may not be significant. Potentially more limiting is the fact that the net increase in female employment for projects that exceed their planned increases must still equal only 40 percent of the anticipated increase, rather than 40 percent of the actual increase in total employment. Not only does this reduce the impact of the quota requirement during the period of the recruitment plan; it may also allow the quota's benefits to be eroded over the longer run.

It is unclear how much is really lost by the decision to hold firms to 40 percent of the planned increase in total employment when total employment expands faster than expected. As noted earlier, underestimating the true employment increase would reduce the amount of location aid in the form of the more attractive depreciation loan. However, this refers to the *maximum* allowable depreciation loan, while the actual incentives faced by firms depend on how actual loan decisions are made. In addition, because the support for net employment increases is a continuing subsidy related to actual employment increases, it provides firms with an incentive to hire women not strictly required by the location aid quota and to avoid the postproject correction in female employment noted above.

Modeling the Impact

The tentative conclusion that the quota has had some positive impact leads to the obvious question: how much? Our efforts here have followed an approach similar to that used in evaluating the impact of minimum wage laws.[44]

We begin by assuming that in the absence of the quota changes in female employment would be determined by such factors as total employment growth and the initial level of female employment relative to total employment, plus an error term that captures the influence of the many factors we cannot observe. There is no need to be dogmatic about the exact form of this relationship; various alternatives are considered below. We call the change in female employment that a firm would choose in the absence of the quota U (for unconstrained).

In addition to what firms would have done without the quota, what

44. Robert H. Meyer and David A. Wise, "The Effects of the Minimum Wage on the Employment and Earnings of Youth," *Journal of Labor Economics*, vol. 1 (January 1983), pp. 66–100.

they are required to do in order to satisfy the quota is obviously important. Let this required increase be R. Fortunately, we know what increase in female employment had been promised when the project was approved and the extent to which the planned increase in total employment had been achieved by 1979. Thus we can calculate R. R is not defined for firms with general exemptions or no employment growth.

Actual changes in female employment, which we denote by A, depend on U and R in a fairly complicated way. If U is greater than R, or if the quota does not apply, A equals U. For example, if a firm is required to hire three women but finds it profitable to hire five, it will hire five, not three—the required increase is simply irrelevant. If, on the other hand, R is greater than U, one might assume all employers obey the quota and hire R women. We make a less extreme assumption, however: we assume that some proportion, P, ignore the quota and hire U women, while the remaining $1 - P$ obey the quota and hire R.

The proportion P is not known in advance; it is estimated from the data. If the quota were completely obeyed, P would equal zero and we would expect many employers to just meet their quota. Not all employers would do so, however; if some firms found it profitable to exceed their quota, they would do so. If the quota were completely ignored (P equal to one), some projects would have increases in female employment below mandated levels, and a few might just meet their quota (if the required change in female employment happened to be what they wanted to do anyway), but there would be no tendency for female employment changes to cluster at the required level.

A technical description of our model is presented in the Appendix to this chapter, where results based on several alternative assumptions about the determinants of U are considered. Our best estimate is that about half of the employers who would otherwise have increased female employment by less than the required amount increased their hiring of women to meet the quota.[45] The corresponding increase in female employment due to the quota is about one-half worker per project. In comparison with the fourteen women working at the average plant at the

45. This might seem inconsistent with the evidence in the table on page 288 that just meeting the quota was much more common than failing to do so (thirty-six versus thirteen projects). The apparent discrepancy is due to the fact that some of the employers would have hired the number of females required by the quota even if the quota did not exist. This fact increases the number shown as just meeting the quota in the table, but is properly accounted for in the more formal calculations described in the Appendix.

preliminary determination or the nearly nine-worker increase in female employment experienced by the average establishment between 1976 and 1979, this is a modest increase. However, the implied 3 or 4 percent increase in female employment in directly affected establishments in Sweden is larger than most studies find for the OFCCP in the United States. Moreover, one should bear in mind that by 1979 (or, for that matter, 1980) the full impact of the quota had not been felt in many cases. As noted above, roughly a sixth of the establishments had experienced no employment growth and nearly another fifth had increased employment but by less than anticipated when the aid application was approved.

Over the longer run, two competing forces will come into play. It is possible that the quota-induced experience with female workers will change employers' perceptions about female workers in general and thus women's employment opportunities will expand. On the other hand, as more firms' employment growth *exceeds* their planned increase, they can move toward their preferred, lower, female share of employment by keeping the number of women at the quota-mandated level as more men are hired. The evidence that thirteen of the thirty-six projects that exceeded their planned increase in total employment continued to have only the number of women required by the quota suggests that this response is not simply a remote theoretical possibility.

Effect of the Quota on Jobs Held by Women

One aspect of the quota requirement not discussed so far is its effect on the kind of jobs performed by women. In particular, does the quota lead firms to place women in nontraditional jobs? Unfortunately, data on this subject are almost nonexistent.

Because compliance with the quota depends upon the numerical increase in female employment, rather than its distribution by occupation, job categories of the women hired by aided firms do not appear to be collected. The recruitment plans do require the firm to indicate the planned occupational distribution of the anticipated new employees. But we learned of no tabulations of these recruitment plan data. Thus we are left with the impressions of those involved with the program.

Early government evaluations of the quota reported varied reactions—some hiring of women into nontraditional jobs, but also instances of firms shuffling their work forces so that new positions would not entail very heavy work.[46] Reports of women requesting a transfer from heavy work to lighter, more traditional work were also noted.

A Labor Market Board representative pointed out that the traditional female share in many industries in the aided areas was so far below 40 percent that a significant expansion of women's work role would be necessary to meet the quota. A labor union representative disagreed, however, estimating that in the recruitment plans he had seen, half or even two-thirds of the women were to be placed in traditionally female jobs.[47]

The various views noted above are no doubt a reflection of three factors. First, the definition of a traditionally female job is often difficult in practice. Second, reliable statistics are unavailable. Third, there seems to be a part-empty, part-full character to the discussion. Some women appear to have been placed in nontraditional jobs (such as mixing cement in the reinforced products plant we visited), while others have been placed in light manufacturing jobs or even nonmanufacturing jobs (clerical or cleaning) within manufacturing establishments.

Domestic Implications

The sex-based employment quota has so far been successful in promoting employment opportunities for Swedish women in companies receiving regional development assistance. Factors that may have contributed to the success of the quota include linkages between AMS-SIND, the County Labor Boards, and the Employment Office; the rigorous enforcement of the program by AMS-SIND; and, more fundamentally, the national commitment Sweden has made to promote equality between the sexes in working life. We suggest that U.S. policymakers examine these components of the Swedish program with a view toward enhancing existing affirmative action and job creation programs. For example, as we discussed above, federally financed employment and training programs in the United States currently have a small role to play

---

46. *Könskvotering vid vissa former av regionalpolitiskt stöd* (Solna, Sweden: Arbetsmarknadsstyrelsen, 1978) [*Sex Quotas and Certain Types of Regional Aid: Report from the Evaluation Group* (Solna, Sweden: National Labor Market Board, 1978)], p. 3; and National Labor Market Board, *Comments on the Follow-up Report*, pp. 2–3.

47. Interview with Hirsch and Westermark, May 19, 1981; and interview with Gösta Karlsson, Swedish Salaried Employees Union, June 4, 1981.

in the training and placement of recruits in carrying out affirmative action goals and even less involvement in the monitoring of referrals to these programs. Admittedly, some government contractors require higher-level skills than training programs provide, and some contracts do not require new hires, particularly if a previous contract is being continued. Nevertheless, by not including local employment and training programs in the follow-up and monitoring of referrals made by these agencies, a valuable enforcement tool may be ignored. Such linkage will be more important if the Job Training Partnership Act succeeds in improving employer satisfaction with training programs and the scale of such programs is expanded.

Secondly, the Swedish program has shown that vigorous enforcement is the key to a successful affirmative action program. For enforcement efforts to be effective, adequate resources must be provided.[48] Moreover, agencies responsible for overseeing affirmative action plans must conduct compliance reviews and resolve class complaints within prescribed time frames.[49] If review of the hiring record of each completed contractor requires unavailable resources, scanning such records in order to give special attention to firms that fail to even approximate their affirmative action goals is probably the next-best alternative.

Lastly, we suggest that the Swedish program has worked because of the visible national commitment of the government to equality between women and men in working life. Although the theory underlying the "dual targeting" or emphasis on both women and men in the promotion of government-backed employment programs (*jämställdhet*) has given way since 1981 to a focus on the more disadvantaged sex, the Swedish government's commitment toward equal employment opportunity appears fixed.[50] Similarly, the U.S. government's commitment toward

48. See U.S. Commission on Civil Rights, *The Federal Civil Rights Enforcement Budget, Fiscal Year 1983* (U.S. Commission on Civil Rights Publications, 1982), pp. 40–50.

49. See *Women's Equity Action League (WEAL)* v. *Bell*, no. 74-1720 (D.D.C. March 11, 1983), and *Alameda County* v. *Brennan*, 381 F. Supp. 125 (N.D. Cal. 1974), *aff'd*, 608 F.2d 1319 (9th Cir. 1979).

50. Berit Rollén, *Equality in the Labour Market between Men and Women—A Task for the National Labour Market Board*, report delivered at the Center for Research on Women, Wellesley College, May 1978, p. 4; Birgitta Wistrand, *Swedish Women on the Move*, ed. and trans. by Jeanne Rosen (Stockholm: Swedish Institute, 1981), pp. 7–8; and interview with Annika Baude, consultant to the project, August 23, 1984. Of course, it remains to be seen whether the shift in 1982 from AMS to SIND as the agency

equal employment opportunity must also remain visible and fixed, so that affirmative action programs may be permitted to work to achieve equality between women and men in the labor market.

Appendix

The relationship presented in the text between the actual change in female employment, A, and the required and unconstrained changes, R and U, is:

If $U > R$ or R is undefined, $A = U$;
If $U = R$, $A = R$;
If $U < R$, $\text{Prob}(A < R) = P$; $\text{Prob}(A = R) = 1 - P$.

R can be computed from knowledge of planned increases in total and female employment. U is not observed; we assume it is determined by $U_i = X_i B + e_i$, where e_i is normally distributed with mean zero and variance $\sigma_1{}^2$.

As noted in the text, we treat observations with A close to R as if the actual change equals the required change. There are two reasons for this complication. First, even a firm that adheres strictly to the quota could experience a small, temporary deviation between R and U (for example, if a female worker quits and is not yet replaced when employment is measured). Second, employment as measured is an integer variable, so we must account for the possibility that A equals R because the unconstrained change in female employment just happened to equal the required level. (With genuinely continuous variables, this occurs with zero probability.) More precisely, we defined $R' = R - 1.5$ and $R'' = R + 1.5$, and treated an observation as "just" meeting the quota if $R' < A < R''$.

Likelihood Function

If $A_i > R''_i$ or if R_i is undefined, we know observation i was not

responsible for administering the quota reflects a change in the Swedish government's policy toward women's equality in the labor market.

constrained by the quota. Its contribution to the log-likelihood function is

$$LLF_i = -\frac{1}{2}\ln{(2\pi\sigma_i^2)} - \frac{1}{2}\left(\frac{A_i - X_iB}{\sigma_i}\right)^2.$$

If $R_i'' > A_i > R_i'$, observation i "just" satisfies the quota. Its contribution to the log-likelihood is

$$LLF_i = \ln\left\{F\left(\frac{R_i'' - X_iB}{\sigma_i}\right) - F\left(\frac{R_i' - X_iB}{\sigma_i}\right)\right.$$
$$\left. + (1 - P)F\left(\frac{R_i' - X_iB}{\sigma_i}\right)\right\}$$
$$= \ln\left\{F\left(\frac{R_i'' - X_iB}{\sigma_i}\right) - PF\left(\frac{R_i' - X_iB}{\sigma_i}\right)\right\},$$

where F is the standard-normal cumulative distribution function. The first two terms in the first line of the above expression represent the case where the unconstrained change in female employment just happens to be that required by the quota, while the last term represents observations that increase their female hiring to reach the quota.

Finally, if $A_i < R_i'$, observation i failed to meet the quota. Its contribution to the log-likelihood is

$$LLF_i = \ln P - \frac{1}{2}\ln{(2\pi\sigma_i^2)} - \frac{1}{2}\left(\frac{A_i - X_iB}{\sigma_i}\right)^2.$$

We assumed that $\sigma_i^2 = \sigma^2 w_i$, where w_i is the average of total employment in 1976 and 1979. This assumption can be justified roughly by thinking of the number of women employed for a given level of total employment as a binomially distributed variable. (This is analogous to weighting sample *proportions* by the square root of the sample size in linear models.) We scaled the w_i's, so that the mean of $w_i^{(1/2)}$ was equal to one.

Determinants of Unconstrained Changes in Female Employment

In choosing the determinants of the unconstrained change in female employment, we assumed that it depended linearly on initial levels of female and total employment and in more complicated ways on the growth of employment. It is convenient to divide the overall change in female employment into two components: the first due to the effects of turnover with a given level of total employment, and the second due to the change in total employment.

Suppose total employment, T, remained constant between 1976 and 1979. If t_F and t_M are the turnover rates of female and male jobs, then $t_F F_{76}$ and $t_M M_{76}$ are the numbers of replacements hired in previously female and male jobs. If h_F and h_M are the proportions of the two types of replacements who are females, $F_{79} = F_{76} - (1 - h_F)t_F F_{76} + h_M t_M M_{76}$. Since $M_{76} = T_{76} - F_{76}$, this can be rewritten

$$F_{79} - F_{76} = -[(1 - h_F)t_F + h_M t_M]F_{76} + h_M t_M T_{76}$$
$$= -[t_F + (h_M t_M - h_F t_F)]F_{76} + h_M t_M T_{76}.$$

If total employment changes, the change in female employment obviously depends on the size of the employment change, and perhaps on the initial female share of total employment, $s = F_{76}/T_{76}$. Thus a general expression for the unconstrained change in female employment is

$$F_{79} = F_{76} = -[t_F + (h_M t_M - h_F t_F)]F_{76} + h_M t_M T_{76}$$
$$+ g(s, T_{79} - T_{76}).$$

In the work reported below, we considered three forms for the function g:

(1) $g(s, T_{79} - T_{76}) = g_0(T_{79} - T_{76}) + g_1 s(T_{79} - T_{76})$;

(2) $g(s, T_{79} - T_{76}) = g_0(T_{79} - T_{76}) + g_1 s(T_{79} - T_{76})$

$$+ g_3(T_{79} - T_{76})^2 + g_4 s(T_{79} - T_{76})^2;$$

(3) $g(s, T_{79} - T_{76}) = g_0(T_{79} - T_{76}) + g_1 s(T_{79} - T_{76})$

$$+ g_3(T_{79} - T_{76})^- + g_4 s(T_{79} - T_{76})^-,$$

where $(T_{79} - T_{76})^-$ is equal to $T_{79} - T_{76}$ when that quantity is negative and is equal to zero otherwise. Thus the third specification allows the marginal effect of a change in total employment to differ for increases and decreases.

Results

Our most important findings are reported in table 1. We report results for five specifications. We begin with the one that seems to fit the data best (column 1), where the impact of employment growth is a quadratic

Table 1. *Determinants of Changes in Female Employment*[a]

		Specification				
Variable	Mean	(1)	(2)	(3)	(4)	(5)
F_{76}	14.47	−0.103	−0.002	−0.100	0.157	0.273
		(0.108)	(0.037)	(0.100)	(0.086)	(0.097)
T_{76}	86.36	0.047	0.042	0.050	0.017	−0.006
		(0.026)	(0.006)	(0.024)	(0.028)	(0.028)
$T_{79} - T_{76}$	18.12	0.098	0.058	0.135	0.277	0.306
		(0.065)	(0.064)	(0.062)	(0.042)	(0.041)
$s(T_{79} - T_{76})$	8.74	0.805	0.941	0.758	−0.078	−0.129
		(0.203)	(0.237)	(0.178)	(0.051)	(0.052)
$(T_{79} - T_{76})^2/100$	61.39	0.190	0.070	0.154	..	..
		(0.123)	(0.077)	(0.119)		
$s(T_{79} - T_{76})^2/100$	50.02	−0.296	−0.175	−0.255	..	..
		(0.175)	(0.177)	(0.159)		
$(T_{79} - T_{76})^-$	−2.52	..	..	..	..	−0.692
		..	..	..	..	(0.400)
$s(T_{79} - T_{76})^-$	−0.40	..	..	..	..	3.632
		..	..	..	..	(4.143)
P		0.488	0.298	0.726	0.458	0.472
		(0.110)	(0.077)	(0.113)	(0.103)	(0.106)
Effect of quota		0.542	0.423	0.195	0.688	0.637
Log-likelihood		−416	−455	−452	−442	−437

a. See text for definitions of variables and specifications. Numbers in parentheses are standard errors. $N = 146$.

function of the change in total employment (specification 2 in the previous section).

The change in female employment growth is negatively related to initial female employment and positively related to initial total employment, as turnover considerations predict. Moreover, the coefficient of F_{76} is larger in absolute value than that of T_{76}, as the simple turnover model predicts. Given the highly nonlinear form of the function relating changes in female employment to total employment, the effect of changing total employment obviously depends on the values of s and $T_{79} - T_{76}$ at which that effect is evaluated. At mean values of the variables, an increase in total employment leads to an increase in unconstrained female employment about three-tenths as large. Moreover, the effect of growing total employment on female employment is stronger where the initial share of female employment is higher.

Given this specification of the determinants of the unconstrained change in female employment, the estimated value of P is 0.488. This means that slightly less than half of those who would otherwise hire fewer than the required number of women do so even in the presence of the quota; slightly more than half bring their number of female workers up to the required level. The overall effect of the quota can be estimated as the difference between the mean of the unconstrained change in female employment for the whole sample—what we estimate would have happened without the quota—and the actual mean change in female employment. The value in column 1 is 0.542, which means that the difference amounted to about one-half of a worker per establishment.

Column 2 presents the results when the variance of the error term is assumed constant for all observations, instead of being proportional to total employment. The main results are qualitatively similar, with the proportion of employers failing to meet the quota a bit smaller but the estimated effect of the quota a bit smaller, too.

In column 3, we adopt a stricter definition of just meeting the quota— only values of A exactly equal to R are so regarded. Predictably, a larger fraction of the observations are regarded as failing to meet the quota, and the estimated impact of the quota is smaller. However, the log-likelihood function is considerably lower for the specification, suggesting there is little reason to prefer it.

In column 4, we consider the consequences of simplifying the specification of the function relating changes in female employment to changes in total employment. Terms involving $(T_{79} - T_{76})^2$ are deleted. The remaining coefficients make less sense, and the hypothesis that the omitted terms' coefficients are zero is soundly rejected by the appropriate likelihood ratio test $[x^2(2) = 51$, compared with a critical value at the 0.01 level of 9.2]. The estimated impact of the quota is, however, little affected by the change.

Finally, we consider the third specification of the effects of changing total employment discussed above: the effect of changing total employment differs according to the *sign* of this change, as well as differing at different initial female employment shares. Once again, the estimated effects of the quota (column 5) are similar to those in column 1. The terms involving $(T_{79} - T_{76})^-$ are jointly significant (comparing columns 4 and 5), but less resoundingly so than when the quadratic terms were added.

The overall impression created by table 1 is that the quota had *some* impact (P is significantly less than one under each specification), but the impact on female employment is not enormous (nearly always about half a female worker per establishment). These are the conclusions we emphasized in the text.

Comments by Nancy S. Barrett

The excellent paper by Brown and Wilcher provides a detailed description of the use of gender quotas in the Swedish program of regional economic development assistance. A major contribution is their thorough and comprehensive description of the mechanics of the Swedish program, which will be useful for equal employment opportunity (EEO) planners in the United States and elsewhere. In addition, they have provided a quantitative impact evaluation in the context of the program's stated goals. This comment is intended to go beyond the Brown and Wilcher analysis to an evaluation of the Swedish program as an EEO instrument, and in particular its lessons for EEO policy in the United States.

At the outset, it is important to recognize that the goal of equal employment opportunity, as well as the broader goals of economic, social, and political equality between men and women, is universally accepted (although not always practiced) in Sweden. EEO policies such as gender quotas as a condition for regional development aid are accepted without rancor by employers and male workers, greatly facilitating the work of EEO enforcement. Because this consensus is lacking in the United States, EEO enforcement is more adversarial than in Sweden, and more detailed rules and regulations are generally required to prevent evasion.

An aspect of Swedish EEO policy that merits imitation is its links with other government programs that benefit firms and male workers. The regional aid program is a case in point, as are the linkages between EEO and government-aided training, relocation, and job-placement programs. If firms and male workers stand to gain from these programs, they are more likely to accept gender quotas than they would under U.S.-style affirmative action programs that are set up as zero-sum games. In the Swedish system everyone wins, while in the U.S. system gains for women are at the expense of males and are perceived as costly to firms.

Of course, the ability of policy planners to make these program linkages is related to the social and political consensus for gender equality. In the United States it would be more difficult to impose gender quotas in programs favored by other constituencies. Experience with so-called targeting in U.S. social programs shows that the "targets" quickly become diffuse and the needs of female workers are not often given priority.

Any observer of the Swedish economy is well aware that equality between men and women may be a goal, but it is not the reality. And one reason why Swedish EEO policies are accepted without rancor is that they rarely force the tough issues as does EEO policy in the United States. The gender quotas described by Brown and Wilcher simply ensure that women receive 40 percent of new jobs created in the program. There are no conditions on wages or on the occupational distributions of women relative to men.

The major problem for women workers both in Sweden and the United States is not finding jobs, but rather finding well-paid jobs. In both countries, women hold over 40 percent of the jobs and men take home roughly 70 percent of the pay. Both countries have managed to absorb very rapid increases in the female work force in the past two decades without a noticeable increase in the relative unemployment of females. True, jobs for women are more problematic in Sweden because of prohibitions on layoffs, which disadvantage new entrants relative to experienced workers. However, this is not as serious as women's low earnings, which result from their continued segregation into low-pay occupations. It is worth noting that the elaborate gender quota scheme described by Brown and Wilcher had a very small impact. The increase in female employment due to the quota was about one-half worker per project, compared with the nearly nine-worker increase in female employment experienced by the average establishment during the evaluation period. The small impact was not due to deliberate evasion, but rather to the fact that most firms would have employed this number of women anyway.

It is most peculiar that in a program designed to promote equal employment opportunity no data are available on occupations or earnings of newly hired workers. The idea expressed by Swedish officials—that occupational data are not useful because it is difficult to define a traditionally female job—is ridiculous. Any occupation that employs more than 65 percent of either gender, for instance, is nontraditional for the other. Most men and women work in such jobs.

The Swedish plan described by Brown and Wilcher provides a good example of how EEO programs can be linked to other programs so as to prevent them from being perceived as a zero-sum game. But it fails to deal with the pay issue, which is by far the most important problem of gender equity in all the industrial countries. To accomplish this, EEO programs must emphasize not only the number of jobs for women but also the quality of those jobs. This means moving women into the higher-pay job categories that have been dominated by men, as well as restructuring traditional female jobs in ways that will make them more productive and improve opportunities for advancement. These have been, and should continue to be, the main emphases of EEO programs in the United States. Clearly, both Sweden and the United States can learn from each other in their separate efforts to achieve the goal of gender equality.

Comments by Helen Ginsburg

Brown and Wilcher have presented a very useful and thought-provoking analysis of Sweden's sex-based employment quotas. The paper is rich in nitty-gritty details about the day-to-day operation of the quota program. These details—too often absent from studies of this sort—stem from the authors' extensive interviews and visits to firms that have implemented the quota.

What has been the impact of the quota on the employment of women? Would all the women hired under the quota have been hired even in the absence of the quota? What are the implications for U.S. domestic programs? These are some of the questions Brown and Wilcher ask. The good news is that, despite numerous exemptions and loopholes, the quota has had a small but measurable increase on the hiring of women by establishments receiving regional employment assistance. Brown and Wilcher estimate that about half of the establishments did hire more women than they would have without the quota, but the increase is estimated to be a mere one-half worker per project, when all projects are included. However, according to Brown and Wilcher, that implies a 3 or 4 percent increase in female employment, more than most studies have attributed to U.S. Office of Federal Contract Compliance Programs. This increase might be higher at present because their data were for 1976 and 1979, and, as they point out, firms may get used to hiring women and thus exceed the quota. In their model, Brown and Wilcher assume that hirings due to attitudinal changes would have taken place anyway and are not counted as quota-induced hirings.

According to Brown and Wilcher, the success of the quota is due mainly to rigorous enforcement, extensive involvement of various government agencies in the labor market, and the national commitment Sweden has made to promote equality in working life. I would add another factor. With about 90 percent of Swedish workers unionized, successful implementation of any labor market program also depends on active union-management cooperation. This is facilitated by the presence of both groups on the National and County Labor Market Boards.

But how successful is success? If I were an unemployed or under-employed Swedish woman in a region where job opportunities for women (and for men) are scarce, I would not be overly encouraged by the relatively small impact of the quota alone. I would be more encouraged by the totality of measures that have helped Swedish women. Thus I would like to expand on and focus on some larger questions: Where does the quota fit into Swedish women's quest for equality? How do Swedish women perceive equality? Have they attained it? What can we learn from the total experience, including but not limited to, the quota?

National Commitment to Full Employment

Sweden's sex-based quota, as Brown and Wilcher point out, is an outgrowth of a national commitment to equality between the sexes in working life. It is also, however, an outgrowth of Sweden's national commitment to full employment, one that is deeply held and cuts across political parties. This commitment is so strong that it is difficult for many Americans to understand it. Full employment is an overriding goal of Swedish society.[51]

Full employment policies developed over many decades, starting in the 1930s when the Social Democrats came into power. (They have been in power since then, except for 1976–82.) Until the end of the 1950s, full employment policy meant general expansion of the economy. Then this Keynesian approach was replaced by one that combines macropolicy with myriad selective policies designed to get at a wide variety of labor market problems facing disadvantaged groups and regions. Government programs, including extensive direct job creation (called relief work)

51. Full employment policies are extensively described and analyzed in Helen Ginsburg, *Full Employment and Public Policy: The United States and Sweden* (Lexington, Mass.: Lexington Books, 1983), chaps. 5–9. Women's role in the labor market is the subject of chap. 7.

and labor market training (neither means-tested) play an integral role in the pursuit of full employment. Commitment to full employment played a major role in developing the quota.

Swedish Women Enter the Labor Force en Masse

The participation of Swedish women in the labor force, especially married women and mothers, rose rapidly in the 1960s and 1970s. In the 1960s unemployment averaged 1.7 percent (adjusted to U.S. concepts) and the Swedish economy was booming.[52] Women helped to relieve labor shortages. Between 1965 and 1979 women made up the entire increase in the Swedish labor force. The labor force participation rate of men fell from 80 percent to 78.5 percent, but for women it climbed from 40.5 to 63.5 percent. At the beginning of this period, women were 37 percent of the labor force but by 1979 they were 45 percent—though many were working only part time.[53]

Here a contrast with U.S. attitudes is helpful in understanding the context of the quota. Although Swedish unemployment in the 1970s was very low by U.S. standards (averaging 2.1 percent), the Swedish economy was no longer booming and it took heroic efforts to maintain these low figures. By 1979 the National Labor Market Board, the main instrument for implementing selective policies, had expenditures amounting to 3 percent of Sweden's gross national product and 7.4 percent of the national government budget.[54]

In the United States, unemployment also rose in the 1970s, averaging 6.2 percent during the decade, compared with 4.8 percent in the 1960s. The structural hypothesis was developed at this time to explain the rise in the jobless rate. Women's increasing share of the labor force, many claimed, had led to higher general rates of unemployment because women's unemployment rates were higher than men's. These overall

52. Ibid., table 5-4, p. 121. (Adjustments were made by the U.S. Bureau of Labor Statistics.)

53. Data for labor force participation of Swedish women are from Sveriges officiella statistik, *Arbetskraftsundersökningarna* (Stockholm: Statistika Centralbyrån) [Swedish Official Statistics, *The Labor Force Surveys* (Stockholm: Statistics Sweden)], various issues.

54. Jan Johannesson and Inga Persson-Tanimura, *Labour Market Policy under Reconsideration: Studies of the Swedish Labour Market and the Effects of Labour Market Policy* (Stockholm: Ministry of Labor, 1984), p. 44. Data refer to fiscal year 1978–79.

unemployment rates of the 1970s were then often considered by policy-makers and economists to be less significant than in earlier periods because women had become a larger proportion of the jobless. Thus the "full employment" unemployment rate was upwardly redefined.[55]

In Sweden, on the other hand, where women's unemployment rates were (and are) also somewhat higher than men's, the response was very different. There was an attempt to provide women with employment despite a softening job market. As a Swedish government bill states, "Full employment can only be ensured through measures which are constantly adjusted to current requirements. Aspirations with regard to the provision of meaningful employment have risen and our efforts must be stepped up accordingly."[56] Thus an additional basis for full employment policy became the greater aspirations of women for work. Women's right to work came to be recognized as equal to that of men. Policy was also geared toward hidden unemployment, including women who were not in the labor market because of lack of jobs or child care. Some unemployed housewives became eligible for limited unemployment benefits. Women were clearly included in the full employment goal in the broadest sense. And the quota is part of the effort to translate the goal into reality.

Regional Policy

Regional policy is an outgrowth of full employment policy as well as of the general ideology of equality. Regional disparities have long existed in Sweden. The original approach was to relocate workers from areas of high unemployment to regions with labor shortages. Thus the government helped workers find jobs in other regions and also provided generous relocation grants and allowances. This is still done. But strong backlash against the policy of migration mounted in the North from Swedes who did not want to leave. So, starting in the mid-1960s, Sweden also embarked on a regional development policy designed to bring jobs to the North and avoid lopsided development. In a region where jobs were not only scarce but were mainly in traditionally male-dominated industries such as forestry, mining, and steel, development should mean

55. For a further discussion, see Ginsburg, *Full Employment and Public Policy,* pp. 25, 33–44.

56. "Swedish Labor Market Policy," *Fact Sheets on Sweden* (Stockholm: Svenska Institutet, May 1979), p. 1.

jobs for women as well as men. Not only were job opportunities for women in the North especially sparse compared with those in cities such as Stockholm, traditional attitudes toward women were also very strong.

Job prospects for women in the North have improved. Nevertheless, regional development policy has not halted the economic problems of the North, although it may have prevented them from worsening. Employment expansion through development policy has had to offset the loss of jobs in forestry and in other industries beset with long-term problems that are concentrated in the North. The quota's potential for success hinges on job growth due to development policy. According to one government report, between mid-1965 and 1978 development policy was responsible for the creation of more than 51,000 jobs[57]—equal to slightly more than 1 percent of the Swedish labor force. A later government study, however, concluded that this estimate was much too high.[58] It is notable, though, that during those years, manufacturing jobs declined in the rest of Sweden but grew in the North. In 1980, 358 employers received first-year support for employment of 1,333 persons, of whom 461 were women.[59]

But many—especially in the North—have been critical of regional policy because it is too meager. Unemployment in the North is still several times higher than elsewhere, even among men. Annual expenditures on regional policy have declined in recent years in real and current kroner. Sweden's annual expenditures on labor market policy as a percentage of GNP have risen since the 1970s, while expenditures on regional policy as a percentage of GNP have fallen.[60]

Other Labor Market Policies

Other labor market policies have been very useful to Swedish women, especially labor market training and so-called relief work—jobs at regular wages created by the government for the unemployed. These are extensive and ongoing programs, which often have about 2 percent of

57. Swedish Ministry of Economic Affairs and Ministry of the Budget, *The Swedish Budget 1980/81* (Stockholm: LiberFörlag, 1980), p. 116.

58. Letter to the author from Eskil Wadensjö, Swedish Institute for Social Research, December 21, 1981.

59. Letter to the author from Jan Johannesson, Swedish Ministry of Labor, July 30, 1984.

60. See Johannesson and Persson-Tanimura, *Labour Market Policy*, pp. 11, 14.

the labor force as participants.[61] They are more heavily concentrated in areas of higher than average unemployment, such as the development regions. Women's share of relief workers rose from 12 percent in 1972 to 41 percent in 1983;[62] there has also been a rapid rise in women's share of labor market trainees since the 1960s. It would be useful to compare the quota's relative contribution to employment of women in the development areas with that of relief work and the expansion of public services. I suspect these latter two programs may have provided more jobs than the quota. Public services are closely related to relief work, which has been a boon to women. Relief work has provided jobs—even though sex segregated—and high-quality programs such as day care and care for the elderly, thereby enabling many women to work outside the home. Ironically, a small program for equality grants—modest subsidies available to employers who train women for men's jobs or men for women's jobs—has had only a very minor impact.

Despite the ideology of equality, the Swedish labor market is still extremely sex segregated. Unfortunately, lack of data prevents Brown and Wilcher from estimating the impact of quotas on the occupations of women hired under the program. It has been reported, however, that women have made some breakthroughs in entering male-dominated industries such as sawmills and cement works.[63] But more specific industry data might be available and useful.

Data on increases in women's labor force participation in these areas are quite encouraging. There has been a significant narrowing of the gap in labor force participation, both between men and women in the forestry counties of the North and between women in these counties and in metropolitan counties. Expansion of public services, partly the result of relief work, has had a considerable impact on the labor force participation of women in the North. By contrast, a major weakness of the quota is its small scale. Further, when the economy of these areas is experiencing difficulties—a typical situation—women don't benefit much be-

61. Jan Johannesson, *On the Composition of Swedish Labour Market Policy* (Stockholm: Ministry of Labor, 1983), pp. 27, 29. The figures for all labor market policy measures are even higher. In 1983, for example, an average of 3.3 percent of the labor force was in the various measures (ibid., p. 7).

62. See *Jämställdhet på arbetsmarknaden: Statistik* (Solna, Sweden: Arbetsmarknadsstyrelsen, 1984) [*Equality in the Labour Market: Statistics* (Solna, Sweden: National Labor Market Board, 1984)], table 12.

63. Letter to the author from Marianne Sundström, Center for Swedish Working Life, November 8, 1984.

cause of the slow job growth; but if establishments that utilize the quota expand more than anticipated, women still do not get much more help because the quota applies only to the planned increment in employment. Another weakness of the quota is that it does not apply to all establishments of the firm, as does U.S. contract compliance. If it did, it would be a more potent national tool, as long as some firms did not then decide not to utilize the development grants.

The Act on Equality between Men and Women

Brown and Wilcher mention the 1980 Swedish Act on Equality between Women and Men at Work, which bans sex discrimination except for "positive discrimination" on behalf of those in an under-represented sex. Class action suits are not allowed. Interestingly, before passage of the act, a Swedish delegation to the United States concluded that Sweden did not need U.S.-style equal opportunity legislation.[64] But others disagreed. The law was passed without the support of the Social Democratic party and despite negative reactions from management and labor. In their objections, unions stated that the traditional Swedish voluntary approach to labor relations is preferable. They had, the unions pointed out, already negotiated equality clauses in their contracts. The law allows these agreements to play a major role. But lack of strong affirmative action seems to prevail. (It would be useful to compare what has happened to women in development area firms covered by the sex discrimination law, but not by the quota, with those in firms covered by the quota. But to get that answer would require another study.)

Progress on Other Fronts

Despite slow progress on some fronts, Swedish women have made considerable progress on others. The wage gap between Swedish women who work full time (many don't) and men has narrowed considerably more than in the United States, mainly due to the trade unions' policy of concentrating on raising wages of lower-paid workers. Though women are notably absent from the higher rungs of both unions and management, their presence in politics is more impressive. About one-fourth of

64. Wistrand, *Swedish Women on the Move*, p. 15. This book covers all aspects of the status of women in Sweden, as does Hilda Scott, *Sweden's "Right to be Human": Sex Role Equality: The Goal and the Reality* (Armonk, N.Y.: M.E. Sharpe, 1982).

parliament is female. Consequently, equality is taken more seriously than in the United States. Further, the Swedish government officially upholds the view that society should be striving toward equality in the sense of each person being self-supporting (each individual's earned income is taxed separately) and toward equality in the home.

Some big questions that have been raised are hardly heard at the official or even the unofficial level in the United States: Can there be equality in the labor market without equality in the home? Can women's role change if men's does not? Swedish women don't think so. Thus, a one-year paid parenthood leave under the social insurance scheme enables mothers or fathers (or both, if shared) to stay home to care for infants. Paid leave under social insurance enables parents to stay home from work to care for sick children. And parents with children under 8 years old have the right to reduce their workday to six hours (with proportionate reduction in earnings). Parental leaves are mostly, though not entirely, used by women, but the proportion of men using them has risen. There is also the call for a six-hour day—not yet implemented—to enable working families to be with their children more, and, it is hoped, to lead to a more equal distribution of work in the home and out of the home by men and women. Perhaps the leading issue is that of publicly subsidized day care. It is extensive, and excellent, though still in short supply. And women do not think you can talk seriously about equality without an expansion of child care facilities.

Conclusion

I agree with Brown and Wilcher that policymakers in the United States should examine the Swedish government's commitment to equality, its strong enforcement mechanism for quotas, and its involvement in day-to-day labor market activities. The aim should be to enhance, not replace, U.S. affirmative actions programs, which need more vigorous enforcement. But to add to that list, we need also to consider Sweden's commitment to full employment and family policies, including day care. These are crucial elements needed to attain equality, which have not been part of U.S. policy. Finally, I would stress more political representation for women. In the present political climate, women in the United States may have to fight harder just to stay in the same place in the labor market and the rest of society.

Conference Participants

with their affiliations at the time of the conference

Katharine G. Abraham *Massachusetts Institute of Technology*
Alice H. Amsden *Harvard University*
Hugh Armstrong *Vanier College*
Isabella Bakker *Status of Women Canada*
Nancy S. Barrett *American University*
Lourdes Benería *Rutgers University*
Barbara R. Bergmann *University of Maryland*
Francine D. Blau *University of Illinois*
Clair Brown *University of California–Berkeley*
Charles Brown *University of Maryland*
Gary Burtless *Brookings Institution*
Susan B. Carter *Smith College*
Peter B. Doeringer *Boston University*
Richard B. Freeman *Harvard University*
Helen Ginsburg *Brooklyn College*
Robert S. Goldfarb *George Washington University*
Nancy M. Gordon *Congressional Budget Office*
W. Lee Hansen *University of Wisconsin*
Heidi I. Hartmann *National Academy of Sciences*
Anne Hill *Rutgers University*
Karen C. Holden *University of Wisconsin*
Maryellen R. Kelley *University of Massachusetts–Boston*
Mark R. Killingsworth *Rutgers University*
Stanley Lebergott *Wesleyan University*
Jonathan S. Leonard *University of California–Berkeley*
Janice F. Madden *University of Pennsylvania*
Julie Matthaei *Wellesley College*

Robert H. Meyer *Brookings Institution*
June A. O'Neill *Urban Institute*
Paul Osterman *Boston University*
Joseph A. Pechman *Brookings Institution*
Marilyn Power *University of New Hampshire*
Albert E. Rees *Sloan Foundation*
Alice M. Rivlin *Brookings Institution*
Mark D. Roberts *University of Maryland*
Elyce J. Rotella *Indiana University*
Louise B. Russell *Brookings Institution*
Isabel V. Sawhill *Urban Institute*
Kathryn K. Shaw *Carnegie-Mellon University*
Margaret C. Simms *Urban Institute*
Elaine Sorensen *University of Massachusetts*
David Stern *University of California–Berkeley*
Myra H. Strober *Stanford University*
Lloyd Ulman *University of California–Berkeley*
Shirley J. Wilcher *National Women's Law Center*

Index